Teacher's Edition

WORLD ENGLISH1

SECOND EDITION

~~Real~~ People • Real Places • Real Language

...her, Author

..., Series Editor

NATIONAL GEOGRAPHIC LEARNING | CENGAGE Learning·

Australia • Brazil • Japan • Korea • Mexico • Singapore • Spain • United Kingdom • United States

World English Level 1 Teacher's Edition
Real People, Real Places, Real Language
Martin Milner, Author
Rob Jenkins, Series Editor

Publisher: Sherrise Roehr

Executive Editor: Sarah Kenney

Senior Development Editor: Margarita Matte

Development Editor: Brenden Layte

Assistant Editor: Alison Bruno

Editorial Assistant: Patricia Giunta

Media Researcher: Leila Hishmeh

Senior Technology Product Managers:
  Scott Rule, Lauren Krolick

Director of Global Marketing: Ian Martin

Senior Product Marketing Manager:
  Caitlin Thomas

Sr. Director, ELT & World Languages:
  Michael Burggren

Production Manager: Daisy Sosa

Content Project Manager: Andrea Bobotas

Senior Print Buyer: Mary Beth Hennebury

Cover Designer: Aaron Opie

Art Director: Scott Baker

Creative Director: Chris Roy

Cover Image: Slow Images/Getty Images

Compositor: MPS Limited

Cover Image

Church Nossa Senhora do Rosário dos
Pretos, Salvador, Brazil

For product information and technology assistance, contact us at
Cengage Learning Customer & Sales Support, 1-800-354-9706
For permission to use material from this text or product,
submit all requests online at **cengage.com/permissions**
Further permissions questions can be emailed to
permissionrequest@cengage.com

World English 1 Teacher's Edition: 978-1-285-84839-6

National Geographic Learning
20 Channel Center Street
Boston, MA 02210
USA

Cengage Learning is a leading provider of customized learning solutions with office locations around the globe, including Singapore, the United Kingdom, Australia, Mexico, Brazil, and Japan.

Cengage Learning products are represented in Canada by Nelson Education, Ltd.

Visit National Geographic Learning online at ngl.cengage.com

Visit our corporate website at www.cengage.com

Printed in Canada
Print Number: 03 Print Year: 2017

CONTENTS

WORLD ENGLISH STUDENT BOOK WALK-THROUGH

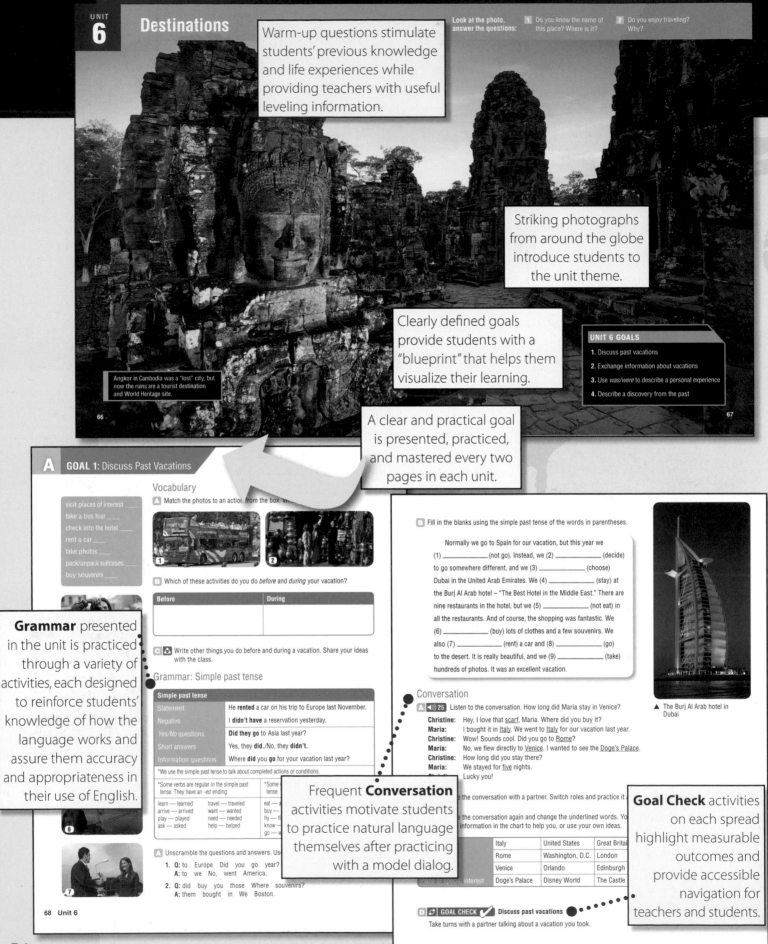

UNIT 6 Destinations

Look at the photo, answer the questions:
1. Do you know the name of this place? Where is it?
2. Do you enjoy traveling? Why?

Warm-up questions stimulate students' previous knowledge and life experiences while providing teachers with useful leveling information.

Striking photographs from around the globe introduce students to the unit theme.

Clearly defined goals provide students with a "blueprint" that helps them visualize their learning.

UNIT 6 GOALS
1. Discuss past vacations
2. Exchange information about vacations
3. Use *was/were* to describe a personal experience
4. Describe a discovery from the past

Angkor in Cambodia was a "lost" city, but now the ruins are a tourist destination and World Heritage site.

66 · 67

A clear and practical goal is presented, practiced, and mastered every two pages in each unit.

A GOAL 1: Discuss Past Vacations

Vocabulary

A Match the photos to an action from the box. Wr...

visit places of interest _____
take a bus tour _____
check into the hotel _____
rent a car _____
take photos _____
pack/unpack suitcases _____
buy souvenirs _____

B Which of these activities do you do *before* and *during* your vacation?

Before	During

C Write other things you do before and during a vacation. Share your ideas with the class.

Grammar presented in the unit is practiced through a variety of activities, each designed to reinforce students' knowledge of how the language works and assure them accuracy and appropriateness in their use of English.

Grammar: Simple past tense

Simple past tense	
Statement	He **rented** a car on his trip to Europe last November.
Negative	I **didn't have** a reservation yesterday.
Yes/No questions	**Did** they **go** to Asia last year?
Short answers	Yes, they **did**./No, they **didn't**.
Information questions	Where **did** you **go** for your vacation last year?

*We use the simple past tense to talk about completed actions or conditions.

*Some verbs are regular in the simple past tense. They have an -ed ending.	*Some... tense.
learn — learned travel — traveled	eat —
arrive — arrived want — wanted	buy —
play — played need — needed	fly — fl
ask — asked help — helped	know —
	go — w

A Unscramble the questions and answers. Use...
1. Q: to Europe Did you go year?
   A: to we No, went America.
2. Q: did buy you those Where souvenirs?
   A: them bought in We Boston.

B Fill in the blanks using the simple past tense of the words in parentheses.

Normally we go to Spain for our vacation, but this year we
(1) _____ (not go). Instead, we (2) _____ (decide)
to go somewhere different, and we (3) _____ (choose)
Dubai in the United Arab Emirates. We (4) _____ (stay) at
the Burj Al Arab hotel – "The Best Hotel in the Middle East." There are
nine restaurants in the hotel, but we (5) _____ (not eat) in
all the restaurants. And of course, the shopping was fantastic. We
(6) _____ (buy) lots of clothes and a few souvenirs. We
also (7) _____ (rent) a car and (8) _____ (go)
to the desert. It is really beautiful, and we (9) _____ (take)
hundreds of photos. It was an excellent vacation.

▲ The Burj Al Arab hotel in Dubai

Conversation

A 🔊 25 Listen to the conversation. How long did Maria stay in Venice?

Christine: Hey, I love that <u>scarf</u>, Maria. Where did you buy it?
Maria: I bought it in <u>Italy</u>. We went to <u>Italy</u> for our vacation last year.
Christine: Wow! Sounds cool. Did you go to <u>Rome</u>?
Maria: No, we flew directly to <u>Venice</u>. I wanted to see the <u>Doge's Palace</u>.
Christine: How long did you stay there?
Maria: We stayed for <u>five</u> nights.
Christine: Lucky you!

Frequent **Conversation** activities motivate students to practice natural language themselves after practicing with a model dialog.

...e the conversation with a partner. Switch roles and practice it a...

...e the conversation again and change the underlined words. Yo...
...information in the chart to help you, or use your own ideas.

	Italy	United States	Great Britain
	Rome	Washington, D.C.	London
	Venice	Orlando	Edinburgh
Place of special interest	Doge's Palace	Disney World	The Castle

D 🔄 **GOAL CHECK** ✓ **Discuss past vacations**
Take turns with a partner talking about a vacation you took.

Goal Check activities on each spread highlight measurable outcomes and provide accessible navigation for teachers and students.

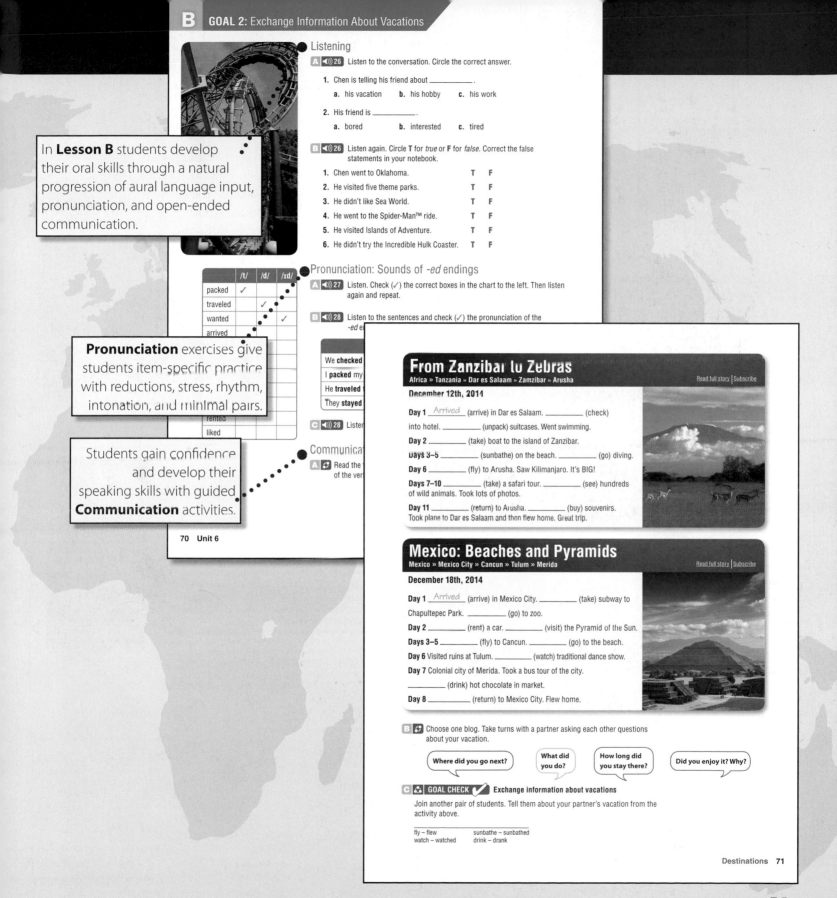

Listening

A 🔊 26 Listen to the conversation. Circle the correct answer.

1. Chen is telling his friend about _____.
   a. his vacation b. his hobby c. his work

2. His friend is _____.
   a. bored b. interested c. tired

B 🔊 26 Listen again. Circle **T** for *true* or **F** for *false*. Correct the false statements in your notebook.

1. Chen went to Oklahoma.   T F
2. He visited five theme parks.   T F
3. He didn't like Sea World.   T F
4. He went to the Spider-Man™ ride.   T F
5. He visited Islands of Adventure.   T F
6. He didn't try the Incredible Hulk Coaster. T F

Pronunciation: Sounds of *-ed* endings

	/t/	/d/	/ɪd/
packed	✓		
traveled		✓	
wanted			✓
arrived			
rented			
liked			

A 🔊 27 Listen. Check (✓) the correct boxes in the chart to the left. Then listen again and repeat.

B 🔊 28 Listen to the sentences and check (✓) the pronunciation of the *-ed* e...

We **checked**
I **packed** my
He **traveled**
They **stayed**

C 🔊 28 Listen

Communica...

A 🔄 Read the
of the ver...

70 Unit 6

From Zanzibar to Zebras

Africa » Tanzania » Dar es Salaam » Zamzibar » Arusha   Read full story | Subscribe

December 12th, 2014

Day 1 _Arrived_ (arrive) in Dar es Salaam. _____ (check) into hotel. _____ (unpack) suitcases. Went swimming.

Day 2 _____ (take) boat to the island of Zanzibar.

Days 3–5 _____ (sunbathe) on the beach. _____ (go) diving.

Day 6 _____ (fly) to Arusha. Saw Kilimanjaro. It's BIG!

Days 7–10 _____ (take) a safari tour. _____ (see) hundreds of wild animals. Took lots of photos.

Day 11 _____ (return) to Arusha. _____ (buy) souvenirs. Took plane to Dar es Salaam and then flew home. Great trip.

Mexico: Beaches and Pyramids

Mexico » Mexico City » Cancun » Tulum » Merida   Read full story | Subscribe

December 18th, 2014

Day 1 _Arrived_ (arrive) in Mexico City. _____ (take) subway to Chapultepec Park. _____ (go) to zoo.

Day 2 _____ (rent) a car. _____ (visit) the Pyramid of the Sun.

Days 3–5 _____ (fly) to Cancun. _____ (go) to the beach.

Day 6 Visited ruins at Tulum. _____ (watch) traditional dance show.

Day 7 Colonial city of Merida. Took a bus tour of the city.

_____ (drink) hot chocolate in market.

Day 8 _____ (return) to Mexico City. Flew home.

B 🔄 Choose one blog. Take turns with a partner asking each other questions about your vacation.

> Where did you go next?
> What did you do?
> How long did you stay there?
> Did you enjoy it? Why?

C ♻ **GOAL CHECK** ✔ **Exchange information about vacations**

Join another pair of students. Tell them about your partner's vacation from the activity above.

fly – flew   sunbathe – sunbathed
watch – watched   drink – drank

In **Lesson B** students develop their oral skills through a natural progression of aural language input, pronunciation, and open-ended communication.

Pronunciation exercises give students item-specific practice with reductions, stress, rhythm, intonation, and minimal pairs.

Students gain confidence and develop their speaking skills with guided **Communication** activities.

C **GOAL 3:** Ask About Lifestyles

> **Language Expansion** sections focus on specific areas that help learners build language strategies and become more competent users of English.

stress-free

Language Expansion: Compound adjectives

A Match the compound adjectives to their meanings.

a. works too much
b. delicious
c. without worries or problems
d. not high in calories
e. makes you happy
f. produced in your own garden
g. all your life
h. not made in a factory

1. mouth-watering _____
2. homemade _____
3. heartwarming _____
4. lifelong _____
5. stress-free _____
6. homegrown _____
7. overworked _____
8. low-calorie _____

B Complete the sentences. Use adjectives from exercise **A**.

1. Kevin and I went to kindergarten together. We are _____ friends.
2. When I was a child, my father had a vegetable garden, so we ate lots of _____ fruit and vegetables.
3. I have to work long hours, and I'm always tired. I think I am _____.
4. My grandmother makes the best _____ chicken soup in the world! It's absolutely _____.

Grammar: Questions with *how*

How much exercise do you get?	**How long** did your grandfather live?
How many cigarettes do you smoke a day?	**How often** do you go to the gym?
old is your father?	

Use **how much** to ask about the quantity of non-countable nouns.
Use **how many** to ask about the quantity of countable nouns.
Use **how old** to ask about age.
Use **how long** to ask about length or a period of time.
Use **how often** to ask about frequency.

D **GOAL 4:** Share Special Travel Tips with Others

Reading

A Read the article. Then answer the questions.

1. Do you think the author enjoys traveling? _____
_____
2. Why should you check the expiration date of your passport? _____
_____
3. Why should you tie a sock to your bag? _____
_____

> **Real Language** information boxes in every unit focus students' attention on frequently used phrases and how to use them.

> **Word Focus** boxes provide definitions of additional vocabulary, useful collocations, and special usage.

5. Airplane food is always good. T F

T F
T F

Word Focus

expiration date = the date a thing comes to an end or can no longer be used

Real Language

We use the expression *share some pointers* to say *give advice.*

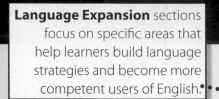

SMART

TRAVELER

EXPERT OPINION

In his book Easy Travel, *Mike Connelly **shares some pointers** on making travel easy:*

DOCUMENTS Make sure you have all your documents: passport, visas, tickets, etc. You should always check the **expiration date** of your passport. Many countries won't let you enter with less than six months left on your passport. Don't forget to buy travel insurance. Medical bills can be very expensive, especially in the United States and Europe. Finally, you should make copies of all your important documents and credit cards and keep them in another bag.

PACKING My advice is—always travel light! I hate to carry heavy bags. Just take the minimum. There is an old saying: *Breakfast in Berlin. Dinner in Delhi. Bags in Bangkok!* So, don't pack anything important in your check-in bag; put important things in your carry-on bag. You don't want to arrive home without your house keys. Another tip—don't use expensive suitcases. People don't steal dirty old bags. Finally, here's a good little tip—tie a sock or brightly colored string to your bag. Why? So you can quickly see your bag on the airport carousel.

THE AIRPORT My first piece of advice is that you should always carry a good book. It helps to pass the time as you wait for your delayed flight. Don't forget to take a sweater or a jacket on the plane. It can get cold on a long night flight. And then there is airline food. Take a snack (cookies or fruit) with you. Sometimes the food is late, sometimes it doesn't arrive at all, and it's never very good.

> Magazine-style readings are a springboard for opinion sharing and personalization, and provide opportunities for students to use the grammar and vocabulary presented earlier in the unit.

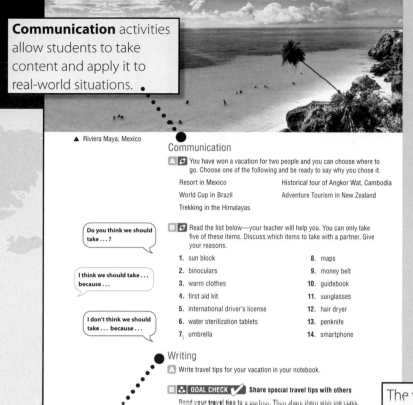

▲ Riviera Maya, Mexico

Communication activities allow students to take content and apply it to real-world situations.

Communication

A 🔁 You have won a vacation for two people and you can choose where to go. Choose one of the following and be ready to say why you chose it.

Resort in Mexico

World Cup in Brazil

Trekking in the Himalayas

Historical tour of Angkor Wat, Cambodia

Adventure Tourism in New Zealand

> Do you think we should take . . . ?

> I think we should take . . . because . . .

> I don't think we should take . . . because . . .

B 🔁 Read the list below—your teacher will help you. You can only take five of these items. Discuss which items to take with a partner. Give your reasons.

1. sun block
2. binoculars
3. warm clothes
4. first aid kit
5. international driver's license
6. water sterilization tablets
7. umbrella
8. maps
9. money belt
10. guidebook
11. sunglasses
12. hair dryer
13. penknife
14. smartphone

Writing

A Write travel tips for your vacation in your notebook.

B ♻ **GOAL CHECK** ✔ **Share special travel tips with others**

Read your travel tips to a partner. Then share them with the class.

Writing activities reinforce the structures, vocabulary, and expressions learned in the unit.

36 Unit 3

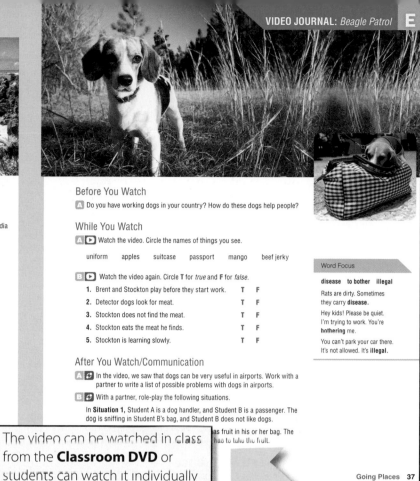

Before You Watch

A Do you have working dogs in your country? How do these dogs help people?

While You Watch

A ▶ Watch the video. Circle the names of things you see.

uniform   apples   suitcase   passport   mango   beef jerky

B ▶ Watch the video again. Circle **T** for *true* and **F** for *false*.

1. Brent and Stockton play before they start work.   T   F
2. Detector dogs look for meat.   T   F
3. Stockton does not find the meat.   T   F
4. Stockton eats the meat he finds.   T   F
5. Stockton is learning slowly.   T   F

After You Watch/Communication

A 🔁 In the video, we saw that dogs can be very useful in airports. Work with a partner to write a list of possible problems with dogs in airports.

B 🔁 With a partner, role-play the following situations.

In **Situation 1**, Student A is a dog handler, and Student B is a passenger. The dog is sniffing in Student B's bag, and Student B does not like dogs.

The video can be watched in class from the **Classroom DVD** or students can watch it individually on the **Student CD-ROM**.

___ as fruit in his or her bag. The ___ has to take the fruit.

Word Focus

disease   to bother   illegal

Rats are dirty. Sometimes they carry **disease**.

Hey kids! Please be quiet. I'm trying to work. You're **bothering** me.

You can't park your car there. It's not allowed. It's **illegal**.

Going Places 37

Students conclude the unit by watching an authentic but carefully-graded National Geographic video clip. This application of students' newly acquired language skills is a part of the on-going unit assessment system and serves as a motivating consolidation task.

This **World English Teacher's Edition** is designed to make your preparation as simple as possible, allowing you to maximize actual classroom teaching time. It features page-by-page suggestions on how to teach the course, answer keys to the Student Book and Workbook, culture notes, extension activities, audio scripts of listening passages not printed in the Student Book, and video scripts.

A snapshot from the course **Scope and Sequence** provides a quick reference as the teacher presents the new unit to students.

The **Unit Theme Overview** provides teachers with all the background information that they will need as they work through the unit. It also gives them a quick preview of the type of activities the students will do throughout the unit.

Step-by-step teaching suggestions are provided on every page of the unit.

Detailed **Grammar** explanations are provided for teacher reference in Lessons A and C.

An additional **Grammar Practice** activity can be used when necessary for re-teaching and review. There are also additional Grammar worksheets at the back of the Teacher's Edition.

UNIT 6 — Destinations

Look at the photo, answer the questions: 1 Do you know the name of this place? Where is it? 2 Do you enjoy traveling? Why?

Angkor in Cambodia was a "lost" city, but now the ruins are a tourist destination and World Heritage site.

UNIT 6 GOALS
1. Discuss past vacations
2. Exchange information about vacations
3. Use was/were to describe a personal experience
4. Describe a discovery from the past

Unit Theme Overview
- The World Tourism Organization compiles an annual ranking of the world's most popular tourist destinations. In 2012, the top country was France, with 83 million international visitors, followed by the United States (67 million), China (58 million), Spain (58 million), Italy (46 million), Turkey (36 million), Germany (30 million), the United Kingdom (29 million), Russia (26 million), and Malaysia (25 million). That's a lot of travelers and a lot of fascinating cross-cultural experiences!
- In this unit, students practice the form, meaning, and uses of the simple past tense in the context of describing past travel experiences. They talk about their own vacation trips and those of others, and learn about an explorer in the past who discovered what is today one of the world's great travel destinations—the amazing ruins of Machu Picchu, in Peru.

Destinations

About the Photo
This photo shows the Bayon, a temple in the ancient city of Angkor Thom in Cambodia. The Bayon stands in the center of Angkor Thom. It has huge faces carved in its central towers, which look down on the city and its visitors. There are thirty-seven main towers in total, and the temple has more than two hundred faces. The faces are of Lokesvara, the "Lord of the World," a Buddhist deity. Built in the late twelfth or early thirteenth centuries, the temple was originally intended for use among all the religions of the kingdom, but it was consecrated as a Buddhist temple. Later, it changed when the state religion went back to Hinduism. Today, the Bayon and Angkor Thom are popular tourist destinations due to their historical and architectural importance. Visitors often visit them along with nearby Angkor Wat.
- Introduce the theme of the unit. Call on students to give the name of a destination they have visited.
- Direct students' attention to the photo. Have students describe what they see.
- Have students work with a partner to discuss the questions.
- Compare answers with the class.
- Ask these questions orally or by writing them on the board for students to answer in pairs: Which place in the world would you like to visit? Why?
- Go over the Unit Goals with the class.
- For each goal, elicit any words students already know and write them on the board; for example, vacation destinations (beach, mountains, etc.), important discoveries, and so forth.

UNIT 6 GOALS	Grammar	Vocabulary	Listening	Speaking	Reading	Writing	Video Journal
• Discuss past vacations • Exchange information about vacations • Use was/were to describe a personal experience • Describe a discovery from the past	Simple past tense I **didn't have** a reservation yesterday. Simple past tense of to be I **was** exhausted.	Travel activities Emphatic adjectives	Listening for general understanding: A vacation	Comparing vacations	National	Writing a travel blog	National

---

LESSON A — Discuss Past Vacations

GOAL 1: Discuss Past Vacations

Vocabulary
- Have students look at the pictures. Say, These people are all taking a vacation. What are they doing? Then have students work individually to number the phrases to correspond with the photos.
- Have students compare answers with a partner.
- Check answers.
- Explain that the prefix un- means not or the opposite. If you unpack a suitcase, you take out the things that you packed.
- Have students work individually to categorize the activities.
- Have students compare answers with a partner, then check answers.
- Divide the class into pairs to take turns talking about their usual activities before and during a vacation.
- Compare answers with the class.

Grammar
- Introduce/review the simple past tense. Say, What did we do in class yesterday? We studied ____. We practiced ____. We learned ____. Elicit more examples from the class with regular verbs like talked, listened, and so forth.
- Go over the information in the chart. Point out the two kinds of verbs. The simple past tense of regular verbs is formed by adding -ed. Most verbs are regular. Some verbs are irregular. They don't use -ed to form the simple past tense. They are all different; students will have to learn them. Go over the irregular verbs in the chart.
- Have students unscramble the questions and answers.
- Have students compare answers with a partner.
- Check answers.

Word Bank: Vacation activities

Before:	During:
buy a map	go for a boat ride
exchange money	go to the tourist information office
get vaccinations	take a walking tour
make train/bus/car reservations	try local foods
	use a phrasebook

Grammar: Simple past tense
The simple past tense is used to talk about actions that were completed in the past. Irregular verbs are those that don't follow the rule in forming the past tense, so they must be learned individually. Practicing with flash cards is a good way to do this. Tell students that if they are unsure about a verb, dictionaries usually have a list of irregular verbs in the back.

Grammar Practice: Simple past tense
Prepare a list of students' names listed in random order on a piece of paper for your own use. Tell students to write three sentences in the past tense about things they did yesterday. Then play a memory game. Call on the first student on your list to say a sentence: Yesterday, I bought a new coat. The second student repeats that sentence and then adds his or her own sentence: Yesterday, Lee bought a new coat, and I read the newspaper. Each student continues in turn until one makes a mistake. Then that student starts over with a new sentence. Play until all students have had several turns. Ask, Who remembered the most sentences?

Vocabulary

A Match the photos to an action from the box. Write the numbers.

visit places of interest ____
take a bus tour ____
check into the hotel ____
rent a car ____
take photos ____
pack/unpack suitcases ____
buy souvenirs ____

B Which of these activities do you do before and during your vacation?

Before	During
pack suitcases	visit places of interest, take a bus tour, check into the hotel, rent a car, take photos, buy souvenirs

C Write other things you do before and during a vacation. Share your ideas with the class.

Grammar: Simple past tense

Simple past tense	
Statement	He **rented** a car on his trip to Europe last November.
Negative	I **didn't have** a reservation yesterday.
Yes/No questions	**Did** they **go** to Asia last year?
Short answers	Yes, they **did**./No, they **didn't**.
Information questions	Where **did** you **go** for your vacation last year?

*We use the simple past tense to talk about completed actions or conditions.

*Some verbs are regular in the simple past tense. They have an -ed ending.

learn — learned	travel — traveled
arrive — arrived	want — wanted
play — played	need — needed
ask — asked	help — helped

*Some verbs are irregular in the simple past tense. They have many different forms.

eat — ate	tell — told
buy — bought	leave — left
fly — flew	say — said
know — knew	see — saw
go — went	take — took

D Unscramble the questions and answers. Use your notebook.

1. Q: to Europe Did you go year? last A: Did you go to Europe last year?
   A: to we No, went America. B: No, we went to America.
2. Q: did buy you those Where souvenirs? A: Where did you buy those souvenirs?
   A: them bought in We Boston. B: We bought them in Boston.

68 Unit 6

Normally we go to Spain for our vacation, but this year we (1) _____ (not go). Instead, we (2) _____ (decide) to go somewhere different, and we (3) _____ (choose) Dubai in the United Arab Emirates. We (4) _____ (stay) at the Burj Al Arab hotel – "The Best Hotel in the Middle East." There are nine restaurants in the hotel, but we (5) _____ (not eat) in all the restaurants. And of course, the shopping was fantastic. We (6) _____ (buy) lots of clothes and a few souvenirs. We also (7) _____ (rent a car and (8) _____ (go) to the desert. It is really beautiful, and we (9) _____ (take) hundreds of photos. It was an excellent vacation.

E Fill in the blanks using the simple past tense of the words in parentheses.

Conversation

▲ Listen to the conversation. How long did Maria stay in Venice?

Christine: Hey, I love that scarf, Maria. Where did you buy it? five nights
Maria: I bought it in Italy. We went to Italy for our vacation last year.
Christine: Wow! Sounds cool. Did you go to Rome?
Maria: No, we flew directly to Venice. I wanted to see the Doge's Palace.
Christine: How long did you stay there?
Maria: We stayed for five nights.
Christine: Lucky you!

F Practice the conversation with a partner. Switch roles and practice it again.

G Practice the conversation again and change the underlined words. You can use the information in the chart to help you, or use your own ideas.

Country	Italy	United States	Great Britain
Capital	Rome	Washington, D.C.	London
Other city	Venice	Orlando	Edinburgh
Place of special interest	Doge's Palace	Disney World	The Castle

▲ The Burj Al Arab hotel in Dubai

GOAL CHECK Discuss past vacations
Take turns with a partner talking about a vacation you took.

Destinations 69

- Have students work individually to complete the paragraph.
- Have students compare answers with a partner.
- Check answers.
- Have students read the questions and answers out loud with a partner.

Conversation
- Have students close their books. Write the question on the board: How long did Maria stay in Venice?
- Play the recording.
- Check answers.
- Play or read the conversation again for the class to repeat.
- Practice the conversation with the class in chorus.
- Have students practice the conversation with a partner and then switch roles and practice it again.
- Tell students to make three new conversations using the information in the chart. Go over the information with the class. Then have them practice the conversations.
- Call on student pairs to present a conversation to the class.

GOAL CHECK
- Have students work with the same partner to talk about a vacation or other trip they took. Remind them to use the simple past tense.

Lesson A 69

T-8

	Goals	Language Focus
UNIT 1 People	• Talk about people	*Her/his name is ____.* *S/he's from ____.* *S/he's a(an) ____.*
UNIT 2 Work, Rest, and Play	• Describe an unusual celebration • Share your ideas with the class	*It's called ____. It's for ____.* *People always . . . on ____*
UNIT 3 Going Places	• Deciding what to take on a trip • Limiting travel needs to one suitcase	*I think we should take . . .* *Don't take . . .*
UNIT 4 Food	• Completing a menu • Ordering meals at a restaurant	*Do you have . . .* *Would you like . . .*
UNIT 5	• Planning a sports center	*I think . . .* *I prefer . . .*

This Teacher's Edition provides additional Communication and Writing practice through classroom materials that can be photocopied. **Communication Activities** include information gap, group work, interview worksheets, simulations and role-plays.

UNIT 2 WORK, REST, AND PLAY

A Look at these unusual celebrations. What do you think people do on these days?

September 5
Be Late for Something Day

July 20
National Ice Cream Day

January 3
Festival of Sleep

May 6
INTERNATIONAL NURSES' DAY

	Writing Tasks	Language Focus
UNIT 1 E-mail Message	• Use *be* in statements and questions • Identify countries, nationalities, and occupations • Use descriptive adjectives	*Are you a new student?* *I'm Chilean.* *Is this class interesting?*
UNIT 2 Describe a Celebration	• List daily activities • Use the simple present tense with *first, next, then,* and *finally* • Write about a celebration	*On my day off, I usually visit friends.* *In the evening, we watch fireworks.*
UNIT 3 Travel Tips	• Practice using pronouns to show possession • Use *should* and other expressions to give travel tips	*These are my keys. They belong to me.* *When you visit my country, you should always . . .*
UNIT 4 Restaurant Menu	• Use *some* and *any* to talk about eating habits • Answer questions ... *many?* • Create a restaurant ...	*In the morning, I usually eat some eggs ...*

The **Writing Program** reinforces and complements the lessons in the Student Book. Writing gives students a chance to reflect on the English they've learned and to develop an indispensable academic skill.

UNIT 6 DESTINATIONS
DESCRIBE A PLACE

A How was your life when you were a child?

When I was a child . . .
1. I wanted ____
2. I didn't want ____
3. I went ____
4. I didn't go ____
5. I learned ____
6. I didn't learn ____

> What did you want when you were a child?
> What did you not want when you were a child?

✓ Take turns. Ask a partner questions about the sentences above.

B When you were a child, what was your favorite place to be? (e.g. your family's kitchen, a park near your house; your grandmother's farm; etc.) Answer these questions about that place.
1. What was your favorite place? ____
2. Why did you like that place? ____
3. How did you get there? ____
4. What did you do there? ____
5. What did you see, hear, and feel in your favorite place? ____

✓ Write about your favorite place when you were a child. Use some of the information above.

DESTINATIONS
UNIT 6

Lesson A GRAMMAR AND VOCABULARY

rent · take a · check in <br> take · visit · unpack · buy

A Complete the expressions for vacation activities.
1. ____ places of interest
2. ____ bus tour
3. ____ to the hotel
4. ____ a car
5. ____ photos
6. ____
7. ____

B Write the past tense of the verb. Be careful! Some verbs have ... and some verbs are irregular.

1. see	saw	9. buy	

The **Grammar Activity** worksheets, new for this edition, provide additional support and practice for the grammar points presented in Lessons A and C in the Student Book units.

Katie: (7) ____ Taj Mahal). It was beautiful!
Eric: What about the food in India? (8) ____ (you/like it)?
Katie: Yes! (9) ____ to some great restaurants).

Lesson D READING AND WRITING

Andy's vacation

To: jj@gomail.com
From: andy2000@hitmail.com
Subject: Good and Bad

Hi Jessica,

You asked about my vacation. There was good and bad.

It was a long trip. The airline was terrible. Everything was late, and the airplane was filthy, with food on the floor and papers everywhere. We flew to the capital city, and then we took a train. We took a boat to get to White Beach. We left home at 5:00 a.m., and we arrived at 10:00 p.m.

The beach was amazing! It really is white, and it's very clean. In fact, it was spotless, and the water was warm and blue. We went swimming every day and walked on the beach. Our hotel was huge but very nice. The food was OK, but the restaurants had only a few different dishes. We had fish every day.

One day, we took a bus tour. It was exhausting! We went to about 20 different ...

The **Workbook** provides additional practice and supports the development of skills through a variety of activities.

DESTINATIONS
UNIT 6

A Circle the correct answer.
1. Andy stayed at ____.
   a. the capital city   b. a beach   c. a small town
2. His trip to White Beach was ____.
   a. easy   b. hard   c. short
3. The hotel was ____.
   a. big   b. dirty   c. fascinating
4. The food wasn't ____.
   a. healthy   b. interesting   c. delicious

B What did Andy think about these things? Check (✓) his opinions.

	☺	☺	☹
1. his vacation			
2. the airplane			
3. the beach			
4. the hotel			
5. the food			
6. the bus tour			
7. the souvenirs			

C You took a vacation in London. Look at the vacation information. ... your friend about it.

... Airport	• see Buckingham Palace
... g hotel	• take a boat trip on the Thames River
... restaurants	• buy souvenirs in famous department stores
... visit the Tower of London	

Overview

The new edition of **World English** uses rich, engrossing National Geographic text, photos, art, and videos to involve students in learning about real people, real places, and real language.

In this edition, newly added TED Talks and Readings also bring some of the world's most important and interesting speakers to the classroom.

Each unit is divided into three two-page lessons, a three-page Reading, Writing, and Communication lesson, and a Video Journal.

A concrete objective at the beginning of every lesson focuses students' attention on what they will be learning. At the end of the lesson, a personalization activity gives students an opportunity to apply what they've learned and lets both teachers and students check student progress.

Unit Opener

Each unit opens with a two-page spread featuring a striking photo. These photos have been chosen both to illustrate the unit theme and to provide material for discussion. Before beginning the unit, teacher and students can describe the picture, name as many things as they can in it, and make guesses about when and where the photo was taken. The two discussion questions then lead students into the topic and introduce several key vocabulary items.

In this Teacher's Edition, a Unit Theme Overview is provided to orient you to the scope of the unit and to give additional information that may be useful in discussing the unit theme. Throughout the lesson notes, For Your Information boxes contain additional facts about the topic of a listening passage, reading, or video.

Vocabulary

Lessons A and C both begin with a short activity presenting lexical items related to the unit theme. In Lesson A, the vocabulary section introduces the core words that students will need to discuss and learn about the unit topic. These are presented in context, with text or pictures to aid students in understanding. After completing the exercises in this section, students have a written record of the meanings of the words, which they can refer to later. The lesson notes in this Teacher's Edition contain a Word Bank of supplementary vocabulary that can be used in activities or taught as enrichment.

Grammar

World English features an explicit grammar syllabus, with individual grammar points tied to the unit theme. Two different grammar points are taught in Lesson A and Lesson C. They are used in the opening presentation of the lessons along with the vocabulary items and then explicitly presented in a box with examples, rules, and usage notes.

Students first do controlled practice with the structure in writing, then freer production in writing, and finally use the structure in controlled speaking practice. Every grammar point is followed by a Conversation section that gives further practice in the use of the structure.

The lesson notes in this Teacher's Edition contain a brief summary of each grammar point for teacher reference, as well an additional Grammar Practice Activity.

New to this edition are Grammar worksheets in the back of the Teacher's Edition. Each unit has two worksheets, one for each of the grammar points in Lessons A and C.

Conversation

Each unit contains two model conversations highlighting both the vocabulary and the grammar for the lesson. Students first listen to the conversation with their books closed and answer one general comprehension question. Next, they listen again while reading the conversation. They are then ready to practice the conversation, taking turns with both roles before making their own conversations based on the model and incorporating specified information along with their own ideas.

Listening

Lesson B starts off with a listening activity. After a warm-up to introduce the subject of the activity, students listen to a conversation, radio program, or interview multiple times, completing a series of written tasks of graded difficulty. The first time, they are asked to listen for the gist or main ideas; subsequent activities ask them to find numbers, details, or further information. A post-listening task helps students to explore and personalize what they've heard.

Audioscripts for all listening activities begin on page T-169.

Pronunciation

The pronunciation component of **World English** emphasizes stress, intonation, reductions, and other features to make learners' English more natural and comprehensible to a wide international audience. Students first learn to recognize a feature of English pronunciation and then to produce it. Examples are presented on the audio recording in the context of the unit theme. Students begin by listening, then repeat with the audio recording, and then practice freer production of the features while interacting with a partner.

If a particular pronunciation point is especially challenging for your students, it can be practiced in a number of ways. You can have the entire class repeat the items in chorus, then the two halves of the class, then rows or columns of students, and finally you can call on individual students to pronounce the items. When students practice in pairs, circulate around the room listening and correcting.

Communication

In contrast to the controlled speaking practice in the Conversation sections, the Communication activities give freer practice with the structures and vocabulary that the students have learned. These activities are designed to allow personal expression, but still within a controlled field of language, so that all students can feel confident of success. While students are doing these activities, you should circulate around the class to help with vocabulary and ideas as needed and to make note of errors and interesting responses to discuss with the class after the end of the activity.

The lesson notes in this Teacher's Edition include Expansion activities for further discussion around the theme of the listening passage. For classes where more practice of free communication is desired, this book also contains 12 Communication Activity Worksheets, which may be photocopied, one for each unit. The activities, which require 15 to 30 minutes of class time each, reinforce the vocabulary and structures from the unit while giving students another opportunity to express their own ideas in English.

Language Expansion

The first part of Lesson C is a Language Expansion activity that is meant to broaden students' vocabulary around the unit theme by introducing a closely related group of lexical items. These are presented in context and are used immediately in writing and then speaking, giving students more options when doing the Grammar and Conversation activities that follow in Lesson C.

Reading

Lesson D is centered around a reading passage, which is followed by a Communication activity that prepares students for writing. All of the reading passages in **World English** are abridged and adapted from authentic articles in National Geographic publications or TED Talks. To help students read for interest and enjoyment, unfamiliar vocabulary is explained either with glosses in a Word Focus box or in a picture dictionary illustration.

The lesson notes in this Teacher's Edition include a Web search activity and a suggestion for a simple project that can be done as a follow-up for each reading passage.

Writing

The writing activities in Lesson D of **World English** flow from the subject of the reading passage and are always preceded by a Communication activity in which students discuss and explore the topic further. This generates ideas and forms a natural prewriting sequence. Writing tasks are short and simple and range from writing single sentences in the lower levels, through writing groups of sentences, on up to writing an entire paragraph.

The writing activities in the units emphasize helping students put their ideas into written form. Where a more structured approach to writing is desired, this Teacher's Edition contains a complete Writing Program, which may be photocopied. These optional writing worksheets, one for each unit, provide instruction and practice in a sequence of writing skills graded to the level of the course.

Video Journal

Each unit of **World English** concludes with an authentic National Geographic three- to four-minute video, with a voice-over that has been specially edited for language learners. The video segments recycle the themes and language of the main unit, bringing them to life in colorful locations around the globe. A Before You Watch activity presents new words that students will hear and gives information about the setting of the video. Students watch the video several times while completing While You Watch activities that ask them first to find general themes and then to locate specific information. They give their response to the video in an After You Watch activity.

The responses to the video draw the strands of the unit together and allow students to demonstrate what they've learned.

TED Talks

In this new edition, students also watch a TED Talk every three units. These videos are accompanied by four-page sections which review the vocabulary and grammar content of the previous three units and also allow students to build upon prior instruction to communicate about issues that affect their community and the world.

Special Features in the Student Book

Real Language This feature highlights high-frequency expressions from everyday language that will make students' speech sound natural and confident. To present them, point out their use in the activity and discuss other situations when they might be useful. If desired, have students work in pairs to create conversations using the expressions.

Word Focus These boxes present and explain additional vocabulary used in an activity, as well as introduce commonly used collocations.

WORLD ENGLISH 1

SECOND EDITION

Real People • Real Places • Real Language

Martin Milner, Author

Rob Jenkins, Series Editor

NATIONAL
GEOGRAPHIC
LEARNING

CENGAGE
Learning·

Australia • Brazil • Japan • Korea • Mexico • Singapore • Spain • United Kingdom • United States

World English Level 1
Real People, Real Places, Real Language
Martin Milner, Author
Rob Jenkins, Series Editor

Publisher: Sherrise Roehr

Executive Editor: Sarah Kenney

Senior Development Editor: Margarita Matte

Development Editor: Brenden Layte

Assistant Editor: Alison Bruno

Editorial Assistant: Patricia Giunta

Media Researcher: Leila Hishmeh

Senior Technology Product Manager: Scott Rule

Director of Global Marketing: Ian Martin

Senior Product Marketing Manager:
   Caitlin Thomas

Sr. Director, ELT & World Languages:
   Michael Burggren

Production Manager: Daisy Sosa

Content Project Manager: Andrea Bobotas

Senior Print Buyer: Mary Beth Hennebury

Cover Designer: Aaron Opie

Art Director: Scott Baker

Creative Director: Chris Roy

Cover Image: Slow Images/Getty Images

Compositor: MPS Limited

Cover Image

Church Nossa Senhora do Rosário dos
Pretos, Salvador, Brazil

For product information and technology assistance, contact us at
Cengage Learning Customer & Sales Support, 1-800-354-9706

For permission to use material from this text or product,
submit all requests online at **cengage.com/permissions**
Further permissions questions can be emailed to
permissionrequest@cengage.com

World English Intro ISBN: 978-1-285-84869-3
World English Intro + CD-ROM ISBN: 978-1-285-84835-8
World English Intro + Online Workbook ISBN: 978-1-305-08954-9

National Geographic Learning
20 Channel Center Street
Boston, MA 02210
USA

Cengage Learning is a leading provider of customized learning solutions with office locations around the globe, including Singapore, the United Kingdom, Australia, Mexico, Brazil, and Japan.

Cengage Learning products are represented in Canada by Nelson Education, Ltd.

Visit National Geographic Learning online at ngl.cengage.com

Visit our corporate website at www.cengage.com

Printed in the United States of America
Print Number: 01 Print Year: 2014

Thank you to the educators who provided invaluable feedback during the development of the second edition of the *World English* series:

AMERICAS

Brazil

Renata Cardoso, Universidade de Brasília, Brasília
Gladys De Sousa, Universidade Federal de Minas Gerais, Belo Horizonte
Marilena Fernandes, Associação Alumni, São Paulo
Mary Ruth Popov, Ingles Express, Ltda., Belo Horizonte
Ana Rosa, Speed, Vila Velha
Danny Sheps, English4u2, Natal
Renata Zainotte, Go Up Idiomas, Rio de Janeiro

Colombia

Eida Caicedo, Universidad de San Buenaventura Cali, Cali
Andres Felipe Echeverri Patiño, Corporación Universitaria Lasallista, Envigado
Luz Libia Rey, Centro Colombo Americano, Bogota

Dominican Republic

Aida Rosales, Instituto Cultural Dominico-Americano, Santo Domingo

Ecuador

Elizabeth Ortiz, COPEI-Copol English Institute, Guayaquil

Mexico

Ramon Aguilar, LEC Languages and Education Consulting, Hermosillo
Claudia García-Moreno Ávila, Universidad Autónoma del Estado de México, Toluca
Ana María Benton, Universidad Anahuac Mexico Norte, Huixquilucan
Martha Del Angel, Tecnológico de Monterrey, Monterrey
Sachenka García B., Universidad Kino, Hermosillo
Cinthia I. Navarrete García, Universidad Autónoma del Estado de México, Toluca
Alonso Gaxiola, Universidad Autonoma de Sinaloa, Guasave
Raquel Hernandez, Tecnológico de Monterrey, Monterrey
Beatriz Cuenca Hernández, Universidad Autónoma del Estado de México, Toluca
Luz María Lara Hernández, Universidad Autónoma del Estado de México, Toluca
Esthela Ramírez Hernández, Universidad Autónoma del Estado de México, Toluca
Ma Guadalupe Peña Huerta, Universidad Autónoma del Estado de México, Toluca
Elsa Iruegas, Prepa Tec Campus Cumbres, Monterrey
María del Carmen Turral Maya, Universidad Autónoma del Estado de México, Toluca
Lima Melani Ayala Olvera, Universidad Autónoma del Estado de México, Toluca
Suraya Ordorica Reyes, Universidad Autónoma del Estado de México, Toluca
Leonor Rosales, Tecnológico de Monterrey, Monterrey
Leticia Adelina Ruiz Guerrero, ITESO, Jesuit University, Tlaquepaque

United States

Nancy Alaks, College of DuPage, Glen Ellyn, IL
Annette Barker, College of DuPage, Aurora, IL
Joyce Gatto, College of Lake County, Grayslake, IL
Donna Glade-Tau, Harper College, Palatine, IL
Mary "Katie" Hu, Lone Star College – North Harris, Houston, TX
Christy Naghitorabi, University of South Florida, St. Petersburg, FL

ASIA

Beri Ali, Cleverlearn (American Academy), Ho Chi Minh City
Ronald Anderson, Chonnam National University, Yeosu Campus, Jeollanam
Michael Brown, Canadian Secondary Wenzhou No. 22 School, Wenzhou
Leyi Cao, Macau University of Science and Technology, Macau
Maneerat Chuaychoowong, Mae Fah Luang University, Chiang Rai
Sooah Chung, Hwarang Elementary School, Seoul
Edgar Du, Vanung University, Taoyuan County
David Fairweather, Asahikawa Daigaku, Asahikawa
Andrew Garth, Chonnam National University, Yeosu Campus, Jeollanam
Brian Gaynor, Muroran Institute of Technology, Muroran-shi
Emma Gould, Chonnam National University, Yeosu Campus, Jeollanam
David Grant, Kochi National College of Technology, Nankoku
Michael Halloran, Chonnam National University, Yeosu Campus, Jeollanam
Nina Ainun Hamdan, University Malaysia, Kuala Lumpur
Richard Hatcher, Chonnam National University, Yeosu Campus, Jeollanam
Edward Tze-Lu Ho, Chihlee Institute of Technology, Now Taipoi City
Soontae Hong, Yonsei University, Seoul
Chaiyathip Katsura, Mae Fah Luang University, Chiang Rai
Byoug-Kyo Lee, Yonsei University, Seoul
Han Li, Aceleader International Language Center, Beijing
Michael McGuire, Kansai Gaidai University, Osaka
Yu Jin Ng, Universiti Tenaga Nasional, Kajang, Selangor
Somaly Pan, Royal University of Phnom Penh, Phnom Penh
HyunSuk Park, Halla University, Wonju
Bunroeun Pich, Build Bright University, Phnom Penh
Renee Sawazaki, Surugadai University, Annaka-shi
Adam Schofield, Cleverlearn (American Academy), Ho Chi Minh City
Pawadee Srisang, Burapha University, Chanthaburi Campus, Ta-Mai District
Douglas Sweetlove, Kinjo Gakuin University, Nagoya
Tari Lee Sykes, National Taiwan University of Science and Technology, Taipei
Monika Szirmai, Hiroshima International University, Hiroshima
Sherry Wen, Yan Ping High School, Taipei
Chris Wilson, Okinawa University, Naha City, Okinawa
Christopher Wood, Meijo University, Nagoya
Evelyn Wu, Minghsin University of Science and Technology, Xinfeng, Hsinchu County
Aroma Xiang, Macau University of Science and Technology, Macau
Zoe Xie, Macau University of Science and Technology, Macau
Juan Xu, Macau University of Science and Technology, Macau
Florence Yap, Chang Gung University, Taoyuan
Sukanda Yatprom, Mae Fah Luang University, Chiang Rai
Echo Yu, Macau University of Science and Technology, Macau

The publisher would like to extend a special thank you to Raúl Billini, English Coordinator, Mi Colegio, Dominican Republic, for his contributions to the series.

Listening	Speaking and Pronunciation	Reading	Writing	Video Journal
Focused listening: Personal introductions	Asking for and giving personal information Contractions of *be*: –'m, –'re, –'s	**National Geographic:** "People from Around the World"	Writing about people's occupations and nationalities	**National Geographic:** "The Last of The Woman Divers"
Focused listening: A radio celebrity interview	Talking about daily schedules and free time Verbs that end in –s	**TED**TALKS "Eric Whitacre: A Virtual Choir 2,000 Voices Strong"	Writing a descriptive paragraph about daily routines Writing Strategy: Word web	**National Geographic:** "Monkey Business"
General listening: Conversations at travel destinations	Giving personal information for travel forms Rising intonation on lists	**National Geographic:** "Smart Traveler"	Writing travel tips	**National Geographic:** "Beagle Patrol"
General and focused listening: Ordering a meal in a restaurant	Role-play: Purchasing food at a supermarket Reduced forms: *Do you have . . .* and *Would you like . . .*	**National Geographic:** "Bugs as Food"	Writing a recipe	**National Geographic:** "Dangerous Dinner"
General and focused listening: Everyday activities vs. today's activities	Talking about what people are doing now Discussing favorite sports Reduced form: *What are you . . .*	**TED**TALKS "Lewis Pugh: My Mind-Shifting Everest Swim"	Writing an e-mail	**National Geographic:** "Cheese-Rolling Races"
General listening: A vacation	Comparing vacations Describing personal experiences Sounds of –*ed* endings	**National Geographic:** "The Cradle of the Inca Empire"	Writing a travel blog	**National Geographic:** "Machu Picchu"

	Unit Goals	Grammar	Vocabulary
UNIT 7 Communication Page 82	• Talk about personal communication • Exchange contact information • Describe characteristics and qualities • Compare different types of communication	Verbs with direct and indirect objects Irregular past tense Sensory verbs	Communication Electronics The senses
UNIT 8 Moving Forward Page 94	• Talk about plans • Discuss long- and short-term plans • Make weather predictions • Discuss the future	Future tense: *be going to* *Will* for predictions and immediate decisions	Short- and long-term plans Weather conditions Weather-specific clothing
UNIT 9 Types of Clothing Page 106	• Make comparisons • Explain preferences • Talk about clothing materials • Evaluate quality and value	Comparatives Superlatives	Clothing Descriptive adjectives Clothing materials

TEDTALKS Video Page 118 **Diana Reiss: Peter Gabriel, Neil Gershenfeld, Vint Cerf: The Interspecies Internet? An Idea in Progress**

	Unit Goals	Grammar	Vocabulary
UNIT 10 Lifestyles Page 122	• Give advice on healthy habits • Compare lifestyles • Ask about lifestyles • Evaluate your lifestyle	Modals (*could, ought to, should, must*); *have to* Questions with *how*	Healthy and unhealthy habits Compound adjectives
UNIT 11 Achievements Page 134	• Talk about today's chores • Interview for a job • Talk about personal accomplishments • Discuss humanity's greatest achievements	Present perfect tense Present perfect tense vs. simple past tense	Chores Personal accomplishments
UNIT 12 Consequences Page 146	• Talk about managing your money • Make choices on how to spend your money • Talk about cause and effect • Evaluate money and happiness	Real conditionals (also called the first conditional)	Personal finance Animals Animal habitats

TEDTALKS Video Page 158 **Michael Norton: How to Buy Happiness**

Listening	Speaking and Pronunciation	Reading	Writing	Video Journal
Focused listening: A radio call-in program	Asking for contact information Describing sights, sounds and other sensations The /b/ and /v/, /l/ and /r/ sounds	**TED**TALKS "Diana Reiss, Peter Gabriel, Neil Gershenfeld, Vint Cerf: The Interspecies Internet? An Idea in Progress"	Writing a text message Make a list	**National Geographic:** "Wild Animal Trackers"
General listening: A talk show	Talking about weekend plans Discussing the weather Reduced form of *going to*	**National Geographic:** "Future Energy"	Writing statements about the future	**National Geographic:** "Solar Cooking"
Focused listening: Shoe shopping	Talking about clothes Shopping—at the store and online Rising and falling intonation	**National Geographic:** "Silk—the Queen of Textiles"	Writing about buying clothes	**National Geographic:** "How Your T-Shirt Can Make a Difference"
General listening: Personal lifestyles	Discussing healthy and unhealthy habits Asking and telling about lifestyles *Should, shouldn't*	**National Geographic:** "The Secrets of Long Life"	Writing a paragraph about personal lifestyle	**National Geographic:** "The Science of Stress"
Listening for general understanding and specific details: A job interview	Interviewing for a job Catching up with a friend Reduced form of *have*	**National Geographic:** "Humanity's Greatest Achievements"	Writing about achievements	**National Geographic:** "Spacewalk"
Listening for specific details: At a travel agency Listening for key information	Making decisions about spending money Talking about important environmental issues Intonation, sentence stress	**TED**TALKS "Michael Norton: How to Buy Happiness"	Write about cause and effect Writing Strategy: Make suggestions	**National Geographic:** "The Missing Snows of Kilimanjaro"

BACKGROUND – LEARNING AND INSTRUCTION

Learning has been described as acquiring knowledge. Obtaining knowledge does not guarantee understanding, however. A math student, for example, could replicate any number of algebraic formulas, but never come to an *understanding* of how they could be used or for what purpose he or she has learned them. If understanding is defined as the ability to use knowledge, then learning could be defined differently and more accurately. The ability of the student to use knowledge instead of merely receiving information therefore becomes the goal and the standard by which learning is assessed.

This revelation has led to classrooms that are no longer teacher-centric or lecture driven. Instead, students are asked to think, ponder, and make decisions based on the information received or, even more productive, students are asked to construct learning or discover information in personal pursuits, or with help from an instructor, with partners, or in groups. The practice they get from such approaches stimulates learning with a purpose. The purpose becomes a tangible goal or objective that provides opportunities for students to transfer skills and experiences to future learning.

In the context of language development, this approach becomes essential to real learning and understanding. Learning a language is a skill that is developed only after significant practice. Students can learn the mechanics of a language but when confronted with real-world situations, they are not capable of communication. Therefore, it might be better to shift the discussion from "Language Learning" to "Communication Building." Communication should not be limited to only the productive skills. Reading and listening serve important avenues for communication as well.

FOUR PRINCIPLES TO DEVELOPING LEARNING ENVIRONMENTS

Mission: The goal or mission of a language course might adequately be stated as the pursuit of providing sufficient information and practice to allow students to communicate accurately and effectively to a reasonable extent given the level, student experiences, and time on task provided. This goal can be reflected in potential student learning outcomes identified by what students will be able to do through performance indicators.

World English provides a clear chart within the table of contents to show the expected outcomes of the course. The books are designed to capture student imagination and allow students ample opportunities to communicate. A study of the table of contents identifies the process of communication building that will go on during the course.

Context: It is important to identify what vehicle will be used to provide instruction. If students are to learn through practice, language cannot be introduced as isolated verb forms, nouns, and modifiers. It must have context. To reach the learners and to provide opportunities to communicate, the context must be interesting and relevant to learners' lives and expectations. In other words, there must be a purpose and students must have a clear understanding of what that purpose is.

World English provides a meaningful context that allows students to connect with the world. Research has demonstrated pictures and illustrations are best suited for creating interest and motivation within learners. National Geographic has a long history of providing magnificent learning environments through pictures, illustrations, true accounts, and video. The pictures, stories, and video capture the learners' imagination and "hook" them to learning in such a way that students have significant reasons to communicate promoting interaction and critical thinking. The context will also present students with a desire to know more, leading to life-long learning.

Objectives (Goals)

With the understanding that a purpose for communicating is essential, identifying precisely what the purpose is in each instance becomes crucial even before specifics of instruction have been defined. This is often called "backward design." Backward design means in the context of classroom lesson planning that first desired outcomes, goals, or objectives are defined and then lessons are mapped out with the end in mind, the end being what students will be able to do after sufficient instruction and practice. Having well-crafted objectives or goals provides the standard by which learners' performance can be assessed or self-assessed.

World English lessons are designed on two-page spreads so students can easily see what is expected and what the context is. The goal that directly relates to the final application activity is identified at the beginning. Students, as well as instructors, can easily evaluate their performance as they attempt the final activity. Students can also readily see what tools they will practice to prepare them for the application activity. The application activity is a task where students can demonstrate their ability to perform what the lesson goal requires. This information provides direction and purpose for the learner. Students, who know what is expected, where they are going, and how they will get there, are more apt to reach success. Each success builds confidence and additional communication skills.

Tools and Skills

Once the lesson objective has been identified and a context established, the lesson developer must choose the tools the learner will need to successfully perform the task or objective. The developer can choose among various areas in communication building including vocabulary, grammar and pronunciation. The developer must also choose skills and strategies including reading, writing, listening, and speaking. The receptive skills of reading and listening are essential components to communication. All of these tools and skills must be placed in a balanced way into a context providing practice that can be transferred to their final application or learner demonstration which ultimately becomes evidence of communication building.

World English units are divided into "lessons" that each consists of a two-page spread. Each spread focuses on different skills and strategies and is labeled by a letter (A-E). The units contain the following lesson sequence:

> A: Vocabulary
> B: Listening and Pronunciation
> C: Language Expansion
> D: Reading/Writing
> E: Video Journal

Additional grammar and vocabulary are introduced as tools throughout to provide practice for the final application activity. Each activity in a page spread has the purpose of developing adequate skills to perform the final application task.

LAST WORD

The philosophy of World English is to provide motivating context to connect students to the world through which they build communication skills. These skills are developed, practiced, and assessed from lesson to lesson through initially identifying the objective and giving learners the tools they need to complete a final application task. The concept of performance is highlighted over merely learning new information and performance comes from communicating about meaningful and useful context. An accumulation of small communication skills leads to true and effective communication outside of the classroom in real-world environments.

People

About the Photo

This photo was taken by Sigit Pamungkas, a photojournalist from Indonesia. The photo shows Muslim women attending evening prayers at a mosque in Surabaya, East Java, Indonesia. It shows the night before Ramadan, an important Islamic celebration. Ramadan is the ninth month of the Islamic calendar. During the month of Ramadan, adults fast from dawn to sunset every day and dedicate a lot of their time to prayer. This photo beautifully captures the women in their white robes and their movement as they kneel to pray, contrasted with the young girl in red, standing still in the center.

- Introduce the theme of the unit. Tell students that in this unit, they will meet real people from many different places.

- Direct students' attention to the photo. Have students describe what they see.

- Have students work with a partner to discuss the questions.

- Have several pairs share their ideas with the class. Write key vocabulary on the board.

- Go over the Unit Goals with the class, explaining as necessary.

- For each goal, elicit any words students already know and write them on the board; for example, expressions like *Nice to meet you*; questions like *What's your name?*; occupations, etc.

UNIT
1
People

A girl in a red dress stands out among Muslim women praying on the eve of Ramadan in East Java, Indonesia.

2

UNIT 1 GOALS	Grammar	Vocabulary	Listening
• Meet people • Ask for and give personal information • Describe different occupations • Describe positive and negative parts of occupations	Review of present tense: *be* *They're Thai.* *He's not a dancer.* *Be* + adjective (+ noun) *It is an easy job.* Possessive adjectives	Occupations Countries Nationalities Descriptive adjectives	Focused listening: Personal introductions

Look at the photo, answer the questions:
1 Who are these people? Share your ideas with a partner.
2 Are they like you? Why or why not?

UNIT 1 GOALS

1. Meet people

2. Ask for and give personal information

3. Describe different occupations

4. Describe positive and negative parts of occupations

Unit Theme Overview

- Students begin their work in **World English** Level 1 by considering some of the things people have in common, and looking at the kinds of information we often exchange with other people when we first meet them.

- In English-speaking countries, one common topic of conversation when people first meet is occupations and the work people do. It is considered a relatively neutral subject at social and business events (asking about a new acquaintance's family, which is appropriate in some cultures, is considered too personal). People ask questions about a person's occupation and if the person enjoys it. Learning how to ask questions is also a very good strategy for lower-level learners because it helps to maintain conversation in a natural way.

Teacher Tip

Going over the Unit Goals is an important stage in the lead-in to each unit. It is helpful for students to know what they are going to be learning so they can activate prior knowledge in English. Activating what students already know about a topic helps them be able to organize and understand the new knowledge.

Speaking	Reading	Writing	Video Journal
Asking for and giving personal information **Pronunciation:** Contractions of *be*: -'m, -'re, -'s	**National Geographic:** "People from Around the World"	Writing about a person and his or her occupation	**National Geographic:** "The Last of the Woman Divers"

3

Meet People

Vocabulary

- Direct students' attention to the map. Tell them they are going to meet people from these places. Go over the names of the countries and nationalities in the box, pronouncing them for students to repeat. Have students look at the pictures and say what the people are doing. Provide vocabulary as necessary.

- Introduce the names of the occupations listed in the box. Pronounce them for students to repeat and explain as necessary. Point out that *police officer* can be used for both *policeman* and *policewoman*.

A • Have students complete the sentences with the nationalities and occupations.

- Have students compare answers with a partner.

- Check answers. Point out that nationalities must have a capital letter in English.

Engage!

- Have pairs rank the jobs from most to least difficult. Have pairs join to make groups of four to share their rankings and talk about the differences they have. Have groups share, and have the class try to agree on a ranking. Write the list on the board.

B • Point out the expression in the Real Language box.

- Read through the conversation with the class. Model the conversation about Norma.

- Divide the class into pairs, and have them make new conversations about the other people pictured in **A**.

- Call on pairs of students to present their conversations to the class.

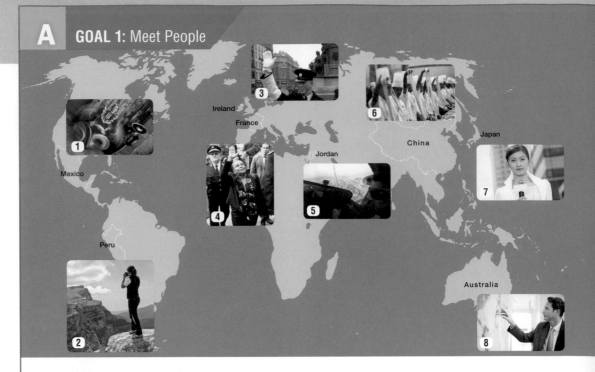

A **GOAL 1:** Meet People

Countries and Nationalities

China — Chinese
Australia — Australian
Jordan — Jordanian
France — French
Mexico — Mexican
Peru — Peruvian
Ireland — Irish
Japan — Japanese

Occupations

~~dancer~~ pilot chef journalist politician
photographer police officer travel agent

Vocabulary

A Fill in the blanks. Use words from the boxes.

1. This is Norma. She's ___Mexican___ and she's a ___dancer___.
2. This is Gabriela. She's ___Peruvian___ and she's a ___photographer___.
3. This is Frank. He's ___Irish___ and he's a ___police officer___.
4. This is Marie. She's ___French___ and she's a ___politician___.
5. This is Yaseen. He's ___Jordanian___ and he's a ___pilot___.
6. This is Chuan Li. He's ___Chinese___ and he's a ___chef___.
7. This is Nanako. She's ___Japanese___ and she's a ___journalist___.
8. This is Nicolas. He's ___Australian___ and he's a ___travel agent___.

B 🔄 Work with a partner. Talk about the people in the pictures.

> Norma is from Mexico.

> Oh, she's Mexican. What does she do?

> She's a dancer.

Engage!

Rank the occupations from most difficult (1) to least difficult (8).

Real Language

We say *What does she/he do* to ask about a person's occupation or job.

4   Unit 1

Word Bank: Occupations

accountant	farmer	pharmacist
architect	firefighter	professor
artist	government employee	reporter
computer programmer	homemaker	salesperson
doctor	musician	scientist
electrician	nurse	secretary
engineer	office worker	writer

Grammar: Be

Subject pronoun + *be*		*Be* contractions	
I **am**		I'm	
You/We/They **are**	Thai.	You're We're They're	Thai.
He/She/It **is**		He's She's It's	

Negative statements with *be*

Subject pronoun	*Be*	Negative	
I	**am**		a dancer.
You/We/They	**are**	not	dancers.
He/She/It	**is**		a dancer.

Yes/No questions

Be	Pronoun		Short answers
Are	you/they	Mexican?	Yes, I **am**. No, I'**m** not.
Is	he/she/it		Yes, they **are**. No, he **isn't**.

A Match the questions and the answers.

1. Are you a doctor? __d__
2. Is she Chinese? __b__
3. Is Ben Australian? __a__
4. Are Mario and Teresa students? __c__

a. Yes, he is.
b. No, she isn't. She's Japanese.
c. Yes, they are. They're from Argentina.
d. No, I'm not. I'm a nurse.

B Fill in the blanks with a pronoun and the correct form of the verb *be*.

1. ___I'm not___ from Japan. I'm from Thailand.
2. ___Are you___ from Indonesia? Yes, I am.
3. Where ___are they___ from? They're from China.
4. ___He isn't___ an engineer. He's a doctor.

Conversation

A 🔊 2 Listen to the conversation. Where is Sean from? *Canada*

Sean: So, Claudia, where are you from?
Claudia: I'm from <u>Chile</u>.
Sean: So, you're <u>Chilean</u>, eh? Sounds cool. Are you from <u>Santiago</u>?
Claudia: Yes, I am. And you, Sean? Where are you from?
Sean: I'm <u>Canadian</u>.
Claudia: Wow! <u>Canada</u>. I'd love to go to <u>Canada</u>. Which city are you from?
Sean: I'm from <u>Toronto</u>.

B 🔁 Practice the conversation with a partner. Switch roles and practice it again.

C 🔁 Change the underlined words and make a new conversation.

D 🔃 **GOAL CHECK** ✓ **Meet people**

Choose an occupation, a nationality, and a country for yourself. Walk around the class and introduce yourself to other classmates.

Real Language

To show surprise and interest we can say:

Formal ⟷ Informal
Really? *Wow!* *Cool!*

People **5**

Grammar

- Review statements with *be*. Tell students, *I am a teacher. What about you?* Elicit, *I am a student/a doctor*. Ask several students.
- Go over the information in the first two charts and elicit more examples. Point out the contractions.
- Review the *Yes/No* questions and short answers in the chart.
- Divide the class into pairs. Have them ask three questions and use short answers.

A • Have students work individually to match the columns.
- Check answers.

B • Have students complete the sentences with pronouns and *be*.
- Check answers.

Conversation

A • Have students close their books. Write the question on the board: *Where is Sean from?*
- Play the recording. 🔊 2
- Check answers.
- Play or read the conversation again for the class to repeat.
- Practice the conversation in chorus. Point out the expressions in the Real Language box.

B • Have students practice the conversation with a partner.

C • Have students work with the same partner to make a new conversation.
- Call on student pairs to present their conversation to the class.

D 🔃 **GOAL CHECK** ✓

- Have students choose a new occupation, nationality, and country.
- Then have them introduce themselves to as many classmates as possible, using the model.

Grammar: Be

The verb *be* presents difficulties for learners whose languages do not have a similar structure. They may produce incorrect sentences such as *He Chinese* or *She a doctor*. If necessary, explain to the class that every English sentence must contain a verb (a word for an action), and that *be* is a verb. Another thing to consider is that many languages do not use an *it* pronoun. Point out the examples using *it*, and explain to students that *it* is used for things that are not people.

Grammar Practice: Be

With the class, make a list of six to eight famous people from other countries. Then have students write sentences about their occupations and nationalities. For example:

Lionel Messi: *He's a soccer player. He's Argentinian.*

Ask For and Give Personal Information

Listening

A • Divide the class into pairs. Have them look at the pictures and read about the people, then guess the missing information.

B • Tell students they are going to hear part of a TV game show. Ask them what usually happens at the beginning of these shows (the players are introduced). Tell them they are going to hear this part of the show.

• Tell students to listen and write the missing information.

• Play the recording. 🔊 3

• Have students compare answers with their partner.

• Play the recording again and check answers. 🔊 3

C • Have students read the list of countries and then listen and write the nationalities.

• Play the recording again. Check answers. 🔊 3

• If desired, play the recording one more time, pointing out the answers as they are heard. 🔊 3

• Ask, *Do you like game shows? Which ones? Who is usually on game shows?*

Pronunciation

• Review the idea of contractions. Explain that we use contractions in fast or informal speaking.

• Point out the difference in pronunciation between the *s* in *it's* and the *s* in *he's* and *she's*. In *it's*, the *s* is pronounced /s/. The *s* is a voiced /z/ in *he's* and *she's*.

A • Tell students to notice the difference in pronunciation between the separate and contracted forms.

• Play the recording one or more times. Call on rows of students to pronounce the pairs. 🔊 4

B **GOAL 2:** Ask For and Give Personal Information

Listening

A 🔄 Look at the pictures. Talk to a partner. Guess the missing information.

B 🔊 3 Listen to the TV game show. Fill in the blanks with the correct information.

1. Name: Kyoko Hashimoro
Nationality: _Japanese_
City: Tokyo
Country: Japan
Occupation: _engineer_

3. Name: Jim Waters
Nationality: _Canadian_
City: Coldstone
Country: _Canada_
Occupation: Farmer

2. Name: Luis Gomez
Nationality: _Peruvian_
City: Lima
Country: _Peru_
Occupation: _doctor_

4. Name: Bianca da Silva
Nationality: _Brazilian_
City: Rio de Janeiro
Country: _Brazil_
Occupation: Musician

C 🔊 3 Listen to the questions in the game show. Write the nationality.

1. Country: Jordan	**Nationality:** _Jordanian_
2. Country: Germany	**Nationality:** _German_
3. Country: Switzerland	**Nationality:** _Swiss_
4. Country: Jamaica	**Nationality:** _Jamaican_

Pronunciation: Contractions of *be*

A 🔊 4 Listen and repeat.

1. I am   I'm
2. you are   you're
3. he is   he's /z/
4. she is   she's /z/
5. it is   it's /s/

For Your Information: Game shows

Game shows are extremely popular in countries around the world. On them, people must answer questions or participate in activities to win money or prizes. On some game shows, contestants compete alone, while others involve teams or playing with celebrities. Countries as diverse as Argentina, Bulgaria, Iceland, Iran, Macedonia, Pakistan, South Africa, and Venezuela all have game shows among their most popular TV programs.

B 🔊 5 Listen. Circle the verb or contraction you hear. Then listen again and repeat.

1. (**I am** | I'm) a teacher.
2. (He is | **He's**) an engineer.
3. (She is | **She's**) a nurse.
4. (**They are** | They're) interesting.
5. (You are | **You're**) welcome.

C 👥 Play round-robin.

Student 1: I'm a dentist.

Student 2: I'm a student, and he's a dentist.

Student 3: I'm a teacher, she's a student, and he's a dentist.

Continue the game for as many occupations as possible.

▲ Andrew is a pilot.

Communication

A 🔄 **Student A** chooses a card from the ones to the right. **Student B** guesses the card by asking *yes/no* questions.

B: Are you 28 years old? **A:** No, I'm not.

B: Are you a doctor? **A:** Yes, I am.

B: Are you Argentinian? **A:** No, I'm not.

B: Is your name Helen? **A:** Yes, it is!

B 👥 Choose a famous person. The others in the group ask *yes/no* questions to guess who you are. They can ask 20 questions.

* Pictures

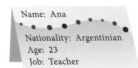

C 👥 **GOAL CHECK** ✔ **Ask for and give personal information**

Interview some of your classmates. Ask their name, their age, and the job they do or want to do.

What job do you want to do?

I want to be a pilot.

Name: Andrew
Nationality: American
Age: 28
Job: Pilot

Name: Pablo
Nationality: Argentinian
Age: 28
Job: Doctor

Name: Mi Hi
Nationality: Korean
Age: 23
Job: Architect

Name: Helen
Nationality: American
Age: 30
Job: Doctor

Name: Kwan
Nationality: Korean
Age: 30
Job: Architect

Name: Ana
Nationality: Argentinian
Age: 23
Job: Teacher

People **7**

Expansion Activity: My class

Have students draw a chart with four columns and the same number of rows as there are people in the class, including the teacher. Have students interview their classmates and you to complete the chart with everybody's name, nationality, age, and occupation (those not working can say *student*). Elicit from students the questions they need to ask, and write them on the board: *What's your name? Where are you from? How old are you? What do you do?*

Describe Different Occupations

Language Expansion

- Introduce the idea of adjectives—words that describe a noun (*a **big** house, a **good** book*). Present the pairs of adjectives under the pictures. Elicit more examples for each adjective (for example, *Who's a rich person? What's a boring job?*).

A • Have students work individually to classify the words.

- Have students compare answers with a partner.

- Check answers by completing the chart on the board.

B • Have students read the sentences and choose an adjective for each one.

- Have students compare answers with a partner and talk about any differences.

- Compare answers with the class.

- Point out the information in the Word Focus box. Ask students, *Which jobs have a good salary?* Write a list on the board.

Grammar

- Go over the information in the first chart and elicit more examples from the students. Say, *Tell me about your job/your classes/this school,* to elicit sentences like: *My job is interesting./My classes are difficult./My school is big.*

- Then go over the information in the second chart and repeat the questions, but have students tell you instead: *It's an interesting job./They're difficult classes./It's a big school.*

- Review the possessive adjectives. Hold up your book and say, *It's my book.* Pick up a student's book, hand it to the student, and say, *It's your book.* Point to a female student, point to her book, and say, *It's her book.* Point to a male student, point to his book, and say *It's his book.*

Language Expansion: Descriptive adjectives

▲ easy   ▲ happy   ▲ unhappy   ▲ interesting   ▲ boring

▲ difficult   ▲ rich   ▲ poor   ▲ safe   ▲ dangerous

Word Focus

salary = money earned through the work you do

A Write the words in the correct column.

Positive		Negative	
happy		unhappy	
rich	safe	poor	dangerous
interesting	easy	boring	difficult

B Read the sentences. Circle an adjective. Compare your answer to your partner's. Discuss any differences.

1. Dan is a travel agent. His job is (interesting | boring).

2. Ana is a police officer. Her job is (safe | dangerous).

3. Mario's job does not have a good **salary.** He is (happy | unhappy).

4. Ismael is a doctor. He is (rich | poor).

5. Gabriela is a teacher. Her job is (easy | difficult).

Grammar: *Be* + adjective (+ noun)

Possessive Adjectives

This is **my** friend.
Is that **your** brother?
His/Her friend comes from Uruguay.
Their parents are nice people.

*Possessive nouns are formed with an apostrophe (') + -s. Laura**'s** friend is from London.

Subject	*Be*	Adjective
My friend	**is**	rich.
His job	**is**	dangerous.
I	**am**	not happy.
My brother's job	**is**	interesting.

Subject	*Be*	Article	Adjective	Noun
It	**is**	an	easy	job.
Your friend	**is**	an	interesting	person.
It	**is**	a	difficult	life.

8   Unit 1

Word Bank: More descriptive adjectives

calm	small
important	traditional
large	unimportant
modern	unpopular
new	worried
old	young
popular	

Victor is an environmentalist. His job is interesting and dangerous.

A Circle the correct word or phrase in parentheses.

1. My father's job is (**interesting** | an interesting). He is a newspaper photographer. It's not (easy | **an easy**) job, but he enjoys it.

2. I am a travel agent. The salary isn't very (**good** | an good). I'm not (**rich** | an rich).

3. John is an engineer. It's (difficult | **a difficult**) job, but it's (interesting | **an interesting**) job.

B Complete the sentences using a possessive adjective.

1. I am a farmer. _____My_____ salary is not very good.

2. Michael is a musician. _____His_____ job is interesting.

3. Susan and Jenny are from Ireland. _____Their_____ nationality is Irish.

4. You are a pilot. I think _____your_____ job is dangerous.

5. Michelle is from Germany. _____Her_____ nationality is German.

C Unscramble the words to write sentences.

1. job friend's is My dangerous.   My friend's job is dangerous.

2. is person. interesting Kim's friend an   Kim's friend is an interesting person.

3. your happy? brother Is   Is your brother happy?

4. rich is not a My father man.   My father is not a rich man.

Conversation

A 🔊 6 Listen to the conversation. What does Graham do?   He's a policeman.

Graham: What do you do, Elsa?
Elsa: I'm <u>an engineer</u>.
Graham: <u>An engineer</u>! That's interesting.
Elsa: Yes, but it's difficult work. And you, Graham? What do you do?

Graham: I'm <u>a policeman</u>.
Elsa: <u>A policeman</u>! Is it dangerous?
Graham: No. In fact, sometimes it's boring.

B 🔄 Practice the conversation with a partner. Switch roles and practice it again. Then change the underlined words and make a new conversation.

C 🔄 **GOAL CHECK** ✓ **Describe different occupations**
Choose an occupation and say two things to your partner about it. Take turns.

A • Have students work individually to choose the correct answers.
• Have students compare answers with a partner.
• Check answers.

B • Have students complete the sentences.
• Have students compare answers with a partner.
• Compare answers with the class.

C • Have students work individually to write the sentences. If necessary, ask, *What do you know about the first word of a sentence?* (It has a capital letter.)
• Have students compare answers with a partner.
• Check answers.

Conversation

A • Have students close their books. Write the question on the board: *What does Graham do?*
• Play the recording. 🔊 6
• Check answers.
• Play or read the conversation again for the class to repeat.
• Practice the conversation with the class in chorus.

B • Have students practice the conversation with a partner and then switch roles and practice it again.

C 🔄 **GOAL CHECK** ✓

• Have students work with a partner, taking turns to talk about an occupation from the previous lessons or another one they know about. Model for the students: *My friend is a bus driver. It's boring and sometimes dangerous.*
• Have several students say something about an occupation.

Grammar Practice: Possessive adjectives

Sit with the class in a circle. The teacher begins by saying, *My name is _____.* The student on your right then says, *His/Her name is _____. My name is _____.* The next student says the names of all of those who have come before (using complete sentences). If a student forgets a name, he or she starts over again with *My name is _____.* Play until all students have had several turns and have learned most of the names.

Grammar: Adjectives

Adjectives generally do not cause difficulty for learners. However, students may occasionally add an -*s* to adjectives that describe plural nouns (*they're interestings books*).

Describe Positive and Negative Parts of Occupations

Reading

- Introduce the topic of the reading. Tell students they are going to read about people in three different countries.

A
- Have students look at the pictures and guess the people's jobs.
- Tell students to read the article the first time and find the people's jobs. Tell them to circle any words they don't understand.
- Check answers.
- Go over the article with the class, answering any questions from the students about vocabulary.

B
- Have students read the article again to mark the statements *true* or *false*.
- Have students compare answers with a partner.
- Check answers.

C
- Have students read the questions.
- Have students compare answers with a partner.
- Tell students to read the article a third time to find the information.
- Check answers.

D **GOAL 4:** Describe Positive and Negative Parts of Occupations

Reading

A Look at the pictures. What do you think these people do? Peter: farmer
Rimii: actress   Tanya: student, musician

B Read the article. Circle **T** for *true* and **F** for *false*.

1. Peter is a pilot.   T (F)
2. Peter's salary is good.   (T) F
3. Rimii is from India.   (T) F
4. She says her work is sometimes interesting.   T (F)
5. Tanya is an engineer.   T (F)
6. She says school is difficult.   T (F)

C Answer the questions.

1. What does Peter do?
   He's a farmer.

2. Is Peter poor?
   No, he isn't.

3. What does Rimii do?
   She's an actress.

4. Is her salary good?
   Yes, it is.

5. Where is Tanya from?
   She's from Boulder, Colorado.

6. Do you think Tanya is happy?
   Answers may vary.

10   Unit 1

PEOPLE FROM AROUND THE WORLD

For some people, their job is interesting, but their salary is not good. For other people, their job is boring, but their salary is good. And then for some lucky people, their job is interesting, and their salary is good.

Let's look at some people and their jobs:

Peter Elworthy is from New Zealand. He is not a pilot; he's a farmer! His farm is very big,

---

For Your Information: New Zealand

New Zealand is a group of islands in the southwestern Pacific Ocean, near Australia. The Polynesian Maori people first reached the islands in about 800 CE. The first European to visit the islands was the Dutch explorer Abel Tasman, in 1642. The two largest islands are made up mostly of mountains and fertile pastures. Because of this, the economy is largely based on farming.

Reading Tip

Students may feel they have to understand the meaning of every word to completely understand a text. Rather than having students look up each word they don't know as they encounter it, have students circle the words they don't understand and keep reading. When students stop to look up a number of words, they lose the thread of meaning. If students circle words and move on, the meaning may become clear through context. For words that do not become clear, allot a specific time for asking and answering vocabulary questions after all the students finish reading.

so he uses an airplane. He says, "I'm happy. My job is interesting, and also the salary is good. And my dog, Shep, can come with me in the airplane."

Rimii Sen is an actress. She is Indian, and she is from Mumbai. "People think an actress's life is exciting, but it is difficult work, and sometimes it is boring. However, the salary is very good!"

Tanya Rogers is a student from Boulder, Colorado, in the United States. She is studying to be an engineer, but she really wants to be a musician. "School is boring, and I love my music. For some musicians, the salary is good, but for most musicians it is not good."

Engineer or musician? What a decision!

People 11

After Reading

Have students bring in a newspaper or magazine photo or an image from the Internet of a person doing his or her job. Divide the class into groups of four or five students, and have the students take turns showing and describing their pictures. Discuss the most interesting/unusual pictures with the whole class.

Describe Positive and Negative Parts of Occupations

Communication

A • Divide the class into pairs and have students write a list of jobs.

• Individually, have students decide if the jobs on their list are interesting or boring and whether they have a good or bad salary. Have them complete the chart.

B • Have students compare their chart with their partner and discuss the differences.

• Compare answers with the class and complete the chart on the board.

Writing

A • Have students look at the pictures and say what they think the people's nationalities and occupations are.

• Have students read about Safi. Ask, *Where is Safi from? What does he do?*

• Write on the board the name and country of someone the students all know. Have students help you write about this person. Write the text on the board.

• Have students complete the information about Angeline and Asef.

• Check answers. For each person, ask about the job; for example, *Is Angeline's job boring or interesting?* etc.

B 🔁 **GOAL CHECK** ✔

• Divide the class into pairs. Have them take turns telling about a friend or family member's occupation.

• Call on students to tell the class about the person's occupation.

D | **GOAL 4:** Describe Positive and Negative Parts of Occupations

Safi

▲ Angeline

▲ Asef

Communication

A 🔁 With a partner, make a list of all the jobs you know. Individually, write them in the boxes in the chart below.

	Good salary	Poor salary
Interesting		*dancer*
Boring		

B 🔁 Compare your answers with your partner's.

Writing

A Look at the people. Write about each person's job and nationality.

Safi: Afghanistan

Safi is ____Afghani____ and *he is a farmer.*

Angeline: Brazil

Angeline is ____Brazilian____ and *she is a (ballet) dancer.*

Asef: Jordan

Asef is ____Jordanian____ and *he is a doctor/nurse.*

B 🔁 | **GOAL CHECK** ✔ **Describe positive and negative parts of occupations**

With a partner, talk about a friend or family member and his or her occupation. Describe good and bad things.

12 **Unit 1**

Teacher Tip: Models for writing

Providing students with a model before asking them to write is helpful. A model text can be used as a framework for producing their own text. As well as having students read the model in the book, it is a good idea to have the class help you write a similar text on the board before they begin to write their own.

A bay on Jeju Island

Before You Watch

A Fill in the blanks. Use the words in the box.

> tour guide   divers   seafood

In Korea, there is a group of woman _____*divers*_____ . They go to the
sea every day to catch _____*seafood*_____ , like octopus and shellfish.
Some of the women are not divers. One of them works with tourists.
She is a _____*tour guide*_____ .

While You Watch

A ▶ Watch the video. Circle **T** for *true* and **F** for *false*.

1. Diving is difficult and dangerous.   (T)   F
2. The water is cold.   (T)   F
3. The divers can stay underwater for
   ten minutes.   T   (F)

4. Sunny Hong is a diver.   T   (F)
5. The women sell the seafood.   (T)   F

After You Watch

A ⚡ Sunny Hong speaks English. She is a tour guide. She is not a diver.
She says, "I am lucky." How can speaking English help *you*?

Communication

A What jobs do women do well? What jobs do men do well? Make a list in your notebook.

B ⚡ Work with a partner. Compare your lists. Are they the same? Do you agree with your partner?

People   **13**

For Your Information: Jeju Island

Jeju Island (also spelled Cheju) is an area of Korea that
developed its own distinctive culture and customs because of
its isolation. It has a much warmer climate than the rest of the
country and produces citrus fruit. One unusual feature of Jeju's
culture is that women have traditionally had roles of authority
in the family because they earned a lot of money, especially
through diving. Today, tourism is the biggest industry in Jeju.
People come to the island for its scenery (a volcanic mountain
with numerous waterfalls), warm climate, and beaches.

Video Journal:
The Last of the Woman Divers

Before You Watch

- Have students look at the pictures
  and say what they see and where
  they think it is. Tell students they
  are going to hear about an unusual
  occupation.

A • Go over the words in the box. Have
  students complete the sentences.

- Check answers.

While You Watch

A • Tell students to watch the video and
  answer *true* or *false*. Have them
  read the statements. Play the video.

- Have students compare answers
  with a partner.

- Check answers.

After You Watch

A • Have students answer the question
  with a partner.

- Discuss the question with the
  whole class. Compile a list on
  the board. Which things are most
  important for the students?

Communication

A • On the board, draw a chart with two
  columns: *Jobs women do well* and
  Jobs men do well. Have students
  write a list of occupations for each
  column. If necessary, have them
  refer back to earlier lessons for the
  names of occupations listed there.

B • Divide the class into pairs and have
  them compare lists and discuss
  any differences.

- Discuss the different jobs that
  students listed, and see whether the
  class agrees with their opinions.
  Point out, *The divers in Jeju Island
  are women. What about divers in
  other countries? Are the women in
  Jeju good divers?*

Work, Rest, and Play

About the Photo

This photo was taken at the Central China Normal University, in Wuhan. It is a large, prestigious university with more than 30,000 students, including more than 1,600 international students. For several years now, the university has allowed parents to spend the first night with their children, sleeping on mats in the gymnasium. Some parents find it hard to get used to the idea of their children leaving home and may even experience what is called "empty nest syndrome," finding themselves feeling alone and missing their children. Staying for the first night helps parents with the transition. It may not be comfortable, but hundreds of families choose to spend their last night together on the university gym floor.

- Introduce the theme of the unit. Ask students, *When do you work? When do you rest? When do you play?*

- Direct students' attention to the photo. Have students describe what they see.

- Have students discuss the questions with a partner.

- Have several students share their ideas. Write them on the board.

- Ask these questions orally or by writing them on the board for students to answer in pairs: *What do you do on workdays? What do you do on weekends?*

- Go over the Unit Goals with the class. For each goal, elicit any words students already know and write them on the board; for example, vocabulary for daily routines (get up, go to work, have lunch, etc.).

Work, Rest, and Play

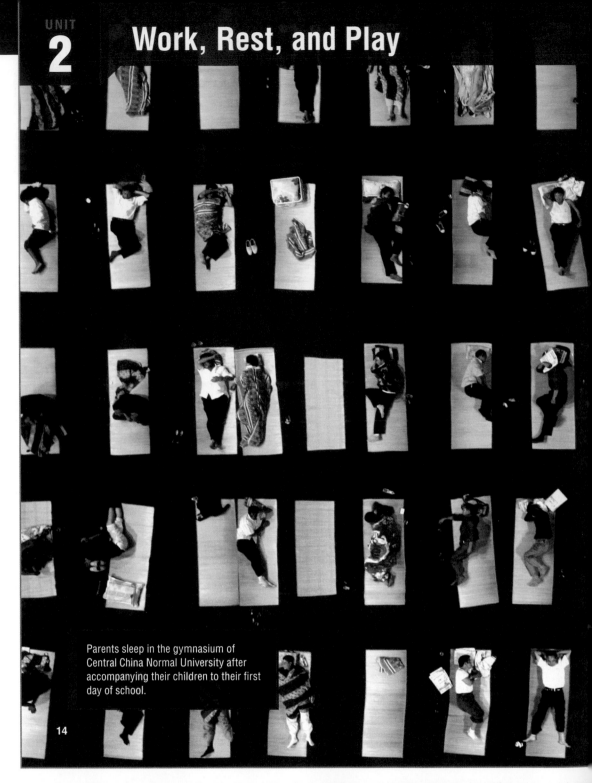

Parents sleep in the gymnasium of Central China Normal University after accompanying their children to their first day of school.

14

UNIT 2 GOALS	**Grammar**	**Vocabulary**	**Listening**
- Talk about a typical day - Talk about free time - Describe a special celebration or festival - Describe daily life in different communities	Review: Simple present tense *Alison **catches** the bus.* Prepositions of time **on** *Saturday,* **in** *the morning,* **at** *five thirty* Adverbs of frequency *We **always** give presents at Christmas.*	Daily activities Party words	Focused listening: Celebrity interview

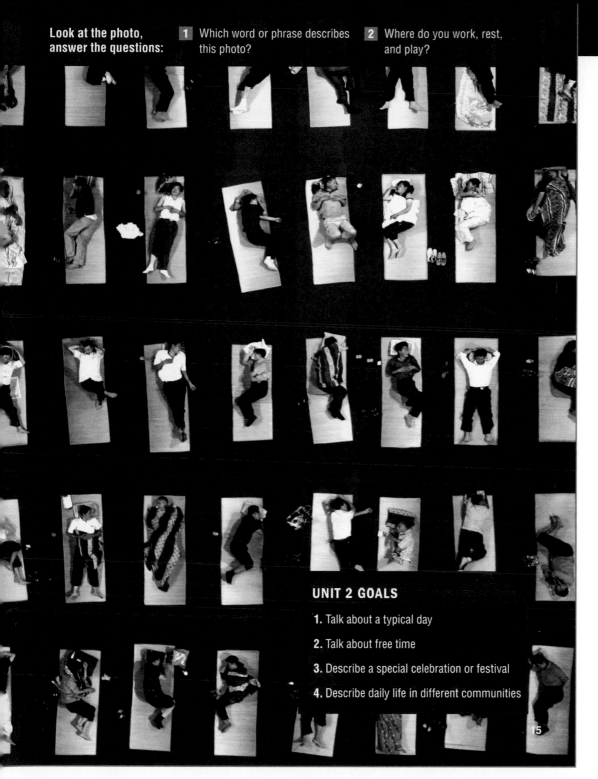

UNIT 2 GOALS

1. Talk about a typical day

2. Talk about free time

3. Describe a special celebration or festival

4. Describe daily life in different communities

Unit Theme Overview

- In this unit, students will learn to talk about regular, repeated activities, using the simple present tense. The sequence of topics discussed moves from the more familiar and universal, to the unique and more specific.

- Students begin by discussing their daily workday activities, which are fairly similar around the world with some important cultural differences (for example, most North Americans like to take a shower in the morning, to start their day feeling clean and fresh, while Japanese people generally bathe at night, to wash away the cares of the day and go to bed relaxed).

- They next consider their free-time activities, which show more individual variation, before considering festivals in their country. Throughout the lessons, they are practicing the language used for the recurring events that make up the fabric of our lives, wherever in the world we live. Students will learn about a virtual choir and think about the daily lives of the participants in an amazing project from TED speaker Eric Whitacre, and finally, students will learn about a special festival in Thailand.

Speaking	Reading	Writing	Video Journal
Talking about daily schedules and free time **Pronunciation:** Verbs that end in -s	**TED Talks:** "Eric Whitacre: A Virtual Choir 2,000 Voices Strong"	Writing a descriptive paragraph about a daily routine	**National Geographic:** "Monkey Business"

Talk About a Typical Day

Vocabulary

- Introduce the topic. Ask, *What do you do on a typical day?* Compile a list on the board.

A • Present the vocabulary in the box by miming or explaining.
- Have students work individually or with a partner to label the pictures.
- Check answers.

B • Have students circle their daily activities.
- Compare answers with the class. For each activity ask for a show of hands from students who do it every day.

C • Have students write a list of other activities they do every day. Provide vocabulary as necessary.
- Call on students to read their list to the class.

D • Have students write the activities that they circled in **A** and the activities on their list from **C** in the order that they do them.

E • Introduce/review the use of *first, next, then, finally* to talk about a sequence of events. Give an example from the daily routine in class: *First, we check our homework. Next, we read the lesson. Then, we practice speaking.*
- Have students talk about their daily routines with a partner.
- Call on students to explain their daily routines to the class.

---

brush your teeth
get up
eat breakfast
go to bed
take a shower
catch the bus
go to the movies
take a nap
watch TV
visit friends
start work
eat out

Vocabulary

A Label the pictures. Use phrases from the box.

a. brush your teeth   b. eat breakfast   c. go to bed

d. catch the bus   e. go to the movies   f. eat out

g. take a nap   h. watch TV   i. visit friends

j. start work   k. get up   l. take a shower

B Circle the activities in exercise **A** that you do every day.

C Make a list of other activities you do every day. Share your list with the class.

First I get up, and **then** I take a shower and brush my teeth.

D In your notebook, write the activities from **A** and **C** that you do, in the order that you do them.

E 🔄 Describe your weekday routine to a partner. Use *first, next, then,* and *finally.*

Word Bank: Daily activities

catch the train/ subway	go to class
clean the house	take a break
cook dinner	take care of children
do chores	sign in/punch in (at work)
drive to work/ school	
eat lunch	wash the dishes

Grammar: Simple present tense

The simple present tense is used for repeated, habitual actions (*I eat vegetables every day.*) and for statements of fact that are always true (*The sun rises in the east.*).

Common errors to watch for include omitting the *-s* or *-es* with the third person singular (*He ~~go~~ to work.*); adding a form of *be* to the verb (*He ~~is go~~ to work every day.*); and forming negative sentences with *no* (*He ~~no go~~ to work every day.*).

Grammar: Simple present tense

Simple present tense	
Statements	**Negative**
I/You **start** work at eight o'clock. Alison **catches** the bus at five thirty. We/They **go** to the movies every Saturday.	I/You **don't start** work at nine o'clock. Alison **doesn't catch** the bus at six thirty. We/They **don't go** to the movies every Friday.
Yes/No questions	**Short answers**
Do you **start** work at eight o'clock? **Does** Alison **catch** the bus at five thirty? **Do** we/they **go** to the movies every Saturday?	Yes, I **do**. No, I **don't**. Yes, she **does**. No, she **doesn't**. Yes, we/they **do**. No, we/they **don't**.

*We use the simple present tense to talk about habits and things that are always true.

A Complete the questions and answers.

Prepositions of time		
on	**in**	**at**
on Saturday(s) on the 4th of July on Valentine's Day on the weekend	in the morning in the afternoon in the evening	at eight o'clock at night

1. **Q:** What time do you _____ get up _____?

   A: I get up _____ at _____ seven o'clock.

2. **Q:** _____ Do _____ you watch TV in the morning?

   A: No, I _____ don't _____ watch TV in the morning.

3. **Q:** Do they _____ go to bed _____ at ten o'clock?

   A: No, they _____ don't go _____ to bed at ten o'clock.

Conversation

A 🔊 7 Listen to the conversation. Does Mia work on Saturday? yes

Omar: So, Mia, you're a <u>secretary</u>.
Mia: That's right.
Omar: What time do you start work?
Mia: At <u>nine o'clock</u>.
Omar: Do you work on Saturday?
Mia: <u>Yes, I do, but we finish work at twelve o'clock on Saturdays.</u>
Omar: What do you do in the evenings?
Mia: <u>I watch TV or go to the movies.</u>

B 🔄 Practice the conversation with a partner. Switch roles and practice it again.

C 🔄 Change the underlined words and make a new conversation.

D 🔄 **GOAL CHECK** ✔ **Talk about a typical day**

Talk with your partner about what you do on Sundays. Mention the times you do each activity.

▲ Sara starts work at her job as a meteorologist at seven o'clock.

Work, Rest, and Play   **17**

Grammar

- Go over the formation of present tense statements. Remind students they must add -s or -es with he/she.
- Ask a student to say three things he or she does every day. Ask the class, What does (Akiko) do every day?
- Go over the formation of negative sentences. Ask a student to say three things he or she doesn't do on Sundays. Ask the class what the student doesn't do.
- Go over the formation of Yes/No questions and short answers. Ask students questions about their daily activities. Elicit short answers.
- Go over the prepositions of time in the chart. Ask students, When do you do your homework/take a shower? and elicit answers with the prepositions of time.

A • Have students work individually to complete the conversations, then check the answers as a class.

Conversation

A • Have students close their books. Write the question on the board: Does Mia work on Saturday?
- Play the recording. 🔊 7
- Check answers.
- Play or read the conversation again for the class to repeat.
- Practice the conversation with the class in chorus.

B • Have students practice the conversation with a partner.

C • Have students work with the same partner to make a new conversation.
- Call on student pairs to present their conversation to the class.

D 🔄 **GOAL CHECK** ✔

- Divide the class into pairs to take turns telling about what they do on Sundays.
- Have several students tell the class about their partners' Sundays.

Grammar: Prepositions of time

Generally speaking, in is used with broader periods of time: in the twentieth century/1976/winter/April/the morning.

On is used with shorter periods of time: on Wednesdays/New Year's Day/March 15th.

At is used with points in time: at 7:30/noon.

Grammar Practice: Simple present tense

Have students interview each other about their usual daily activities. Then have each student write five sentences about his or her partner's activities. Call on students to read an interesting sentence to the class.

Talk About Free Time

Listening

A • Have students look at the picture and describe what they see. Ask, *What do you think his job is?*

• Tell students they are going to hear an interview with an actor about his activities on one day of the week. Have them read the question.

• Play the recording one or more times. 🔊 8

• Check answers.

B • Tell students to listen again to the interview and answer the questions. Go over the questions with them.

• Play the recording one or more times. 🔊 8

• Have students compare answers with a partner.

• Check answers.

• Tell the class, *Bob Hardy is famous. Is his Sunday like yours? Do you think famous people do normal things? Why or why not?*

Pronunciation

A • Remind the class that with *he* or *she*, verbs in the simple present tense take -*s* or -*es* at the end. Point out that the -*s* has different pronunciations (/s/ after a voiceless sound, /z/ after a voiced sound, and /ɪz/ after the letters *ch*, *sh*, *s*, or *z*). Tell them to listen to the pronunciations.

• Play the recording. 🔊 9

• Point out the differences in pronunciation.

• Play the recording again and have students mark the sound they hear. 🔊 9

• Check answers.

B **GOAL 2:** Talk About Free Time

Listening

A 🔊 8 Listen to the interview. What is Bob talking about? Circle the correct answer.

    a. his daily routine   (**b.** his free time)   **c.** his work

B 🔊 8 Listen again. Circle the correct answer.

1. On Sundays, Bob gets up at _____.

    a. eight o'clock   (**b.** nine o'clock)   **c.** ten o'clock

2. In the morning he _____.

    (**a.** takes a nap)   **b.** visits friends   **c.** goes to a movie

3. What does he do in the afternoon?

    a. He has lunch.   (**b.** He watches sports on TV.)   **c.** He visits friends.

4. What does he do in the evening?

    a. He watches TV.   (**b.** He goes out for dinner.)   **c.** He visits friends.

Pronunciation: Verbs that end in -*s*

A 🔊 9 Listen and check (✓) the correct column.

	Ends with /s/	Ends with /z/	Ends with /ɪz/
starts	✓		
comes		✓	
catches			✓
watches			✓
gets	✓		
eats	✓		
goes		✓	

18   Unit 2

For Your Information: Leisure activities

Free time is spent in different ways in different countries and cultures around the world. In the United States, a recent survey showed that reading was the number one free-time activity. This was followed by watching TV, then spending time with family. In a United Kingdom survey on leisure-time activities, watching TV and videos was the most popular pastime and listening to the radio came in second. In a similar survey conducted in Japan, the most popular free-time activity was eating out. The second most popular activity was driving. Karaoke, which ranked fourth, was more popular than watching videos, which came in fifth. Listening to the radio or music ranked sixth.

B 🔊 9 Listen again. Repeat the words.

C ⟳ Use the verbs from exercise **A** and write sentences. Have your partner read your sentences and check the pronunciation.

Communication

A Use the cues to write questions.   Answers may vary.

1. go to the movies / Saturdays *Do you go to the movies on Saturdays?*

2. get up / eight o'clock / the weekend *Do you get up at eight o'clock on the weekend/on weekends?*

3. watch TV / Sunday mornings *Do you watch TV on Sunday mornings?*

4. take a nap / afternoon / weekend *Do you take a nap in the afternoon on the weekend/on weekends?*

5. eat out / weekend *Do you eat out on the weekend/on weekends?*

B 👥 Interview two classmates. Use the questions in exercise **A**. Write *yes* or *no* in the chart.

Question	Classmate's name	Classmate's name
1.		
2.		
3.		
4.		
5.		

C ⟳ Tell a partner about the interviews.

> Ana goes to the movies on Saturdays, and so does Sebastian.

> Ana goes to the movies on Saturdays, but Sebastian doesn't.

> Ana doesn't go to the movies on Saturdays, but Sebastian does.

> Ana doesn't go to the movies on Saturdays, and neither does Sebastian.

D ⟳ **GOAL CHECK** ✔ **Talk about free time**

Talk with a partner about your free time.

> What do you do in your free time?

Word Focus

We use *so do/does* to connect two affirmative sentences.

We use *neither do/does* to connect two negative sentences.

We use *but* when the sentences are different.

B • Tell students to listen again and repeat the words.
• Play the recording. 🔊 9
• Have students practice reading the words to a partner. Walk around and help with difficulties.

C • Have students write sentences with the verbs from **A**.
• Have students exchange their sentences with a partner and read the sentences out loud. Walk around and help with difficulties.
• Call on several students to read a sentence.

Communication

A • Have students write questions using the prompts.
• Have students compare answers with a partner.
• Check and write the questions on the board.

B • Have students interview two classmates using the questions from **A**.
• Have students complete the chart with their classmates' information.

C • Point out the information in the Word Focus box.
• Model the sample dialog with a student.
• Divide the class into pairs and have them tell each other about the people they interviewed. Remind them to use *so, but,* and *neither.*
• Have several students share sentences with the class.

D ⟳ **GOAL CHECK** ✔

• Have students change partners. Have them tell their new partners about what they do in their free time and when they usually do it.

Teacher Tip

When checking answers to exercises that focus on accuracy (for example, the grammar exercises), it is helpful to write the correct answers on the board as well so that students can check that they have written the correct answers in their book or notebook. For some students, only hearing the answers may not be enough, they need to see them as well. Students can also be involved in writing the answers on the board and then the class can check them together.

Expansion Activity

Have students work with a partner to prepare an imaginary interview with a famous person, asking about his or her activities on a Saturday or a Sunday. Have students role-play the interview.

Describe a Special Celebration or Festival

Language Expansion

A • Have students look at the photos and say what they see.

• Have students work individually to read the captions and the text about celebrations.

• Ask, *What countries does the text talk about?* (India, the United States, Italy) *What are the celebrations there called?* (Diwali, Independence Day, Carnival)

• Go over the meanings of the words in blue.

B • Have students work individually to fill in the correct words.

• Have students compare answers with a partner.

• Check answers.

C • Divide the class into pairs and have students discuss the questions.

• Draw a chart on the board with three columns: *fireworks, costumes, presents*. Have students share their answers and complete the chart with the different celebrations.

C **GOAL 3:** Describe a Special Celebration or Festival

People in India enjoy Diwali, the Festival of Lights. They decorate streets and houses in many colors.

In the United States, Americans end their Independence Day celebrations with **fireworks**.

In Venice, people wear **costumes** and cover their faces with **masks** to celebrate Carnival.

Language Expansion: Party words

A Read the text and captions. Pay attention to the words in **blue**.

> All around the world, people need to **celebrate**. During the week we work, on weekends we rest, but we also need to have **fun**. **Festivals** are special celebrations. During festivals people dance, sing, wear different clothes, eat special food, and give **presents** to friends and family.

B Complete the sentences with the words in **blue**.

1. We watch the _____ fireworks _____ on New Year's Eve.
2. I love parties. You can dance and sing. It's _____ fun _____!
3. At Halloween, children wear _____ costumes _____ and _____ masks _____ to cover their faces.
4. We _____ celebrate _____ Christmas on the 24th and 25th of December.
5. I always give my mother _____ presents _____ on her birthday.
6. I like to _____ decorate _____ the house for holidays.

C Discuss the following questions about your country with a partner.

1. Do you watch fireworks? If so, when?
2. Do you wear costumes? If so, when?
3. Do you give presents? If so, when?

20   Unit 2

For Your Information: Famous festivals

Las Fallas (Valencia, Spain): Huge paper figures and scenes are built on the streets and then burned on March 19.

Hogmanay (Edinburgh, Scotland): People celebrate New Year's Eve with parades, fireworks, and noisy parties.

Jidai Matsuri (Kyoto, Japan): People dress in costumes from all eras of the city's history and parade through the streets.

Calgary Stampede (Calgary, Canada): The city sponsors a huge rodeo with cowboy competitions, food, and music.

Songkran (Thailand): People celebrate the Thai New Year by throwing water on each other in the streets.

Dragon Boat Festival (Hong Kong): Dragon-shaped boats filled with rowers and drummers have races.

Camel Fair (Pushkar, India): Thousands of camels and their owners gather to race and celebrate.

Grammar: Adverbs of frequency

0% ———————————————————————————————————— 100%

never	sometimes	often	always

Word order			
Subject	**Adverb of frequency**	**Verb**	
We	**always**	give	presents at Christmas.
We	**never**	dance	in the streets at Christmas.
Subject	*Be*	**Adverb of frequency**	
Christmas	is	**always**	in December.
Carnival	is	**usually**	in February or March.

*We use adverbs of frequency to say how often we do something.   *Adverbs of frequency come **before** the verb unless the verb is *be*.

A Unscramble the words to make sentences. Write the sentences.

1. always We have a on Thanksgiving. turkey   We always have a turkey on Thanksgiving.

2. Valentine's Day. never I send cards on   I never send cards on Valentine's Day.

3. sometimes on visit our We neighbors New Year's.   We sometimes visit our neighbors on New Year's.

4. Nur his forgets wife's sometimes birthday.   Nur sometimes forgets his wife's birthday/Nur forgets his wife's birthday sometimes.

5. is in summer. It hot usually   It is usually hot in summer.

B 🔁 Take turns. Tell a partner which sentences in exercise **A** are true for you.

Conversation

A 🔊 10 Listen to the conversation. Does Chuck have a family meal on New Year's Eve? no

Diego: What do you do on New Year's Eve?
Chuck: Well, we sometimes go downtown. There are fireworks. It's really pretty. Other people invite friends to their house and they have a party.
Diego: Do you give presents to your friends and family?
Chuck: No, we never give presents on New Year's Eve.
Diego: Do you have a meal with your family?
Chuck: No, we do that on Christmas. On New Year's Eve we just have a party!

> **Real Language**
>
> We say we *party* when we have fun with family or friends.

B 🔁 Practice the conversation with a partner. Switch roles and practice it again.

C 🔁 Change the underlined words and make a new conversation.

D 🔁 **GOAL CHECK** ✔ Describe a special celebration or festival

Talk with a partner about your favorite celebration or festival.

Grammar: Adverbs of frequency

Adverbs modify (give more information about) the action in the verb of a sentence. Frequency adverbs answer the question, *How often?*

The most common error to watch out for is in word order: *He ~~gets up sometimes~~ early. I ~~never am~~ late.*

Grammar Practice: Adverbs of frequency

With the class, make a list of festivals and celebrations in the students' countries, including birthdays. Tell each student to choose one celebration they enjoy and one celebration they don't enjoy very much. Have them write five sentences about what they do for each celebration, using adverbs of frequency. (Give examples: *I don't like New Year's Eve. I always stay home. I usually go to bed early!*) Call on students to read one of their lists to the class. What are their favorite celebrations? What are their least favorite?

Grammar

- Direct students' attention to the line with percentages. Tell the class, *I always get up early. What about you?* Elicit, *I sometimes/never/usually get up early.* Continue with other unit vocabulary.
- Go over the information in the chart.

A • Have students work individually to write the sentences. Remind them that adverbs come after *be*, but before other verbs.
- Have students compare answers with a partner, then check answers as a class.

B • Divide the class into pairs to talk about the things in **A** that they do (or don't do).
- Compare answers with the class.

Conversation

A • Have students close their books. Write the question on the board: *Does Chuck have a family meal on New Year's Eve?*
- Play the recording. 🔊 10
- Check answers.
- Play or read the conversation again for the class to repeat. Point out the Real Language box. Explain that we *party* (using *party* as a verb) is informal language. 🔊 10
- Practice the conversation with the class in chorus.

B • Have students practice the conversation with a partner and then switch roles.

C • Have students work with the same partner to make a new conversation.
- Call on student pairs to present their conversation to the class.

D 🔁 **GOAL CHECK** ✔

- Have students change partners and then talk about what they do for their favorite celebration or festival.

Describe Daily Life in Different Communities

Reading

A • Have students look at the pictures and describe what they see.

• Have students identify the kind of music they see. Then have them discuss their answers with a partner.

• Compare answers with the class.

B • Divide the class into pairs and have students talk about the kinds of music they like and when and where they listen to music.

• Have several students share their answers with the class. Write a list of different types of music on the board.

C • Have students read the statements. Point out the words in the Word Bank.

• Have students read the article and choose the correct words to complete the sentences.

• Have students compare answers with a partner.

• Check answers.

D GOAL 4: Describe Daily Life in Different Communities

Reading

A 🔁 Look at the pictures. What kind of music does each show? Discuss with a partner.
Suggested answers:

opera, classical, rock

B 🔁 In pairs, talk about your favorite types of music. When and where do you listen to music?

C Read the article. Choose the correct answer.

1. As a child, Eric Whitacre wanted to be _____ .

   a. a teacher   c. a composer
   b. in a band ✓

2. When Eric Whitacre _____ for the first time, it surprised him.

   a. wrote music
   b. sang with a choir ✓
   c. met a conductor

3. He became a famous conductor and _____ .

   a. composer ✓   c. student
   b. singer

4. _____ makes it possible for people all over the world to join Eric Whitacre's virtual choir.

   a. Pop music   c. The Internet ✓
   b. College

5. The people in the choir are united by _____ .

   a. a love of singing ✓   c. family
   b. living near each other

> **WORD BANK**
> **choir** group of people that sing together
> **choral** related to a choir
> **composer** person who writes music
> **conductor** person who leads a choir
> **virtual** on computers or on the Internet

TED Ideas worth spreading

Eric Whitacre Composer/Conductor

A VIRTUAL CHOIR 2,000 VOICES STRONG

The following article is about Eric Whitacre. After Unit 3, you'll have the opportunity to watch some of Whitacre's TED Talk and learn more about his idea worth spreading.

Eric Whitacre is a **composer** and **conductor.** He is excited about using **choral** music to join people together from all around the world.

As a child, Eric Whitacre lived in a small town with many farms. He loved music. He didn't know how to read music, but he often played instruments. He always wanted to be part of a rock or pop band. Years later, he went to college. There he met the conductor of the college's **choir.** At first, Eric didn't want to join the choir, but finally he did.

The first time that Eric Whitacre sang with the choir, it was a big surprise. He thought that choral music was beautiful and interesting. He learned how to read music, and then he began to write musical pieces. He became a successful composer and conductor.

Whitacre's choir is very unusual because it's completely **virtual.** The Internet makes this possible. The members of the choir don't know each other. They are different ages, from different countries, and have different professions. But they are united by their love of singing and their desire to be part of a worldwide community that makes beautiful music.

For Your Information: Eric Whitacre

Eric Whitacre is a conductor and composer from the United States. Whitacre grew up in a small farming town, but always had a passion for music. In college, he joined the choir and that experience had such an impact on him that he began writing choral pieces. He went on to study at the Juilliard School, a prestigious performing arts school in New York City. Whitacre wrote his first choral work in his early twenties and has received Grammy nominations for his work. However, he recently has become known for his virtual choir. Whitacre had the idea in response to a fan posting a video on YouTube of herself singing one of his pieces. This project has been hugely successful in uniting singers of all ages from around the world to sing. Whitacre's work has shown how technology can be used to bring people together in a positive way. The virtual choir has created a sense of community among people who have never met, and will probably never meet, but who can still be part of the same incredible choir.

"The most transformative experience I've ever had . . . I felt for the first time in my life that I was part of something bigger than myself."

— Eric Whitacre

A choir blends many voices together to make music.

23

Reading Tip

As well as going over the meanings of words that students do not understand, it is also important to check the pronunciation of any unfamiliar words. *Choir is* one word that has a difficult pronunciation. The pronunciation is /kwaɪr/, and students might need the pronunciation modeled several times before they can say it comfortably.

After Reading

Have students work individually or in pairs to search online for more information about Eric Whitacre and his virtual choir. Have them tell the class what they found.

Writing

A • Have students look at the photo and describe what they see. Tell them this person is in the virtual choir. Introduce the idea of *lifestyle*. Ask, *What do you think her life is like? What does she do on a typical day?* Write students' ideas on the board.

• Have students complete the paragraph, then check answers as a class.

B • Copy the *morning routine* word web onto the board. Focus students' attention on the Writing Strategy. Explain how organizing ideas before writing is a helpful strategy to write more effectively.

• Have students complete the word web.

• Have students share their ideas and complete the word web on the board.

C • Have students make a word web about their daily routine.

• Then have them write a paragraph describing their day.

• Have students talk about how the singer's lifestyle is similar to or different than their own.

Communication

A • Have students tell you anything they remember about Eric Whitacre. Write their ideas on the board. Ask, *Is he happy? Does he like his job?*

• Have students read the directions and discuss the questions with a partner.

B ⟳ **GOAL CHECK** ✔

• Divide the class into pairs. Have them pick a singer from the virtual choir and write a paragraph describing the singer's daily routine. Then they should discuss how the singer's lifestyle is similar to and different from their own.

• Have several pairs share their paragraph with the class.

D **GOAL 4:** Describe Daily Life in Different Communities

Writing

> **Writing Strategy**
>
> A word web can help you brainstorm and organize ideas before you write.

A Complete the paragraph about a singer's morning routine.

In the morning, I ____*get up*____ early, around 6:30. Next to my room is the bathroom, where I ___*take a shower*___. Then, I ___*eat breakfast*___ in the kitchen. I never watch TV at breakfast; I often _____*listen*_____ to music.

B Fill in the word web with activities that are related to morning routines.

C ⟳ Make a word web about your daily routine. Then write a paragraph describing your day. With a partner, talk about how the singer's lifestyle is the same or different than yours.

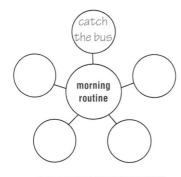

catch the bus

morning routine

> The virtual choir enables people who begin their daily routines at very different times to come together and make music. At 8 a.m. in the United States, Melody is waking up. What time is it for Georgie and Cheryl Ang? What do you think they are doing?

Communication

A ⟳ Eric Whitacre always spent a lot of his free time making music. Now he's a famous composer and conductor. With a partner, talk about the following: What do you love to do in your free time? What is your dream job? Are they related?

B ⟳ **GOAL CHECK** ✔ **Describe daily life in different communities**

Read the paragraph on the left. Pick a singer from the virtual choir. Imagine his or her daily routine. With a partner, write a paragraph describing the day. Talk about how the singer's lifestyle is the same or different than yours.

Georgie from England   **Cheryl Ang from Singapore**   **Melody Myers from the U.S.**

24   Unit 2

Teacher Tip: Starting and ending group and pair work

To make group and pair work go smoothly, it's helpful to use clear signals for beginning and ending the task.

• Write starting and ending times on the board (Group work starts: 10:15. Group work ends: 10:25.)

• Tell your students that group work ends when you clap your hands three times.

• Train your students that when they see you raise your hand, they should also raise their hands and stop talking. The room will fall silent without you interrupting.

VIDEO JOURNAL: *Monkey Business* **E**

Monkeys in Lopburi

Before You Watch

A You are going to watch a video about a monkey festival. Circle five words or expressions you think you will hear in the video. Answers may vary.

food	take a nap
dance	watch TV
visit friends	water
presents	tourist

While You Watch

A ▶ Watch the video. Circle **T** for *true* or **F** for *false*.

1. The monkey festival is on the last Sunday in November. (T) F
2. The monkeys dance. T (F)
3. The people give the monkeys lots of food. (T) F
4. The monkeys cut the electric and telephone cables. (T) F

B ▶ Watch the video again and answer the questions.

1. In which country is Lopburi? Thailand

2. What do the people do for the monkey festival? They take food and water to the monkeys, dance, and have parades.

3. What is the first goal of the festival? to feed the monkeys

4. What is the second goal of the festival? for the tourists

After You Watch

The monkeys of Lopburi are interesting because in other countries, monkeys don't live with people. They are **wild**. But in Lopburi, they live with people. They are **tame.**

A Write the animals from the box in the correct column. Add other animals. Answers may vary.

birds cats cows	
lions horses elephants	

Wild	Tame
lions, elephants, birds, horses	cats, dogs, horses, birds, cows

---

Video Journal: *Monkey Business*

Before You Watch

A • Have students look at the photo and describe what they see.

• Have students read the directions and circle the words and expressions they think they will hear in the video.

While You Watch

A • Have students read the statements.

• Play the video and have students answer *true* or *false*.

• Have students compare answers with a partner. Play the video again as necessary.

• Check answers and confirm the words from **Before You Watch A**

B • Have students read the questions and write any answers they already know.

• Play the video again and have students confirm or complete their answers.

• Have students compare answers with a partner. Play the video again as necessary.

• Check answers.

After You Watch

A • Have students read the information. Ask, *Do wild animals live with people? What about tame animals?*

• Have students write the animals in the correct column of the chart.

• Have students compare answers with a partner. Have them add other animals to the chart.

• Check answers by completing the chart on the board.

For Your Information: The Monkey Festival

In Thailand, monkeys are revered because they are considered descendants of the monkey god Hanuman. The Thai people believe monkeys bring good luck and wealth, so in the town of Lopburi, macaque monkeys roam the streets freely and are fed by the local people. But on the last Sunday of November every year, a banquet is organized for the monkeys at the Phra Prang Sam Yot temple. Large amounts of fruit and other foods are beautifully arranged at the temple for the monkeys. The Monkey Festival is not only important to the local people, it also attracts a lot of tourists, which is good for the local economy.

Going Places

About the Photo

This photo was taken by Kani Polat in the Cappadocia region of Turkey. Hot air balloon rides are a popular tourist attraction in this UNESCO World Heritage site. The region was once covered in volcanic ash, but erosion from wind and water swept the lighter material away and exposed cones, pillars, and chimneys of rock. Some of the structures reach as high as 40 meters (130 feet) tall. The region has been inhabited since between 1800 and 1200 BCE. Around the fourth century CE, the people who lived there began to build tunnels right into the rock. The result is a unique network of underground urban areas used as homes, churches, and for storage. In some places, entire towns with up to eight levels of tunnels can be found.

- Introduce the theme of the unit. Ask students, *What are some ways to travel?* Elicit *airplane, bus, train, car.*

- Direct students' attention to the photo. Have them describe what they see.

- Have students work with a partner to answer the questions. Then, compare answers as a class.

- Ask these questions orally or by writing them on the board for students to answer in pairs: *What are some places in your country that you travel to? How do you usually travel?*

- Go over the Unit Goals with the class.

- For each goal, elicit any words students already know and write them on the board; for example, possessive adjectives (*my, your,* etc.), travel destinations, different forms of transportation, etc.

Hot air balloons fill the sky above the Cappadocia region of Turkey.

26

UNIT 3 GOALS	Grammar	Vocabulary	Listening
• Identify possessions • Ask for and give personal travel information • Give travel advice • Share special travel tips with others	Possession *It* **belongs** *to Ali. It's* **his.** *Should* for advice *You* **should** *bring a credit card.* **Should** *I take a taxi?*	Travel preparations and stages Travel documents and money	General listening: Conversations at the check-in counter, immigration, and hotel reception

Unit Theme Overview

- Travel is one of the world's largest industries, and it's growing larger every year. In 2012, over 3 billion passengers traveled by airplane alone, and it's virtually impossible to say how many used trains, ships, and other modes of transportation. Travel can provide English learners with an opportunity to use their new language skills. Even learners who stay at home are more and more likely to encounter foreign travelers who use English as a language for international communication.

- In this unit, students learn vocabulary pertaining to international travel, especially air travel. They talk about travel preparations and learn how to give advice about travel, while gaining information that may be useful to them on future trips.

UNIT 3 GOALS

1. Identify possessions

2. Ask for and give personal travel information

3. Give travel advice

4. Share special travel tips with others

27

Speaking	Reading	Writing	Video Journal
Giving personal information for travel forms **Pronunciation:** Rising intonation in lists	**National Geographic:** "Smart Traveler: Expert Opinion"	Writing travel tips	**National Geographic:** "Beagle Patrol"

Identify Possessions

Vocabulary

A
- Have students look at the pictures and say what they see.
- Go over the phrases, explaining the vocabulary as needed.
- Have students work with a partner to number the pictures in order. If many students are unfamiliar with air travel, have them do the exercise in groups, or do it together as a whole class.
- Check answers. In some cases, students might have a slightly different order than the given answers. For example, when traveling, you can take a cab from the airport (10), or you can take a cab to the airport (3).

B
- Have students work individually to fill in the sentences with expressions from **A**.
- Have students compare answers with a partner.
- Check answers.

C
- Have students read the questions and write down their answers. Provide vocabulary as needed.
- Have students share their answers with the class. In large classes, have students share in small groups.

A **GOAL 1:** Identify Possessions

Vocabulary

A In what order do you do these things when you travel? Number the pictures.
Answers may vary. Suggested answers:

⑩ ▲ take a taxi

① ▲ buy your ticket

⑥ ▲ board the airplane

④ ▲ go through security

⑨ ▲ claim your baggage

⑦ ▲ go through immigration

⑧ ▲ go through customs

③ ▲ check in

⑤ ▲ buy duty-free goods

② ▲ pack your bags

B Complete the sentences. Use a phrase from exercise **A**.

1. After you ___go through customs___ , you can leave the airport.
2. Do I have to take off my shoes when I ___go through security___ ?
3. At the airport, the first thing you do is ___check in___ .
4. Many people ___buy duty-free goods___ like perfume and chocolates at the airport.
5. When you ___board the airplane___ , you can only take a small bag.
6. Make sure you don't take the wrong bag when you ___claim your baggage___ at the carousel.

C What do you do when you are waiting for a plane? What do you do on the plane? Use a dictionary or ask your teacher for help. Share your ideas with the class.

28   Unit 3

Word Bank: On the airplane

aisle	lavatory
beverage cart	overhead bin
captain	passenger
emergency exit	seat
flight attendant	seat belt
in-flight movie	tray table

Grammar: Possession

English shows possession in a number of ways. Three are presented here: Possessive adjectives modify a noun (*my/his/your bag*). Possessive pronouns take the place of a noun (*mine/his/yours*). *Belong to* + object pronoun is a verb showing possession. (*The dog belongs to them.*) In addition, there are possessive nouns (covered elsewhere), which are formed with *-'s* (*Mark's car*). If a possessive noun is plural, there is only an apostrophe added to the end. (*That is the Johnsons' car.*)

Grammar: Possession

Possessive adjective	Possessive pronoun	*Belong to*	
my	mine		me.
your	yours		you.
his	his	It **belongs to**	him.
her	hers	They **belong to**	her.
our	ours		us.
their	theirs		them.

Real Language

To ask about possession, we can say *Whose _____ is this?*

A Complete the conversations. Use a word or phrase for possession.

1. **A:** Excuse me, is this _____your_____ bag?   **B:** No, it's not _____mine_____.

2. **A:** Is this Anna's bag?   **B:** No, _____hers_____ is green.

3. **A:** _____Whose_____ ticket is this?   **B:** I think it _____belongs to_____ Shawn.

B Answer the questions using *belong to* and a possessive pronoun.

1. Whose passport is this? (Ali) It belongs to Ali. It's his.

2. Whose keys are these? (my keys) They belong to me. They're mine.

3. Whose camera is this? (my sister's) It belongs to my sister. It's hers.

4. Whose bags are these? (John and Lucy's) They belong to John and Lucy. They're theirs.

5. Whose tickets are these? (Logan's and mine) They belong to Logan and me. They're ours.

Conversation

A 🔊 11 Listen to the conversation. Who does the bag belong to?

Anna: Whose <u>bag</u> is this?   *the woman*
Bill: It's not mine.
Anna: Maybe it's Jim's. Is this your <u>bag</u>, Jim?
Jim: No, mine is <u>black</u>.
Anna: Well, whose is it?
Bill: Maybe it belongs to this woman. Excuse me, does this <u>bag</u> belong to you?
Woman: Yes, it's mine. Thank you so much.

B 👥 Practice the conversation in a group of four students. Switch roles and practice it again.

C 🔄 Change the underlined words and make a new conversation.

D 👥 **GOAL CHECK** ✔ Identify possessions

Give a personal item, like your pen or watch, to the teacher. The teacher will then give you someone else's personal item. You have to find the owner.

> Do you know whose watch this is?

> Does this watch belong to you?

> Is this your watch?

Grammar

- Present/review the possessive adjectives. Hold up your book and say, *Here is my book.* Pick up a student's book, hand it back, and say, *Here is your book.* Call on students to form similar sentences.
- Present/review the possessive pronouns. Hold up your book, and say, *It's mine.* Call on students to form similar sentences.
- Introduce *belong to*. Hold up various items and say, *It belongs to you/her.* Point out the Real Language box. Then hold up items and say, *Whose (book) is this?* to elicit, *It belongs to him,* etc.

A • Have students work individually to complete the conversations, then check answers.

B • Have students work individually to write sentences, then check answers.

Conversation

A • Have students close their books. Write the question on the board: *Who does the bag belong to?*
- Play the recording. 🔊 11
- Check answers.
- Play or read the conversation again for the class to repeat.
- Practice the conversation with the class in chorus.

B • Have students practice the conversation in groups.

C • Have students work with the same group to make a new conversation.
- Call on several groups to present their conversations to the class.

D 👥 **GOAL CHECK** ✔

- Have each student give you a personal item. Redistribute the items and have students identify the items' owners.
- Have students say who items belong to; for example, *That pen belongs to her/Ana.*

Grammar Practice: Possession

Have students bring scissors and old magazines with pictures (fashion, technology, sports, cooking, etc.) to class, to be cut up and shared. Divide the class into groups of three or four students and give them five minutes to look through the magazines and cut out pictures of ten things they would like to own (for example, a pair of shoes, a camera, skis). Have each group put all their pictures in a pile, mix them, and then figure out whose picture each one is, using possessive pronouns: *Is this yours? No, it's his. That's not mine,* and so on.

Ask For and Give Personal Travel Information

Listening

A • Have students look at the picture. Ask, *Where is this place? Do you want to go there? Do you go in an airplane from here to get there?*

• Tell students they are going to hear three conversations. They should listen and find the place discussed in each conversation.

• Play the recording one or more times. 🔊 12

• Check answers.

B • Tell students to listen again to answer *true* or *false*. Have them read the statements.

• Play the recording one or more times. 🔊 12

• Have students compare answers with a partner.

• Check answers.

Pronunciation

• Explain that in English, when we say a sentence containing a list of things, our voice rises when we say each thing on the list, and falls when we say the last thing on the list.

A • Tell students to listen to the sentences and read along in their books.

• Point out the numbers chart. Tell students that when we talk about dates we use ordinal numbers like those in the second and third columns. Point out the numbers in item #2.

• Play the recording. 🔊 13

• Tell students to listen again and repeat the sentences. Play the recording one or more times.

• Call on rows or columns of students to repeat the sentences. Then call on individual students to repeat the sentences.

B   GOAL 2: Ask For and Give Personal Travel Information

▲ Rome is one of the most popular places to travel to in the world.

Listening

A 🔊 **12**   Listen to the conversations. Where do the conversations take place?

Conversation 1 _c_   **a.** hotel reception

Conversation 2 _b_   **b.** immigration

Conversation 3 _a_   **c.** check-in counter

B 🔊 **12**   Listen again. Circle **T** for *true* and **F** for *false*.

Conversation 1

1. The man books a window seat.   (T)   F
2. The man has two bags.   T   (F)

Conversation 2

1. This is the woman's first visit to the United States.   (T)   F
2. The woman is staying in the United States for three weeks.   T   (F)

Conversation 3

1. The man is staying at the hotel for one night.   (T)   F
2. The man has one bag.   T   (F)

one	first	1st
two	second	2nd
three	third	3rd
four	fourth	4th
five	fifth	5th
ten	tenth	10th
twenty	twentieth	20th
thirty-one	thirty-first	31st

Pronunciation: Rising intonation on lists

A 🔊 **13**   Listen and repeat the sentences.

1. I'm going to London, Paris, Rome, and Madrid.

2. I'll be in Rome on June 21st, 22nd, and 23rd.

3. In Rome, I want to visit the Colosseum, the Vatican, and the Spanish Steps.

4. To get around, I can take the metro, a taxi, or a Vespa.

30   Unit 3

B 🔄 Practice these sentences with a partner.

1. When we are in Peru, we are going to visit Lima, Cusco, and Machu Picchu.
2. We'll be in Cusco on the 4th, 5th, and 6th of October.
3. To get from Cusco to Machu Picchu, you can take a train, bus, or taxi.
4. The taxi is quick, clean, and expensive.

Communication

A 🔄 Take turns. Ask a partner questions to fill out the immigration form below with his or her information.

> What is your first name?

> My first name is Wahid.

Department of Immigration **PERMISSION TO ENTER**	
1. First name	8. Principal destination in this country
2. Middle name	
3. Family name	9. Hotel and/or street address
4. Date of birth	
5. Place of birth	10. Entry date
6. Nationality	11. Departure date
7. Country of residence	12. Reason for visit

FORM 12a/PTO (Revised08)
[Pursuant to Section 211(d)(3) of the IPA]

B 🔄 **GOAL CHECK** ✔ **Ask for and give personal travel information**

Work with a new partner. Tell your new partner about your previous partner, using the information on the form in exercise **A**.

> His destination is . . .

▲ Children in the Plaza de Armas, Cusco, Peru

Going Places **31**

B • Have students look at the picture at the bottom of the page and describe what they see.
• Have students practice saying the sentences to a partner.
• Call on students to say a sentence for the class.

Communication

A • Introduce the activity. Ask students if they have ever traveled to another country. Were there special papers to fill out? Explain that this is a form from an English-speaking country. Go over the information asked for on the form.
• Divide the class into pairs. Tell students that they will fill out the form using their partner's information (not their own!). Go over the questions they will ask: *What's your first name/nationality/ principal destination?* and so forth. On the board, write, *How do you spell that?* and *Could you repeat that, please?* Finally, tell students they can give true answers or make up answers if they want.
• Walk around, helping as needed.

B 🔄 **GOAL CHECK** ✔

• Assign students new partners, and have them tell their new partner about the person they interviewed in **A**.
• Have several students tell the class about the person their partner told them about.

Expansion Activity

Have students work with a partner to prepare and practice role-playing one of the situations they heard in the **Listening** section (a hotel reception desk, the immigration area of an airport, or an airline check-in counter). Have student pairs present their conversations to the class.

Give Travel Advice

Language Expansion

A • Introduce the names of the documents shown in the pictures. Ask which ones the students have and use.

• Have students work individually to complete the sentences with the names of documents.

• Have students compare answers with a partner.

• Check answers.

• Tell the class, *I'm going to (Japan).* Ask, *What documents do I need?* Elicit, *You need an airline ticket/ a visa,* etc. Talk about various countries.

B • Go over the expressions for giving an opinion. Explain that we say, *I think* and *The best idea is* to give our opinions. We say, *I don't agree* and *I agree* to react to another person's opinion.

• Go over the expressions for giving a reason. Explain that if stores *don't accept* a form of money, you can't use that form of money to buy things there.

• Have students talk with a partner about the best kinds of money to take on a trip.

• Compare answers with the class. Talk about other forms of money that people use while traveling, such as ATM/debit cards (to get money from machines).

C • Have students read the directions. Ask, *What things can you do online when you're planning a vacation?* Have students write a list of things they can do online.

• Model the conversation with a student. Point out the use of *should.* Have students role-play the situation with a partner. Monitor and provide vocabulary as necessary.

• Have several pairs share their conversation with the class.

C GOAL 3: Give Travel Advice

▲ travel insurance

▲ international driver's license

▲ visa

▲ credit cards

▲ passport

Language Expansion: Travel documents and money

A Complete the sentences. Use the names of the travel documents.

1. You need a(n) ___international driver's license___ to drive a car in a foreign country.

2. In some countries, you need a(n) ___visa___ to enter.

3. It's a good idea to buy ___travel insurance___. Medical bills are expensive.

4. Your ___passport___ is your photo ID in any foreign country.

5. You can buy a(n) ___airline ticket___ on the Internet. But you need to write down or print the confirmation number.

B ⟳ Talk to a partner. What is the best form of money to take on your trip? Why?

Give an opinion

> I think credit cards are good.

> The best idea is to take . . .

Give a reason

> People steal . . .

> . . . don't accept . . .

> People lose cash.

▲ airline ticket

▲ cash

C ⟳ Your father is planning a vacation. He usually uses a travel agent. You think he should do the planning online.

1. Write a list of the things he can get online, for example, hotel reservations and museum tickets.

2. With a partner, role-play persuading your father to buy online.

> You should book a hotel online because it is cheaper.

> No, you should ask a travel agent, so you know the hotel is safe.

32 Unit 3

Word Bank:
Exchanging money

bills	currency
buy/sell rate	exchange office
coins	exchange rate
commission	receipt

Grammar: Imperatives and *should* for advice

We use *should* and *shouldn't* to give advice. *Should* + base form of the verb is a tactful or "soft" way of giving advice. It means that the speaker thinks this would be a good idea.

Grammar: *Should* for advice

Should				
Subject	*Should*	Adverb of frequency	Verb	Complement
You	**should**	(always)	make	a copy of your passport.
You	**shouldn't**		wear	expensive jewelry.

*We use *should/shouldn't* to give advice.

Questions with *should*			
Should	Subject	Verb	Complement
Should	I	take	a taxi from the airport?

*We use questions with *should* to ask for advice.

A Ask for advice. Read the responses and write the questions.

1. **Q:** <u>Should I take the shuttle bus to the airport?</u>
   A: Yes, you should. The shuttle bus is quick and cheap.

2. **Q:** <u>Should I bring (take) a sweater to the beach?</u>
   A: No, you shouldn't. It is hot at the beach. You don't need a sweater.

3. **Q:** <u>Should I use a credit card?</u>
   A: Yes, you should. Credit cards are accepted in a lot of shops.

4. **Q:** <u>Should I use (carry) cash?</u>
   A: No, you shouldn't. It's dangerous to carry cash.

B  Ask the questions in exercise **A** and give different advice. Take turns with a partner.

Conversation

A 🔊 14 Listen to the conversation. What does Claudia want from the United States? *a nice present/a watch*

Ayumi: Hi, Claudia. You know the USA. Can you give me some advice? I'm going to New York in January.
Claudia: Lucky you! How can I help?
Ayumi: First: Should I buy travel insurance?
Claudia: Yes, you should. Hospitals and doctors are very expensive in the U.S.
Ayumi: OK. That's another $200. What about clothes? What should I take?
Claudia: You should take a warm sweater and some gloves and a scarf.
Ayumi: Hmm, that's another $100.
Claudia: Oh, just one more thing! Don't forget to buy me a nice present, like a new watch.
Ayumi: Oh no! That's another $500! Traveling is expensive!

B Practice the conversation with a partner. Switch roles and practice it again.

C Change the underlined words and make a new conversation.

D **GOAL CHECK** ✔ **Give travel advice**

Discuss travel tips for visitors to your country. Think about the following topics.

- transportation
- how to carry money
- Can you drink the water?

▲ Washington Square Park, New York City

Going Places 33

Grammar Practice: *Should*

Have students work with a partner. Ask them to write a list of six problems; for example: *1. I don't have any cash. 2. I'm cold.*

Match two pairs and have them take turns reading a problem from their lists. The other pair needs to provide advice using *should*. Then do a class check. Elicit the most original advice from each of the groups.

Grammar

- Introduce *should* for giving advice. Point out that *should* is used with the base form of the verb. Say, *I am from (Brazil). I want to take a vacation in your country. Please give me advice.* Elicit ideas, such as, *You should come here in the summer.*

A
- Have students work individually to write the questions.
- Have students compare answers with a partner, then check answers as a class.

B
- Divide the class into pairs and have them take turns asking and answering the questions, using their own ideas for advice.
- Call on student pairs to present a question and answer to the class.

Conversation

A
- Have students close their books. Write the question on the board: *What does Claudia want from the United States?*
- Play the recording. 🔊 14
- Check answers.
- Play or read the conversation again for the class to repeat.
- Practice the conversation with the class in chorus.

B
- Have students practice the conversation with a partner.

C
- Have students work in the same pairs to make a new conversation.
- Call on several pairs to present their conversation to the class.

D **GOAL CHECK** ✔

- Divide the class into pairs. Have students read the directions and then discuss tips with their partner.
- Write three categories on the board: *transportation, money,* and *water/food.* Have student pairs share their advice and write their ideas on the board.

Share Special Travel Tips with Others

Reading

- Introduce the topic of the reading. Ask students, *When you travel, do you take a lot of things? Or do you travel light? Why?*

- Focus students' attention on the Real Language and Word Focus boxes.

- Have students read the article quickly to get the main idea. Tell them to circle any words they don't understand.

- Go over the article with the class, answering any questions about vocabulary.

A • Tell students to reread the article and answer the questions.
- Have students compare answers with a partner.
- Check answers.

B • Tell students to read the statements and answer *true* or *false*. Have them reread the article if necessary.
- Have students compare answers with a partner.
- Check answers.

D GOAL 4: Share Special Travel Tips with Others

Reading

A Read the article. Then answer the questions.

1. Do you think the author enjoys traveling? <u>Yes (because he knows a lot about travel).</u>

2. Why should you check the expiration date of your passport? <u>Many countries won't let you enter with less than six months left on your passport.</u>

3. Why should you tie a sock to your bag? <u>So you can quickly see your bag on the airport carousel.</u>

4. Why should you take a good book when you travel? <u>It helps to pass the time as you wait for a flight.</u>

B Circle **T** for *true* and **F** for *false*.

1. You need a lot of documents to travel. Ⓣ F

2. You need to take a lot of clothes in your bag. T Ⓕ

3. Bags can be hard to identify at the airport. Ⓣ F

4. Flights are never late. T Ⓕ

5. Airplane food is always good. T Ⓕ

Word Focus

expiration date = the date a thing comes to an end or can no longer be used

---

Real Language

We use the expression *share some pointers* to say *give advice.*

---

34 Unit 3

SMART

Additional Vocabulary

bill = a paper that says you must pay a certain amount of money

delayed = late

medical = related to doctors and hospitals

minimum = the smallest amount you can have

snack = food eaten between meals

For Your Information: Travel tips

Here are more travel tips from experts:

- Always put your name and your itinerary inside each bag that you check in when flying. Name tags can fall off of lost bags, and the airline checks inside the bag for information about the owner.

- Drink a lot of water on the plane. The air inside is very dry, and the water will make you feel much better. Don't drink coffee or tea because they make your body even drier.

- On a long flight, sleep as much as you can. If you arrive in the morning, try to stay awake all day and go to bed at your usual time. If you feel tired, don't sleep for more than an hour during the day. This helps your body adjust to the new time.

- For your return flight, call the airline the day before you travel. Ask if the flight time has changed.

TRAVELER

EXPERT OPINION

In his book Easy Travel, *Mike Connelly shares some pointers on making travel easy:*

DOCUMENTS Make sure you have all your documents: passport, visas, tickets, etc. You should always check the **expiration date** of your passport. Many countries won't let you enter with less than six months left on your passport. Don't forget to buy travel insurance. Medical bills can be very expensive, especially in the United States and Europe. Finally, you should make copies of all your important documents and credit cards and keep them in another bag.

PACKING My advice is—always travel light! I hate to carry heavy bags. Just take the minimum. There is an old saying: *Breakfast in Berlin. Dinner in Delhi. Bags in Bangkok!* So, don't pack anything important in your check-in bag; put important things in your carry-on bag. You don't want to arrive home without your house keys. Another tip—don't use expensive suitcases. People don't steal dirty old bags. Finally, here's a good little tip—tie a sock or brightly colored string to your bag. Why? So you can quickly see your bag on the airport carousel.

THE AIRPORT My first piece of advice is that you should always carry a good book. It helps to pass the time as you wait for your delayed flight. Don't forget to take a sweater or a jacket on the plane. It can get cold on a long night flight. And then there is airline food. Take a snack (cookies or fruit) with you. Sometimes the food is late, sometimes it doesn't arrive at all, and it's never very good.

Going Places 35

Reading Tip: Using authentic material

Reading "real English" can be a motivating factor for many students. Opinion pieces and lists of tips for certain activities are popular in many magazines and newspapers, as well as on Web sites. Have students read other opinion pieces like this article and report their findings back to the class.

After Reading

Divide the class into groups of three or four students. Have each group choose a topic such as food, shopping, transportation, or health and create a poster for visitors with tips and illustrations. Have each group stand up in front of the class to present and explain their poster.

Share Special Travel Tips with Others

Communication

A
- Have students look at the picture and describe what they see. Ask, *Do you want to go on vacation here?*
- Divide the class into pairs and have them decide which vacation they would choose. Remind them that they need to give their reasons.
- Have each pair find another pair who has chosen a different vacation, if possible. Have them explain their reasons for choosing their vacation to each other.
- Have several pairs share their reasons with the class.

B
- Model the questions and statements with several students, using different items from the list.
- With the same partner, have students discuss which items from the list to take.
- Have several pairs share which items they want to take and their reasons for taking each item with the class.

Writing

A
- Choose one of the vacations from **Communication A** and write it on the board. Ask, *What travel tips can you give me for this vacation?*
- Have students help you write a list of tips on the board.
- Have students write travel tips for their vacation individually.

B 🔗 **GOAL CHECK** ✔

- Divide the class into pairs. Have them read their tips to each other and compare ideas.
- Call on students to read their vacation travel tips to the class.

D **GOAL 4:** Share Special Travel Tips with Others

▲ Riviera Maya, Mexico

Communication

A ♻ You have won a vacation for two people and you can choose where to go. Choose one of the following and be ready to say why you chose it.

Resort in Mexico	Historical tour of Angkor Wat, Cambodia
World Cup in Brazil	Adventure tourism in New Zealand
Trekking in the Himalayas	

> Do you think we should take . . . ?

> I think we should take . . . because . . .

> I don't think we should take . . . because . . .

B ♻ Read the list below—your teacher will help you. You can only take five of these items. Discuss which items to take with a partner. Give your reasons.

1. sun block
2. binoculars
3. warm clothes
4. first-aid kit
5. international driver's license
6. water sterilization tablets
7. umbrella
8. maps
9. money belt
10. guidebook
11. sunglasses
12. hair dryer
13. penknife
14. smartphone

Writing

A Write travel tips for your vacation in your notebook.

B ♺ **GOAL CHECK** ✔ **Share special travel tips with others**

Read your travel tips to a partner. Then share them with the class.

Teacher Tip: Encouraging the use of English

A common challenge in monolingual classes is motivating students to use only English in group work. Here are some approaches to consider:

- Explain the rationale for using only English. Tell students, *We learn to speak English by speaking English.* If appropriate, tell students about your own language-learning experiences.

- Establish a clear policy. For example, you might tell students, *It's OK to ask questions in your native language, but for all other things we use only English.*

- Set an example for the students. Use only English for instructions and classroom management.

Before You Watch

A Do you have working dogs in your country? How do these dogs help people?

While You Watch

A ▶ Watch the video. Circle the names of things you see.

(uniform) (apples) (suitcase) passport (mango) (beef jerky)

B ▶ Watch the video again. Circle **T** for *true* and **F** for *false*.

1. Brent and Stockton play before they start work.   (T)   F
2. Detector dogs look for meat.   (T)   F
3. Stockton does not find the meat.   T   (F)
4. Stockton eats the meat he finds.   T   (F)
5. Stockton is learning slowly.   T   (F)

Word Focus

disease   **to bother**   **illegal**

Rats are dirty. Sometimes they carry **disease.**

Hey, kids! Please be quiet. I'm trying to work. You're **bothering** me.

You can't park your car there. It's not allowed. It's **illegal.**

After You Watch/Communication

A In the video, we saw that dogs can be very useful in airports. Work with a partner to write a list of possible problems with dogs in airports.

Answers may vary. Suggested answers:

B With a partner, role-play the following situations.

In **Situation 1,** Student A is a dog handler, and Student B is a passenger. The dog is sniffing in Student B's bag, and Student B does not like dogs.

In **Situation 2,** Student A is a passenger that has fruit in his or her bag. The fruit is a gift. Student B is the dog handler and has to take the fruit.

Some people are afraid of dogs.

The dogs want to eat all the food.

The dogs find the wrong food.

The dogs make noise.

The dogs make the airport dirty.

Going Places   37

Video Journal: *Beagle Patrol*

Before You Watch

A • Introduce the idea of working dogs. Have students discuss different kinds of working dogs that they might know about (for example, search dogs who look for lost people, guard dogs who bark to alert their owners when strangers come near, etc.).

While You Watch

A • Point out the information in the Word Focus box.
- Tell students to watch the video the first time and circle the things they see.
- Play the video.
- Have students compare answers with a partner.
- Check answers.

B • Tell students to watch the video again and answer *true* or *false.* Have the students read the statements.
- Play the video.
- Check answers.

After You Watch/ Communication

A • Divide the class into pairs and have them work together to list possible problems.
- Compare answers with the class.

B • Divide the class into pairs. Have them role-play the two situations.
- Call on several pairs to present one of the situations to the class.

For Your Information: Beagles

The beagle is a small-to-medium-sized dog that was originally used for hunting. Beagles weigh 18 to 35 pounds (8 to 16 kilograms) and have markings of brown, black, and white. Although the modern breed of beagles was developed in England in the 1830s, dogs similar to beagles were used for hunting in ancient Greece! Beagles are known for their excellent sense of smell and their ability to follow the trail of a scent. This makes them very well-suited as detector dogs. They are also popular pets because they are small and have a calm personality. Probably the most famous beagle in the world is Snoopy, the dog in the well-known comic strip *Peanuts.*

A Virtual Choir 2,000 Voices Strong

Before You Watch

- With books closed, have students share what they remember about Eric Whitacre (from the reading in Unit 2). Ask, *Who is Eric Whitacre? What does he do? What does he write? What does he do that is unusual?* Write students' answers on the board.

A • Have students look at the pictures and match them to the correct words.
- Have students compare answers with a partner.
- Check answers.

B • Divide the class into pairs and have them think of an example for *singer, conductor, choir,* and *piano.*
- Have pairs share their examples and write a list on the board.

C • Have students read the sentences and write the correct words to complete the sentences.
- Have students compare answers with a partner.
- Check answers.

D • Tell students they are going to watch a TED Talk. Have them read the instructions. Ask, *What's a virtual choir? What do you think you will hear about in the TED Talk?* Write students' ideas on the board.
- Have students write three things a person should do to start a virtual choir and share their list with a partner.
- Compare answers with the class.

TEDTALKS

Eric Whitacre Composer/Conductor
A VIRTUAL CHOIR 2,000 VOICES STRONG

Before You Watch

A Write the correct word under each picture.

| singer | conductor | choir | piano |

1. conductor
2. singer
3. piano
4. choir

> Eric Whitacre's idea worth spreading is that technology and music can connect us in wonderful, unexpected ways. Watch Whitacre's full TED Talk on TED.com.

D You are going to watch a TED Talk about a virtual choir. What do you think you will see in the video? What things do you think a person should do if they are going to start an online community? Discuss them with a partner.

> **You should have a computer.**

While You Watch

A ▶ Look at the pictures and quotes on the next page. Then watch the TED Talk. As you watch, put the pictures in order. Write the number in the box under the picture.

B ▶ Watch the TED Talk again. Complete the sentences using the words from the box.

| connect | singers | Malta |
| Sleep | Britlin | Jordan |

1. A girl named ___Britlin___ posted a video for Eric Whitacre. Her video gave Eric the idea for the first virtual choir.

2. Eric created a virtual choir to ___connect___ people around the world.

3. The second virtual choir had 2,051 ___singers___.

4. The second virtual choir had singers from many countries, such as Jordan/Malta and Malta/Jordan.

5. Eric Whitacre chose a piece called "___Sleep___" for the second virtual choir.

B 🔄 Work with a partner. Try to think of one example each for items 1–4 in exercise **A**. Share your answers with the class.

C Complete the sentences using the words from the box.

> **community** group of similar people
> **connection** relationship
> **post** put information up
> **record** store music so it can be listened to later
> **virtual** on a computer

1. The sisters had a very strong ___connection___.
2. Please ___record___ your music for him.
3. People who live in a neighborhood are part of the ___community___.
4. The video game had a ___virtual___ world that players could play in.
5. I will ___post___ this information on the Web site for my classmates.

38

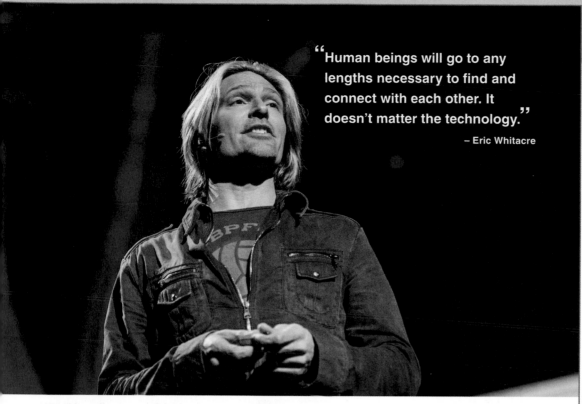

> " **Human beings will go to any lengths necessary to find and connect with each other. It doesn't matter the technology.** "
>
> – Eric Whitacre

While You Watch

A • Have students look at the pictures and read the quotes. Tell them to number the pictures as they watch the talk.

• Play the talk.

• Have students compare answers with a partner.

• Check answers.

B • Have students read the sentences. Tell them to complete the sentences with words from the box as they watch the talk. Play the talk again.

• Have students compare answers with a partner.

• Check answers.

[1] "I had this idea. If I could get 50 people to all do this same thing, sing their parts—soprano, alto, tenor, and bass—wherever they were in the world, post their videos to YouTube, we could cut it all together and create a virtual choir."

[3] "I just couldn't believe the poetry of all of it—these souls all on their own desert island, sending electronic messages in bottles to each other."

[4] "For Virtual Choir 2.0 . . . our final tally was 2,051 videos from 58 different countries. From Malta, Madagascar, Thailand, Vietnam, Jordan, Egypt, Israel, as far north as Alaska, and as far south as New Zealand."

[2] "I posted a conductor track of myself conducting. And it's in complete silence when I filmed it, because I was only hearing the music in my head, imagining the choir that would one day come to be."

39

Viewing Tip

Encourage students to take notes as they watch. Note taking is a useful strategy for students, and one which they can use both in and out of class while they are listening to spoken English. Writing down key words, numbers, dates, etc., can help them understand both the main idea and details of what they hear.

After You Watch

A • Have students read the statements and correct the false information.

• Have students compare answers with a partner. Play the talk again as necessary.

• Check answers.

B • Ask, *Why is Eric Whitaker's virtual choir unusual? Where is a conductor usually when he is conducting a choir?*

• Divide the class into small groups and have them discuss other occupations that could be done virtually.

• Have each group share their ideas and write a list on the board.

C • Say, *I want to be in Eric Whitacre's next virtual choir. What advice can you give me?* Write one or two pieces of advice on the board. As necessary, remind students to use *You should . . . .*

• Have students read the directions and then write six pieces of advice with a partner.

• Have pairs share their advice and add it to the list on the board.

TEDTALKS

Eric Whitacre Composer/Conductor
A VIRTUAL CHOIR 2,000 VOICES STRONG

Virtual Choir 2.0

After You Watch

A Read the sentences. Correct the false information. *Answers will vary.*

1. A choir has to use the Internet. _____*virtual choir*_____

2. In Eric Whitacre's virtual choir, all the singers record their videos at ~~the same time~~. *different times*_____

3. In their testimonials, the singers said that being in the virtual choir ~~did not make~~ them feel connected to other people around the world. _*made*_____

4. All of the members of the choir ~~are now good friends~~, even though they live in different countries and do not meet in person. _*sang together*_____

B Most conductors work with singers in person, but Eric Whitacre conducts a choir online. With a group, take turns naming occupations. For each one, discuss whether it is possible for people in the occupation to work in a virtual way.

Teacher
- Teachers usually work in person.
- It is also possible for them to work in a virtual way. Teachers can teach online.

C Someone you know wants to be part of Eric Whitacre's next virtual choir. What advice would you give? With a partner, brainstorm a list of verbs (*be, learn, post,* etc.). Use *should/shouldn't* and the verbs to write five pieces of advice in your notebook.

40

Rural Alaska

D 🔁 One woman in the virtual choir lives in rural Alaska, 400 miles from the nearest town. What do you think her life is like? Why is the choir important to her? How do music and technology connect her with people around the world? Discuss with a partner.

E 🔀 Do you like to do the following things online, in person, or both? Add your own idea. Then answer by placing a check (✓) in the appropriate box. Then interview your classmates about what they prefer. Write each classmate's initials in the appropriate box. Share with the class.

	Virtual world	In person	Both
1. play games			
2. take classes			
3. talk to family			
4. shop			
5. explore the world			
6. _____			

F Pick one of the activities in exercise **E**. Write a short paragraph about why you think it is better to do that activity online or in person. Use some of the words provided.

to live nearby/far away	to connect	to spend time together/alone
to feel lonely/alone	to meet	

Challenge! 🔀 What other virtual choirs has Eric Whitacre conducted? Visit TED.com to find out. Then share what you learned with a group. Be sure to include the name of the musical piece, the number of singers, the number of countries, and a short description of the piece. Use at least two descriptive adjectives.

41

Ideas Worth Spreading

With books closed, have students share what they remember about Eric Whitacre. Ask, *What is his message? What does he want to tell people? What does his choir accomplish? How?*

- Have students read the information in the Ideas Worth Sharing box on page 38 again. Remind them that they can watch the whole talk at TED.com to help them develop their listening skills.

D • Have students look at the picture and describe what they see.

- Tell students to read the information and the questions. Divide the class into pairs and have them discuss the questions.

- Have different pairs share their answers with the class.

E • Students should read the directions and complete the chart for themselves. Remind them to add an activity of their own.

- Have students interview a partner and write their information in the chart.

- Have students tell the class about their partner's preferences.

F • Tell students to read the directions and the phrases in the box. Ask, *Do you prefer to play games online or in person?* Have students help you start writing a paragraph on the board; for example, *I prefer to play games online to meet new people . . .*

- Have students write a paragraph individually about their preferences.

- Have students exchange paragraphs with a partner and compare their opinions.

Challenge

- With their books closed, have students say why Whitacre's virtual choir is special. Ask, *How do the people in the choir feel? How does Whitacre feel? How are they able to sing all together?* Write their ideas on the board.

- Have students find out about Whitacre's other virtual choirs outside of class and share what they learned with their classmates.

Food

About the Photo

This photo shows spices arranged on a tabletop. A spice is a dried vegetable substance, such as a seed, fruit, root, or bark, that is used to color or flavor food. The study of herbs and spices dates back to at least the year 3000 BCE, in Egypt. Early scholars studied spices for medicine, cosmetics, and cooking. The spice trade started in the Middle East and has existed for at least 4,000 years. At one point, it was one of the most profitable trades in the world and was very important in the development of trade routes, cultural exchange, and alliances between nations. Some of the earliest spices include cinnamon and ginger. As well as adding a distinct flavor to food, spices are useful as preservatives and can also make food healthier by adding antioxidants. The spices in this photo include cayenne pepper, curry, garlic, paprika, and sea salt.

- Direct students' attention to the photo. Have students describe what they see.
- Have students discuss the questions with a partner.
- Compare answers with the class, compiling a list of favorites on the board.
- Go over the Unit Goals with the class, explaining as necessary.
- For each goal, elicit any words students already know and write them on the board; for example, food vocabulary, restaurant expressions, etc.

A colorful blend of spices is displayed in a variety of measuring spoons. People around the world use spices to flavor and preserve food.

42

UNIT 4 GOALS	Grammar	Vocabulary	Listening
• Give a recipe • Order a meal • Talk about diets • Discuss unusual foods	*Some* and *any* with count and non-count nouns *We don't have **any** milk. There is **some** cheese.* *How much* and *How many* with quantifiers: *lots of, a few, a little* ***How many** oranges do you need? **A few.***	Food Diets	General and focused listening: In a restaurant

Unit Theme Overview

- Food is a complex and interesting topic, with cultural, social, health, and even moral aspects. Our food preferences are shaped not only by personal taste, but also by custom, habit, and our physical environment.

- This unit presents several different facets of food around the world. Students begin by looking at individual foods and describing the ingredients in favorite dishes, practicing the use of quantifiers and count/non-count nouns. Next, they talk about food in restaurants and ordering meals there. Another lesson brings in the theme of diet and health and why people eat certain kinds of food. Students also consider the cultural side of food and talk about foods that are considered delicious in some countries and disgusting in others.

UNIT 4 GOALS

1. Give a recipe
2. Order a meal
3. Talk about diets
4. Discuss unusual foods

43

Speaking	Reading	Writing	Video Journal
Role-play: Purchasing food at a store Role-play: Ordering from a menu **Pronunciation:** Reduced forms: *Do you have . . .* and *Would you like . . .*	**National Geographic:** "Bugs as Food"	Writing a recipe	**National Geographic:** "Dangerous Dinner"

Give a Recipe

Vocabulary

- Go over the names of the foods in the picture. Ask, *Which of these foods do you like? Which foods do you eat often?*

A • Have students work individually to choose the correct description for each group of foods.

- Check answers.

B • Divide the class into pairs and have them add other foods to each group.

- Have pairs share their lists, and write a list for each food group on the board.

Grammar

- Go over the information about count and non-count nouns. Explain that non-count nouns are things that we see as a whole and don't count individually (for example, *water, air, cheese*). Look at the foods and drinks in the illustration and give/elicit examples of each (count: *eggs, bananas, peppers*; non-count: *milk, butter, juice*).

- Explain to students that there are some irregular nouns that do not follow the common rule of adding -*s* or -*es* to make a plural; for example, one child–two children, one man–two men.

- Present the information about *some* and *any*. Elicit examples from the picture from students; for example, *There are some potatoes. There aren't any pears.* etc.

A · GOAL 1: Give a Recipe

drinks dairy products
vegetables fruit
protein meat

Vocabulary

A Talk to a partner. Choose a word or phrase from the box to describe each group of foods.

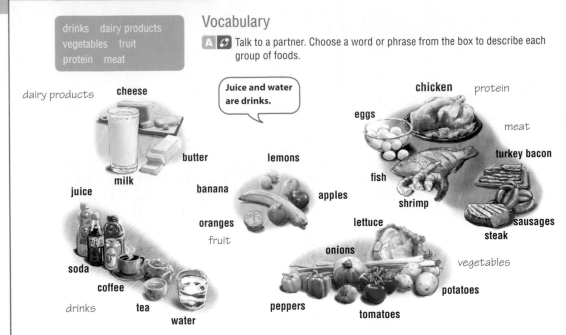

Juice and water are drinks.

Grammar: *Some* and *any* with count and non-count nouns

Count and non-count nouns

Singular	Plural
This is a lemon.	Those are lemons.
This is milk.	~~Those are milks.~~

*For nouns you can count, we add -*s* or -*es* to form the plural.
*Nouns you cannot count don't have a plural form.

B With your partner, think of some other foods you know and write them in the correct group. Then share them with the class.

Some and *any*

	Count nouns		Non-count nouns
	Singular	**Plural**	
Statement	We need an apple.	There are **some** oranges on the table.	There is **some** cheese on the table.
Negative	We don't have a lemon.	There aren't **any** bananas at the store.	We don't have **any** milk.
Question	Do we have a red pepper?	Are there **any** eggs?	Do you have **any** butter?

*You can also use *some* for questions with *could*.
Could I have **some** milk?

44 Unit 4

Word Bank: More foods

dairy: (sour) cream, yogurt

fruit: cherries, grapes, mangoes, melon, nectarines, peaches, strawberries

protein: beans, beef, mutton, tofu, turkey

vegetables: beans, cabbage, carrots, cucumbers, eggplant, squash

Grammar: *Some* and *any*

Some is used in positive sentences, *any* is used in questions and negatives, and *some* and *any* are both used in questions that make offers. This rule has been simplified somewhat but will always produce grammatical sentences. Native speakers generally use *some* in offers when they anticipate a positive answer: *Do you want some ice cream?* They use *any* when they anticipate a negative answer: *Do you want any more ice cream, or should I put it away?*

count: eggs, sausages, oranges, bananas, apples, lemons, potatoes, peppers, tomatoes, onions

A In your notebook, write the food words from the picture in two columns: *Count nouns* and *Non-count nouns*.

non-count: milk, butter, cheese, fish, shrimp, chicken, steak, turkey bacon, lettuce, soda, tea, coffee, water, juice

B 🔀 Add other food words to the chart. Use a dictionary if necessary. Share your words with your group.

C Complete the sentences with *some* or *any*.

1. Do we have ___*any*___ tomatoes?
2. Pass me ___*some*___ apples, please.
3. There isn't ___*any*___ milk in the fridge.
4. I think there is ___*some*___ cheese on the table.
5. There aren't ___*any*___ eggs.
6. Could I have ___*some*___ water, please?

Conversation

A 🔊 15 Listen to the conversation. What do you need to make a Spanish omelet?

Lee:	Let's make a Spanish omelet.
Diana:	Great. What do we need?
Lee:	OK. It says here you need some olive oil. Do we have any olive oil?
Diana:	No, we don't, but it doesn't matter; we have some corn oil. That will do.
Lee:	Next, we need some potatoes, a large onion, and a red pepper.
Diana:	We don't have a red pepper.
Lee:	Never mind. We can use a green pepper.
Diana:	OK. And then we need some eggs. Four eggs.
Lee:	OK! Let's begin!

oil, potatoes, an onion, a pepper, and 4 eggs

> **Real Language**
>
> We can use *never mind* or *it doesn't matter* to show something is not important.

> **Word Focus**
>
> Names of fractions:
> $\frac{1}{2}$ = one-half
> $\frac{1}{3}$ = one-third
> $\frac{1}{4}$ = one-fourth or one-quarter

B 🔄 Practice the conversation with a partner. Switch roles and practice it again.

C 🔄 Choose a new recipe and repeat the conversation.

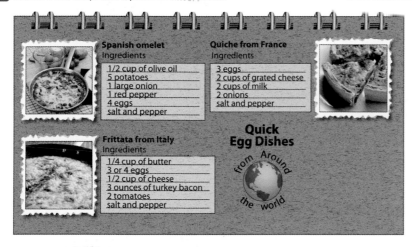

Spanish omelet
Ingredients
1/2 cup of olive oil
5 potatoes
1 large onion
1 red pepper
4 eggs
salt and pepper

Quiche from France
Ingredients
3 eggs
2 cups of grated cheese
2 cups of milk
2 onions
salt and pepper

Frittata from Italy
Ingredients
1/4 cup of butter
3 or 4 eggs
1/2 cup of cheese
3 ounces of turkey bacon
2 tomatoes
salt and pepper

Quick Egg Dishes from Around the world

D 🔄 **GOAL CHECK** ✔ **Give a recipe**

Tell a partner the name of a dish you like. Explain the recipe by describing the ingredients you need to prepare it.

Food **45**

A
- Have students work individually to classify the items in the illustration.
- Have students compare answers with a partner.
- Check answers.

B
- Have students work individually or in pairs to add words to the chart.
- Have students share their lists in small groups.
- Have groups share some of their words with the class.

C
- Have students work individually to complete the sentences.
- Have students compare answers with a partner.
- Check answers.

Conversation

A
- Have students close their books. Write the question on the board: *What do you need to make a Spanish omelet?*
- Focus students' attention on the Real Language box.
- Play the recording. 🔊 15
- Check answers.
- Play or read the conversation again for the class to repeat.
- Practice the conversation with the class in chorus.

B
- Have pairs practice the conversation and then switch roles and practice it again.

C
- With the class, go over the recipes. Ask, *What ingredient is in all of the recipes?* (eggs)
- Go over the words for fractions in the Word Focus box. Explain that fractions are often used in recipes.
- Have students work with a partner to make a new conversation about one of the other recipes.
- Call on student pairs to present their conversations to the class.

D 🔄 **GOAL CHECK** ✔

- Have pairs talk about dishes they like and explain the recipes.

Grammar Practice: *Some* and *any* with count and non-count nouns

Ask a student, *What's in your bag?* and start writing a list on the board: *two books, some paper, a pen . . .* Tell students to write a list of everything in their bag/purse/backpack without looking inside it. Give them a few minutes to write, and then match them with a partner. Have them give their list to their partner, who will read it out loud while they check what's actually inside. Who made the most accurate list?

Order a Meal

Listening

A • Tell students they are going to hear a conversation in a restaurant. Point out the information in the Word Focus box. Go over the terms *waiter* and *customer*. Students should listen to find the number of customers.

• Play the recording one or more times. ◄)) 16

• Check answers.

B • Tell students to listen again to find what the customers ordered. Go over the items on the menu with the class. Explain that *filet mignon* (fi-LAY meen-YAWN) is a French name for a kind of steak. The pronunciation can be shown phonetically as /ˈfɪleɪ ˈmiːnjɒn/.

• Have students compare answers with a partner.

• Play the recording one or more times. ◄)) 16

• Check answers.

B **GOAL 2:** Order a Meal

▲ A busy restaurant in Guilin, China

Listening

A ◄)) 16 Listen to the **waiter** taking an order from **customers**. How many customers are there? *two*

B ◄)) 16 Listen again and write the food and drink that each person ordered.

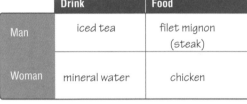

	Drink	Food
Man	iced tea	filet mignon (steak)
Woman	mineral water	chicken

Word Focus

waiter = A *waiter* is a person who works in a restaurant and serves food and drinks.

customer = A *customer* is a person who buys goods or services.

Menu

Appetizers

Chicken 'n Cheese
Deep-fried chicken served with fresh tomatoes and sliced Cheddar cheese

Vegetable Soup
Made from fresh vegetables

Main Dishes

Seashore Shrimp
Grilled shrimp served with peppers and boiled rice

Butter-Baked Chicken
Roasted half-chicken in a lemon sauce served with carrots and potatoes

Filet Mignon
8 oz. grilled tenderloin steak, served with iceberg lettuce and your favorite salad dressing

Drinks
Mineral water, iced tea, coffee

46   Unit 4

For Your Information: Restaurant expressions

The waiter might say:

Are you ready to order?

What would you like to drink?

Our special today is (fried chicken).

Is everything all right? (when coming back to the table to check if diners need anything during the meal)

Would you care for any dessert?

A customer might say:

How is (the fish) cooked?

What kind of (soup) do you have?

Could you please bring me (some butter)?

Excuse me, this dish is cold/too salty/not what I ordered.

Could we have the check/bill, please?

C 🔊 16 Listen again. Who asked these questions?

1. Are you ready to order? _waiter_
2. Do you have any mineral water? _woman_
3. What would you recommend? _woman_
4. Does the filet mignon come with salad? _man_
5. Anything else? _waiter_

Pronunciation: Reduced forms *Do you have . . .* and *Would you like . . .*

A 🔊 17 Listen to the full form and the reduced form.

B 🔊 18 Listen and check (✓) the correct column. Then listen again and repeat.

	Full form	Reduced form
1. Do you have a pen?		✓
2. Would you like some more bread?	✓	
3. Do you have any paper?	✓	
4. Would you like some coffee?		✓
5. Do you have any change?		✓

Communication

A 🔄 With a partner, role-play the following situation.

Student A You work in a supermarket. Serve the customer.

Student B You want to make one of the egg dishes on page 45. Ask for the food you need from the sales assistant.

B 🔄 | **GOAL CHECK** ✔ **Order a meal**

Work with a partner. Choose roles and role-play. Switch roles and role-play again.

Student A You are a customer in a restaurant. Order a meal from the menu on page 46.

Student B You are the waiter. Take the customer's order.

Food **47**

Expansion Activity

With the class, brainstorm the menu for a restaurant, including appetizers, main dishes, and drinks, and write it on the board. If desired, use this menu for the role-play activity for Goal 2.

C
- Tell students to listen to the conversation one more time and write down the person who asked each question.
- Play the recording one or more times. 🔊 16
- Have students compare answers with a partner, then check answers.

Pronunciation

A
- Remind students that when we speak quickly in English, some words and sounds can become "reduced"—pronounced differently.
- Tell students to listen to the full and reduced forms of the two expressions.
- Play the recording. 🔊 17

B
- Tell students to listen to the sentences and mark the pronunciation they hear.
- Play the recording one or more times. 🔊 18
- Have students compare answers with a partner, then check answers.
- Play the recording again and have students repeat. 🔊 18

Communication

A
- Write the following sentences on the board for students to refer to: *May I help you?/I'd like . . . / Anything else?*
- Divide the class into pairs and have them role-play the conversation in a supermarket, then change roles and practice again with a different egg recipe from page 45.
- Call on student pairs to present a conversation to the class.

B 🔄 | **GOAL CHECK** ✔
- Divide the class into pairs. Have them role-play the situation using the menu on page 46. Write expressions from the For Your Information box on page 46 on the board for students to refer to.
- Call on student pairs to present to the class.

Talk About Diets

Language Expansion

- Introduce the idea of special diets. *Why do people eat special diets? What kinds of special diets do students know about?*

- With the class, read the menus for the two kinds of diets. Point out that one has foods with a lot of fiber, and the other has foods with a lot of protein. Clarify the meanings of *fiber* and *protein* if necessary.

- Ask students which foods from the menus they eat regularly/like/don't like.

A • Have students work individually to classify the foods, referring to the menus to help them.

- Have students compare answers with a partner.

- Check answers.

B • Copy the chart onto the board. With the class, brainstorm other foods to add to the chart.

▲ broccoli

▲ cauliflower

▲ beans

▲ whole-wheat bagel

▲ breakfast cereal

▲ nuts

Language Expansion: Diets

Many people eat a special diet. Sometimes, people go on a diet to lose weight and sometimes so that they will feel healthier. Here are two diets: a high-fiber diet and a high-protein diet. The first has a lot of food that contains fiber, for example, whole wheat, brown rice, and maize. The second has a lot of food that contains protein, like meat, fish, and cheese.

	High-fiber diet	High-protein diet
Breakfast	1 bowl of high-fiber breakfast cereal or 2 slices of whole-grain bread or 1 whole-grain bagel fruit	4 slices of turkey bacon or 2 sausages 3 eggs a glass of milk
Snack	popcorn or dried fruit	1 hamburger (without the bread) or 2 beef hot dogs (without the bread)
Lunch or Dinner	vegetables dried pea, bean, or lentil soup berries nuts	1 large steak or chicken cheese

A Write the names of the foods on the page in the correct column.

High-fiber diet	High-protein diet
broccoli, cauliflower, beans, whole-wheat bagel, breakfast cereal	hamburger, tuna salad, nuts

▲ hamburger

▲ tuna salad

B Add the names of other high-fiber and high-protein foods you know to the chart.

Possible answers: High fiber: apples, oranges, lettuce, potatoes, red peppers, green peppers
High protein: milk, eggs, fish, shrimp, chicken, steak, bacon, sausages

48   Unit 4

Word Bank: Nutrition words

balanced diet
calorie
carbohydrate
fat
mineral (iron, calcium)
serving

vegan diet (no meat, fish, eggs, milk, honey, or any foods from animals)

vegetarian diet (no meat or fish)

vitamin (A, D)

Grammar: *How much* and *How many* with quantifiers

To use *How much* and *How many* and *lots of/a few/a little* correctly, students need to have a solid grasp of the count/non-count distinction. Many common errors result from confusing the two, such as ~~How much egg do we need?~~ and ~~How many milk do you drink?~~ For many non-count nouns, English has units that make them countable—for example, *milk/glasses of milk, lettuce/heads of lettuce, cheese/slices of cheese.*

Grammar: *How much* and *How many* with quantifiers: *lots of, a few, a little*

	Information question	Quantifiers	
		++++	+
Count	**How many** oranges do you need?	I need **lots of** oranges.	I need **a few** oranges.
Non-count	**How much** milk do we have?	We have **lots of** milk.	We have **a little** milk.

*We use *lots of* and *a few* to answers questions about quantity.
*We use *a little* to answer questions about small quantities we cannot count.

A Complete the sentences using *a little* or *a few*.

1. There is only ___a little___ tuna salad in the fridge.

2. We only need ___a few___ apples.

3. Please bring ___a few___ bananas.

4. I only take ___a little___ sugar in my coffee.

5. There are just ___a few___ peppers left.

B Fill in the blanks with *How much, How many, lots of, a few,* or *a little*.

1. Q: ___How many___ potatoes would you like?　A: Just ___a few___, thanks.

2. Q: ___How much___ steak do we need?　A: There are eight of us, so we need ___lots of___ steak.

3. Q: ___How much___ broccoli would you like?　A: I'm not very hungry. Just ___a little___.

4. Q: ___How many___ apples do we need?　A: About 20. We eat ___lots of___ apples.

C With a partner, use the words in exercise **A** on page 48 to ask and answer questions.

Conversation

A 🔊 19 Listen to the conversation. Can Pat eat popcorn? Yes (She can eat lots of popcorn.)

Kim: You're looking good.
Pat: Thanks, Kim. I'm on a special diet. It's a high-fiber diet.
Kim: High fiber? You mean lots of bread and fruit?
Pat: That's right.
Kim: How much bread can you eat for breakfast?
Pat: I can eat two slices of whole-grain bread for breakfast or one bowl of high-fiber cereal.
Kim: And what about snacks?
Pat: No problem. I can eat lots of popcorn and dried fruit.
Kim: Mmm, sounds like a delicious diet. Maybe I'll join you.

> **How much cauliflower would you like?**
>
> **Just a little.**

B Practice the conversation with a partner. Switch roles and practice it again.

C Make a new conversation for the high-protein diet.

D | **GOAL CHECK** ✓ **Talk about diets**

With a partner, have a conversation about your own diet or another diet you know.

Food **49**

Grammar

- Go over the information in the chart. Ask, *How much coffee/juice do you drink? How many eggs/desserts do you eat?* Elicit answers with *a few/a little/lots.* Have students ask you questions.

A • Have students work individually to complete the sentences.
- Have students compare answers with a partner, then check answers.

B • Have students work individually to complete the sentences.
- Have students compare answers with a partner, then check answers.

C • Divide the class into pairs to ask and answer questions using the food on page 48 and quantity expressions. Model with several students. Students can also use the words on page 44.
- Call on different students to ask a classmate a question.

Conversation

A • Have students close their books. Write the question on the board: *Can Pat eat popcorn?*
- Play the recording. 🔊 19
- Check answers.
- Play or read the conversation again for the class to repeat.
- Practice the conversation with the class in chorus.

B • Have students practice the conversation with a partner.

C • Have students work with the same partner to make a new conversation about a high-protein diet.
- Call on several pairs to present their conversation to the class.

D | **GOAL CHECK** ✓

- Divide the class into new pairs to talk about their own diet or another kind of diet they know about. Provide vocabulary as necessary.

Grammar Practice: *How much* and *How many* with quantifiers

Write these words on the board: *coffee, desserts, vegetables, water, milk, meat, eggs, fruit.*

Divide the class into pairs and have them ask their partner questions with *How much/How many* about each thing: *How much coffee do you drink?* Then call on students to tell the class if their partner has a healthy diet, and why: *She eats a lot of fruit.*

Discuss Unusual Foods

Reading

- Introduce the topic of the reading. Ask students, *What strange things do people eat in other countries?* Write answers on the board.
- Ask students to think about any things that they eat in their country that people in other countries might not like.

A
- Look at the photos with the class and talk about students' reactions.
- Call on students to answer the question.

B
- Point out the vocabulary in the Word Focus box.
- Have students read the article. Tell them to circle any words they don't understand.
- Go over the article with the class, answering any questions from the students about vocabulary.
- Explain, if necessary, that the article talks about laws for selling food. For example, the United States government says that people can sell chocolate if it has less than 60 bits of bugs in it (per 100 grams).
- Have students work individually to answer the questions.
- Have students compare answers with a partner.
- Check answers.

Reading

A Look at the photos. Do people eat insects in your country?

B Read the article. Answer the questions.

1. What insects are on the menu in the restaurant? <u>crickets, ant eggs, silkworms</u>

2. In Thailand, are insects luxury food? <u>no</u>

3. How many bits of insects are allowed in peanut butter? <u>30</u>

4. What does the author order? <u>chocolate-covered crickets</u>

5. Do you like to eat insects? Give your reasons. <u>Answers will vary.</u>
_____
_____
_____

▲ Crickets, grasshoppers, and other insects-on-a-stick are for sale at a Donghaumen Night Market near Wangfujing Dongcheng, Beijing, China.

Word Focus

luxury = A *luxury* is something we do not really need.

unintentionally = When something happens *unintentionally*, we don't mean for it to happen.

New York City, USA

BUGS AS FOOD

I am sitting in an expensive New York restaurant, and I read the menu. I can't believe my eyes! Chocolate-covered crickets. Wow! I can also order Ant Egg Soup or Silkworm Fried Rice. And it's expensive—$25 for 5 crickets!

I don't like the idea of eating insects. However, in many countries insects are not **luxury** food. They are part of an everyday diet. In Thailand, open-air markets sell silkworms and grasshoppers. Movie theaters in South America sell roasted ants as snacks instead of popcorn.

Additional Vocabulary

estimate = to guess or calculate

contain = have inside

hey = people use this word to get other people to listen to them

---

For Your Information: Edible insects

Insects are eaten in some cultures of Africa, Asia, Australia, and South America. In other cultures, eating insects is uncommon or even taboo. Over 1,200 kinds of insects are eaten, most commonly grasshoppers, crickets, and ants. Arachnids like tarantulas and scorpions are also eaten in some countries. Sometimes, they are eaten for their nutrients or they are used as a condiment or snack. One problem with eating insects is that their bodies may contain a high concentration of pesticides. Today, foods containing insects (such as gourmet chocolates) can be ordered online, and there are even Web sites with recipes for cooking insects.

I am probably eating insects without knowing it, anyway. "It's estimated that the average human eats half a kilogram (1.1 pounds) of insects each year, **unintentionally**," says Lisa Monachelli, director of youth and family programs at New Canaan Nature Center in Connecticut. "For example, in the United States, chocolate can have up to 60 bits of bugs (like legs and heads) per 100 grams. Tomato sauce can contain 30 fly eggs per 100 grams, and peanut butter can have 30 insect bits per 100 grams."

Well, if I am eating insects anyway . . . I decide to order the chocolate-covered crickets, and hey, they taste good.

People eat bugs for food all over the world.

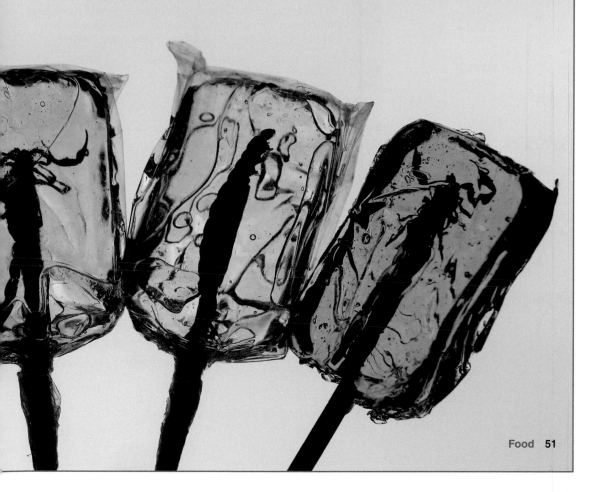

Reading Tip

Remind students that the title, pictures, and captions with an article can help them understand the text. Encourage them to always read the title first, and to look at the pictures and captions, and think about what information they are going to find in the text before they read. Using the information outside the text itself is a good strategy students can use to help them understand what they read.

After Reading

Have students work in small groups to prepare a poster about a traditional food in their city or country. The poster should include a description, pictures, and directions for making the food. Display the posters on the classroom walls.

Discuss Unusual Foods

Communication

A • Have students look at the picture. Ask, *What is this? Do people eat snakes? Do you eat snakes?*

• Have students read the information and identify any of the foods on the list that they eat in their country.

• Have students complete the chart with the delicacies.

B • Divide the class into pairs and have them compare their charts. Have them explain their decisions.

• Have several students share with the class which food they would or would not eat.

C ⚫ **GOAL CHECK** ✓

• Have students write a list of food that visitors to their country might find strange.

• Have students tell the class about the unusual foods they listed. Encourage the rest of the class to ask questions about the food each student talks about. In large classes, divide the class into smaller groups to share their unusual foods.

Writing

A • Have students read the recipe for fried rattlesnake. Explain vocabulary as necessary.

• Have students write a recipe for one of the unusual foods from the list they wrote in **Communication C.** Provide vocabulary as necessary.

• Have students exchange recipes with as many classmates as time allows, then ask them, *Which recipe would you like to try? Definitely not try? Might you try?*

rattlesnake

Communication

Many countries have unusual food. At least, it is unusual to visitors to the country. To the people of the country, it is not unusual. In fact, it is often special food—a delicacy. Here are some examples. Do you eat any of these in your country?

Texas, USA	**Rattlesnake**
Mexico	**Ceviche—uncooked fish**
China	**Bird's nest soup**
Scotland	**Haggis—sheep's stomach**
France	**Frog's legs**
Saudi Arabia	**Sheep's eyeballs**

A Write the delicacies in the chart.

I would **definitely** eat this. ☺	I **might** eat this. 😐	I would **never** eat this. ☹

> I would never eat haggis.

Fried Rattlesnake

1. Catch and kill a rattlesnake.
2. Remove the skin and intestines.
3. Cut it into 5-cm pieces.
4. Fry it in very hot oil.
5. Eat it!

B 🔄 Read your answers from the chart to your partner.

C ⚫ **GOAL CHECK** ✓ Discuss unusual foods

Make a list of delicacies that visitors to your country might find unusual. Share it with the class. Answer questions from the class.

Writing

A Write a recipe for one of the delicacies in exercise **C.**

52 Unit 4

For Your Information: Pufferfish

Pufferfish are the second most poisonous animal in the world (only a species of frog is more toxic). There are more than 120 kinds of puffers, and they live in the sea and in marine estuaries. The skin and some internal organs contain the poison. Fishermen have to wear gloves when handling pufferfish.

These fish are called puffers because when danger approaches, they are able to fill their bodies with more water so that they look much bigger. The poison in a puffer's body is produced from bacteria in its food, so puffers that are raised in an aquarium do not develop any toxins.

whale shark

Video Journal:
Dangerous Dinner

Before You Watch

Ⓐ • Have students work with a partner to answer the questions about the different kinds of fish, and discuss which ones are dangerous and why. Compare answers with the class.

While You Watch

Ⓐ • Tell students to watch the video and answer *true* or *false*. Have students read the statements.

• Play the video.

• Check answers.

Ⓑ • Tell students to watch the video again and answer the questions. Have students read the questions.

• Play the video.

• Check answers.

After You Watch

Ⓐ • Divide the class into pairs and have them discuss the questions.

• Compare answers with the class.

▲ great white shark

▲ stingray

▲ stonefish

▲ pufferfish

Before You Watch

Ⓐ 🔁 Work with a partner. Discuss these questions.

1. Which of these fish can kill you?   2. How can they kill you?

1. The great white shark, stonefish, and pufferfish can kill people.

While You Watch

2. The great white shark kills with its teeth. The others kill with poison.

Ⓐ ▶ Watch the video. Circle **T** for *true* and **F** for *false*.

1. The pufferfish is not expensive.   T Ⓕ
2. Chef Hayashi has a license to prepare *fugu*.   Ⓣ F
3. About 30 people die every year because they eat *fugu*. T Ⓕ
4. American General Douglas MacArthur introduced a test for *fugu* chefs.   Ⓣ F
5. Tom likes the *fugu*.   Ⓣ F

Ⓑ Answer the questions.

1. Is Tom worried about eating *fugu*? _____ *Yes, he is.* _____
2. When did Chef Hayashi get his license? _____ *in 1949* _____
3. How does *fugu* poison kill a person? _____ *The person can't breathe.* _____
4. How many people can a tiger *fugu* kill? _____ *30* _____

After You Watch

Ⓐ 🔁 Discuss these questions with a partner.

1. Why do you think people like to eat *fugu*?
2. Would you eat *fugu*?

Food   53

Teacher Tip: Errors in spoken English

Giving immediate corrections to students during group and pair work is not always effective. Students are too involved in the activity and won't retain the correct information. **Instead:**

• Make notes on errors frequently heard during the activity, and give a mini-lesson after the activity, contrasting the error and the correct form.

• Listen to different groups in rotation, write down important errors, and give the list to the group members to correct.

• Note sentences with errors during the activity, and write them on the board. Together, the class identifies the errors and corrects them.

• For all of these activities, it's best NOT to include the name of the student who made the error. Students generally recognize their own sentences even without names.

Sports

About the Photo

This photo shows expert climbers Hazel Findlay and Alex Honnold climbing the sea cliffs of Acadia National Park, Maine, in the United States. This cliff is called Great Head and is about 30.5 meters (100 feet) high. Having the ocean right below them felt "very dramatic and intense," said Findlay. The photo was taken by photographer and climber Tim Kemple. Kemple specializes in photographing extreme sports athletes in action. He travels the world taking photos of surfers, snowboarders, BASE jumpers, mountain bikers, and more. To get the steep angle of this shot, with the ocean below and the two climbers, Kemple rappelled down the cliff from above.

- Introduce the theme of the unit. Ask students how many sports they can name in English, and write the names on the board.

- Direct students' attention to the photo. Have students describe what they see.

- Have students discuss the questions with a partner.

- Compare answers. Add any different sports to the list on the board.

- Ask these questions orally or by writing them on the board, for students to answer in pairs: *Which sports do you watch? Which sports events do you go to?*

- Go over the Unit Goals with the class.

- For each goal, elicit any words students already know and write them on the board; for example, sports vocabulary, daily activities, frequency words (*often, always*), actions happening now, etc.

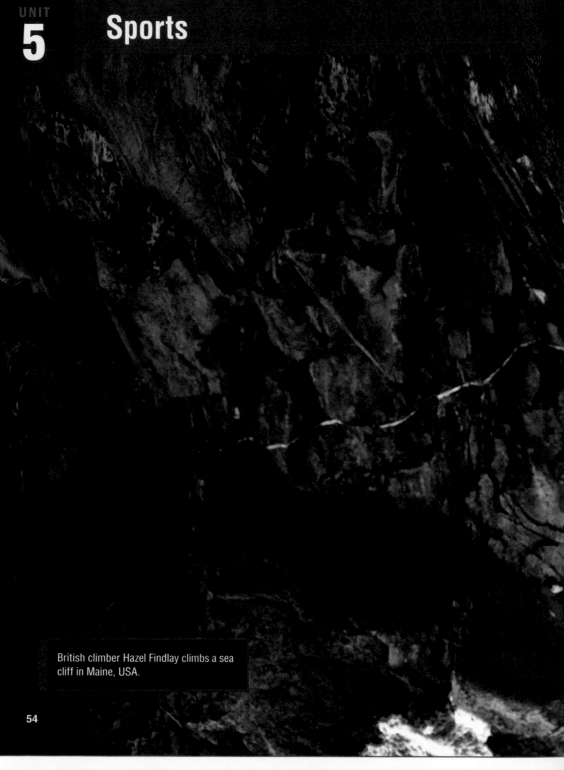

UNIT
5 **Sports**

British climber Hazel Findlay climbs a sea cliff in Maine, USA.

54

UNIT 5 GOALS	Grammar	Vocabulary	Listening
• Describe activities happening now • Compare everyday and present-time activities • Talk about favorite sports • Discuss adventures	Present continuous tense ***Are*** you ***studying*** right now? Stative verbs I ***like*** to be outdoors.	Playing sports Team sports Individual sports	General and focused listening: Everyday activities vs. today's activities

Look at the photo, answer the questions:

1 What is this sport?

2 What sports do you play? What sports would you like to play?

Unit Theme Overview

- The world of sports includes everything from children kicking a soccer ball behind their house to the parade of top-notch athletes entering the stadium at the opening ceremony of the Olympic Games. Sports may be played individually or on teams, indoors or outdoors, by professionals or amateurs. This unit covers a broad variety of sports and invites students to consider the ones they enjoy most and why they enjoy them.

- Students begin by practicing use of the present continuous tense to talk about activities in progress and then learn to contrast these activities with routines and habits. They discuss their preferences in sports and learn to use stative verbs for feelings and mental states. They also read about one athlete, TED speaker Lewis Pugh, and the amazing challenge he undertook to draw attention to climate change.

UNIT 5 GOALS

1. Describe activities happening now

2. Compare everyday and present-time activities

3. Talk about favorite sports

4. Discuss adventures

55

Speaking	Reading	Writing	Video Journal
Talking about what people are doing now Discussing favorite sports **Pronunciation:** Reduced form of *What are you . . .*	**TED Talks:** "Lewis Pugh: My Mind-Shifting Everest Swim"	Writing an e-mail	**National Geographic:** "Cheese-Rolling Races"

Describe Activities Happening Now

Vocabulary

A • Have students look at the pictures and describe what they see.

• Have students work individually to read the conversations and label the photos with the words in blue.

• Check answers.

B • Have students work with a partner to read the descriptions and write the activities from **A**.

• Check answers.

A GOAL 1: Describe Activities Happening Now

Vocabulary

A Read the conversations. Use the words in blue to label the photos.

Anna is studying for a test. She is bored and tired, so she is calling some friends.

Anna:	Hi! What's up? What are you doing?
Bridget:	We're at the beach. Kenny's swimming and the others are playing soccer. How about you? What are you doing?
Anna:	I'm studying! Grrrr!

Anna:	Hi Jill. What are you doing?
Jill:	I'm at Eagle Rocks with Antonia and Pete. They're climbing and I'm hiking. It's really cool. Why don't you come?
Anna:	I can't. I'm studying for a test.

Anna:	Hi Leyla. What's happening?
Leyla:	Hi. I'm at the gym. I'm taking a break. Mary and Catalina are here, too. Mary is lifting weights and Catalina is jogging. What are you doing?
Anna:	I'm studying. Boring!!!

1. taking a break

2. swimming

3. climbing

4. hiking

5. lifting weights

6. jogging

7. playing soccer

B 🔄 Take turns. Read the clues to a partner. Guess an activity from exercise **A**. Write your answer.

1. You do this in the gym. lifting weights

2. You do this in a swimming pool. swimming

3. You play this with a ball. playing soccer

4. It is like running. jogging

5. You do this in the mountains. hiking/climbing

6. You do this when you are tired. taking a break

56 Unit 5

Word Bank: Adventure sports

bungee jumping

kayaking

mountain biking (bicycling)

paragliding

scuba diving

skydiving

white-water rafting

Grammar: Present continuous tense

The present continuous tense is used for actions that are in progress at the time of speaking and actions that are not completed. It contrasts with the simple present tense, which is used to talk about routines and things that are always true. It is formed with *be* and the *-ing* form of the verb.

Grammar: Present continuous tense

	Present continuous tense	
Statement	I **am playing** soccer	right now.
Negative	They **are not taking** a break	at the moment. now.
Yes/No question	**Are** you **studying**	right now? at the moment?
Wh- question	What **are** you **doing**	now?

*We use the present continuous tense to talk about things that are happening at the moment.

A Complete the message. Use the present continuous tense of the verbs given.

Webcam 1: Everest Base Camp

Hi everyone. At last, we are at base camp on Mt. Everest.

Sherpa Parbat (1) ___is cooking___ (cook) dinner.

Smells great, Parbat! Matteo and Sherpa Tensing (2)
___are checking___ (check) the ropes. And here's Ben. It looks

like he (3) ___is writing___ (write) in his daily diary. He

never misses a day. And Dan? What (4) ___is he doing?___

(do)? Ah, typical Dan. He (5) ___is taking___ (take) a nap.

Conversation

A 🔊 **20** Listen to the conversation. What are the twins doing? They're playing soccer.

Mom: Hey, it's quiet today. Where are the kids?
Dad: Well, Mario's playing basketball in the yard.
Mom: What's Carla doing?
Dad: She's swimming in the pool.
Mom: And the twins? What are they doing?
Dad: Uhh . . . I don't know.
Mom: Hey, you two! What are you doing?
Twins: We're playing soccer!

B 🔄 Practice the conversation with a partner. Switch roles and practice it again.

C 🔄 Make a new conversation using other sports.

D 🔄 **GOAL CHECK** ✔ **Describe activities happening now**

Talk to a partner. What are your family and friends doing now?

Sports 57

Grammar Practice: Present continuous tense

Mime an action and tell the class to guess what you're doing, using the present continuous tense: *You're playing tennis. You're watching a scary movie.* Tell the class when they have guessed correctly. Divide students into pairs and have them plan a similar mime for the class to guess. When all pairs are ready, have one student from each pair come to the front of the class and present their mime. At the end of the activity, talk about any funny/difficult/surprising mimes.

Grammar

- Present/review the present continuous tense. Tell the class, *Right now, I'm standing. I'm talking. What are you doing?* Elicit, *I'm studying/listening/writing*, and so on. Point to students and ask, *What is he/she doing? What are they doing?*

- Go over the information in the chart.

A • Have students work individually to complete the message.

- Have students compare answers with a partner.

- Check answers.

Conversation

A • Have students close their books. Write the question on the board: *What are the twins doing?*

- Play the recording. 🔊 **20**

- Check answers.

B • Play or read the conversation again for the class to repeat.

- Practice the conversation with the class in chorus.

- Have students practice the conversation with a partner and then switch roles and practice it again.

C • Have students work with the same partner to make a new conversation about the people, using different sports.

- Call on student pairs to present their conversations to the class.

D 🔄 **GOAL CHECK** ✔

- Have students tell their partners about the activities their friends and family members are doing now, using the present continuous tense.

- Call on students to say a sentence about their partner's family or friends for the class.

Compare Everyday and Present-Time Activities

Listening

A
- Have students look at the pictures and describe what they see.
- Tell students they are going to hear three telephone conversations. They should listen the first time to find what the people are talking about.
- Play the recording one or more times. 🔊 21
- Check answers.

B
- Tell students to listen again to find what the people in the conversations usually do.
- Play the recording one or more times. 🔊 21
- Have students compare answers with a partner.
- Check answers.

C
- Tell students to listen again to the conversations and write what the people are doing today.
- Play the recording one or more times. 🔊 21
- Have students compare answers with a partner.
- Check answers.

B **GOAL 2:** Compare Everyday and Present-Time Activities

Listening

A 🔊 **21** Listen to the phone calls. The people are talking about _____.

   a. what they usually do

   b. what they are doing at the moment

   c. both

▲ go to the movies   ▲ go ice skating   ▲ study

▲ go to a ball game   ▲ play basketball   ▲ fix the roof

B 🔊 **21** Listen again. What do these people usually do? When?

  1. Alan and Karen usually _go to the movies_ on _____Fridays_____.

  2. Khaled usually _____studies_____ in the _____evening_____.

  3. Liam usually _goes to the ball_ on _____Sundays_____.
                               game

C 🔊 **21** Listen again. What are they doing today?

  1. Alan and Karen _are ice skating_____.

  2. Khaled _is playing basketball_____.

  3. Liam _is fixing the roof_____.

58 Unit 5

Word Bank: Sports words

champion	player
coach	point
game	referee
goal	score
fan	scoreboard
league	team
match	uniform

▲ A group of boys play volleyball at sunset.

Pronunciation: Reduced form of *What are you . . .*

A 🔊 22 Listen to the full form and the reduced form.

B 🔊 23 Listen and check (✓) the correct column.

	Full form	Reduced form
1. What are you reading?	✓	
2. What are you thinking?		✓
3. What are you playing?		✓
4. What are you cooking?	✓	
5. What are you writing?		✓

C 🔊 23 Listen again. Repeat the sentences.

D 🔄 Practice this conversation using the reduced form. Repeat the conversation using *eat, read,* and *write*. Replace the underlined words.

A: What are you doing?

B: I'm <u>cooking</u>.

A: What are you <u>cooking</u>?

B: I'm <u>cooking rice</u>.

Communication

A 👥 One member of the group mimes a sport. The other members of the group try to guess the sport.

B 🔄 **GOAL CHECK** ✓ **Compare everyday and present-time activities**

Work with a partner. What are you doing now? What do you do at this time on a Sunday?

Are you playing volleyball?

Yes, I am.

Sports   59

Pronunciation

A • Review the idea that when we speak quickly in English, some words and sounds are "reduced"— pronounced differently.

• Usually, unstressed vowels are reduced to /ə/. For example, *you* changes from /ju/ to /jə/.

• Tell students to listen to the full and reduced forms of the expression.

• Play the recording. 🔊 22

B • Tell students to listen and check the pronunciation they hear.

• Play the recording. 🔊 23

• Have students compare answers with a partner, then check answers.

C • Play the recording for students to repeat the sentences. Then have them practice in pairs. 🔊 23

• Call on students to read the sentences in both forms.

D • Model the conversation.

• Divide the class into pairs and have them practice the conversation with the four verbs.

• Remind them that using the reduced form sounds more natural in spoken English.

• Have several pairs present the conversation to the class.

Communication

A • Divide the class into groups of five or six. Have one student mime an activity and the others guess the mime, using the present continuous tense. Model for the class by miming and having them guess.

• Have a few students mime an activity for the class to guess.

B 🔄 **GOAL CHECK** ✓

• Have students write a list of what they usually do on Sundays.

• Divide the class into pairs to talk about what they're doing now and what they usually do on Sundays.

• Call on students to tell the class about their partner's activities.

Lesson B   59

Expansion Activity

Collect magazine photos of people doing leisure activities, one for each group of four to five students. Put students in groups and give each group a picture. Tell students that the person in the picture is on vacation. Have a "secretary" in each group write down sentences about what the person is doing.

Then have groups imagine an interesting or unusual job for the person in the picture (for example, spy, actor, race-car driver). What does he or she usually do at work? The "secretary" writes down the group's answers on the other side of the paper. (Spy: *He travels to foreign countries. He looks for secrets.*)

Talk About Favorite Sports

Language Expansion

A • Have students look at the pictures and name the sports.

• Introduce the idea of team sports (sports you play as part of a group) and individual sports (sports where one person plays against another person). Elicit examples from the class. Then talk about indoor and outdoor sports and elicit examples.

• Go over the names of the sports in the box. Have students work individually to list the sports in the correct section of the chart.

• Have students compare answers with a partner.

• Check answers.

B • Divide the class into groups of three to four students and have them think of another way to categorize sports—for example, expensive sports or dangerous sports. They should make a list of sports in that category.

• Have each group read its list to the class, without saying the name of the category. The class must then guess the category.

C • Go over the explanations in the Word Focus box.

• With the class (or in groups), have students list more names of sports in the appropriate categories.

Language Expansion: Team sports and individual sports

A Write the following sports in the correct box according to the categories.

> baseball   gymnastics   football   volleyball
> ice hockey   diving   skateboarding   golf

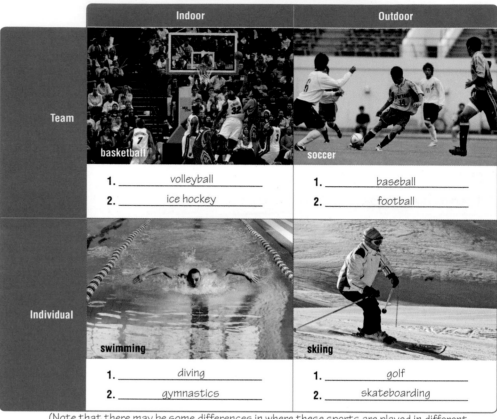

	Indoor	Outdoor
Team	basketball	soccer
	1. _volleyball_	1. _baseball_
	2. _ice hockey_	2. _football_
Individual	swimming	skiing
	1. _diving_	1. _golf_
	2. _gymnastics_	2. _skateboarding_

(Note that there may be some differences in where these sports are played in different countries—for instance, ice hockey can be an outdoor sport in Canada, but not in Brazil.)

Word Focus

We use *play* for team games—for example, *I play soccer.*

We use *go* for individual sports—for example, *I go swimming.*

B Work in groups. Make a chart with new ways to categorize sports. Have the other groups guess the names of your categories.

C Write the names of more sports.   Answers will vary.

play	soccer,	basketball, field hockey, lacrosse, tennis
go	swimming,	skiing, sailing, running, dancing

Word Bank: More sports

archery	martial arts
bowling	ping-pong (table tennis)
boxing	
cycling	racquetball
handball	rock climbing
horseback riding	tennis
horse racing	track and field
	wrestling

Grammar: Stative verbs

Stative verbs are verbs for feelings, senses, emotions, and mental states. They do not describe *actions* that take place, but *states.* (Some books refer to them as *nonaction verbs.*) They are not used in the continuous tenses (present continuous, past continuous, etc.), except with certain special meanings:

Dr. Diaz is <u>seeing</u> a patient now. (= meeting with)
She's <u>having</u> problems with her computer. (= experiencing)

Grammar: Stative verbs

Stative verbs			
like	Why do you **like** outdoor sports? I **like** to be outdoors.	know	You **know** I can't swim.
hate	I **hate** indoor sports.	want	I don't **want** to go bungee jumping.
think	I **think** indoor sports are boring.	need	You **need** a lot of equipment.
prefer	Do you **prefer** outdoor sports?	cost	The equipment **costs** a lot of money.

*We usually do not use stative verbs in the present continuous tense.

A Circle the correct form of the verb in parentheses.

1. Skiing is expensive. It (is costing | (costs)) a lot of money.
2. I (am needing | (need)) a new soccer shirt.
3. The kids ((are playing) | play) in the garden at the moment.
4. I don't like team games. I (am preferring | (prefer)) individual sports.

B Write the correct form of the verb in parentheses.

1. Ashira ___doesn't like___ (not like) to go swimming.
2. I ___am playing___ (play) golf right now. Can I call you back?
3. I like rock climbing but my friend ___hates___ (hate) it.
4. Frederick can't come. He ___is fixing___ (fix) the car.

Conversation

A 🔊 24 Listen to the conversation. Does Adrian want to try rock climbing? no

Adrian: Why do you like rock climbing?
Kris: I hate to be indoors all the time.
Adrian: Me too, but it looks dangerous. I don't want to die.
Kris: Me neither! That's why we use ropes.
Adrian: Do you need a lot of equipment?
Kris: Yes, you do, and it costs a lot of money.
Adrian: So it's expensive and dangerous! Well, I think it's a crazy sport. Definitely not for me.

B 🔄 Practice the conversation with a partner. Switch roles and practice it again. Then change the sport and make a new conversation.

C 🔄 **GOAL CHECK** ✔ **Talk about favorite sports**

Tell a partner about your favorite sport. Say why you like it.

> **Real Language**
>
> We say *me too* to agree with a positive statement and *me neither* to agree with a negative statement.

Sports 61

Grammar

- Go over the information in the chart. Explain that stative verbs are verbs for feeling and thinking. We don't use them in the present continuous tense.

A • Have students work individually to choose the correct form of the verb.
- Have students compare answers with a partner.
- Check answers.

B • Have students work individually to complete the sentences with the correct form of the verb.
- Have students compare answers with a partner.
- Check answers.
- Focus students' attention on the Real Language box.

Conversation

A • Have students close their books. Write the question on the board: *Does Adrian want to try rock climbing?*
- Play the recording. 🔊 24
- Check answers.

B • Play or read the conversation again for the class to repeat.
- Practice the conversation with the class in chorus.
- Have students practice the conversation with a partner and then switch roles and practice it again.
- Have students work with the same partner to make a new conversation about the people, using a different sport.
- Call on student pairs to present their conversations to the class.

🔄 **GOAL CHECK** ✔

- Divide the class into pairs and have them explain why they like their favorite sports.
- Call on students to tell the class about their partner's favorite sports.

Grammar Practice: Stative verbs

Have students work with a partner to write a questionnaire with five questions using stative verbs. (For example, *What sport do you hate? Do you want to go bungee jumping?*) Both partners should write a copy of their questionnaire. When all student pairs are finished, they should exchange questionnaires with another pair and answer the questions they receive. Then they should give the questionnaires back to the pair who wrote the questions. Finish with a whole-class discussion of interesting questions and answers.

Discuss Adventures

Reading

A • Have students look at the pictures and describe what they see.

• Have students read the directions and match the sentences to the pictures.

• Check answers.

B • Point out the words in the Word Bank. Have students read the article and find sentences with stative verbs.

• Have students compare answers with a partner.

• Check answers.

C • Have students read the statements.

• Have students read the article and choose *true* or *false*.

• Have students compare answers with a partner.

• Check answers.

D GOAL 4: Discuss Adventures

Reading

A Lewis Pugh is an activist who does remarkable things to call attention to **environmental** problems. Look at the photos. Match what he and his team are doing to the photos.

 1. _____d_____

 2. _____b_____

 3. _____c_____

 4. _____a_____

a. He is swimming.   c. They are hiking.
b. He is speaking.   d. They are rowing.

B Read the article with a partner. Underline the sentences with stative verbs.

C Circle **T** for *true* or **F** for *false*.

1. Lewis Pugh is not a very good swimmer.   T (F)

2. Mt. Everest is the tallest mountain on Earth.   (T) F

3. Lake Imja is at the bottom of Mt. Everest.   T (F)

4. A glacier is really the same thing as a lake.   T (F)

5. Lewis Pugh thinks that people can protect the environment.   (T) F

WORD BANK

environment where we live; what is around us; the air, land, sea
glacier a huge area of moving ice
global warming a rise in the earth's temperature causing the climate to change
melting becoming water because of heat

62   Unit 5

TED Ideas worth spreading

Lewis Pugh Adventurer/Environmentalist

MY MIND-SHIFTING EVEREST SWIM

The following article is about Lewis Pugh. After Unit 6, you'll have the opportunity to watch some of Pugh's TED Talk and learn more about his idea worth spreading.

Lewis Pugh is a famous swimmer, but not in the way you might think. In 2007 he swam across the North Pole in water that was so cold his fingers were frozen. Why did Pugh do this? Well, he wants people to pay attention to **global warming** and the problems it is causing.

As a boy, Lewis visited national parks and he learned how fragile and amazing the Earth is. Now he wants to protect the Earth and draw attention to the problems facing it. He decided to swim in water near the North Pole to bring attention to the **melting glaciers** and icecap. Lewis said that the swim was so scary and painful that it would be his last time swimming in freezing water. But when he heard about Lake Imja, near Mt. Everest, high in the Himalayas, he decided to swim in cold water again.

Mt. Everest is the tallest mountain in the world and swimming there is very difficult. It's so high that it's hard to breathe. You feel sick and your head hurts. Because of global warming, glaciers on Mt. Everest are melting and leaving lakes behind, like Lake Imja. This means there's less water for people who need it in nearby countries like China, India, Pakistan, and Bangladesh.

Lewis says he learned two lessons from swimming at Mt. Everest. First, he learned that people can unintentionally do a lot of damage. We do things that hurt the Earth because we know no other way to live. Second, he learned that if we change the way we think, we can do things we didn't think were possible. We can all do something to protect our environment if we change the way we think and think more about our future.

For Your Information: Lewis Pugh

Lewis Pugh is a maritime lawyer, an activist for saving the world's oceans, and a pioneer swimmer. Pugh was the first person to swim across a section of ocean near the North Pole, and later, across a glacial lake on Mt. Everest. He carries out these dangerous swims in order to draw attention to the environmental problems being caused by climate change—specifically, how it is affecting the oceans of the world. Pugh firmly believes that we can achieve the impossible if we put our minds to it; he demonstrates this through his pioneer swimming expeditions. However, his message goes beyond that. He wants people to take action. He wants to change the way we live and treat our planet in order to stop climate change and the resulting environmental issues, such as melting glaciers and rising sea levels and temperatures. As a speaker, Pugh has worked with some of the most important organizations in the world, encouraging them to take actions that will prevent harm to the environment.

"I heard about the Himalayas and the melting of the glaciers because of climate change."

"Very few things are impossible to achieve if we really put our whole minds to it."

– Lewis Pugh

63

Reading Tip

In small groups or pairs, students can work together to come up with their own comprehension questions about the article. Then they exchange their questions with another group and return their answers for checking.

After Reading

Have students use the Internet to find out what other oceans and lakes Lewis Pugh has swum in around the world. Have students report back to the class.

Communication

A • Have students look at the lists of activities and equipment and match them.

• Have students compare answers with a partner.

• Check answers.

B • Have students read the sentences and complete them with the correct verbs from the box.

• Have students compare answers with a partner.

• Check answers.

C • Elicit from students other examples of dangerous sports. Write a few on the board.

• Divide the class into pairs and have students discuss the questions.

• Have several pairs share their answers with the class.

Writing

A • Have students read the quotation in the box. Ask, *How do you think Pugh felt when he started his swim?*

• Have students suggest other dangerous sports, and write them on the board.

• Choose one sport and tell students you want to try this sport. Have students help you begin writing an e-mail on the board, telling a friend about the sport.

• Have students write their own e-mails individually about a dangerous sport they want to try.

B 🔲 **GOAL CHECK** ✓

• Have students exchange e-mails with a partner and discuss how their dangerous sport e-mails are similar or different.

• Have students tell the class about their partner's dangerous sport e-mail.

D **GOAL 4:** Discuss Adventures

A lake created by a melted glacier in the Himalayas

Communication

A Match the equipment to the activity. Write the correct number.

1. a ball   _1_ playing soccer

2. boots   _5_ ice hockey

3. a bathing suit _4_ hiking

4. a backpack   _3_ swimming

5. skates   _2_ mountain climbing

B Complete the sentences with the correct verbs. Use the words in the box.

> fishing   climbing
> swimming   jogging

1. We love the water. We are going _swimming_ tomorrow.

2. Ahmed wants to catch and eat some shrimp. He is going _fishing_.

3. They like the mountains. They are going _climbing_ this weekend.

4. Jill would like to exercise in the park. She is going _jogging_ today.

C 🔄 Lewis Pugh swims in dangerous conditions. What other sports can be dangerous? How are they dangerous? Have you ever played a dangerous sport? Which one? Discuss with a partner.

> "We all got down onto the ice, and I then got into my swimming costume and I dived into the sea. I have never in my life felt anything like that moment. I could barely breathe. I was gasping for air."

Writing

A Read Lewis Pugh's quote. Then write an e-mail to a friend about a dangerous sport that you'd like to try.

B 🔄 **GOAL CHECK** ✓ **Discuss adventures**

Share your e-mail with a partner. How are they the same? How are they different?

cheese rolling

Before You Watch

A 🔄 Which of these unusual sports would you like to try? Why? Discuss with a partner.

While You Watch

A ▶ Fill in the blanks. Use the words in the box. Watch the video and check your answers.

> injuries cold
> spectators winner

▲ octopush

1. The first ____winner____ of the day is Craig Brown.
2. One year, one of the cheeses went into the ___spectators___.
3. It's not just spectators who get injured—competitors do as well, especially when it's _____cold_____ or there hasn't been much rain.
4. Cheese-rolling spectator: "It's when the ground is really hard . . . that's when the ____injuries____ are going to happen."

▲ sepak takraw

After You Watch

A 🔄 Discuss these questions with a partner.

1. Why do you think people join the cheese-rolling race?
2. Do they want the cheese?
3. Do they want to have fun?
4. Are they crazy?

Communication

A 🔄 Role-play the following situation.

Student A is a competitor in the cheese-rolling race.

Student B interviews him or her.

> Why do you come?

> Where do you come from?

Sports 65

Video Journal: *Cheese-Rolling Races*

Before You Watch

A • Have students work with a partner to talk about the sports in the pictures and which ones they would like to try.

• Compare answers with the class.

While You Watch

A • Tell students to watch the video the first time and fill in the blanks with words from the box.

• Play the video.

• Play the video again for students to check their answers.

• Check answers.

After You Watch

A • Divide the class into pairs and have them talk about the questions.

• Compare answers with the class.

Communication

A • Divide the class into new pairs. Have them role-play the situation. Point out the model questions.

• Have students swap roles and role-play the situation again.

For Your Information: Unusual sports

Cheese-rolling is a sport that was invented in a town in England. A big round cheese rolls down a hill, and people run down the hill after it.

Octopush is an underwater form of hockey. Two teams try to push a puck across the bottom of a swimming pool into a goal.

Sepak takraw is popular in Southeast Asia. Two teams of three players use their feet, knees, and heads to send a ball over a net.

Teacher Tip: Helping groups finish at the same time

A common situation in group work is that one group completes the task long before the others—or long after. Here are some approaches you can take.

With a group that finishes too quickly:

• Check to be sure they have understood the task and completed all parts correctly.

• Give them additional questions.

• Have the group prepare a written report of their ideas, answers, etc.

With a group that finishes too slowly:

• Tell them to omit parts of the task.

• Take over briefly as discussion leader to help them move along.

• Set a time limit. Tell them, *I'll ask for your answers in five minutes.*

Destinations

About the Photo

This photo shows the Bayon, a temple in the ancient city of Angkor Thom in Cambodia. The Bayon stands in the center of Angkor Thom. It has huge faces carved in its central towers, which look down on the city and its visitors. There are thirty-seven main towers in total, and the temple has more than two hundred faces. The faces are of Lokesvara, the "Lord of the World," a Buddhist deity. Built in the late twelfth or early thirteenth centuries, the temple was originally intended for use among all the religions of the kingdom, but it was consecrated as a Buddhist temple. Later, it changed when the state religion went back to Hinduism. Today, the Bayon and Angkor Thom are popular tourist destinations due to their historical and architectural importance. Visitors often visit them along with nearby Angkor Wat.

- Introduce the theme of the unit. Call on students to give the name of a destination they have visited.

- Direct students' attention to the photo. Have students describe what they see.

- Have students work with a partner to discuss the questions.

- Compare answers with the class.

- Ask these questions orally or by writing them on the board for students to answer in pairs: *Which place in the world would you like to visit? Why?*

- Go over the Unit Goals with the class.

- For each goal, elicit any words students already know and write them on the board; for example, vacation destinations (beach, mountains, etc.), important discoveries, and so forth.

Angkor in Cambodia was a "lost" city, but now the ruins are a tourist destination and World Heritage site.

66

UNIT 6 GOALS	Grammar	Vocabulary	Listening
• Discuss past vacations • Exchange information about vacations • Use *was/were* to describe a personal experience • Describe a discovery from the past	Simple past tense *I didn't have* a reservation *yesterday.* Simple past tense of *to be* *I was* exhausted.	Travel activities Emphatic adjectives	Listening for general understanding: A vacation

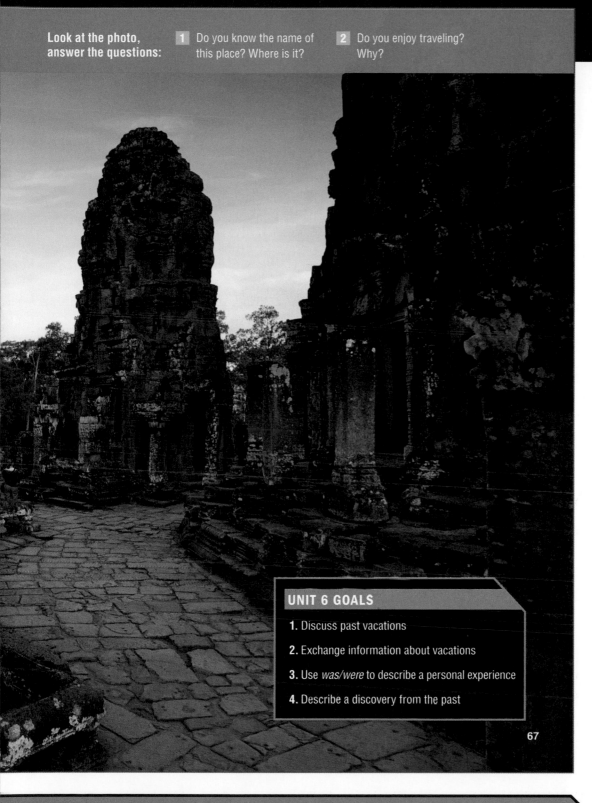

Look at the photo, answer the questions:

1 Do you know the name of this place? Where is it?

2 Do you enjoy traveling? Why?

Unit Theme Overview

- The World Tourism Organization compiles an annual ranking of the world's most popular tourist destinations. In 2012, the top country was France, with 83 million international visitors, followed by the United States (67 million), China (58 million), Spain (58 million), Italy (46 million), Turkey (36 million), Germany (30 million), the United Kingdom (29 million), Russia (26 million), and Malaysia (25 million). That's a lot of travelers and a lot of fascinating cross-cultural experiences!

- In this unit, students practice the form, meaning, and uses of the simple past tense in the context of describing past travel experiences. They talk about their own vacation trips and those of others, and learn about an explorer in the past who discovered what is today one of the world's great travel destinations—the amazing ruins of Machu Picchu, in Peru.

UNIT 6 GOALS

1. Discuss past vacations

2. Exchange information about vacations

3. Use *was/were* to describe a personal experience

4. Describe a discovery from the past

67

Speaking	Reading	Writing	Video Journal
Comparing vacations Describing personal experiences Describing the past **Pronunciation:** Sounds of *-ed* endings	**National Geographic:** "The Cradle of the Inca Empire"	Writing a travel blog	**National Geographic:** "Machu Picchu"

Discuss Past Vacations

Vocabulary

A
- Have students look at the pictures. Say, *These people are all taking a vacation. What are they doing?* Then have students work individually to number the phrases to correspond with the photos.
- Have students compare answers with a partner.
- Check answers.
- Explain that the prefix *un-* means *not* or *the opposite*. If you unpack a suitcase, you take out the things that you packed.

B
- Have students work individually to categorize the activities.
- Have students compare answers with a partner, then check answers.

C
- Divide the class into pairs to take turns talking about their usual activities before and during a vacation.
- Compare answers with the class.

Grammar

- Introduce/review the simple past tense. Say, *What did we do in class yesterday? We studied ____. We practiced ____. We learned ____.* Elicit more examples from the class with regular verbs like *talked, listened,* and so forth.
- Go over the information in the chart. Point out the two kinds of verbs. The simple past tense of regular verbs is formed by adding *-ed.* Most verbs are regular. Some verbs are irregular. They don't use *-ed* to form the simple past tense. They are all different; students will have to learn them. Go over the irregular verbs in the chart.

A
- Have students unscramble the questions and answers.
- Have students compare answers with a partner.
- Check answers.

Vocabulary

A Match the photos to an action from the box. Write the numbers.

visit places of interest	_6_
take a bus tour	_1_
check into the hotel	_5_
rent a car	_7_
take photos	_3_
pack/unpack suitcases	_4_
buy souvenirs	_2_

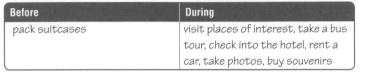

B Which of these activities do you do *before* and *during* your vacation?

Before	During
pack suitcases	visit places of interest, take a bus tour, check into the hotel, rent a car, take photos, buy souvenirs

C Write other things you do before and during a vacation. Share your ideas with the class.

Grammar: Simple past tense

Simple past tense	
Statement	He **rented** a car on his trip to Europe last November.
Negative	I **didn't have** a reservation yesterday.
Yes/No questions	**Did they go** to Asia last year?
Short answers	Yes, they **did**./No, they **didn't**.
Information questions	Where **did** you **go** for your vacation last year?

*We use the simple past tense to talk about completed actions or conditions.

*Some verbs are regular in the simple past tense. They have an *-ed* ending.		*Some verbs are irregular in the simple past tense. They have many different forms.	
learn — learned	travel — traveled	eat — ate	tell — told
arrive — arrived	want — wanted	buy — bought	leave — left
play — played	need — needed	fly — flew	say — said
ask — asked	help — helped	know — knew	see — saw
		go — went	take — took

A Unscramble the questions and answers. Use your notebook.

1. **Q:** to Europe Did you go year? last
   A: to we No, went America.

   A: Did you go to Europe last year?
   B: No, we went to America.

2. **Q:** did buy you those Where souvenirs?
   A: them bought in We Boston.

   A: Where did you buy those souvenirs?
   B: We bought them in Boston.

Word Bank: Vacation activities

Before:
buy a map
exchange money
get vaccinations
make train/bus/car reservations

During:
go for a boat ride
go to the tourist information office
take a walking tour
try local foods
use a phrasebook

Grammar: Simple past tense

The simple past tense is used to talk about actions that were completed in the past. Irregular verbs are those that don't follow the rule in forming the past tense, so they must be learned individually. Practicing with flash cards is a good way to do this. Tell students that if they are unsure about a verb, dictionaries usually have a list of irregular verbs in the back.

B Fill in the blanks using the simple past tense of the words in parentheses.

Normally we go to Spain for our vacation, but this year we (1) ___didn't go___ (not go). Instead, we (2) ___decided___ (decide) to go somewhere different, and we (3) ___chose___ (choose) Dubai in the United Arab Emirates. We (4) ___stayed___ (stay) at the Burj Al Arab hotel – "The Best Hotel in the Middle East." There are nine restaurants in the hotel, but we (5) ___didn't eat___ (not eat) in all the restaurants. And of course, the shopping was fantastic. We (6) ___bought___ (buy) lots of clothes and a few souvenirs. We also (7) ___rented___ (rent) a car and (8) ___went___ (go) to the desert. It is really beautiful, and we (9) ___took___ (take) hundreds of photos. It was an excellent vacation.

▲ The Burj Al Arab hotel in Dubai

Conversation

A 🔊 25 Listen to the conversation. How long did Maria stay in Venice?

Christine:	Hey, I love that <u>scarf</u>, Maria. Where did you buy it?
Maria:	I bought it in <u>Italy</u>. We went to <u>Italy</u> for our vacation last year.
Christine:	Wow! Sounds cool. Did you go to <u>Rome</u>?
Maria:	No, we flew directly to <u>Venice</u>. I wanted to see the <u>Doge's Palace</u>.
Christine:	How long did you stay there?
Maria:	We stayed for <u>five</u> nights.
Christine:	Lucky you!

five nights

B 🔁 Practice the conversation with a partner. Switch roles and practice it again.

C 🔁 Practice the conversation again and change the underlined words. You can use the information in the chart to help you, or use your own ideas.

Country	Italy	United States	Great Britain
Capital	Rome	Washington, D.C.	London
Other city	Venice	Orlando	Edinburgh
Place of special interest	Doge's Palace	Disney World	The Castle

D 🔁 **GOAL CHECK** ✔ **Discuss past vacations**

Take turns with a partner talking about a vacation you took.

B • Have students work individually to complete the paragraph.
• Have students compare answers with a partner.
• Check answers.
• Have students read the questions and answers out loud with a partner.

Conversation

A • Have students close their books. Write the question on the board: *How long did Maria stay in Venice?*
• Play the recording. 🔊 25
• Check answers.

B • Play or read the conversation again for the class to repeat.
• Practice the conversation with the class in chorus.
• Have students practice the conversation with a partner and then switch roles and practice it again.

C • Tell students to make three new conversations using the information in the chart. Go over the information with the class. Then have them practice the conversations.
• Call on student pairs to present a conversation to the class.

D 🔁 **GOAL CHECK** ✔

• Have students work with the same partner to talk about a vacation or other trip they took. Remind them to use the simple past tense.

Grammar Practice: Simple past tense

Prepare a list of students' names listed in random order on a piece of paper for your own use. Tell students to write three sentences in the past tense about things they did yesterday. Then play a memory game. Call on the first student on your list to say a sentence: *Yesterday, I bought a new coat.* The second student repeats that sentence and then adds his or her own sentence: *Yesterday, Lee bought a new coat, and I read the newspaper.* Each student continues in turn until one makes a mistake. Then that student starts over with a new sentence. Play until all students have had several turns. Ask, *Who remembered the most sentences?*

Exchange Information About Vacations

Listening

- Have students look at the picture and say what it is and where you would find one. Ask, *Do you like to go on roller coasters?*
- Introduce the topic. Ask, *Do you tell your friends about your vacations? Do you like to hear about their vacations? Why or why not?*

A • Tell students they are going to hear a conversation between two friends. Have them read the questions.
  - Play the recording. 🔊 26
  - Check answers.

B • Tell students to listen again to answer *true* or *false*. Go over the statements.
  - Play the recording one or more times. 🔊 26
  - Check answers.

Pronunciation

A • Explain to students that the *-ed* ending on regular past-tense verbs has different pronunciations in different words. Tell students to listen to the recording and check the sound they hear.
  - Play the recording one or more times. 🔊 27
  - Have students compare answers with a partner.
  - Check answers.

B • Tell students to listen to the recording and check the sound they hear.
  - Play the recording one or more times. 🔊 28
  - Have students compare answers with a partner.
  - Check answers.

C • Tell students to listen again and repeat the sentences.
  - Play the recording. 🔊 28

B GOAL 2: Exchange Information About Vacations

Listening

A 🔊 26 Listen to the conversation. Circle the correct answer.

1. Chen is telling his friend about _____ .
   a. his vacation   **b.** his hobby   **c.** his work

2. His friend is _____ .
   a. bored   **b.** interested   **c.** tired

B 🔊 26 Listen again. Circle **T** for *true* or **F** for *false*. Correct the false statements in your notebook.

1. Chen went to Oklahoma. .... T **(F)**
2. He visited five theme parks. .... T **(F)**
3. He didn't like Sea World. .... **(T)** F
4. He went to the Spider-Man™ ride. .... T **(F)**
5. He visited Islands of Adventure. .... **(T)** F
6. He didn't try the Incredible Hulk Coaster. ... T **(F)**

Pronunciation: Sounds of -ed endings

A 🔊 27 Listen. Check (✓) the correct boxes in the chart to the left. Then listen again and repeat.

	/t/	/d/	/ɪd/
packed	✓		
traveled		✓	
wanted			✓
arrived		✓	
played		✓	
needed			✓
asked	✓		
helped	✓		
visited			✓
rented			✓
liked	✓		

B 🔊 28 Listen to the sentences and check (✓) the pronunciation of the *-ed* ending.

	/d/	/t/	/ɪd/
We **checked** into the hotel.		✓	
I **packed** my bags.		✓	
He **traveled** to Europe.	✓		
They **stayed** at an expensive hotel.	✓		

C 🔊 28 Listen again and repeat the sentences.

Communication

A 🔄 Read the travel blogs on the next page. Fill in the gaps with the past tense of the verbs in parentheses.

70   Unit 6

For Your Information: Orlando

Orlando is a city in Florida in the United States. It is a major tourist destination, with an estimated 57 million tourists visiting each year. They come to Walt Disney World, SeaWorld, Universal Studios Florida, a large number of golf courses, and one of the biggest shopping malls in the United States. The city also has several important art museums. The population is around 250,000 people, with about 2 million people in the metro area.

From Zanzibar to Zebras

Africa » Tanzania » Dar es Salaam » Zamzibar » Arusha

Read full story | Subscribe

December 12th, 2014

Day 1 _Arrived_ (arrive) in Dar es Salaam. _Checked_ (check) into hotel. _Unpacked_ (unpack) suitcases. Went swimming.

Day 2 _Took_ (take) boat to the island of Zanzibar.

Days 3–5 _Sunbathed_ (sunbathe) on the beach. _Went_ (go) diving.

Day 6 _Flew_ (fly) to Arusha. Saw Kilimanjaro. It's BIG!

Days 7–10 _Took_ (take) a safari tour. _Saw_ (see) hundreds of wild animals. Took lots of photos.

Day 11 _Returned_ (return) to Arusha. _Bought_ (buy) souvenirs. Took plane to Dar es Salaam and then flew home. Great trip.

Mexico: Beaches and Pyramids

Mexico » Mexico City » Cancun » Tulum » Merida

Read full story | Subscribe

December 18th, 2014

Day 1 _Arrived_ (arrive) in Mexico City. _Took_ (take) subway to Chapultepec Park. _Went_ (go) to zoo.

Day 2 _Rented_ (rent) a car. _Visited_ (visit) the Pyramid of the Sun.

Days 3–5 _Flew_ (fly) to Cancun. _Went_ (go) to the beach.

Day 6 Visited ruins at Tulum. _Watched_ (watch) traditional dance show.

Day 7 Colonial city of Merida. Took a bus tour of the city. _Drank_ (drink) hot chocolate in market.

Day 8 _Returned_ (return) to Mexico City. Flew home.

B 🔄 Choose one blog. Take turns with a partner asking each other questions about your vacation.

> **Where did you go next?**

> **What did you do?**

> **How long did you stay there?**

> **Did you enjoy it? Why?**

C 🔆 **GOAL CHECK** ✔ **Exchange information about vacations**

Join another pair of students. Tell them about your partner's vacation from the activity above.

fly – flew	sunbathe – sunbathed
watch – watched	drink – drank

Destinations **71**

Communication

A
- Introduce the idea of blogs—Web sites where people write about their experiences and ideas and post pictures for other people to see. Ask if students ever read/write blogs. What are some popular topics? (travel, politics, family life)
- Have students read the travel blogs and complete them with the past tense of the verbs. Point out to students that in notes and diaries, we can use the verb without the subject (*Arrived, Took,* etc.).
- Have students compare answers with a partner.
- Check answers.

B
- Assign a role to each student. Have them look over "their" blog. Answer any questions about vocabulary.
- Model the questions with a student.
- Have students take turns asking about each other's vacation. Walk around the class, helping as needed.

C 🔆 **GOAL CHECK** ✔

- Combine student pairs into groups of four and have each student tell the group what they heard from their partner in the previous activity.
- Finish with a whole-class discussion. Which trip would students like to take? Why?

Expansion Activity

Tell students to imagine they are foreign tourists on vacation in their country. Have them write a short e-mail to a friend about what they did on one day of their trip. Have students read their e-mails to a partner. Then call on students to read their e-mails to the class.

Use *Was/Were* to Describe a Personal Experience

Language Expansion

- Introduce the idea of emphatic adjectives—"strong" adjectives. For example, *excellent* means *very, very good*. Go over the adjectives in the chart.

A
- Have students work individually to describe each picture with adjectives, then check answers.

B
- Have students work individually to complete the sentences.
- Have students compare answers with a partner, then check answers.

Grammar

- Go over the information in the chart about the simple past tense of *to be* (*was* and *were*). Elicit more examples from the class. Ask, *How was your day yesterday?* (*It was good/bad/boring*, etc.) *How were your English classes last year?* (*They were easy/interesting/hard*, etc.)

- *Was* can be pronounced two ways. If the word is alone or at the end of an utterance, it will be pronounced /wɑz/. The following examples may be used:

  *Yes, I **was.***

  *I think Mary **was.***

  In the negative, the /wɑz/ quality is retained: *No, I **wasn't** /wɑzənt/.*

  However, in questions or affirmative statements, *was* is pronounced /wəz/ and is tied to the next word:

  *I **was** happy.*

  ***Was** I right?*

  *Mary **was** sick.*

A
- Have students work individually to match the columns, then check answers.
- Have students read the questions and answers with a partner.

Adjectives	Emphatic adjectives
good/nice	excellent outstanding magnificent amazing
bad	awful terrible horrible
interesting	fascinating
tiring	exhausting
dirty	filthy
clean	spotless
big	enormous huge

Language Expansion: Emphatic adjectives

A Write two or three emphatic adjectives below each picture.

filthy

horrible

huge

enormous, amazing, magnificent

B Use emphatic adjectives to complete the text.   Answers may vary.

We had an (1) _____exhausting_____ vacation. We visited six European countries in six days. My favorite country was Italy. Rome is a (2) _____magnificent_____ city. There is so much to see: museums, churches, ruins. We stayed in a (3) _____spotless_____ hotel. Everything about it was perfect. It had an (4) _____enormous_____ swimming pool and very friendly people.

Grammar: Simple past tense of *to be*

Simple past tense of *to be*	
Statement	I **was** exhausted.
Negative	The food **wasn't** great.
Information questions	Why **was** your vacation awful?
Yes/No questions	**Were** they tired?
Short answers	No, they **weren't**.

A Match the questions and the answers.

1. Were you tired? __d__
2. Where were they? __b__
3. Was the weather good? __e__
4. Was he late? __a__
5. Were the rooms clean? __c__

a. No, he wasn't. He was on time.
b. They were in Peru.
c. No, they weren't. They were filthy.
d. Yes, I was. I was exhausted.
e. Yes, it was. It was excellent.

Word Bank: Emphatic adjectives

afraid–terrified

cold–freezing

happy–delighted

hot–boiling

hungry–starving

sad–miserable

surprised–astonished

Grammar: Simple past tense of *to be*

Was and *were* are used for states and situations in the past.

Yes/No questions are formed by inverting subject and verb:

He was happy. Was he happy?

Wh- questions are formed by adding the *Wh-* word to inverted subject and verb:

He was sad. Why/When was he sad?

B Complete the sentences with *was* or *were*.

1. We didn't enjoy our vacation. The weather _____was_____ very bad.
2. How _____was_____ the food?
3. _____Were_____ you tired when you got home?
4. I _____was_____ really interested in the ruins. They were amazing.
5. _____Was_____ the hotel clean?

C Complete the sentences with the correct forms of *to be*.

Last year we went diving at Pulau Sipadan, Malaysia.

It (1) ____was____ amazing! There (2) ____were____

lots of turtles, and we saw some hammerhead sharks,

as well. We also went to Barracuda Point, but unfortunately,

there (3) ____weren't____ any barracuda. It (4) ____was____

the wrong time of year. We stayed at the Dive Center and

the food (5) ____was____ excellent. The rooms

(6) ____were____ spotless.

▲ A diver in Pulau Sipadan

D ⟳ Write three questions about exercise **C** to ask your partner.

Conversation

A ◀))) 29 Listen to the conversation. What was good about the vacation? the food

Alex: How was your vacation?
Mike: It was terrible.
Alex: Why? What happened?
Mike: Well, first of all, the weather was <u>bad</u>. It rained nonstop for two weeks.
Alex: Oh, no.
Mike: And the hotel was <u>dirty</u>. It was full of cockroaches.
Alex: Yuck! And how was the food?
Mike: Actually, the food was <u>good</u>.
Alex: Well, at least you enjoyed something.
Mike: Not really. I had a bad stomach and couldn't eat. Some vacation!

B ⟳ Practice the conversation with a partner. Switch roles and practice it again.

C ⟳ Practice again and change the underlined adjectives to emphatic adjectives.

D ⟳ **GOAL CHECK** ✔ Use *was/were* to describe a personal experience

Tell a partner about a good or bad experience you had.

The weather was awful.

The food was excellent.

Destinations **73**

B • Have students work individually to fill in *was* or *were*.
• Have students compare answers with a partner.
• Check answers.

C • Have students look at the picture and describe what they see.
• Have students complete the text with the correct form of *be*.
• Have students compare answers with a partner.
• Check answers.

D • Have students write questions about the vacation in **C.** For example, *What animals did you see? Did you see any barracuda?*
• Divide the class into pairs to ask and answer the questions.
• Have several students ask one of their questions for the rest of the class to answer.

Conversation

A • Have students close their books. Write the question on the board: *What was good about the vacation?*
• Play the recording. ◀))) 29
• Check answers.

B • Play or read the conversation again for the class to repeat.
• Practice the conversation with the class in chorus.
• Have students practice the conversation with a partner and then switch roles and practice it again.

C • Have student pairs practice again, substituting emphatic adjectives for the underlined words.

D ⟳ **GOAL CHECK** ✔

• Divide the class into pairs and have them take turns sharing a good or bad experience from the past.
• Call on students to share something interesting they heard from their partner.

Grammar Practice: Simple past tense of *to be*

Write these sentence stems on the board and have students copy them onto paper:

1. _____ was born in another city.
2. _____ was very busy yesterday.
3. _____ wasn't home last night.
4. _____ was absent from class last week.

Add other sentence stems relevant to your class.

Have students walk around the class with paper and pencil asking questions with *Were you _____?* and filling in classmates' names for sentences that apply to them. Have students ask follow-up questions. (*Where were you born? What did you do?* etc.) Have them return to their seats when they have filled in all the spaces. Finish with a whole-class discussion of interesting answers.

Describe a Discovery from the Past

Reading

A • Have students look at the black and white photos and describe what they see. Discuss with the class when they think the photos were taken.

B • Have students read the article. Tell them to note any words they don't understand. Point out the words in the Word Focus box.

• Go over the article with the class, answering any questions from the students about vocabulary.

• Have students read the article again to find the emphatic adjectives.

• Check answers.

C • Have students identify the regular and irregular past simple verbs.

• Have students compare answers with a partner.

• Check answers.

D • Have students read the article again to find the answers to the questions.

• Check answers.

Additional Vocabulary

ancient = very old

modern = new

D GOAL 4: Describe a Discovery from the Past

Reading

A Look at the black and white photos. When do you think these photos were taken? 1912

B Read the article. Underline the emphatic adjectives. *exhausting, magnificent, outstanding, amazing, enormous*

C Underline the regular simple past verbs and circle the irregulars.

D Answer the questions.

1. Did Hiram Bingham discover Inca ruins in Ollantaytambo? *no*

   _____

2. How much did he pay Arteaga? _____
   50 cents per day

3. Was the climb to Machu Picchu easy?
   no

4. Where did they eat? *in a little grass hut*

   _____

▲ A man stands at the walls of the main temple.

Word Focus

hut = a small house
ruins = old buildings that have fallen down
to clear = to cut down

---

74   Unit 6

Machu Picchu, Peru
THE CRADLE OF THE

INCA EMPIRE

For Your Information: Machu Picchu

The city of Machu Picchu was built by the Incas around 1460 but was abandoned after only 100 years. Scientists are not sure why this happened, but they think it may have been because its inhabitants were wiped out by smallpox brought by the Spanish. Because the city was hidden high in the mountains, it was never found or destroyed by the Spanish.

The city is located on a high area between two mountains. The building technique (called dry stone because it is made without mortar) used by the Incas allows the stones to move slightly in an earthquake. As a result, the walls remained in good condition for centuries.

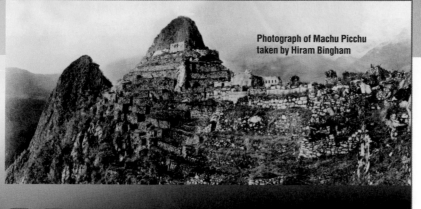

Photograph of Machu Picchu
taken by Hiram Bingham

Reading Tip

Have students look at the pictures that accompany a text and talk about what they think a text will be about. Have a discussion about what students see in the pictures to get them thinking about the content and ready to read.

Most people travel for vacations, but some people travel to explore and discover new places. In 1911, Hiram Bingham, an American archaeologist, traveled to Peru where he discovered Machu Picchu, the lost city of the Incas. Read his report of the discovery.

In 1911, I went to Cuzco in Peru looking for ancient Inca **ruins.** We left Cuzco and traveled to the modern city of Urubamba. We then continued down the Urubamba River until we came to the beautiful little town of Ollantaytambo. We continued down the river, and six days after we left Cuzco, we arrived at a place called Mandorpampa. A man came and introduced himself as Arteaga, and I asked him about ruins. He told us of some ruins in the mountains, called Machu Picchu. I offered to pay him 50 cents per day to take us to the ruins, and he agreed.

The next day, we crossed the river and began an exhausting climb. At noon we arrived at a little grass **hut.** The people there were very friendly and gave us some boiled potatoes and cool water. The view was magnificent, the water was delicious, but there were no ruins. However, we continued upward until at last we arrived on top of the mountain. Immediately, we found some ancient Inca walls made of white stone. I knew at once that this was a truly amazing discovery.

I returned to Machu Picchu in 1912, and we began **to clear** the forest. We started to see the ruins, and they were outstanding. The walls are made from enormous stones, and as we continued to clear the forest, we discovered more and more ruins. At last, the lost city of Machu Picchu appeared before us.

Destinations 75

After Reading

Have students search online for tourist information about Machu Picchu. How do people go there today? What can they see? Have each student tell the class one interesting fact they learned.

Describe a Discovery from the Past

Communication

A • Have students close their books. Write on the board, *Stonehenge*, or show an image. Elicit what students know about it and write their ideas on the board.

• Divide the class into small groups and have them complete the chart with as much information as they can.

B • Copy the chart onto the board and have groups share their ideas and complete the chart. Complete and correct information.

Writing

A • Have students read the directions.

• Individually, have them write a paragraph about one of the other places in the chart.

• Have students exchange papers with a partner. Ask them to mark corrections and suggestions for improvements on their partner's paper.

• If desired, have students rewrite their papers, to be collected for grading.

B ⟲ **GOAL CHECK** ✔

• Divide the class into pairs and have them talk about another explorer in a different place. If necessary, brainstorm examples on the board, such as Marco Polo's trip to China, Roald Amundsen walking to the South Pole, or Edmund Hillary and Tenzing Norgay climbing Mount Everest.

D **GOAL 4:** Describe a Discovery from the Past

The Pyramids of Giza

Communication

A 👥 Work with a group and fill in as much information in the chart as you can.

	Stonehenge	Pyramids of Giza	A ruin in your country
Where is it?	in England	Giza, Egypt	
What was it?	a burial ground	a sacred burial chamber	
Who built it?	Ancient Britons	Ancient Egyptians	
When was it built?	3000 BCE–2000 BCE	2550 BCE	

B 👥 Share your information with the class and write in any new information from classmates.

Writing

A Write a travel blog about one of the places from the chart. Use your notebook for extra space if needed.

_____

_____

_____

_____

B ⟲ **GOAL CHECK** ✔ **Describe a discovery from the past**

Talk to a partner about a discovery from the past that you know about.

76 Unit 6

For Your Information: Tourism at Machu Picchu

Today, Machu Picchu is one of the most important tourist destinations in South America and in the world. It is a UNESCO World Heritage site. Every year, over a million people visit the site. There is a lot of concern over the damage that this tourism causes, with people walking on ancient paths and stone and leaving their trash behind. Air pollution is caused by the buses and other vehicles that bring the visitors. Experts say that steps must be taken to preserve this amazing city.

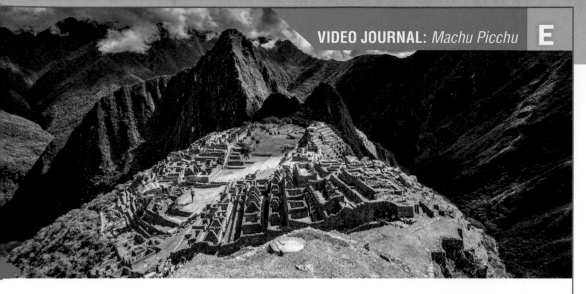

Before You Watch

A Fill in the blanks. Use the words in the box to complete the video summary.

tourists   environment
quiet   business

Video summary

When Hiram Bingham discovered Machu Picchu, it was a (1) ___quiet___

place. Now, many (2) ___tourists___ go to Machu Picchu every day. Some

people say it is good for (3) ___business___, but other people say it is bad for

the (4) ___environment___ .

While You Watch

A ▶ Watch the video. Circle **T** for *true* and **F** for *false*.

1. Machu Picchu is a popular tourist destination.	Ⓣ	F
2. Machu Picchu is sometimes known as the Lost Town of the Incas.	T	Ⓕ
3. Conservationists think tourism is good for Machu Picchu.	T	Ⓕ
4. Jose wants more people to come to Machu Picchu.	Ⓣ	F

After You Watch

A 🔁 Discuss these questions with a partner.

1. What are the big tourist attractions in your country?
2. Are there any problems with tourism in your country? What are they?
3. Do you think tourism is good or bad? Give reasons.

> **Tourists buy souvenirs and stay in hotels.**

> **That's good. It brings money to the country.**

Video Journal: *Machu Picchu*

Before You Watch

- Review what students learned about Machu Picchu in the reading. Where is it? Who built it? Who found it again?

A • Have students work individually to complete the video summary with the vocabulary in the box.

- Have students compare answers with a partner.
- Check answers.

While You Watch

A • Tell students to watch the video the first time and choose *true* or *false*. Go over the statements.

- Play the video.
- Have students compare answers with a partner.
- Check answers.

After You Watch

A • Have students discuss the questions with a partner. Then compare answers with the class, making lists on the board.

Teacher Tip: Roles in group work

It can be helpful to assign roles to students in each group. Some possibilities:

Leader—asks questions and keeps the discussion on topic

Secretary—takes notes on the group's ideas

Reporter—tells the group's answers to the class

Recorder—records the number of times each group member speaks and tells each member how often they spoke when the activity ends

Be sure to rotate these roles often.

My Mind-Shifting Everest Swim

Before You Watch

A • Have students look at the pictures and describe what they see.

• Tell students to decide which place they would like to visit and why. Encourage them to make notes of their ideas.

• Have students discuss their choice and reasons with a partner.

• Have several students share their choice and reasons with the class.

B • Ask students to share what they remember about Lewis Pugh (from the Reading in Unit 5). Ask, *Who is Lewis Pugh? What does he do? Why?* Write students' answers on the board. Tell students they are going to watch one of Pugh's TED Talks.

• Go over the words in the box. Direct students' attention to the definitions in the Word Bank. Have students complete the summary using the words in the box.

• Have students compare answers with a partner.

• Check answers.

C • Have students read the directions and the questions.

• Divide the class into small groups and have them look at the pictures and discuss the questions.

• Compare answers with the class. On the board, write students' ideas about what they think they will see in the TED Talk.

While You Watch

A • Have students look at the pictures and read the quotations. Tell them to number the pictures as they watch the talk.

• Play the talk.

• Have them compare answers with a partner.

• Check answers.

TEDTALKS

Lewis Pugh Adventurer/Environmentalist
MY MIND-SHIFTING EVEREST SWIM

Before You Watch

A ⚡ Look at the pictures. Which of these places would you like to visit? Why? Research the places if needed. Tell a partner. Do you share the same answers?

Greenland

Patagonia, Chile

Mt. Everest, Nepal

Santa Cruz, Argentina

B Use the words in the box to complete the TED Talk summary.

symbolic	humility	aggressive
Sherpas	debrief	sustainable

WORD BANK
aggressive to do something with a lot of force
battleground a place where there are a lot of problems or conflict
debrief to talk about something after it is done
humility thinking you are not more important than other people or things
instability a situation that can change at any time
Sherpas people who live in the Himalayas and work as mountain guides
sustainable something that will last a long time
symbolic representing something
tactical something that is smartly planned

> Lewis Pugh's idea worth spreading is that we can do something to stop climate change; we just need to take it seriously. That's why he swam across Lake Imja, a place that should be made of ice. Watch Pugh's full TED Talk at TED.com.

TED Talk Summary

Lewis Pugh swims in cold places because it is ____*symbolic*____ of saving the environment. He wants Earth to be ____*sustainable*____, or around forever. Lewis decided to swim in a lake high on Mt. Everest in the Himalayas. ____*Sherpas*____ helped him climb the big mountain to Lake Imja. After a failed first attempt, Lewis had a ____*debriefing*____ to discuss the best way to swim at 5,300 meters (17,400 feet) above sea level. He is usually very ____*aggressive*____ when he swims because he wants to finish quickly and get out of the cold water. But this time he showed ____*humility*____ and swam slowly.

C ♣ Look closely at the pictures in exercise **A** again. All of these places used to be completely covered in snow and ice. Discuss the following questions as a group.

What do you think is happening to the snow and ice in the pictures? Why? What do you think you will see in the TED Talk?

While You Watch

A ▶ Watch the TED Talk. Put the quotes in order. Write the number in the boxes provided.

78

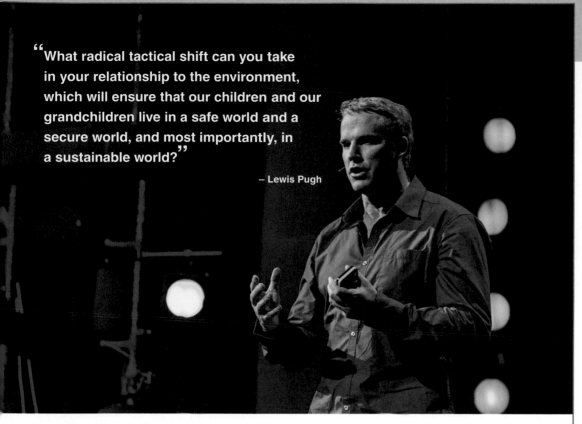

> "What radical tactical shift can you take in your relationship to the environment, which will ensure that our children and our grandchildren live in a safe world and a secure world, and most importantly, in a sustainable world?"
>
> — Lewis Pugh

1 "And I remember getting out of the water and my hands feeling so painful and looking down at my fingers, and my fingers were literally the size of sausages."

2 "I heard about this lake, Lake Imja. This lake has been formed in the last couple of years because of the melting of the glacier."

3 "And so I decided to walk up to Mt. Everest, the highest mountain on this earth, and go and do a symbolic swim underneath the summit of Mt. Everest."

4 "And I swam across the lake. And I can't begin to tell you how good I felt when I came to the other side."

79

For Your Information: Global warming

Throughout the history of Earth, natural cycles and events have caused the climate to change. However, the latest round of changes cannot be explained by these factors alone. The only way to describe these drastic changes is by looking at an increase in man-made greenhouse gases like carbon dioxide.

Some effects of this increase in temperature include melting ice caps and glaciers, higher sea levels, more extreme weather and storms, and changes in animal habitats and life cycles. In the future, many scientists fear that these effects will become far worse and also cause floods, droughts, animal and plant extinctions, and a rapid spread of certain diseases.

As more and more people become aware of the problems, a worldwide movement is underway to stop global warming. Activists like Lewis Pugh play an important role in educating the public about this important issue.

After You Watch

A • Have students read the questions. Tell them to answer them as they watch the talk.

• Play the talk again.

• Have them compare answers with a partner.

• Check answers.

B • Have students read the sentences and the names of the places in the box. Tell them to complete the sentences with the correct places as they watch the talk.

• Play the talk again.

• Have students compare answers with a partner.

• Check answers.

C • Have students read the sentences and complete them with an appropriate emphatic adjective from the box.

• Have them compare answers with a partner.

• Check answers.

TEDTALKS

Lewis Pugh Adventurer/Environmentalist
MY MIND-SHIFTING EVEREST SWIM

After You Watch

A Watch the TED Talk again. Circle the correct answer for each question.

1. What are the Himalayas?		big lakes	(big mountains)
2. How long did Lewis swim at the North Pole?		(19 minutes)	30 minutes
3. What is melting in the Himalayas?		(glaciers)	lakes
4. How many people depend on water from the Himalayas?		(2 billion)	1 million
5. What is the world's population?		9 billion	(6.8 billion)

B Fill in the names of the places from the words in the box.

Lake Imja	North Pole	Bangladesh
Mt. Everest	Himalayas	

1. In 2007, Lewis Pugh swam at the _____North Pole_____.

2. The glaciers in the _____Himalayas_____ are melting.

3. The highest mountain on Earth is _____Mt. Everest_____.

4. _____Lake Imja_____ is very high, near the top of Mt. Everest.

5. China, India, Pakistan, and _____Bangladesh_____ are countries near the Himalayas.

C Use the emphatic adjectives to complete the sentences.

exhausting	fascinating	enormous
excellent	awful	

1. Mt. Everest isn't small. It's a(n) _____enormous_____ mountain.

2. His story wasn't boring. It was _____fascinating_____.

3. Lewis Pugh survived his North Pole swim. He must be a(n) _____excellent_____ swimmer.

4. Swimming for a very long time, especially in cold conditions, isn't easy. It is _____exhausting_____.

5. When Lewis Pugh first tried the swim, he had to stop. He felt _____awful_____.

80

A melting ice field

D Lewis Pugh completed his amazing swims to call attention to the problem of global warming. Here are some things caused by global warming. Write the correct captions under the pictures. Have you seen any of these things before? Give examples and discuss with a partner.

Effects of Global Warming

Animals in Danger	Huge Storms
No Water	Floods

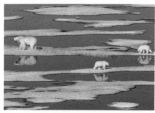

1. _____Animals in Danger_____

2. _____Huge Storms_____

3. _____Floods_____

4. _____No Water_____

E Make a list of things of things you can do to protect the environment. Discuss as a group. Share your list with other groups.

Challenge! Look at the pictures from exercise **D** again. Research other effects of global warming. Make a list. Then research what your country is doing to address the problem of global warming. Is it enough? Write an essay with your ideas to share with the class.

81

Ideas Worth Sharing

- With books closed, have students share what they remember about Lewis Pugh. Ask, *What is his message? What does he want to tell people? What does he want people to do? Why? What does he think we need to do to change things?*

- Have students read the information in the Ideas Worth Sharing box on page 78 again. Remind them that they can watch the whole TED Talk and other talks by Pugh at TED.com to help them develop their listening skills.

D • Write on the board, *global warming*. Ask, *What do you know about global warming?* Write students' ideas on the board.

- Have students read the directions and match the pictures to the problems caused by global warming.

- Have students discuss the problems and give more examples with a partner.

- Have pairs share their ideas with the class.

E • Divide the class into groups of three students and have them discuss what they can do to protect the environment. Have each group write a list.

- Have groups join together to form groups of six students and share their lists.

- Compare lists as a class, and write a list on the board.

Challenge

- Have students use the Internet to research other effects of global warming and make a list (this can be done in or outside of class depending on resources). Have students share their list with the class.

- Have students do follow-up research to find out what their country is doing about the issues related to global warming. This can be done individually or in pairs/ small groups. Have students share what they found out with the class.

- As a class, discuss whether the country is doing enough and what else the students think could be done. Write the ideas on the board. Have students help you begin an essay.

- Have students write their own essay.

- Have students exchange essays with a partner and compare ideas.

Communication

About the Photo

This photo by Petra Warner was taken at Wolf Park in Indiana, USA. Wolf Park is a non-profit organization devoted to research, habitat conservation, and education about wolves, foxes, coyotes, and bison. In this picture, a staff member howled and Warner was ready to capture the wolves' response.

- Direct students' attention to the photo. Have students describe what they see.

- Introduce the theme of the unit. Ask, *What do you know about wolves? How do they communicate?*

- Have students work with a partner to discuss the questions.

- Compare answers with the class.

- Ask these questions orally or by writing them on the board for students to answer in pairs: *What ways do you communicate? What's your favorite way to communicate?*

- Go over the Unit Goals with the class, explaining as necessary.

- For each goal, elicit any words students already know and write them on the board; for example, topics we talk about in personal communication, information that is contact information, adjectives for characteristics and qualities (people/things), vocabulary for different types of communication (cell phone, text message, etc.), and so forth.

Wolves may howl to let other wolf packs know to stay away from their territory, or just to let others know where they are.

82

UNIT 7 GOALS	Grammar	Vocabulary	Listening
• Talk about personal communication • Exchange contact information • Describe characteristics and qualities • Compare different types of communication	Verbs with direct and indirect objects *I sent **Mike** an **e-mail**.* Sensory verbs *It **feels** soft.*	Communication Electronics The senses	Listening for specific information: A radio call-in program

UNIT 7 GOALS

1. Talk about personal communication

2. Exchange contact information

3. Describe characteristics and qualities

4. Compare different types of communication

83

Unit Theme Overview

• Communication is the field of human activity that has changed and developed the most in recent years. Smartphones, the Internet, e-mail, and social media have all changed our daily lives. Some new technologies, such as answering machines, became popular, then quickly became obsolete. At the same time, older ways of transmitting messages are still used and appreciated. Many people still enjoy receiving a letter in the mail or settling down to read the newspaper.

• This unit begins by considering common ways to communicate and giving students the vocabulary they need to discuss them. Students learn to exchange contact information, such as telephone numbers and e-mail addresses. They then talk about verbs for feeling and sensing—ways that the body takes in information. Finally, they look at the different ways that animals communicate, and watch a video about how technology is being used in animal conservation work.

Speaking	Reading	Writing	Video Journal
Asking for contact information Describing senses and sensations Compare ways to communicate **Pronunciation:** /b/ and /v/, /l/ and /r/	**TED Talks:** "Diana Reiss: The Interspecies Internet? An Idea in Progress"	Writing a text message	**National Geographic:** "Wild Animal Trackers"

Talk About Personal Communication

Vocabulary

A • Have students look at the pictures and identify which ones they use.

• Go over the words in the box. Then have students work individually to use them to label the pictures.

• Tell students that *e-mail* can be spelled in two different ways. *E-mail* (with a hyphen) is used in this book, but *email* (without a hyphen) is also correct.

• Check answers.

B • Have students classify the words from **A** in the correct column of the chart. Point out that students might have different ideas.

• Have students compare answers with a partner.

• Check answers by completing the chart on the board. Discuss any differences students have.

Grammar

• Review the object pronouns (*me, you, him, her, it, us, them*).

• Ask students, *Did you send someone an e-mail yesterday? Who?* Elicit names. Write on the board:

   I sent/my friend/an e-mail.

   I sent/Lara/an e-mail.

   I sent/her/an e-mail.

• Elicit more examples from the class.

• Go over the information in the chart. Point out that the indirect object (the person who receives the action) comes first in this type of sentence.

A GOAL 1: Talk About Personal Communication

Vocabulary

A Label the pictures. Use the words in the box.

> e-mail fax smartphone TV letter
> newspaper ad social media text message

1. _____e-mail_____

2. _____fax_____

3. _____text message_____

4. _____social media_____

B Write the words from exercise **A** in the correct column.

	Inexpensive	Expensive
fast	e-mail, text message, social media	smartphone TV, fax
slow	letter	newspaper ad

Grammar: Verbs with direct and indirect objects

(Subject) + verb	Indirect object	Direct object
I sent	Mike	an e-mail.
My parents bought	me	a smartphone.
I am writing	Helen	a text message.
Find	me	his number, please.
I didn't fax	him	the report.
Give	me	a call.

5. _____letter_____

6. _____TV_____

7. newspaper ad

8. smartphone

Word Bank: E-mail vocabulary

attachment	recipient
Bcc (blind courtesy copy)	reply
body	send
Cc (courtesy copy)	sender
header	signature file

Grammar: Verbs with direct and indirect objects

In a sentence, a verb may have both a direct object (the object the action is done to) and an indirect object (the person for whom the action is done).

Two different patterns are possible. The direct object can also come first, with the indirect object preceded by *for* or *to*:

   I sent an e-mail to her.   *I baked a cake for her.*

A Unscramble the words to write sentences. Underline the indirect objects.

1. sent a I fax. Barbara
   I sent Barbara a fax.

2. sent My brother an me e-mail.
   My brother sent me an e-mail.

3. address. me his Find e-mail
   Find me his e-mail address.

4. new Jim a computer. I bought
   I bought Jim a new computer.

5. a your mom Give call.
   Give your mom a call.

Irregular past tense	
Present	**Past**
buy	bought
send	sent
write	wrote
find	found
get	got

B Read the situations and make requests. Use the verbs in parentheses.

Situation	Request
1. You lost your friend's phone number.	(send) Please send me your phone number.
2. You want your friend to call his father.	(give) Please give your father/him a call.
3. You want your parents to buy your sister a printer.	(buy) Please buy my sister/her a printer.
4. You want your friend to pay you by check.	(write) Please write me a check.

C Ask your partner how, and how often, they communicate with other people

Conversation

A 🔊 2 Listen to the conversation. How does Ken communicate with Chris? by e-mail and text message

Ken: Hey, Chris. I sent you <u>an e-mail</u> yesterday and you didn't answer.
Chris: <u>E-mail</u>? What <u>e-mail</u>? You didn't send me an <u>e-mail</u>.
Ken: Come on! You got it. Then I sent you <u>a text message</u>.
Chris: <u>Text message</u>? What <u>text message</u>? You didn't send me a <u>text message</u>, either. Honest!
Ken: OK, well you've got no excuses now. Where's the $15 you owe me?
Chris: $15? What $15?

Real Language

We can use *Come on!* to show impatience.

B Practice the conversation with a partner. Switch roles and practice it again.

C Change the underlined words and practice it again.

D **GOAL CHECK** ✓ **Talk about personal communication**

Write a list of types of personal communication that you use and another list of types of personal communication that you don't use. Compare your lists with a partner.

Communication 85

Grammar Practice: Verbs with direct and indirect objects

Have students write sentences with direct and indirect objects about the last time they used these ways of communicating:

send an e-mail	*call on the phone*
write a letter	*send a card*

For example, *I called my brother.* Call on students to read sentences to the class. Remind students to use the correct form of the simple past as necessary.

- Present the irregular past-tense verbs in the chart.

A • Have students work individually to unscramble the sentences.
- Check answers.

B • Have students work individually to write a sentence for each situation.
- Check answers.

C • Divide the class into pairs and have students discuss how and how often they communicate with a partner; for example, *I call my mom every day*.
- Have several students tell the class about their partner's communication habits.

Conversation

A • Have students close their books. Write the question on the board: *How does Ken communicate with Chris?*
- Play the recording. 🔊 2
- Check answers.

B • Play or read the conversation again for the class to repeat.
- Direct students' focus to the Real Language box.
- Practice the conversation with the class in chorus.
- Have students practice the conversation with a partner then switch roles and practice it again.

C • Have students work with the same partner to make a new conversation.
- Call on student pairs to present their conversations to the class.

D **GOAL CHECK** ✓

- Have students work individually to write a list of ways they communicate with other people and another list of personal communication that they don't use.
- Divide the class into pairs to compare and discuss their lists.
- Discuss students' most and least popular ways of communicating.

Exchange Contact Information

Listening

A
- Have students look at the pictures and describe what they see. Ask, *What is this man doing? What's his job?*
- Tell students they are going to hear a radio program. Have them read the question.
- Play the recording one or more times. 🔊 3
- Check answers.

B
- Tell students to listen again to find and write all the contact information in the chart. Go through the chart to point out what they must find. Go through the information in the chart and explain how we pronounce the symbols and abbreviations.
- Play the recording one or more times. 🔊 3
- Have students compare answers with a partner.
- Check answers.

C
- Divide the class into pairs and have them take turns reading and writing down the contact details.
- Call on students to read each set of contact information aloud while other students write the details on the board.

Written	Pronounced
@	at
-	hyphen
<u>Sydney</u>	underscore
/	slash
\	backslash
St.	street
Ave.	avenue

B   GOAL 2: Exchange Contact Information

Listening

A 🔊 3 Listen to the radio program. Circle the correct answer.

This is a _____ .

a. talk show   **b.** music show   **c.** call-in program

B 🔊 3 Listen again and complete the chart.

Phone number	34-36-29-18-34
Fax number	34-30-14-76-22
E-mail address	kingstownradio@coolmail.com
Text message (SMS) address	333 317-3476
Mailing address	Kingstown Radio, 25 Main Street, Kingstown

C 🔄 Below is the contact information of some famous places. Take turns reading them aloud with a partner using the correct pronunciation.

1. Bennelong Point, Sydney, New South Wales, Australia. Tel. + 61 29250 7111 www.sydneyoperahouse.com e-mail: infodesk@sydneyoperahouse.com

2. 1600 Pennsylvania Ave. NW, Washington DC, 20500, USA. Tel. 1 202 456 1111 www.whitehouse.gov e-mail: comments@whitehouse.gov

3. 5 Avenue Anatole France, 75007, Paris, France. Tel. 33 08 92 70 12 39 www.tour-eiffel.fr

86   Unit 7

For Your Information: Giving contact details

E-mail addresses: If there are no spaces in a multiword address, you can clarify by saying, *That's all one word.* The symbol "–" is pronounced *dash* and "." is *dot* in e-mail and Internet addresses.

Phone numbers: These are sometimes preceded by an *area code* if you are calling from another city.

Phone numbers are usually pronounced as single digits with a pause between each two or three digits. The number 0 is usually said as *oh*. For example: (304) 922-0768 is *area code three-oh-four (pause) nine-two-two (pause) oh-seven (pause) six-eight*.

Pronunciation: /b/ and /v/, /l/ and /r/

A 🔊 4 Listen and circle the word that you hear.

/b/	/v/	/l/	/r/
1. (bat)	vat	1. alive	(arrive)
2. berry	(very)	2. (blush)	brush
3. (best)	vest	3. flee	(free)
4. ban	(van)	4. fly	(fry)
5. boat	(vote)	5. (lane)	rain
6. bowels	(vowels)	6. lead	(read)
7. (bale)	veil	7. (lice)	rice
8. (bent)	vent	8. (light)	right
9. (best)	vest	9. long	(wrong)
10. bet	(vet)	10. play	(pray)

B 🔄 Take turns reading one of the words from each pair to your partner. Your partner has to identify which word you read.

Communication

A Write your contact information in column one of the chart.

B 👥 Ask three of your classmates for their contact information. Complete the chart.

	Me	Classmate 1	Classmate 2	Classmate 3
Name				
Home phone number				
Cell phone number				
E-mail address				
Mailing address				

C 🔄 **GOAL CHECK** ✔ **Exchange contact information**

Give the contact details of a friend or family member to a partner.

Real Language

When we want someone to repeat something, we can say: *Sorry, I missed that* or *Could you repeat that, please?*

When we want someone to say a word letter by letter, we can say: *Could you spell that, please?*

Pronunciation

A
- Go over the different sounds /b/ and /v/, /l/ and /r/. Tell students to listen to the pairs and circle the word they hear.
- Pairs of words with only one different sound are called *minimal pairs.*
- Play the recording one or more times. 🔊 4
- Check answers.

B
- Have students take turns saying a word from each pair for their partner to identify.
- Have different students say a word from each pair and have the class identify which word it is.

Communication

A
- Have students write down their contact information in the column for *Me*. Help as needed with any problems in the section for *Mailing address*. Tell students that they can make up a number or address if they don't want to give their real information.

B
- Model the activity. Ask a student, *What's your e-mail address?* and write down the information. On the board, write the sentences, *What's your _____?* and *Sorry, I don't have one.* Model the expressions and questions in the Real Language box.
- Have students walk around the class with their books, exchanging contact information. Tell them to sit down when they've completed the chart.
- Ask, *Who has an unusual/interesting e-mail address? What is it?*

C 🔄 **GOAL CHECK** ✔

- Have students work individually to write a list of a friend's or family member's contact information.
- Divide the class into pairs and have them share this information by asking and answering each other's questions. They should only refer to their lists if necessary.

Expansion Activity

Have students make an e-mail and/or phone number list of all their classmates. Dictate a list of all students' names for them to write down on a sheet of paper, and then have them circulate around the classroom asking for and giving information.

Describe Characteristics and Qualities

Language Expansion

- Go over the names of the senses with the class. Give/elicit more examples of characteristics we identify by using each sense: sight, hearing, taste, smell, and touch.

A • Divide the class into pairs and have them discuss which sense is used for each characteristic.
- Compare answers with the class.

B • Have students work with the same partner to list other things they can see, hear, taste, smell, and touch.
- Compare answers with the class, making lists on the board.

Grammar: Sensory verbs

- Go over the verbs in the chart. Point out that they are used to talk about things that we are perceiving.

C | **GOAL 3:** Describe Characteristics and Qualities

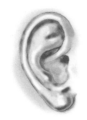
▲ sight

▲ hearing

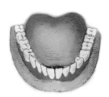
▲ taste

▲ smell

▲ touch

Language Expansion: The senses

With the senses, we perceive (*see, notice, feel*) characteristics and qualities of people, animals, places, and things.

A 🔄 Look at the senses to the left. Discuss the following question with a partner. What senses do you use to identify these characteristics?

▲ **sweet** *taste* ▲ **loud** *hearing* ▲ **soft** *touch* ▲ **green** *sight*

▲ **dirty** *sight* ▲ **bad** *smell* ▲ **salty** *taste* ▲ **wet** *touch*

B 🔄 Work with a partner to make a list of other things you can perceive with your senses.

Grammar: Sensory verbs

Subject	Verb	Adjective
The food	**smells**	delicious.
It	**feels**	soft.
You	**look**	cold.
It	**tastes**	salty.
He	**sounds**	tired.

*Sensory verbs are stative verbs.
*They are usually followed by an adjective.
*They are not used in the simple progressive tense.

88 Unit 7

Word Bank:
Sensations

hearing: musical, quiet

sight: dark, light

smell: pungent, smoky, sweet

taste: bitter, sour, spicy

touch: cold, hard, hot, rough, smooth

Grammar: Sensory verbs

With these linking (or copular) verbs of sensation, the subject of the sentence is the thing that is producing the sensation. These are all stative verbs, which are not normally used in continuous tenses.

▲ People in this market in Phonsavan, Laos, use many senses at the same time.

A Complete the sentences with sensory verbs.

1. That car can't be safe. It ___looks/sounds___ very old.
2. Listen to the CD player! It ___sounds___ terrible.
3. What are you cooking? It ___smells/tastes___ delicious.
4. Hey, you changed your hair. It ___looks___ great.
5. I don't like these French fries. They ___taste___ too salty.
6. I prefer this sweater. It ___feels/looks___ soft.

B 🔁 Take turns with a partner. Describe the photo above by making statements with *looks, sounds, tastes, smells, feels,* and an adjective.

Sample answers:
The market looks crowded. It sounds noisy. The chicken tastes great. The food smells good. The sun feels warm.

Conversation

A 🔊5 Listen to the conversation. What's wrong with Bill and Susan's milk? It smells terrible. It tastes awful.

Susan:	I think there is something wrong with this <u>milk</u>.
Bill:	It looks OK to me.
Susan:	Smell it! It smells <u>terrible</u>.
Bill:	Mmm. It doesn't smell too bad. How does it taste?
Susan:	I'm not going to taste it!
Bill:	OK, let me try. Ugh, you're right. It tastes <u>awful</u>.

B 🔁 Practice the conversation with a partner. Switch roles and practice it again.

C 🔁 Change the underlined words and make a new conversation.

D 🔁 GOAL CHECK ✔ **Describe characteristics and qualities**

Work with a partner. Use sensory verbs to describe your classroom and your classmates.

Communication 89

A • Have students work individually to complete the sentences with sensory verbs from the box on page 88. Point out that more than one verb may be correct.
• Have students compare answers with a partner.
• Check answers.

B • Divide the class into pairs and have them describe the picture at the top of the page; for example, *The food tastes spicy.*
• Have different pairs say something about the picture. Write the sentences on the board and correct as necessary with students' help.

Conversation

A • Have students close their books. Write the question on the board: *What's wrong with Bill and Susan's milk?*
• Play the recording. 🔊5
• Check answers.

B • Play or read the conversation again for the class to repeat.
• Practice the conversation with the class in chorus.
• Have students practice the conversation with a partner and then switch roles and practice it again.

C • Have students work with a partner to make a new conversation.
• Call on student pairs to present their conversation to the class.

D 🔁 **GOAL CHECK** ✔

• Divide the class into pairs and have them talk about people and things around them using the sensory verbs they have learned. Call on students to tell the class one of the things they noticed.

Grammar Practice:
Sensory verbs

Have students write one sentence about something they like using each verb of sensation (*feel, smell, taste, look, sound*). Give an example: *These shoes feel comfortable.* Have them share their sentences with a group.

Compare Different Types of Communication

Reading

A • Introduce the topic of the reading. Ask students how animals communicate (for example, by sounds and moving their bodies).

• Have students read the directions and complete the chart.

• Have them compare and discuss answers with a partner.

• Compare answers with the class. Most animals use more than one sense to communicate, so answers will vary.

B • Have students look at the photo of the dolphin; ask, *What do you know about dolphins?* Write students' ideas on the board.

• Divide the class into pairs and have them discuss the questions. Tell them to talk about dolphins and the animals in the chart in **A.**

• Have several pairs share their ideas with the class.

C • Have students read the statements. Point out the words in the Word Bank. Have students read the article and choose if the statements are true or false.

• Have students compare answers with a partner.

• As a class, have students correct the false information.

• Check answers.

D **GOAL 4:** Compare Different Types of Communication

Reading

A 🔄 Animals use all their senses, but for many animals, one of the senses is the most important. Check (✓) one box for each animal and compare with a partner.

	By sight	By sound	By smell
1. dogs			✓
2. ants	✓		
3. whales		✓	
4. peacocks	✓		
5. wolves			✓
6. bees		✓	

B 🔄 Read the article. With a partner, discuss these questions: Are dolphins intelligent? Do they have feelings? Do the same for the other animals listed in exercise **A.**

C Read the sentences. Are they true or false? Circle **T** for *true* or **F** for *false*.

1. People are self-aware. Ⓣ F

2. Scientists do experiments to gain information. Ⓣ F

3. When two people talk, it is **interspecies** communication. T Ⓕ

4. When you use your brain, you are using cognition. Ⓣ F

5. You usually recognize people you have never seen before. T Ⓕ

6. Some animals whistle to communicate. Ⓣ F

WORD BANK
ability what someone or something is able to do
cognition mental activities (thinking, understanding, learning, remembering)
experiment scientific test
interspecies between species
recognize to know because of previous experience
self-aware aware of oneself
whistle high, loud sound

90 Unit 7

TED Ideas worth spreading

Diana Reiss Scientist

THE INTERSPECIES INTERNET? AN IDEA IN PROGRESS

The following article is about Diana Reiss. After Unit 9, you'll have the opportunity to watch some of Reiss and her colleagues' TED Talk and learn more about their idea worth spreading.

What happens when you give a dolphin a mirror or a computer keyboard? Just ask Diana Reiss. She studies the **cognition** and communication of dolphins. Scientists believe that dolphins and other animals are **self-aware** and have emotions. They are able to think, learn, and remember.

Diana Reiss showed these **abilities** in her research with dolphins and elephants. Reiss used a mirror in her studies. The animals **recognized** themselves in the mirror. That shows that they are self-aware.

Reiss also made a special keyboard that could work underwater. The keyboard had keys that the dolphins could touch. When touched, the computer would make a whistle and the dolphins got a fun object or activity. In the **experiment,** the dolphins learned to use the keyboard all by themselves. They played with the keyboard, copied the **whistles,** and learned which keys to touch to get what they wanted.

Diana Reiss's keyboard experiment showed that dolphins have cognitive abilities and can use them to communicate. But that experiment was many years ago. Now, she is interested in what today's technology can show us about animal minds. What do you think of an orangutan using an iPad? Or other animals being connected through the Internet?

For Your Information: Dolphins

Dolphins are sea mammals that live in shallow parts of the oceans near land. They range in size from 4–30 feet (1.2–9.5 meters). Dolphins eat smaller animals like fish and squid. Scientists believe that they are one of the most intelligent animals. Dolphins live together in groups called *pods.* They swim together and help other members of their pod if they are sick or injured. They communicate with other dolphins by using sounds like whistles and clicks. Because of their friendly appearance and playful behavior, dolphins are very popular in movies and cartoons, and they are among the most popular exhibits at aquariums around the world.

Many scientists think dolphins have emotions and recognize themselves.

"How do we explore intelligence in this animal that's so different from us?"

– Diana Reiss

91

Reading Tip

Being able to understand referents, such as pronouns, in a text is a valuable reading skill. When reading a text, take time to stop and ask students what a pronoun refers to. Tell students to take the pronoun and replace it with the proper noun and see if the sentence makes sense. Referents in this reading include *they, she, and them.*

After Reading

Have students find out more about Diana Reiss's research on animal communication and report back to the class about what they find.

Writing

A • Elicit different types of communication from students and write a list on the board; for example, *e-mail, text message, social media, phone call*, etc.

• Have students complete the chart individually and then discuss with a partner. Have them compare any differences in their answers.

• Have several students share with the class one of their partner's answers.

B • Ask, *Do you send text messages? Who do you send them to? Do you write differently in text messages?* Give an example, and explain what abbreviations are. Remind students that these abbreviations should only be used in text messaging.

• Have students read the text messages and match them to the correct situation from the chart in **Writing A.**

• Check answers and have students tell you the full messages (without abbreviations). Write it on the board as a conversation.

Communication

A • Divide the class into pairs and have them make a list of the ways humans communicate. Then have them choose an animal and list the ways it communicates.

B 🔁 **GOAL CHECK** ✔

• Review the idea of animal communication and list examples on the board.

• Divide the class into pairs and have them talk about similarities and differences between animal and human communication.

• Compare ideas with the class.

D GOAL 4: Compare Different Types of Communication

Dolphins can communicate with each other using a keyboard. Do you think they can communicate with people?

Writing

A 🔁 What type of communication would you use in these situations? Text message, e-mail, letter, or social media? Fill in the first column and then ask your partner. Discuss any differences.

You want to . . .	Me	My partner
1. . . . send a photo to your parents.		
2. . . . thank your grandmother for a birthday present.		
3. . . . keep in touch with some friends in Brazil.		
4. . . . invite a friend to do something with you.		
5. . . . send an assignment to your teacher.		

B 🔁 People often use abbreviations. Do you understand these messages? Which situation from exercise **A** do they match? With a partner, write a new text conversation. Explain your abbreviations to the class. *Situation 4*

Hi. HRU?

GREAT. WRUD?

NOTHING. WANNA GO TO THE MOVIES TN?

IDUNNO. GOTTA FINISH MY PROJECT.

OK LMK.

OK CU LATER.

Communication

A 🔁 With a partner, make a list of some of the other ways humans communicate. Then pick an animal and list the way it communicates.

B 🔁  **GOAL CHECK** ✔ **Compare different types of communication**

With your partner, compare human communication with animal communication. How are they the same? How are they different? Share your ideas with the class.

92 Unit 7

An elephant and rhinoceros in the African bush

Before You Watch

A Match the words to the definitions.

1. conservationist _b_
2. increase _c_
3. decrease _d_
4. to track _a_

a. to follow wild animals
b. a person who protects wild animals
c. to get (or make) bigger
d. to get (or make) smaller

While You Watch

A ▶ Watch the video. Circle **T** for *true* and **F** for *false*.

1. In the video, you see lions. **T** F
2. Louis Liebenberg is trying to collect information about the animals. **T** F
3. The Bushmen and the conservationists speak the same language. T **F**
4. The small computer that the Bushmen use is called the Cyber Tracker. **T** F
5. Louis Liebenberg makes maps from the information. **T** F

After You Watch

A 🔁 The Cyber Tracker is a quick way of recording information about wild animals. Can you think of other uses for the Cyber Tracker? Discuss with a partner.

Communication **93**

Teacher Tip: Checking answers

There are many ways to check students' answers to activities, all with advantages and disadvantages.

- Teacher reads the answers out loud, students check their work—the fastest way, but with the least student involvement
- Teacher calls on students to give their answers—also fast, but may make students feel anxious
- Students correct each other's work—gives students more responsibility, but they may not correct all mistakes
- Volunteers each write the answer to one question on the board—gives the class an opportunity to work with common errors, but uses a lot of class time
- Teacher corrects outside of class—an opportunity for detailed feedback, but requires a lot of work from the teacher

---

Video Journal:
Wild Animal Trackers

Before You Watch

A • Have students look at the picture and read the caption. Tell them they are going to watch a video about animal conservation.

• Have students work individually to match the words and meanings, using a dictionary as needed.

• Check answers.

While You Watch

A • Tell students to watch the video the first time and choose *true* or *false*. Have them read the statements.

• Play the video.

• Have students compare answers with a partner.

• Play the video again as necessary.

• Check answers.

After You Watch

A • Divide the class into pairs and have them talk about the question.

• Compare answers with the class. (For example, tourists could use the Cyber Tracker to read information about animals.)

For Your Information:
Bushmen

The Bushmen are an ethnic group of indigenous people who live in many countries of southern Africa, from South Africa north to Mozambique and Angola. Traditionally, they lived by hunting and gathering plants, although starting in the 1950s, they changed to farming. In the past, they lived in small groups that traveled together in search of food. Their society was very egalitarian, with chiefs having very little power and men and women having equal status. Today, there are about 90,000 Bushmen.

UNIT
8   **Moving Forward**

As global trade has increased, port cities like Singapore have become more and more important.

94

Moving Forward

About the Photo

This photo was taken by Justin Guariglia for the National Geographic book, *Life in Color*. The photo shows the vast amount of shipping containers waiting to be transported around the world at the Port of Singapore Authority. Located at the tip of the Malay Peninsula in Southeast Asia, the port maintains 1,600 cranes, 29,000 staff, and moves 160,000 containers daily.

With the theme being Moving Forward, this photo reflects movement on a global scale. As global trade, communication, and travel grow, so does cultural understanding and the exchange of ideas among people around the world.

- Focus students' attention on the unit title. Ask them what they think it means and what the unit is about. Write their ideas on the board.

- Direct students' attention to the photo. Have students describe what they see.

- Have students work with a partner to discuss the questions. Explain that *looking forward* means you are happy about something in the future.

- Compare answers with the class.

- Ask these questions orally or by writing them on the board for students to answer: *Do you like to talk and think about the future? Why or why not?*

- Go over the Unit Goals with the class, explaining as necessary.

- For each goal, elicit any words students know and write them on the board; for example, plans for the future (studies, travel, jobs, personal events, etc.), weather vocabulary, etc.

UNIT 8 GOALS	Grammar	Vocabulary	Listening
• Talk about plans • Discuss long- and short-term plans • Make weather predictions • Discuss the future	Future—*be going to* **We're going to** *buy a new car tomorrow.* *Will* for predictions and immediate decisions *I think it* **will** *rain this afternoon.*	Plans Weather conditions Weather-specific clothing	Listening for general understanding: A talk show

Look at the photo, answer the questions:

1 Why do you think shipping ports are important?

2 Are you looking forward to the future? Why?

UNIT 8 GOALS

1. Talk about plans

2. Discuss long- and short-term plans

3. Make weather predictions

4. Discuss the future

95

Unit Theme Overview

- People in almost every country are fascinated with the future. They flock to science fiction movies to see visions of what our lives could be like a hundred years from now. They read analyses of what the stock market will do or who will win the next soccer World Cup. They pick up the newspaper or visit a Web site to find out what the weather will be like tomorrow or three days from now. There is even a branch of social science called *futurology* dedicated to understanding future trends, predicting what is likely to continue, and what will be new. Futurologists look at possible, probable, and preferable scenes in the future. They also use computer simulations to look at the possible results of current decisions.

- Learning to talk about the future in English is complex because unlike some other languages, English uses a number of different structures to talk about future time. In this unit, students are introduced to two of them: *going to* for plans and predictions and *will* for predictions. They consider many different aspects of the future, from their own personal short- and long-term plans, to tomorrow's weather, to new technology in the future and how it will affect us.

Speaking	Reading	Writing	Video Journal
Talking about weekend plans	**National Geographic:** "Future Energy"	Writing statements about the future	**National Geographic:** "Solar Cooking"
Discussing the weather			
Pronunciation: Reduced form of *going to*			

Talk About Plans

Vocabulary

A
- Have students look at the pictures and describe what they see.
- Tell students they are going to learn expressions for future plans. Go over the phrases in the box.
- Have students work individually to write the number of the correct phrase for each picture.
- Check answers.
- Ask, *Which of these plans are in your future?*

B
- Discuss the meanings of short-term (close in the future—for example, in the next week or month) and long-term (far away in the future—for example, next year). Have students work individually to categorize the plans from **A**.
- Have students compare answers with a partner.
- Check answers by completing the chart on the board.

C
- Have students work individually to rank the long-term plans in the chart from most important to least important.
- Divide the class into pairs and have them discuss their answers.
- Compare answers with the class.

Grammar

- Introduce the structure. Tell students (for example), *I have lots of plans for the weekend. On Friday night, I'm going to have dinner at a restaurant. On Saturday morning, I'm going to clean my house. On Saturday afternoon, I'm going to go shopping.* Ask questions like, *What are you going to do on Friday night/Saturday?* Elicit answers with *going to.*
- Go over the information in the chart.

Vocabulary

A Number the pictures to match the phrases from the box.

1. study for the next test	4. buy a new car	7. buy my own house
2. get a new job	5. have children	8. speak English fluently
3. do the laundry	6. clean the house	

Add word Bank

I don't want to have children now. I'm too young.

I need to buy a new car. My car is really old.

B Write the plans from exercise **A** in the correct column.

Short-term plans	Long-term plans
clean the house, study for the next test, do the laundry	buy a new car, buy my own house, have children, get a new job, speak English fluently

C 🔄 Number the long-term plans in order of importance to you (1 for the most important plan). Compare your list with a partner's list. Give reasons.

Grammar: Future—*be going to*

Be going to		
Statements	We**'re going to** buy a new car tomorrow.	
Negatives	He**'s not going to** get a new job next year.	
Yes/No questions	**Are** you **going to** do the laundry this weekend?	Yes, I am. No, I'm not.
Wh- question	When **are** you **going to** pay the phone bill?	On Tuesday.

*We can use *be going to* to talk about our plans for the future.
*We also use these time expressions: *tomorrow, next Saturday / week / year.*

96   Unit 8

Word Bank: Future plans

apply to college/university/graduate school

change careers

get engaged

get married

learn to drive/cook/swim

start a business

study abroad

take tennis/Spanish/computer lessons

start/take up skiing/playing the guitar/writing poems

Grammar: *Future—be going to*

English uses a variety of ways to talk about future time. One of them is *be going to*, which is used to talk about plans and intentions. It is also used informally for making predictions, which will be covered in Lesson C of this unit. One common error to watch out for is omitting the *be* verb: ~~We going to watch videos.~~

A Match the questions and the answers.

1. Where are you going to have lunch today? __c__
2. Are you going to invite Ajay to the party? __a__
3. What are you going to do on Saturday? __d__
4. When is Nicola going to arrive? __e__
5. Is it going to rain this evening? __b__

a. Yes, I am. He loves dancing.
b. Maybe. I would take an umbrella.
c. At Luigi's.
d. We're going to go ice skating.
e. Her plane arrives at five o'clock.

B Complete the conversation with *be going to* and the verbs in parentheses.

A: Hey! I just won $100!

B: Wow! What __are you going to do__ (you do) with it?

A: Well, first, I __'m/am going to buy__ (buy) my mother some flowers.

B: Great. She __'s/is going to love__ (love) those.

A: And then, I __'m/am going to give__ (give) my sister $10.

B: And the rest?

A: I __'m/am going to put__ (put) it in the bank.

B: __Are you going to buy__ (you buy) anything for yourself?

A: Maybe. But not now.

C ⚡ Look at the pictures on page 96. Take turns asking a partner questions about the phrases.

> **When/Where/How/Why are you going to . . . ?**

Conversation

A 🔊 6 Listen to the conversation. Is Kiri going to go to the beach? yes

Mai: Hi, Kiri. What are you going to do this weekend?

Kiri: Well, I'm going to <u>study for the test</u> and <u>do the laundry</u>. Why? Why do you ask?

Mai: We're going to <u>go to the beach</u>. Do you want to come?

Kiri: Mmm, I'm not sure. I'd love to, but . . . you know . . . work.

Mai: Come on. It's going to be fun!

Kiri: Well, maybe I can <u>study for the test</u> tonight. And I can <u>do the laundry</u> when we come back.

Mai: So you're going to come?

Kiri: Sure!

B 🔄 Practice the conversation with a partner. Switch roles and practice it again.

C 🔄 Change the underlined words and practice it again.

D 🔄 **GOAL CHECK** ✔ Talk about plans

Tell a partner your plans for this weekend.

> **Real Language**
>
> We can say *Mmm* or *I'm not sure* to show uncertainty.

> **I'm going to go hiking this weekend.**

Moving Forward 97

A • Have students work individually to match the columns.
• Have students compare answers with a partner.
• Check answers.

B • Have students work individually to complete the conversation.
• Have students compare answers with a partner.
• Check answers.

C • Divide the class into pairs and have students ask and answer questions about the plans in the pictures on page 96. Point out the sample question structure in the speech bubble and model with several students and possibilities.
• Have several students tell the class about one of their partner's plans.

Conversation

A • Have students close their books. Write the question on the board: *Is Kiri going to go to the beach?*
• Play the recording. 🔊 6
• Check answers.

B • Play or read the conversation again for the class to repeat.
• Direct students' attention to the Real Language Box.
• Practice the conversation with the class in chorus.
• Have students practice the conversation with a partner and then switch roles and practice it again.

C • Have student pairs think of new information to substitute for the underlined words. Then have them make a new conversation.
• Call on student pairs to present their conversations to the class.

D 🔄 **GOAL CHECK** ✔

• Divide the class into pairs and have them share their weekend plans.
• Call on students to tell the class about their partner's plans.

Grammar Practice: *Future—be going to*

Have students take a piece of paper and make seven columns with the days of the week at the top. This is their "calendar" for next week. Then have them write an activity (real or imaginary) for five of the seven days (such as, *see a movie, study English,* etc.). Have students work with a partner to plan an activity (such as, *have a cup of coffee*) they want to do together. They should not look at their partner's calendar. Model sentences like, *I'm going to do the laundry on Monday night* and *What are you going to do on Tuesday night?* When all student pairs have finished, call on students to talk about their plans.

Discuss Long- and Short-Term Plans

Listening

A • Have students look at the picture. Ask, *What does he do?*

• Tell students they are going to hear an interview with a famous singer. Have them read the question.

• Play the recording one or more times. 🔊 7

• Check answers.

B • Tell students to listen again to the conversation and choose *true* or *false*. Read through the statements with the class.

• Play the recording one or more times. 🔊 7

• Check answers.

• Ask, *What do you think? Is his life going to change with a baby? Why?*

C • Have students correct the false statements in **B**.

• Check answers.

Pronunciation

A • Remind students that many words and sounds in English are reduced when we are speaking quickly. Tell students to listen to the reduced form of *going to.*

• Play the recording. 🔊 8

• Ask, *What does the reduced form of* going to *sound like?* (gonna) Point out that *gonna* is used only in speaking, NEVER in writing.

• Play the recording again and have students repeat. 🔊 8

B • Tell students to listen and check the pronunciation they hear, full or reduced.

• Play the recording one or more times. 🔊 9

• Check answers.

C • Have students say the sentences to a partner using either the full or the reduced form. Their partner identifies which form they are using.

B **GOAL 2:** Discuss Long- and Short-Term Plans

Listening

A 🔊 7 Listen to the interview with a pop singer. Is he talking about his short-term plans or long-term plans? *short-term plans*

B 🔊 7 Listen again and circle **T** for *true* and **F** for *false*.

1. Pedro is going to record his new album in ~~June~~. T (F)
2. You can buy Pedro's new album ~~in stores~~. T (F)
3. Pedro is going to take a break in the summer. (T) F
4. Pedro is ~~going~~ to do a world tour this year. T (F)
5. Alicia is going to have a baby in July. (T) F
6. The baby isn't going to change Pedro's life. (T) F
7. Pedro is going to start making a film at the end of the year. (T) F

C Correct the *false* sentences in exercise **B** in your notebook.
   1. January; 2. on the Internet; 4. not going

Pronunciation: Reduced form of *going to*

A 🔊 8 Listen and repeat.

B 🔊 9 Listen to the sentence and check (✓) the correct box.

	Full form	Reduced form
1. When are you going to finish?	☐	✓
2. They're not going to like it.	☐	✓
3. We're going to leave at three thirty.	✓	☐
4. I'm going to take a shower.	☐	✓
5. Are you going to take a taxi?	✓	☐
6. What are you going to do this weekend?	✓	☐
7. I'm not going to go to the meeting.	☐	✓
8. When is Saleh going to arrive?	✓	☐

C 🔄 Take turns reading the sentences in exercise **B** with either the *full form* or the *reduced form*. Your partner has to say which form you used.

For Your Information: Life changes from having children

According to experts, having a baby, especially a first baby, changes many aspects of one's life. It can cause pressure in the relationship with one's partner and may require change and adjustment in both parents' career goals. It can have both positive and negative effects on friendships, as well as affecting relationships with your own parents and your in-laws. It even brings changes in people's identity and sense of who they are.

A hang glider soars above Yosemite National Park in the United States.

Communication

A What are your short-term and long-term plans? Check (✓) the correct column.

Short-term plans			
Are you going to . . .	Yes, I am.	I'm not sure.	No, I'm not.
eat out tonight?			
go to a party this weekend?			
play or watch a sport this evening?			
rest this weekend?			

Long-term plans			
Are you going to . . .	Yes, I am.	I'm not sure.	No, I'm not.
start your own business?			
learn another language?			
move to another country?			
buy a new car?			

B 🔁 With a partner, take turns asking and answering the questions in exercise **A.** Then ask a *Wh*- question.

C 🔁 **GOAL CHECK** ✔ Discuss long- and short-term plans

Tell a partner your plans for tonight and your plans for the next five years. Use the words in the box to help you.

> **Are you going to start your own business?**

> Yes, I am.

> **What type of business?**

> I'm not sure. Maybe a hang gliding school.

tomorrow	next weekend
next week	next month
next year	in five years

Communication

A • Have students look at the picture and describe what they see. Ask, *Are you going to do something like this in the future?*

• Have students work individually to mark their short-term and long-term plans.

B • Divide the class into pairs and explain the activity: They should ask the questions in **A,** and after each question they should ask for more information. Go over the example conversation. Model with a student. On the board, write the question words *who/where/when/why/what* to prompt them in asking *wh-* questions.

• Have students discuss the questions with their partner. Walk around the class, helping as needed.

• Call on students to tell the class about one plan their partner has.

C 🔁 **GOAL CHECK** ✔

• Have students work with a partner to talk about two future plans: one for the short term and one for the long term.

• Point out the time expressions in the box.

• Call on students to tell the class about one of their plans.

Expansion Activity

Have students choose one of their long-term plans and write several sentences about it, answering questions that begin with *who/where/when/why/what.* Divide the class into groups of three to four and have students share their work with their group.

Make Weather Predictions

Language Expansion

- Write on the board, *weather*. Elicit any words students know to describe the weather.

- Go over the adjectives for weather conditions in the box. Ask students, *How is the weather today?* Elicit, *It's (hot and sunny).* Ask, *How's the weather in January/April/August/October?*

- Go over the vocabulary for clothing. Ask, *Which things do you need today/for rain/for cold weather/at the beach?*

Ⓐ
- Have students work individually to complete the sentences.
- Have students compare answers with a partner.
- Check answers.

Grammar

- Explain that another way to make predictions in English is with *will*. Go over the information in the chart.

Ⓐ
- Have students work individually to complete the sentences.
- Have students compare answers with a partner.
- Check answers.

C   **GOAL 3:** Make Weather Predictions

▲ raincoat

Language Expansion: Weather conditions

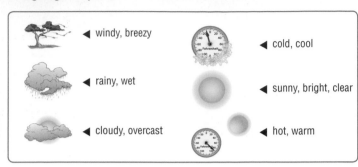

- windy, breezy
- rainy, wet
- cloudy, overcast
- cold, cool
- sunny, bright, clear
- hot, warm

We use adjectives to describe the weather. *Today is **sunny** and **warm**.*

Ⓐ Complete the sentences. Use the words on this page.

1. It's not going to rain tomorrow. You don't need to take your <u>umbrella/raincoat/rain boots</u> or your <u>raincoat/umbrella/rain boots</u>

▲ umbrella   ▲ sunglasses

2. Put on your sweater. It's going to be ____<u>cool/cold</u>____ outside.

3. The weather forecast says it's going to be cloudy today. You don't need to take your ____<u>sunglasses</u>____ .

4. It's going to be <u>sunny/bright/hot</u> and <u>sunny/bright/hot</u> tomorrow, so don't forget your sun hat.

▲ rain boots   ▲ swimsuit

Grammar: *Will* for predictions and immediate decisions

▲ sun hat   ▲ scarf

Will		
Statements	I think it **will** rain this afternoon. It **will** be windy tomorrow.	
Negatives	Don't take your sweater. I'm sure it **will not (won't)** be cold.	
Yes/No questions	**Will** it be windy?	Yes, it **will**./No, it **won't**.

*We use *be going to* and *will* to make predictions.
*We only use *will* to make an immediate decision. **A:** The phone is ringing. **B:** OK, I will answer it.

Ⓐ Complete the sentences using *will* or *be going to*.

1. **A:** You're looking happy.
   B: Yes, I ____<u>'m/am going to</u>____ buy a new car this afternoon.

2. **A:** Oh no! It's starting to rain.
   B: I ____<u>'ll/will</u>____ get an umbrella.

3. **A:** This is heavy.
   B: Wait, I ____<u>'ll/will</u>____ help you.

4. **A:** You have to get up at five o'clock tomorrow.
   B: Yes, I ____<u>'m/am going</u>____ to go to bed early tonight.

▲ sweater

100   Unit 8

Word Bank: More weather adjectives

chilly/freezing

foggy

humid

muggy

snowy

stormy

Grammar: *Will* for predictions and immediate decisions

Another structure English uses to talk about future time is *will*. In this lesson, *will* is introduced as an alternative to *going to* for making predictions. *Will* is slightly more formal than *going to*. *Will* is also used to talk about decisions made at the time of speaking: *The phone is ringing. I'll answer it.* In everyday speech, *will* is generally used in its contracted form. Using the full form can make speakers sound overly formal.

B Rewrite the questions using *be going to* or *will*.

be going to	will
1. Is it going to rain tomorrow?	Will it rain tomorrow?
2. Is it going to be sunny this afternoon?	Will it be sunny this afternoon?
3. Are we going to have a hot summer this year?	Will we have a hot summer this year?
4. What is the weather going to be like on the weekend?	What will the weather be like on the weekend?
5. Is it going to be overcast tomorrow?	Will it be overcast tomorrow?
6. Are we going to finish the book before the end of the year?	Will we finish the book before the end of the year?
7. Are temperatures going to rise in the next 100 years?	Will temperatures rise in the next 100 years?
8. Are you going to get good grades?	Will you get good grades?

C With a partner, take turns asking and answering the questions in exercise **B**.

D Write some predictions about your life. Use *be going to* and *will*.   Answers will vary.

1. I _____ have a happy life.

2. I _____ live to be 100 years old.

3. I _____ find an interesting job.

4. I _____ speak perfect English one day.

Conversation

A 🔊 10 Listen to the conversation.

Andrew: Do we have everything ready for the beach?
Barbara: Sure. Everything's ready.
Andrew: Do you think it's going to rain?
Barbara: No, they say it's going to be hot.
Andrew: Are you going to take your umbrella?
Barbara: No, I said it's going to be hot. It's not going to rain.
Andrew: No, I mean your beach umbrella for the sun.
Barbara: Oh, I see. Yes, that's a good idea.

B 🔄 Practice the conversation with a partner. Switch roles and practice it again.

C 🔄 Circle the predictions. Change *be going to* to *will* and practice it again.

D 🔄 **GOAL CHECK** ✔ **Make weather predictions**

Talk to a partner. What is the weather like now? What is it going to be like tomorrow?

Do you think it will rain?

No, they say it will be hot.

Will you take your umbrella?

No, I said it will be hot.

It won't rain.

B • Have students work individually to rewrite the sentences.

• Have students compare answers with a partner.

• Check answers.

C • Divide the class into pairs and have them ask and answer the questions in **B.**

D • Have students complete the sentences, making predictions about their own lives.

• Have students compare answers with a partner.

• Have several students share one of their predictions with the class.

Conversation

A • Have students close their books.

• Play the recording for students to listen to. 🔊 10

B • Play or read the conversation again for the class to repeat.

• Practice the conversation with the class in chorus.

• Have students practice the conversation with a partner and then switch roles and practice it again.

C • Have students work with their partner to find the predictions and change them to *will.*

• Check answers.

• Have students practice the new conversation with a partner.

D 🔄 **GOAL CHECK** ✔

• Have students discuss the questions with a partner.

• Compare answers with the class.

Grammar Practice: *Will* for predictions and immediate decisions

Divide the class into groups of three or four. Assign each group one of these topics: food, clothes, schools, houses, TV (more than one group can have the same topic). Tell each group to think about life 20 years from now and write as many predictions about their topic as they can with *will.* Set a time limit (for example, five minutes). Then ask one member of each group to read the group's predictions to the class.

Discuss the Future

Reading

- Introduce the topic of the reading. Ask students, *What are some kinds of energy that we use?* Elicit/give words like *oil, gas, electricity*, and so forth.

A
- Divide the class into pairs and have them discuss the questions. Tell them that they will find the answers in the article.
- Direct students' attention to the Word Focus box.
- Have students read the article to check their guesses. Tell them to circle any words they don't understand.
- Check answers.
- Go over the article with the class, answering any questions from the students about vocabulary.

B
- Have students underline the sentences from the reading that have *will* and *be going to*.
- Check answers.

C
- Have students work individually to answer the questions.
- Have students compare answers with a partner.
- Check answers.

D
- Talk about other kinds of renewable energy the students may be familiar with; for example, water power, wood and other natural fuels, and geothermal power (power from the earth's heat). Ask, *Which ones do we use here? What do people use them for?* Ask students to make predictions about energy in the future with *will*.
- Divide the class into pairs and have them discuss the question.
- Have several pairs share their answers with the class.

D | **GOAL 4:** Discuss the Future

Reading

A ⚡ Discuss these questions with a partner. Then read and check your answers.

1. What are fossil fuels? *coal, oil, and natural gas*
2. What is alternative energy? *solar power and wind power*

B Read the article. Underline *will* and *be going to*.

C Answer the questions.

1. How much energy will we need in 2100?
   three times as much as today, 960 billion kilowatt hours per day
2. What are three problems with solar power? *It's expensive. It needs a lot of space. It doesn't work at night.*
3. What are two problems with wind energy? *Turbines are ugly and the wind doesn't blow all the time.*
4. Does Michael Pacheco think there will be enough energy in the future?
   He doesn't know.

D ⚡ How do you think people will get energy in the future? Solar, wind, fossil fuels, or another way? Discuss with a partner.

Word Focus

alternative = something different

cost-effective = something *cost-effective* saves money

renewable = something you can use again and again

ugly = not beautiful

FUTURE ENERGY
WHERE WILL WE GET OUR ENERGY?

We are going to have a big energy problem in the future. Today, the world uses 320 billion kilowatt-hours of energy a day. By 2100, we will use three times as much energy. How will we get the energy? Today, we get a lot of energy from fossil fuels: coal, oil, and natural gas. But fossil fuels are dirty, and they will not last forever. In the long term, we will have to find **alternatives**. We will need **renewable** energy.

SOLAR POWER

Near Leipzig in Germany, there is a field with 33,500 solar panels. It produces enough energy for 1,800 homes. That's a lot of energy! However, there are problems. One problem is that solar energy is expensive, but the price is falling. "Thirty years ago it was **cost-effective** on satellites," says Daniel Shugar, president of PowerLight Corporation. "Today, we can use it for houses and businesses." He says that in the future most houses will have solar panels. There are other problems with solar power. It needs a lot of space, and, of course, it doesn't work at night.

For Your Information: Renewable energy facts

- Enough sunlight falls on the earth's surface in one hour to meet the world's energy demands for a whole year.
- More than 300,000 homes added solar power in 2013, with the number of installations expected to reach 362,000 by 2016.
- Albert Einstein won the Nobel Prize in 1921 for his work on producing electricity from sunlight.
- One wind turbine produces enough electricity for 300 homes.
- People in China used wind power to grind grain in 200 BCE.
- To produce wind power, the wind must blow at least 14 mph (20 kph).

WIND POWER

On a cloudy day in Denmark, a wind turbine is producing clean, renewable electricity. Right now, wind power is the best of the alternative energy sources. But again, there are problems. Some people think wind turbines are **ugly**. And, of course, there are days when there is no wind.

So, how will our grandchildren get their energy? "We're going to need everything we can get from solar, everything we can get from wind," says Michael Pacheco, director of the National Bioenergy Center, part of the National Renewable Energy Laboratory (NREL) in Golden, Colorado, "And still the question is: Can we get enough?"

Moving Forward 103

Reading Tip: Scanning
After students read the text and begin to answer the questions, they will need to refer back to the reading. Tell students not to reread the entire text, but scan it just for the information they need instead. Scanning is reading just for specific information without reading irrelevant information.

After Reading

Have students work in pairs to search online for information about a place where people are now using one of these forms of renewable energy: solar, wind, biomass, geothermal, or water. Have them tell the class about the place and what people are doing with that form of energy. Ask the class which energy source they think is best and why.

Discuss the Future

Communication

A • Have students read the chart and the questions. Have them add two more questions and then complete the chart with their own answers.

• Have students work with a partner. Tell them to ask each other the questions and compare and discuss their answers.

• Compare answers as a class.

Writing

A • Have students read the directions and the example text.

• Have students write their own text about the events in the chart in **A.**

• Walk around helping as necessary.

B **GOAL CHECK** ✔

• Divide the class into groups of three to four students and have them share their ideas from their paragraphs. Appoint a secretary in each group to write down the most interesting ideas.

• Call on the secretaries to present two to three ideas to the class.

D **GOAL 4:** Discuss the Future

The surface of Mars

Communication

A 🔁 Write more questions in the chart. Fill in the first column with your answers, and then ask your partner the questions. Compare and discuss your answers.

In the future, do you think . . .	Me			Partner		
	Yes	Maybe	No	Yes	Maybe	No
1. . . . people will live under the sea?						
2. . . . there will be enough food for everyone?						
3. . . . we will find a cure for cancer?						
4. . . . most houses will have solar panels?						
5. . . . people will travel to Mars?						
6. . . . wars will end?						
7.						
8.						

Writing

A Write when you think these events will happen in your notebook.

In the next 50 years, I think we will find a cure for cancer, maybe most houses will have solar panels, but I don't think people will travel to Mars.

Maybe by 2100 people will . . .

B **GOAL CHECK** ✔ **Discuss the future**

Join two or three other students and discuss your ideas about the future.

104 Unit 8

For Your Information: Solar cooking

There are many different types of solar cookers— more than 65 different designs are available today, and people are inventing their own variations every day. All of them work in similar ways. Some kind of reflective material concentrates sunlight in a small cooking area, where a black surface turns the light into heat. A clear material lets light enter but keeps the heat inside, so it can cook the food. Solar cooker projects are being carried out around the world. For example, in Lesotho, in southern Africa, women have started bakeries that use solar ovens. In Sudan, refugees in camps make their own solar cookers from local materials. And in India, entire villages have started cooking all their food in solar ovens.

solar cooking

Video Journal: *Solar Cooking*

Before You Watch

A 🔁 Look at the pictures. Discuss these questions with a partner.

1. What fuels can you use to cook food? *gas, electricity, and wood*

2. What fuel do you use to cook food? *Answers will vary.*

While You Watch

A ▶️ Watch the video. Check (✓) the correct box.

Benefits of solar ovens	Health	Environmental
1. You don't have to cut down trees.	☐	✓
2. African women don't have to walk a long way to collect firewood.	✓	☐
3. There is no smoke.	☐	✓
4. Solar ovens can be used to make water clean.	✓	☐
5. Solar ovens don't cause pollution.	☐	✓

After You Watch/Communication

A 🔁 With a partner, make a list of what you need to make a solar oven. Write instructions on how to make the oven. Use drawings if needed. Then, role-play the following situation.

Student A
You are running a workshop in Africa. You have to explain the benefits of using solar ovens. Some of the participants have doubts.

Student B
You are a participant in the workshop. Your mother cooked with wood and you cook with wood. You have doubts about changing. Ask questions.

▲ gas

▲ electricity

▲ firewood

▲ solar energy

▲ wind

Moving Forward 105

Video Journal: *Solar Cooking*

Before You Watch

A • Have students look at the pictures and answer the questions with a partner.

• Compare answers with the class.

While You Watch

A • Tell students to watch the video and mark the answers. Point out that more than one answer may be correct. Have the students read the statements.

• Play the video.

• Have students compare answers with a partner.

• Check answers. The answers given are suggestions. For example, items 3 and 5 can also be considered health issues.

After You Watch/ Communication

A • Divide the class into pairs and have them make a list of items needed to make a solar oven. Compare lists with the class, and write a list on the board.

• Have pairs write instructions for making the oven. Encourage them to use drawings to support the instructions.

• Have students read the situation. Divide the class into pairs and assign them A or B. Have them read their role. Give them a few minutes to write down ideas and questions to ask based on their role.

• Have students role-play the workshop situation.

• Have several pairs present their role-play to the class.

Teacher Tip: Giving students more responsibility

Giving students responsibility for everyday classroom tasks can not only lighten the teacher's workload but can also help students feel more involved. Here are some tasks that your students may be able to perform:

• handing back homework
• distributing papers
• calling the class to order at the beginning
• setting up audio equipment
• erasing/washing the board

9

Types of Clothing

About the Photo

This photo shows a Bedouin family in the city of Saint Catherine, in the Sinai Peninsula of Egypt. The family is celebrating after a wedding and wearing traditional clothing. Bedouin weddings usually take place at family homes and may last up to five days. The photo was taken by American photojournalist Amy Toensing.

The Bedouin are traditionally nomads who herd sheep and goats with their camels across the deserts of the Sinai, the Negev, and Arabia. Today many Bedouin families have settled in towns and adapted to the modern world. However, the Bedouin culture is still respected and valued, and the Bedouin are known for their hospitality and honor.

- Introduce the theme of the unit. Ask students, *What are you wearing today? Where did you buy it?*

- Direct students' attention to the photo. Have students describe what they see. If students don't mention clothes, ask, *What is he/she wearing?*

- Have students work with a partner to discuss the questions.

- Compare answers with the class.

- Ask these questions: *Where do you think these people get their clothes? Where do you go shopping for clothes?*

- Go over the Unit Goals with the class, explaining as necessary.

- For each goal, elicit any words students already know and write them on the board; for example, adjectives for describing, verbs for preferences (like, love, don't like, etc.), clothing materials (cotton, nylon, etc.), and so on.

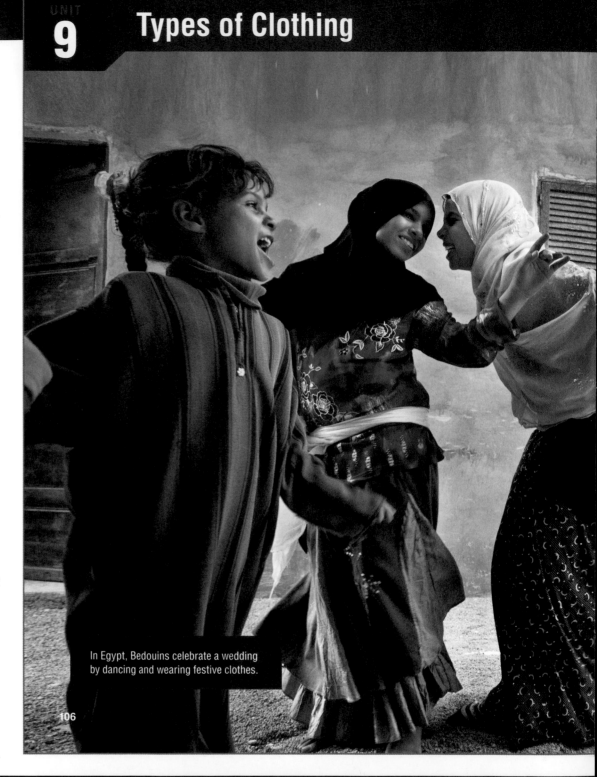

In Egypt, Bedouins celebrate a wedding by dancing and wearing festive clothes.

106

UNIT 9 GOALS	Grammar	Vocabulary	Listening
• Make comparisons • Explain preferences • Talk about clothing materials • Evaluate quality and value	Comparatives *This dress is **prettier than** that one.* Superlatives *The cotton pajamas are* **the cheapest.**	Clothing Descriptive adjectives Clothing materials	Listening for specific information: Shoe shopping

UNIT 9 GOALS

1. Make comparisons

2. Explain preferences

3. Talk about clothing materials

4. Evaluate quality and value

107

Unit Theme Overview

- Along with so many other things, types of clothing and the way we shop for clothes have changed in recent years. With the Internet, new styles and fads move around the world faster than ever; the globalization of manufacturing has reduced prices of clothing and made it possible for people to afford a greater variety of clothing than previously. And online shopping makes it possible for people in even small or remote places to purchase the latest fashions and seek out clothing that matches their tastes exactly. This globalization has also exposed people to clothing styles from around the world.

- In this unit, students acquire basic vocabulary for clothing and learn to talk about their tastes and preferences by making comparisons. They practice superlatives and use them while practicing the language they need for shopping in stores. Finally, they will learn the history and culture behind the most exotic and treasured of clothing materials—silk. Students will then learn some of the consequences of the manufacture of clothing.

Speaking	Reading	Writing	Video Journal
Talking about clothes Shopping—at the store and online **Pronunciation:** Rising and falling intonation	**National Geographic:** "Silk—The Queen of Textiles"	Writing about favorite clothes	**National Geographic:** "How Your T-Shirt Can Make a Difference"

Make Comparisons

Vocabulary

- Go over the vocabulary for types of clothing presented in the illustrations. Ask if students are wearing any of the items.

A • Divide the class into pairs and have them label the pictures with words from the box.
- Check answers, and have students repeat the clothing words.

B • Have students work individually to find the adjectives that describe clothes in the sentences.
- Have students compare answers with a partner.
- Check answers.
- Go over the meanings of the adjectives with the class.

C • Have students work individually to find the opposite of each adjective.
- Have students compare answers with a partner.
- Check answers.

D • Have students work individually to complete the sentences with the adjectives from **C.**
- Have students compare answers with a partner.
- Check answers.

A | **GOAL 1:** Make Comparisons

tie jeans skirt shirt
suit jacket pants hat
sneakers T-shirt socks
blouse coat handbag
shoes hat belt gloves

Vocabulary

A 🔄 Work with a partner and label the pictures with words from the box.

B Underline the adjectives that describe clothes.

1. a. Fatima is wearing a <u>heavy, handmade</u> sweater, and she's warm.
    b. Charles is wearing a <u>light, poor-quality</u> coat, and he's cold.
2. a. John wore an <u>expensive, formal, business</u> suit to the interview.
    b. Andrew wore a <u>cheap, casual</u> jacket. Guess who got the job!

C Match the opposites.

1. formal __e__   a. cool
2. outdated __c__   b. expensive
3. cheap __b__   c. fashionable, stylish
4. warm __a__   d. heavy
5. handmade __f__   e. casual, informal
6. light __d__   f. machine-made

D Complete the sentences with the words in exercise **C.**

1. It's going to be cold tomorrow. You should take a ____warm____ jacket.
2. You can't wear those ____outdated____ jeans. You should buy stylish ones.
3. ____Handmade____ clothes are more expensive than machine-made clothes.
4. Looks are important, so I always wear a ____formal____ suit when I meet clients.

108   Unit 9

Word Bank: More clothing

belt	sweatpants
coat	sweatshirt
(neck)tie	tank top
sandals	tights
scarf	underwear
shorts	vest

Grammar: Comparatives

Comparative forms of adjectives

Adjectives with one syllable Add -er.	cheap	Machine-made sweaters are **cheaper than** handmade sweaters.
Adjectives that end in -y Change the -y to i and add -er.	pretty	I like that dress, but this one is **prettier**.
Adjectives with two or more syllables Use more or less before the adjective.	beautiful	Eleanor is **more beautiful than** Eva.
	expensive	These suits are **less expensive than** those.
Irregular comparatives	good	Shopping in a store is **better than** shopping online.
	bad	My grades are **worse than** yours.

*The comparative form is often followed by *than*.
*Use *much* to make a comparison stronger. *This coat is **much better than** the other one.*

A Complete the sentences. Use the comparative form of the word in parentheses.

1. I prefer the green handbag, but it is <u>more expensive than</u> (expensive) the blue purse.

2. These jeans are <u>nicer than</u> (nice) those ones.

3. These shoes are <u>more formal than</u> (formal) those ones.

4. This sweater is <u>lighter than</u> (light) that one.

5. I think the blue blouse is <u>prettier than</u> (pretty) the black one.

Conversation

A 🔊 11 Listen to the conversation. Danny and Edris are shopping. What is Danny looking for? *(formal) shoes*

Edris: Look at these blue shoes. They look nice.
Danny: I don't know. I need something more formal. They're for work.
Edris: What about these black ones?
Danny: Mmm, I'm not sure. They're a little expensive.

Edris: Look! Here are some cheaper ones.
Danny: Yes, they're very nice. Oh, they're a size 10. Do they have them in a smaller size?
Edris: Yes, here is a size 9.
Danny: Perfect.

B 🔁 Practice the conversation. Switch roles and practice it again.

C 🔁 Change *shoes* to a singular item of clothing, for example *blouse*, and practice the conversation. Don't forget to change the agreements:

*Look at **this** blue blouse. **It** look**s** nice.*

D **GOAL CHECK** ✔ Make comparisons

Write sentences comparing the clothes that you like to wear with the clothes that your parents like to wear.

> **Real Language**
>
> We can say *I don't know* or *I'm not sure* to show uncertainty.

> **I like to wear jeans. My father likes to wear a suit.**

Types of Clothing   **109**

Grammar: Comparatives

English forms the comparative of adjectives in two different ways: with -er (for short adjectives) and with *more* (for long adjectives). Students occasionally use a combination of both, erroneously: ~~He is more taller than I am.~~ They may also need to be reminded of spelling changes: big→ bigger; happy → happier.

Grammar Practice: Comparatives

Bring magazines to class. Divide students into groups of three. Have groups compare the different articles of clothing worn by people in the magazines, using comparative adjectives: *That green sweater is more fashionable than the blue one.*

Grammar

- Introduce the structure. Show pictures of two people or draw on the board two people who are opposites in height, weight, and age. Ask students, *Who is taller/younger/thinner/heavier/older?*
- Go over the information in the chart. Give/elicit more examples of each type of adjective.

A • Have students work individually to fill in the comparative adjectives.
- Check answers.
- Direct students' attention to the Real Language box.

Conversation

A • Have students close their books. Write the question on the board: *What is Danny looking for?*
- Play the recording. 🔊 11
- Check answers.

B • Play or read the conversation again for the class to repeat.
- Practice the conversation with the class in chorus.
- Have students practice the conversation with a partner and then switch roles and practice it again.

C • Have students work with the same partner to make a new conversation using a singular item of clothing. Point out the changes they will need to make.
- Call on student pairs to present their conversations to the class.

D 🔁 **GOAL CHECK** ✔

- Have students write a list of clothing they wear and clothing their parents wear.
- Have one student read the model aloud.
- Have students write sentences comparing their clothes and their parents' clothes.
- Have students share their sentences with a partner.

Explain Preferences

Listening

- Introduce the topic by asking, *Where do you go to buy shoes? Do you like shopping for shoes? Why or why not?*

A
- Tell students they are going to hear a conversation in a shoe store. Have them read the question. Play the recording one or more times. 🔊 12
- Check answers.

B
- Have students complete the sentences with the comparative form of the adjectives.
- Have students compare answers with a partner.
- Listen again and check answers. Write the correct forms on the board. 🔊 12

C
- Tell students to listen again to find the information. Go over the questions.
- Play the recording one or more times. 🔊 12
- Have students compare answers with a partner.
- Check answers.

Listening

A 🔊 12 Listen. What is the woman buying? *(blue) shoes*

B 🔊 12 Fill in the blanks with comparatives using the adjectives in parentheses. Listen and check your answers.

1. **Shopper:** Do you have anything less formal?

   Sales attendant: Yes, these are _____ *more casual* _____ (casual).

2. **Shopper:** Do you have a _____ *bigger* _____ (big) size?

   Sales attendant: How about these? Are they _____ *better* _____ (good)?

3. **Shopper:** Do you have anything _____ *less expensive* _____ (expensive)?

   Sales attendant: Something _____ *cheaper* _____ (cheap)?

C 🔊 12 Listen again and answer the questions.

1. How many pairs of shoes does the woman try on? _____ *two* _____

2. How much do the white shoes cost? _____ *$80* _____

3. How much do the black shoes cost? _____ *$75* _____

4. What size shoes does the woman wear? _____ *7 or 7 1/2* _____

5. What color are the shoes that the woman buys? _____ *blue* _____

110   Unit 9

For Your Information: Shoe sizes

Different countries use different systems of shoe sizes. Here are some common equivalents.

Women:			Men:		
Metric	**US**	**UK**	**Metric**	**US**	**UK**
36	5–5.5	2–2.5	41	7–7.5	6.5–7
37	6–6.5	3–3.5	42	8–8.5	7.5–8
38	7–7.5	4–4.5	43	9–9.5	8.5–9
39	8–8.5	5–5.5	44	10–10.5	9.5–10
40	9–9.5	6–6.5	45	11–11.5	10.5–11

Pronunciation: Rising and falling intonation

A 🔊 **13** Listen to the sentences. Write arrows to show rising or falling intonation.

1. Which swim suit is cheaper? The blue one or the red one?
2. Whose dress is prettier? Karen's or Mia's?
3. Which is easier? Shopping online or in a store?
4. Which do you think is warmer? The sweater or the jacket?

B 🔊 **13** Listen again. Repeat the sentences.

Communication

A Compare shopping online to shopping in a store. Write sentences using the comparatives of the adjectives. Answers may vary.

1. safe _Shopping in a store is safer than shopping online._
2. quick _Shopping online is quicker than shopping in a store._
3. cheap _Shopping in a store is cheaper than shopping online._
4. easy _Shopping online is easier than shopping in a store._

B 🔄 Where should these people shop—online or in a store? Compare answers with your partner and give reasons. Answers may vary.

	Online	In store
1. Jenny needs a new dress for her birthday party tonight.		✓
2. Hamadi lives in a small village, a long way from the city.	✓	
3. Kenji isn't sure which smartphone to buy.	✓	
4. Albert is 85 years old and can't walk very far.	✓	
5. Rosa doesn't have a credit card.		✓
6. Mario hates waiting in line.	✓	

C 🔄 Discuss these questions with a partner.

1. What are the advantages and disadvantages of shopping online?
2. What are the advantages and disadvantages of shopping in a store?

D 🔄 **GOAL CHECK** ✔ **Explain preferences**

Add two more items to the list. What things do you prefer to buy online? What things do you prefer to buy in a store? Why? Share your ideas with a partner.

> I like to buy books online because it is cheaper.

> I like to buy books in a store because I can look at them.

	Online	In store
1. books		
2. clothes		
3. shoes		
4. camera		
5.		
6.		

Types of Clothing **111**

Talk About Clothing Material

Language Expansion

A • Go over the materials and clothing in the pictures. Point out more examples of clothes that students are wearing that are made out of the different materials.

• Divide the class into pairs and have them talk about the clothes in the pictures, describing them and giving their opinions.

• Have several students give their opinion about different items to the class.

B • Go over the symbols and terms in the clothing care instructions. Explain that *bleach* is a kind of liquid that we use to make clothes white, and a *tumble dryer* is a machine that makes clothes dry. To *dry clean* clothes, you take them to a special shop.

• Have students work individually to read the statements and choose *true* or *false*.

• Have students compare answers with a partner.

• Check answers.

• Ask students if they have any clothing that requires special cleaning or drying instructions.

Grammar

• Review comparative adjectives. Remind students that they are used when we talk about how two things are different.

• Introduce the structure. Ask a number of students, *How tall are you?* (If necessary, teach them, *I'm five foot eight* or *one meter seventy*, etc.) Say, *(Name) is the tallest student in our class.* Ask students, *Who has long hair?* Say, *(Name) has the longest hair.* Continue with other examples as appropriate—oldest/youngest student, and so on.

• Go over the information in the chart. Give/elicit more examples for each pattern.

C **GOAL 3:** Talk About Clothing Materials

> I really like that black leather jacket.

Language Expansion: Clothing materials

A ⚡ Take turns describing the clothes in the pictures to a partner.

100% Cotton Made in USA	100% Wool Made in Scotland	Man-made Fiber Made in Taiwan	100% Leather Made in Argentina	Pure Silk Made in China
Machine Wash, HOT Permanent Press	Hand Wash	Hand Wash	Do Not Wash	Dry-clean
Bleach as Needed	Do Not Bleach	Do Not Bleach		Do Not Bleach
Tumble Dry, MEDIUM	Dry Flat	Tumble Dry, MEDIUM		Dry Flat
Iron, Steam, or Dry, with HIGH HEAT	Iron, Steam, or Dry, with LOW HEAT	Do Not Iron		Iron, Steam or Dry, with LOW HEAT

B Read the different care instructions above. Circle **T** for *true* and **F** for *false*.

1. You can use bleach with cotton.   (T)   F
2. You can dry wool in a tumble dryer.   T   (F)
3. You have to dry-clean silk.   (T)   F
4. You can iron cotton.   (T)   F
5. You shouldn't wash leather.   (T)   F

Grammar: Superlatives

Superlative forms of adjectives		
Adjectives with one syllable Add -*est*.	cheap	The cotton pajamas are **the cheapest.**
Adjectives that end in -*y* Change the -*y* to *i* and add -*est*.	pretty	Helen is **the prettiest** girl in the class.
Adjectives with two or more syllables Use *most* or *least* before the adjective.	beautiful	These are **the most beautiful** shoes in the store.
Irregular superlatives	good	Turner's is **the best** shoe store in town.
	bad	Jon is a bad soccer player, but Tony is **the worst.**

Word Bank: More clothing materials

canvas	nylon
corduroy	polyester
denim	rayon
fleece	suede
linen	vinyl

Grammar: Superlatives

Superlative adjectives are used to compare an item with a group to which it belongs. Often the group is stated in the sentence:

Yoshi is the tallest student in the class.

Sometimes the group is not stated in the sentence:

Yoshi is the tallest.

Superlative adjectives are normally used with *the*. Common errors with superlatives include spelling mistakes and incorrect use of *most* and -*est*.

A Complete the sentences. Use the superlative form of the adjective in parentheses.

1. These are _____the most expensive_____ (expensive) shoes in the store.
2. Which is _____the warmest_____ (warm) jacket? The red one, the brown one, or the blue one?
3. Granger's Discount Store has _____the best_____ (good) prices.
4. These are _____the most formal_____ (formal) shoes that we have.

B Write sentences in your notebook using the pairs of adjectives in the box.

	price	weight	warmth	texture
silk	++++	+	++	++++
wool	+++	++++	++++	+
cotton	++	+++	+++	+++
man-made fiber	+	++	++	++

cheap / expensive
light / heavy
warm / cool
rough / smooth

Answers will vary. Sample answers: Cotton is lighter than wool, but silk is the lightest material.
1. Wool is usually more expensive than cotton, but silk is the most expensive material.

Conversation

A 🔊 14 Listen to the conversation. Why doesn't Pablo like the leather jacket? It's very heavy and expensive.

Pablo:	Excuse me, could you help me? I'm looking for a jacket.
Sales assistant:	Certainly, sir. I have some over here.
Pablo:	Mmm, very nice. Which is the warmest?
Sales assistant:	Well, these GORE-TEX® jackets are the warmest. They're waterproof and not too expensive.
Pablo:	No, I don't really like man-made material.
Sales assistant:	Well, we have some nice leather jackets.
Pablo:	No, I don't really like leather. It's very heavy, and I guess they are the most expensive.
Sales assistant:	Yes, they are. The cheapest is $250.

B 🔄 Practice the conversation. Switch roles and practice it again.

C 🔄 Work with a partner to make a new conversation using a different piece of clothing.

D 🔄 **GOAL CHECK** ✔ **Talk about clothing materials**

Talk with your partner. You are going on a trekking vacation and you're buying clothes. What material would you choose for the clothes in the box? Why?

hat   jacket   boots
pants   socks   shirt

Grammar Practice: Superlatives

Divide the class into groups of three. Tell them they are going to play a geography game in teams. First, they must write the questions correctly, and then they must answer them together. Give them an example: If you say *old city,* they should write, *What's the oldest city in the world?* Appoint one member in each group to be the "secretary" for the group. Dictate the following: *1. large/country, 2. tall/mountain, 3. long/river, 4. cold/place, 5. expensive/city, 6. big/city.* Group members work together to form the correct questions and then answer them. You can have the "secretaries" write the questions and answers on the board for scoring, or you can collect the papers for checking and announce the scores later. Give 1 point for a correct question and 1 point for a correct answer. Answers: 1. Russia; 2. Mount Everest; 3. the Nile River, though the Amazon River is the largest; 4. Antarctica; 5. Singapore; 6. Tokyo

A • Have students work individually to write the superlative adjectives.
• Have students compare answers with a partner.
• Check answers.

B • Have students look at the information in the chart. Ask questions, for example, *Which material is the cheapest? Which is heavier: cotton or man-made fiber?* etc.
• Have students read the example and write sentences comparing the materials, using the adjectives in the box.
• Have students compare sentences with a partner.
• Check answers.

Conversation

A • Have students close their books. Write the question on the board: *Why doesn't Pablo like the leather jacket?*
• Play the recording. 🔊 14
• Check answers.

B • Play or read the conversation again for the class to repeat.
• Practice the conversation with the class in chorus.
• Have students practice the conversation with partners and then switch roles and practice it again.

C • Have students choose a different item of clothing and make a new conversation.
• Call on student pairs to present their conversations to the class.

D 🔄 **GOAL CHECK** ✔

• Have students read the directions. Make sure they understand *trekking* (traveling on foot from one place to another in mountainous areas).
• Divide the class into pairs and have them decide the material they would choose for each item.
• Call on students to explain their choices to the class.

Evaluate Quality and Value

Reading

- Have students look at the pictures and describe what they see.
- Introduce the topic of the reading. Ask students, *What kinds of clothes are made of silk?* (dresses, blouses, scarves, neckties)

A
- Divide the class into pairs and have them discuss the questions.
- Compare answers as a class.

B
- Point out the vocabulary that is defined in the Word Focus box.
- Have students read the article. Tell them to circle any words they don't understand.
- Go over the article with the class, answering any questions from the students about vocabulary.
- Tell students to read the article again and find the answers to the questions.
- Have students compare answers with a partner.
- Check answers.

Reading

A 🔁 Discuss these questions with a partner.

1. What do you know about silk?
2. Where does it come from?
3. Do you have any clothes made from silk?
4. Is it cheap or expensive?

B Read the article. Answer the questions.

1. Which is the most expensive—cotton, wool, or silk? <u>silk</u>

2. Which country is the biggest producer of silk? <u>China</u>

3. Why does Shen think that old silks are more beautiful than modern silks? <u>In ancient times, weaving was done from the heart.</u>

4. Why do the workers put the cocoons into hot water? <u>to make them softer</u>

▲ silkworms

Word Focus

cocoon = a small bag of silk made by the silkworm
commerce = business, to make money
loom = a machine for making textiles
steel = a strong, hard metal
tomb = a place where dead people are buried

SILK
—THE QUEEN OF TEXTILES

Cotton is cool; wool is warm. They're practical. But silk? Silk is soft; it is smooth; it is sophisticated—the queen of textiles. It is also possibly the most expensive material in the world. In ancient Rome, it was more expensive than gold. But it is strong as well—a thread of silk is stronger than **steel.**

I wanted to discover more about this mysterious material, so I went to China. China is where the secret of silk was discovered more than 4,000 years ago, and it is still the biggest producer of silk in the world.

Additional Vocabulary

ancient = from a long time ago

discover = find out about

fibers = lines of material in cloth

mysterious = not easy to understand

prepare = make

producer = maker

sophisticated = not simple

textile = cloth

For Your Information: Silk

After the secret of making silk was discovered in China, silk production spread to Korea and India, then across Asia to Europe. Today, over 30 countries produce silk. The biggest producers of silk are China (54 percent of world production), India (14 percent), and Japan (11 percent). Silk is used in many types of clothing, but it is also used in parachutes, umbrellas/parasols, and bicycle tires.

Reading Tip

When discussing a text as a class, it is important to keep all students engaged by using different types of questions. Ask advanced speakers open-ended questions that need some explanation, such as *Why do people wear silk?* If beginners have difficulty with open-ended questions, try questions that can be answered with a word or phrase, or try multiple-choice questions.

The first person I visited was Shen Congwen, advisor on ancient textiles to the Palace Museum in Beijing. He showed me some ancient silk that workers found in a **tomb** in Jianglin. It was still beautiful. He told me that he thinks old silks are more beautiful than modern silks. "In ancient times, weaving was done from the heart. In modern times, weaving is done for **commerce.**"

So, how do you make silk? The first problem is that the silkworm only eats leaves from one tree—the mulberry tree. "It is easier to prepare food for a human than a silkworm," says Toshio Ito, a Japanese silkworm expert.

Silkworms only live for about 28 days, but in that time they increase in weight 10,000 times. Then, they make a **cocoon.** Workers collect the cocoons and kill the silkworms with steam. Then, they put the cocoons into hot water to soften them. Next, they pull the fibers from the cocoon and spin them to make silk thread. Finally, they weave the thread into cloth on machines called **looms.**

But why is silk so expensive? Well, it takes 110 cocoons to make a tie, 630 cocoons to make a blouse, and 3,000 cocoons to make a kimono. That's many hours of hard work. But many people believe silk's beauty is worth it.

Types of Clothing 115

After Reading

Have students search online for an item of silk clothing that they like (for instance, a necktie, shirt, or dress). Remind them NOT to enter any credit card information and to be careful NOT to buy anything. Ask them to print a copy of the Web page and write a few sentences about why they chose that item.

Evaluate Quality and Value

Writing

A • Ask students to think about their favorite piece of clothing and why they like it. Tell them they are going to write about this item. Go over the questions and have students write down their answers about their favorite piece of clothing.

• Have students write a composition about the item they have chosen.

• Have students exchange papers with a partner. Ask students to mark corrections and suggestions for improvements on their partners' papers.

• If desired, have students rewrite their papers, to be collected for grading.

Communication

A • Have students read the directions and look at the information in the table. Ask, *How much does machine-made silk cost? Which is the cheapest silk? Which is more expensive: machine-made or artificial silk?*

• Divide the class into pairs and assign them role A or B. Have them read their role and then write down a few ideas of what they will say. Remind them to write notes to help them, not complete sentences/questions.

• Have students role-play the situation.

• Have several pairs perform their role-play for the class.

B | **GOAL CHECK** ✔

• Have students look at the four categories and rank them according to what is important to them when clothes shopping.

• Have students compare their ranking with a partner and explain their reasons. Have them discuss any differences.

• Have several students explain their ranking to the class.

D | **GOAL 4:** Evaluate Quality and Value

▲ Silk threads being woven into clothing

Writing

A Write a paragraph in your notebook about your favorite piece of clothing. Answer the questions.

- What is it made from?
- When did you get it?
- Why do you like it?
- Where did you get it?
- How much did it cost?

Communication

A 🔁 With a partner, role-play the following situation.

Student A
You are a sales assistant in a textile shop. Try to sell the handmade silk.

Student B
You are a customer. You want 5 meters of cloth for some curtains. You can spend about $200.

Types of silk	Handmade silk	Machine-made silk	Artificial silk (acetate)
Price	$55–$100 per meter	$25–$35 per meter	$15–$25 per meter

B 🔁 | **GOAL CHECK** ✔ **Evaluate quality and value**

When you are buying clothes, what is most important to you? Rank the following:

_____ where it is made _____ the price

_____ the quality _____ the color

Compare your answers with a partner and discuss any differences.

Teacher Tip: Sharing students' work

There are a number of ways that students can share their work with their classmates:

• Give oral presentations in front of the class.

• Make large posters to display in front of the class.

• Tape students' papers around the classroom walls and allow time for students to walk around and read their classmates' work.

• Have students write or draw on transparencies and show these to the class on an overhead projector.

• Photocopy students' papers into a class magazine/newspaper and make a copy for each student.

A cotton field

Before You Watch

A Complete the passage using the words from the Word Focus box.

> 1 gallon = 3.8 liters
> 1 liter = .26 gallons

It takes about 140 liters of water to make a cup of coffee. The farmer uses water

to grow the coffee. Then water is used to (1) _____manufacture_____ the coffee in a factory and also to

(2) _____transport_____ the coffee to you. It also takes (3) _____energy_____ to make your

cup of coffee; gas on the farm and electricity in the factory. This puts carbon into the air, which is called a

(4) _____carbon footprint_____. One cup of coffee puts more than 100 grams of carbon into the atmosphere.

B Guess how many liters of water it takes to produce a cotton T-shirt. Watch the video and check your guess.

a. 700 liters   **b.** 1,700 liters   **c.** 2,700 liters

While You Watch

A ▶ Watch the video and answer the questions in your notebook.

1. How much water does a person drink per day? *3 liters*

2. List four ways your cotton T-shirt uses energy. *growing, manufacturing, transporting, caring for*

3. How many gallons of water does it take to do one load of wash? *40*

4. How can you reduce your T-shirt's carbon footprint? *don't dry or iron it*

After You Watch

A 🔀 There are many ways to reduce your carbon footprint. You can use public transportation, ride a bicycle, or buy local vegetables. With a group, think of other ways you can reduce your carbon footprint. Share your ideas with the class.

> **Word Focus**
>
> **carbon footprint** = the amount of carbon a person puts into the atmosphere
>
> **energy** = power from electricity, coal, gas, etc. It makes machines work.
>
> **manufacture** = to make something, usually in a factory
>
> **transport** = move things from one place to another, usually by truck, boat, or airplane

Types of Clothing 117

Video Journal:
How Your T-Shirt Can Make a Difference

Before You Watch

A • Have students look at the picture and describe what they see. Ask, *What is made from this plant?*

• Have students read the definitions in the Word Focus box and then complete the paragraph.

• Have students compare answers with a partner.

• Check answers.

B • Have students read the question and predict the answer.

• Have students watch the video and confirm their answer.

• Play the video.

• Check answers.

While You Watch

A • Have students read the questions and answer any they can.

• Have students watch the video again and check their answers.

• Have students compare answers with a partner.

• Check answers. Play the video again as necessary.

After You Watch

A • Have students read the directions and write a list of other ways of reducing their carbon footprint.

• Have students compare their list with a partner.

• Compare ideas as a class, and write a list on the board.

> **Writing and Speaking Tip**
>
> Remind students that brainstorming ideas and taking notes before they do a writing or speaking activity are good strategies to help them be successful. Point out that they should write key words and phrases at this stage, not complete ideas.

For Your Information: Carbon footprints

Your carbon footprint is how much greenhouse gas is produced directly or indirectly from your activities. When you drive your car, wash your clothes, or heat (or cool) your house, carbon dioxide (CO_2) is generated and released into the atmosphere. For example, a gallon of gasoline consumed by your car emits 8.7 kg of CO_2. The food and goods you buy also contribute to your carbon footprint because their production and transportation to you emitted CO_2. Understanding our personal carbon footprint and knowing how big it is are important because carbon dioxide is one of the greenhouse gases that causes global warming. On the Internet, there are Web sites where you can calculate your carbon footprint and get suggestions on how to reduce it.

The Interspecies Internet? An Idea in Progress

Before You Watch

A • Point out the pictures and ask students to describe what they see. Have students share what they remember about Diana Reiss (from the reading in Unit 7). Ask, *Who is Diana Reiss? What does she do? What is she interested in?* Write students' ideas on the board. Tell students they are going to watch a TED Talk with Reiss and other members of her project.

• Have students read the words and the definitions and match them.

• Have students compare answers with a partner.

• Check answers.

B • Go over the words in the Word Bank. Have students complete the sentences using the words.

• Have students compare answers with a partner.

• Check answers.

C • Divide the class into pairs and have them discuss the questions.

• Have several pairs share their ideas with the class.

D • Write on the board, *Interspecies Internet*. Have students say what they think it means.

• Have students read the directions and write down three things they think they will hear in the talk.

• Divide the class into pairs and have them compare their lists.

• Compare answers with the class. On the board, write their ideas about what they will see in the TED Talk.

TEDTALKS

Diana Reiss, Peter Gabriel, Neil Gershenfeld, and Vint Cerf
THE INTERSPECIES INTERNET? AN IDEA IN PROGRESS

Before You Watch

A Match the items to create complete sentences.

1. Communication is . . .   _d_
2. The Internet is . . .   _b_
3. The senses are . . .   _a_
4. Species are . . .   _c_

a. how a person or animal receives information about their environment.

b. a system of computer networks.

c. groups of animals that are similar.

d. using words, sounds, or signs to exchange information, thoughts, or feelings.

B Look at the words in the box. Choose the correct word to complete each sentence.

> **WORD BANK**
>
> **alien** a creature from outer space
> **bonobo** a rare, intelligent ape related to the chimpanzee
> **interact** to communicate with
> **interface** system linking two things
> **interplanetary** between different planets
> **interspecies** between different species
> **sentient** a being capable of experiencing the world through its senses

1. A computer has an ___interface___ to connect to the Internet.

2. Creatures that can think are called ___sentient___.

3. A creature from another world is called a(n) ___alien___.

4. People from around the world ___interact___ using the Internet.

5. Something that connects many planets is ___interplanetary___.

> Diana Reiss, Peter Gabriel, Neil Gershenfeld, and Vint Cerf's idea worth spreading is that the Internet isn't just for humans—animals should have access too. Watch the full TED Talk at TED.com.

6. People and gorillas can communicate using ___interspecies___ communication.

7. A ___bonobo___ is a type of very intelligent ape.

C Can you think of a situation where people and animals communicate, or animals communicate with other animals? Can you think of a situation where you communicate with a machine? Discuss your ideas with a partner.

D You are going to watch a TED Talk about a new idea for an Interspecies Internet. Write down three things you think you will see in the video. Share your ideas with a partner.

While You Watch

A Watch the TED Talk. Put the images on the next page in order. Write the number in the box.

B Write down two or three ideas from each speaker. After the TED Talk, discuss the ideas with a partner.

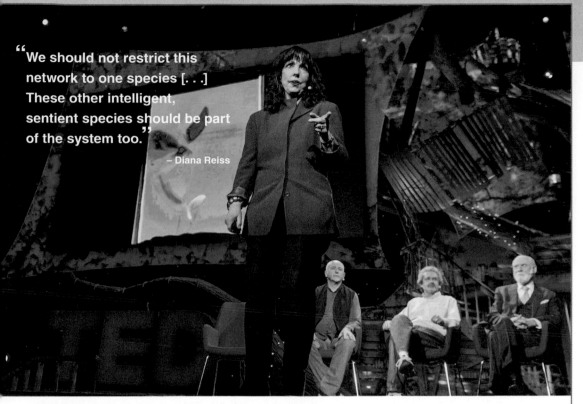

"We should not restrict this network to one species [. . .] These other intelligent, sentient species should be part of the system too."

– Diana Reiss

While You Watch

A • Have students look at the pictures and read the quotes. Tell them to number the quotes as they watch the talk.

• Play the talk.

• Have them compare answers with a partner.

• Check answers.

B • Have students write down two or three of the most interesting ideas from each speaker.

• Have students compare answers with a partner.

• Call on pairs to share ideas and make a class list of the main ideas for each speaker.

2 "We thought, perhaps the most amazing tool that man's created is the Internet, and what would happen if we could somehow find new interfaces, visual-audio interfaces that would allow these remarkable sentient beings that we share the planet with access?"

1 "I work with a lot of musicians from around the world, and often we don't have any common language at all, but we sit down behind our instruments, and suddenly there's a way for us to connect."

3 "We participate in the Apps for Apes program Orangutan Outreach, and we use iPads to help stimulate and enrich the animals."

4 "Now, there is a project that's underway called the Interplanetary Internet . . . What we're learning with these interactions with other species will teach us, ultimately, how we might interact with an alien from another world."

119

After You Watch

A • Have students read the names and the descriptions. Tell them to match them as they watch the talk. Play the talk again.

• Have them compare answers with a partner.

• Check answers.

B • Copy the chart onto the board. Have students help you write predictions for the first idea; for example, *Some animals will be able to play musical instruments.*

• Divide the class into pairs and have them write predictions for each idea.

TEDTALKS

Diana Reiss, Peter Gabriel, Neil Gershenfeld, and Vint Cerf
THE INTERSPECIES INTERNET?
AN IDEA IN PROGRESS

After You Watch

A Watch the TED Talk again. Match each speaker with the correct description.

1. _d_ Peter Gabriel
2. _b_ Neil Gershenfeld
3. _a_ Vint Cerf
4. _c_ Diana Reiss

a. He thinks that the Interspecies Internet can also be used to communicate with life on other planets.

b. He showed how the Interspecies Internet can work by video conferencing with animals.

c. She showed that dolphins can recognize themselves.

d. He played music with a bonobo.

B Read the list of ideas presented by the TED speakers. Then work with a partner to make two predictions for each idea. Answers will vary.

Idea	Predictions
1. communicating with other species using music	a. b.
2. the Interspecies Internet	a. b.
3. the Internet of Things	a. b.
4. the Interplanetary Internet	a. b.
5. communication with aliens	a. b.

120

An orangutan interacts with a tablet.

C 🔷 Get together with another pair. Take turns sharing your predictions. Explain which of the outcomes you find most interesting and why. Share your ideas with the class.

D 🔷 Think about how *you* communicate. Read the list of modes of communication below. Then, with a group, talk about which are the two best and worst ways to communicate with friends. Why?

e-mail	text message	in person
social media	letter	phone
letter	video conferencing	

E 🔷 With your group, imagine that you are going to communicate with the following animals. How does each animal communicate? Why does each animal communicate? Do you think you would be able to communicate with each one? If so, how? Share your ideas with the class.

bonobo	elephant
dolphin	orangutan
dog	cat
parot	bee

Challenge! 🔄 Diana Reiss has been doing experiments with dolphins since her first dolphin-keyboard experiment in the 1980s. Read more about her at TED.com. Find her TED Talk "Thinking Dolphin" online. With a partner, pick one more part of her work to share with the class. Do more research if needed.

121

C
- Join pairs together to make groups of four and have them compare and discuss their predictions. Have them decide which are the most interesting and explain why.
- Compare answers as a class and write the predictions in the chart on the board. Have students help correct any difficulties with *will/be going to* as necessary.
- Have each group say which prediction they think is the most interesting and why.

D
- In the same group, have students read the list of ways to communicate.
- Have each group make a list of the two best and worst ways for communicating with a friend and discuss why.
- Have each group share their list and explain their reasons. Discuss any differences.

E
- Ask, *What's the best way to communicate with a dolphin?* Write students' ideas on the board. Ask, *What could you communicate with a dolphin? What would you want the dolphin to do? What things would you and the dolphin like? How would you both feel?*
- In the same groups, have students discuss each animal and how and what they would communicate.
- Compare ideas as a class and write them on the board.

Challenge
- Have students read more about Diana Reiss and her work (this can be done in or outside of class depending on resources and time). Encourage them to watch the TED Talk "Thinking Dolphin" outside of class.
- Divide the class into pairs and have them choose one part of Reiss's work to research further (in or outside of class). Have each pair share what they found out with the class.

Ideas Worth Sharing
- With books closed, have students share what they remember about Diana Reiss and the other speakers (provide their names if the students can't: Peter Gabriel, Neil Gershenfeld, and Vint Verf). Ask, *What is their message? How do they think communicating with other species will help us in the future?* Write their ideas on the board.
- Have students read the information in the Ideas Worth Sharing box on page 118 again. Remind them that they can watch the whole talk at TED.com to help them develop their listening skills.

Lifestyles

About the Photo

This photo was taken by David Doubilet, a highly acclaimed underwater photographer from New York. Taken at dusk in the Dampier Strait in Indonesia, it shows fishermen standing on their wooden boats, and at the same time, the underwater world of the fish is viewable. To achieve a shot like this, Doubilet half-submerges his camera lens in the water, so the two worlds can be photographed in the same image. This gives a view of the calm surface with fishermen quietly at work beneath the evening sky, while also showing the world below the surface where there is the intense movement of hundreds of small fish.

- Introduce the theme of the unit. Explain that your lifestyle is your way of living—all the things you do every day.

- Direct students' attention to the photo. Have students describe what they see.

- Have students work with a partner to discuss the questions.

- Compare answers with the class.

- Ask these questions orally or by writing them on the board for students to answer in pairs: *What are the most important things for a healthy lifestyle? Are our lifestyles healthier now than they were in the past?*

- Go over the Unit Goals with the class, explaining as necessary.

- For each goal, elicit any words students already know and write them on the board; for example, (un)healthy food vocabulary, exercise and sports vocabulary, etc.

A fisherman stands in a wooden boat on calm water. Below his boat, baitfish shine in the waters of the Dampier Strait in Indonesia.

122

UNIT 10 GOALS	**Grammar**	**Vocabulary**	**Listening**
• Give advice on healthy habits • Compare lifestyles • Ask about lifestyles • Evaluate your lifestyle	Modals (*could, ought to, should, must*); *have to* You **have to** stop smoking. Questions with *how* **How** often do you exercise?	Healthy and unhealthy habits Compound adjectives	Listening for general understanding: Personal lifestyles

Look at the photo, answer the questions:

1 What does the photo show about the fisherman's lifestyle?

2 What is your lifestyle like? Can you improve it?

Unit Theme Overview

- The concept of "lifestyle" was first developed in 1929 by the psychologist Alfred Adler, but it became popular in the 1970s. The term refers to the overall way that a person lives. A person's lifestyle is made up of a complex collection of personal choices and customs imposed by society. Our environment and our culture limit the range of choices that we can make.

- This unit focuses on one particular aspect of lifestyle: the habits and choices that affect our health. Here, again, lifestyle has both personal and social components. People's choices about food, exercise, and other daily activities have an impact on their health, but there are also cultures in the world where people enjoy unusually long and healthy lives due to culturally-imposed customs.

- In this unit, students begin by discussing healthy personal habits and giving advice. They compare lifestyles and learn to ask questions to get more details. Finally, they learn about cultural patterns that seem to promote good health—and others that seem to hinder it.

UNIT 10 GOALS

1. Give advice on healthy habits

2. Compare lifestyles

3. Ask about lifestyles

4. Evaluate your lifestyle

123

Speaking	Reading	Writing	Video Journal
Discussing healthy and unhealthy habits Giving advice for improving habits **Pronunciation:** *Should, shouldn't*	**National Geographic:** "The Secrets of Long Life"	Writing a paragraph about personal lifestyle	**National Geographic:** "The Science of Stress"

Give Advice on Healthy Habits

Vocabulary

• Go over the sentences with the class, pointing out the expressions in blue and explaining as necessary. Ask questions for further practice: *Are you in good shape? Do you eat a lot of junk food?*

A • Have students work individually to fill in the words.

• Have students compare answers with a partner.

• Check answers.

B • Go over the names for the activities in the pictures. Ask different students, *Do you drink lots of water? Do you usually get eight hours of sleep at night?* etc.

• Have students work individually to classify the activities into the chart.

• Have students compare answers with a partner.

• Check answers.

• Point out that these expressions can also be formed as verbs: *I sunbathe. I drink lots of water.* Ask students to tell you one healthy/ unhealthy thing they do. (*I run every day./I eat lots of sugar.*)

A GOAL 1: Give Advice on Healthy Habits

Vocabulary

Alicia has a healthy lifestyle. She's in good shape because she works out at the gym every day. She eats healthy food, like fresh fruits and vegetables.

Robert doesn't have a good lifestyle. He's in bad shape because he never gets any exercise. He eats too much junk food, so he's overweight.

A Complete the sentences with the words in blue.

1. I need to exercise more. I'm in ___bad shape___.
2. Helen doesn't have a ___healthy___ diet. She eats a lot of junk food.
3. I have a healthy ___lifestyle___. I don't smoke and I exercise regularly.
4. I need to change my diet. I eat too much ___junk food___.
5. Jane is looking much better. She ___works out___ and eats healthy food, like vegetables and fruit. Soon she'll be in ___good shape___.

B Write the activities in the correct column in the chart below.

▲ cycling

▲ smoking

▲ watching lots of TV

▲ drinking lots of water

▲ getting eight hours of sleep every night

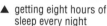
▲ sunbathing

▲ eating a balanced diet

▲ eating lots of sugar

Healthy	Unhealthy
cycling	smoking
drinking lots of water	watching lots of TV
getting eight hours of sleep every night	sunbathing
eating a balanced diet	eating lots of sugar

124   Unit 10

Word Bank: Healthy and unhealthy habits

Healthy:
avoiding stress
getting fresh air
going for a walk every day
going to the doctor for a check-up
playing tennis/basketball/soccer
taking vitamins

Unhealthy:
drinking sugary drinks
eating a lot of salty/fatty food
getting angry often
not wearing a seat belt in the car
playing too many computer/video games
staying up late

Grammar: Modals (*could, ought to, should, must*); *have to*

Make suggestions	Give advice	Express obligation
You **could** stop smoking.	You **should/ought to** stop smoking.	You **must/have to** stop smoking.
! gentle	!! strong	!!! very strong

A Write advice for the following situations in your notebook.

1. Tell your sister to stop smoking. !!! *You have to/must stop smoking.*
2. Tell your father to go on a diet. !! *You ought to/should go on a diet.*
3. Tell your friend to stop watching so much television. ! *You could stop watching so much television.*
4. Tell your brother to get more exercise. !! *You ought to/should get more exercise.*
5. Tell your mother to get more sleep. ! *You could get more sleep.*
6. Tell your friend to stop sunbathing. !!! *You have to/must stop sunbathing.*

B ⟳ Write the advice you would give to these people in your notebook. Then compare your advice with your partner's. Discuss differences.

1. Aisha wants to lose weight.
2. Yun wants to be on the Olympic swimming team.
3. Arata works too much.
4. Jaime needs some money.
5. Jack isn't happy at work.
6. Sam wants to get better grades.

Conversation

A ◀)) 15 Listen to the conversation. Why does Alex want to lose weight? *His clothes don't fit.*

Alex: I need to lose some weight. My clothes don't fit anymore. What should I do?
Faisal: Well, instead of watching TV all day, you could get more exercise.
Alex: Like what?
Faisal: Like cycling, or you could work out at the gym.
Alex: I don't have time. I'm too busy.
Faisal: OK. Then you could change your diet. Eat something healthier, like fruit.
Alex: You mean, no more hamburgers! Oh no!
Faisal: OK. Buy some bigger clothes then.

B ⟳ Practice the conversation with a partner. Switch roles and practice it again.

C ⟳ **GOAL CHECK** ✔ **Give advice on healthy habits**

Ask your partner questions about the activities on page 124. Then give your partner advice.

Real Language

We use *like what?* to ask for an example. We can use *like* to give an example.

> Do you get eight hours of sleep every night?

> No, I don't.

> You should get more sleep.

Lifestyles   125

Grammar

- Introduce the structures. Tell the class, *Mr. X is a teacher at our school. He smokes 30 cigarettes every day. What would a student say to him?* Have students read the chart. Elicit, *You could stop smoking.* Ask, *What would his friend say to him?* (*You should/ought to stop smoking.*) *What would his doctor say to him?* (*You must/have to stop smoking.*)

A
- Have students work individually to write a sentence for each situation.
- Check answers.

B
- Have students write advice for each situation.
- In pairs, have students compare their advice and discuss any differences.
- Have several students share their advice and write it on the board. Have the class help you correct the sentences as necessary.

Conversation

A
- Have students close their books. Write the question on the board: *Why does Alex want to lose weight?*
- Play the recording. ◀)) 15
- Check answers.
- Direct students' attention to the Real Language box.

B
- Play or read the conversation again for the class to repeat.
- Practice the conversation with the class in chorus.
- Have students practice the conversation with partners and then switch roles and practice it again.

C ⟳ **GOAL CHECK** ✔

- Divide the class into pairs and have them ask each other questions using the pictures on page 124, and give advice. Model the example with several students.
- Call on students to tell the class the advice they gave to their partner.

Grammar: Modals (*could, ought to, should, must*); *have to*

Telling other people what to do can be a sensitive situation, and native speakers use modals to make an idea less forceful and more polite, depending on their relationship with the other person.

Grammar Practice: Modals (*could, ought to, should, must*); *have to*

Have students work with partners to write a letter to a newspaper column about a health problem. When all pairs have finished, have them exchange letters with another pair. Tell them that they are now "doctors" and should write a reply.

Compare Lifestyles

Listening

A • Have students look at the pictures and describe the people. Have them read the directions and then rank the three people's lifestyles from healthy to unhealthy. Tell them to listen and find the answer.
  • Play the recording one or more times. 🔊 16
  • Check answers.

B • Tell students to listen to the three people again and find the information.
  • Play the recording one or more times. 🔊 16
  • Have students compare answers with a partner.
  • Check answers.

C • Have students work with partners to make recommendations for the three people.
  • Compare answers with the class.

Pronunciation

A • Tell students to listen to the pronunciations of *should* and *shouldn't* in the sentences.
  • Play the recording one or more times. 🔊 17
  • Point out that the letter *l* in *should* and *shouldn't* is not pronounced.

B • Tell students to listen to the conversations and circle the correct word.
  • Play the recording one or more times. 🔊 18
  • Have students compare answers with a partner.
  • Check answers.

C • Divide the class into pairs and have them choose and practice one of the conversations.
  • Call on two different pairs to present each conversation to the class.

B   GOAL 2: Compare Lifestyles

Listening

▲ Ben

▲ Maggie

▲ Anita

A ♻ 🔊 16 Look at the photos. Guess who is healthy or unhealthy. Rank the people from healthy lifestyle to unhealthy lifestyle. Compare your answers with your classmates. Listen and check.

Maggie ———— Anita ———— Ben

Healthy lifestyle ⟵——————————————⟶ **Unhealthy lifestyle**

B 🔊 16 Listen again and answer the questions.

1. Does Ben exercise every day? <u>no</u>
2. Does Ben smoke? <u>yes</u>
3. What exercise does Maggie do? <u>She swims.</u>
4. Name two things that Maggie has for breakfast. <u>any two of: whole-meal bread, honey, yogurt, high-fiber cereal</u>
5. Where does Anita get her vegetables? <u>from her garden</u>
6. What is Anita's one bad habit? <u>She drinks a lot of coffee.</u>

C 🔄 Work with a partner. What advice would you give to Ben, Maggie, and Anita on how to improve their lifestyles?

Pronunciation: *Should, shouldn't*

A 🔊 17 Listen to the sentences. Notice the difference between *should* and *shouldn't*.

I **should** get more sleep.   They **shouldn't** eat junk food.

B 🔊 18 Listen to the conversations and circle *should* or *shouldn't*.

Conversation 1

Lorena: What can I do to improve my image?
Zuleja: Well, you (should |(shouldn't)) change your hairstyle. Your hair looks great!
Lorena: And what about my clothes?
Zuleja: I think you ((should)| shouldn't) buy some more fashionable clothes. You ((should)| shouldn't) wear less makeup as well.

Conversation 2

Bill: What can I do to change my image?
Adrian: I think you ((should)| shouldn't) shave your beard, but you (should |(shouldn't)) change your hairstyle.
Bill: And what about my clothes?
Adrian: You ((should)| shouldn't) buy some new clothes.

C 🔄 Choose one of the conversations and practice with a partner.

126   Unit 10

For Your Information: Components of a healthy lifestyle

Research has found that six habits are closely linked with a longer life. They are:

1. Eating breakfast every day
2. Avoiding snacks between meals
3. Keeping an ideal weight
4. Regular exercise
5. Sleeping 7–8 hours per night
6. Not smoking.

People aged 55 to 64 who practiced all of these habits were found to be as healthy as younger people, age 25 to 34, who followed only one or two of them. There is more information about healthy lifestyles in the Workbook Reading for this unit.

Fresh vegetables are part of a healthy diet.

Communication

A 👥 Answer the questions for yourself. Then survey two classmates.

Lifestyle choices	Me		Classmate 1 Name _____		Classmate 2 Name _____	
Do you play computer games?	Yes → No	____ hours per day	Yes → No	____ hours per day	Yes → No	____ hours per day
Do you eat fresh vegetables?	Yes → No	____ per day	Yes → No	____ per day	Yes → No	____ per day
Do you spend time on social media?	Yes → No	____ hours per day	Yes → No	____ hours per day	Yes → No	____ hours per day
Do you work out every day?	Yes → No	____ hours per day	Yes → No	____ hours per day	Yes → No	____ hours per day
Do you drink coffee or tea every day?	Yes → No	____ cups per day	Yes → No	____ cups per day	Yes → No	____ cups per day
Do you eat sugary foods?	Yes → No	____ per day	Yes → No	____ per day	Yes → No	____ per day

B 🔁 Tell a partner about you and the classmates you interviewed.

C 👥 Tell your group about your lifestyle.

D 👥 GOAL CHECK ✔ **Compare lifestyles**

As a group, decide who has the best lifestyle and give reasons.

> Ramona and I never play computer games, but Alfredo plays for about two hours per day.

> Salma works out in the gym every day for two hours and doesn't eat sugary foods.

> Yahir eats five pieces of sugary food per day and never works out. Salma has a much better lifestyle.

Lifestyles **127**

Communication

A • Have students answer the questions in the survey.

• Have students move around the classroom and ask two classmates the questions.

B • Divide the class into pairs and have them tell each other about themselves and the two people they interviewed. Point out the model.

C • Divide the class into groups of three or four students and have them discuss their lifestyles.

D 👥 GOAL CHECK ✔

• With the same group, have students decide who has the best (healthiest) lifestyle and explain why. Point out the examples and ask, *Why does Salma have a better lifestyle than Yahir?*

• Have each group share their decision and reasons with the class.

Expansion Activity

Have students work with partners to prepare a role-play about lifestyles: one person has an unhealthy lifestyle and the other tries to help with it. They should decide who the two people are (for example, two friends, or doctor and patient) and use appropriate language in their role-play. When all student pairs are ready, call on them to present their role-plays to the class.

Ask About Lifestyles

- Have students look at the picture and describe what they see. Ask, *What kind of lifestyle does she have: healthy or unhealthy? What do you think she does to have a healthy lifestyle?*

Language Expansion

A • Read through the list of adjectives. Point out that each one is formed from two other words. When this happens, the new word is called a *compound*.

- Have students work individually to match the columns.
- Have students compare answers with a partner.
- Check answers.

B • Have students work individually to complete each sentence with the compound adjectives from **A**.

- Have students compare answers with a partner.
- Check answers.
- Elicit more sentences using these adjectives. Ask questions like, *Do you have a lifelong friend? What kinds of homemade food do you like? Who is overworked?*

Grammar

- Go over the information in the chart about the formation of these questions. Remind students that they already know questions like *How old (are you)?* and *How much/ How many?*
- Ask several students questions, and call on students to ask questions to their classmates.

C **GOAL 3:** Ask About Lifestyles

stress-free

Language Expansion: Compound adjectives

A Match the compound adjectives to their meanings.

a. works too much
b. delicious
c. without worries or problems
d. not high in calories
e. makes you happy
f. produced in your own garden
g. all your life
h. not made in a factory

1. mouth-watering __b__
2. homemade __h__
3. heartwarming __e__
4. lifelong __g__
5. stress-free __c__
6. homegrown __f__
7. overworked __a__
8. low-calorie __d__

B Complete the sentences. Use adjectives from exercise **A**.

1. Kevin and I went to kindergarten together. We are ____lifelong____ friends.
2. When I was a child, my father had a vegetable garden, so we ate lots of ____homegrown____ fruit and vegetables.
3. I have to work long hours, and I'm always tired. I think I am ____overworked____.
4. My grandmother makes the best ____homemade____ chicken soup in the world! It's absolutely ____mouth-watering____.

Grammar: Questions with *how*

How much exercise do you get?	How long did your grandfather live?
How many cigarettes do you smoke a day?	How often do you go to the gym?
How old is your father?	

*We use **how much** to ask about the quantity of non-countable nouns.
*We use **how many** to ask about the quantity of countable nouns.
*We use **how old** to ask about age.
*We use **how long** to ask about length or a period of time.
*We use **how often** to ask about frequency.

128 Unit 10

Word Bank: Compound adjectives

fat-free

left-handed/right-handed

low-salt/high-protein

middle-aged

world-famous

Grammar: Questions with *how*

How is used with adjectives (*How old, How long*) and adverbs (*How often*) to make questions. In this lesson, the only adverb presented is *often*, an adverb of frequency. Other adverbs can also be used with this structure, including adverbs of manner (*How <u>well</u> do you speak English?*).

A Match the questions and the answers.

1. How often does Mike go swimming? _e_
2. How old is Akuru's grandmother? _a_
3. How much junk food do you eat? _d_
4. How long do you think you will live? _b_
5. How many cigarettes does Mario smoke a day? _c_

a. She's about 95.
b. Until I'm 80.
c. About 15.
d. Not much.
e. Once a week.

B Write the questions.

Questions

1. How often do you go to the gym?
2. How old are you?
3. How long will it take?
4. How much do you weigh?

Answers

We go to the gym three times a week.
I am 27 years old.
I think it will take about two hours.
I weigh 168 pounds.

C 🔁 Write five *Wh-* questions in your notebook. Ask your partner the questions. *Possible Wh- questions: Who are they? What homegrown vegetables do you eat? Why do you eat homegrown vegetables? Who is overworked? Why is he/she overworked? What low-calorie food do you eat?*

Conversation

A 🔊 19 Listen to the conversation. What's the problem with Mr. Lopez?
He is overworked; he can't sleep and is always tired.

Doctor:	Good morning, Mr. Lopez. How can I help you?
Mr. Lopez:	Hello, doctor. I'm always tired, but when I go to bed I can't sleep.
Doctor:	OK. How long have you had this problem?
Mr. Lopez:	Since I started my new job.
Doctor:	What do you do?
Mr. Lopez:	I'm in advertising.
Doctor:	How many hours do you work?
Mr. Lopez:	I work about 80 hours a week.
Doctor:	80 hours! That's a lot. And how much exercise do you get?
Mr. Lopez:	Not much. I don't have the time.
Doctor:	OK. It seems to me that you are overworked. You need to work less and find time to get more exercise. Maybe you should look for a more stress-free job.

B 🔁 Practice the conversation with a partner. Switch roles and practice it again.

C 🔁 Change the underlined problem to create and practice a new conversation.

D 🔁 **GOAL CHECK** ✔ **Ask about lifestyles**

Ask a partner about his or her lifestyle.

A • Have students work individually to match the columns.
• Have students compare answers with a partner.
• Check answers.

B • Have students work individually to write the question for each answer.
• Have students compare answers with a partner.
• Check answers.
• Have students practice saying the questions and answers with a partner.

C • Write a few examples on the board to remind students of the structure of *Wh-* questions. Have students write five *Wh-* questions.
• Have students ask and answer the questions with a partner.
• Call on different students to ask questions and have other students answer.

Conversation

A • Have students close their books. Write the question on the board: *What's the problem with Mr. Lopez?*
• Play the recording. 🔊 19
• Check answers.

B • Play or read the conversation again for the class to repeat.
• Practice the conversation with the class in chorus.
• Have students practice the conversation with a partner and then switch roles and practice it again.

C • Have each pair make a new conversation, using their own ideas for solving a different problem.
• Call on student pairs to present their conversations to the class.

D 🔁 **GOAL CHECK** ✔

• Divide the class into pairs and have them ask each other at least three questions with *how*.
• Call on students to tell you something they learned about their partners.

Grammar Practice:
Questions with *how*

Have students work with partners to practice a role-play of a reporter interviewing a famous person about his or her lifestyle. The reporter should ask at least three questions with *how*. When all student pairs are ready, call on them to present their role-plays to the class.

Evaluate Your Lifestyle

Reading

- Introduce the topic of the reading. Ask students, *Who is the oldest person in your family? How old is he or she?*

A
- Divide the class into pairs and have them talk about the questions.
- Point out the words in the Word Focus box. Have students read the article to check their answers to the second question. Tell them to circle any words they don't understand.
- Go over the article with the class, answering any questions from the students about vocabulary.

B
- Tell students to read the article again and answer the questions.
- Have students compare answers with a partner.
- Check answers.
- Ask students about the oldest people they know. Do they follow any of these habits? Is their health good?

Additional Vocabulary

cancer = a very serious disease that kills many people

experts = people who know a lot about a subject

generally = usually

mental = in your mind

nutrients = vitamins and other healthy things in food

sumo wrestling = a Japanese sport

waist = middle of the body

D | **GOAL 4:** Evaluate Your Lifestyle

Reading

A Discuss the questions with a partner.

1. Do you want to live to be 100 years old?
2. What do you think you should do to live to be 100 years old?

B Answer the questions.

1. A long, healthy life depends on mainly two things. What are they? _genes and good habits_

2. Why do men live longer in Sardinia than in the United States? _The men have a more stress-free life._

3. How old was Ushi the last time the writer visited her? _98_

4. How often should you exercise? _every day_

5. What are the advantages of growing your own vegetables? _You eat healthier food and get exercise._

Word Focus

genes = parts of the body that determine physical characteristics

joke = to say something that is not serious

perfume = liquid that smells good

prevent = to avoid

run away = to leave

Sardinia, Italy and Okinawa, Japan

THE SECRETS OF LONG LIFE

A long, healthy life is no accident. It begins with good **genes,** but it also depends on good habits. If you have a healthy lifestyle, experts say you may live up to ten years longer. So what is the secret of a long life?

I visited places in the world where many people live to be 100 years old, including Sardinia in Italy and Okinawa in Japan. Sardinians and Okinawans live longer, have fewer illnesses, and enjoy long, healthy lives.

SARDINIANS

First, I went to Sardinia, where many people, especially men, live longer than in other parts of the world. Generally, women live longer than men. In fact, in America, there are four times as many 100-year-old women as men. However, in Sardinia, an equal number of men and women reach 100.

For Your Information: Sardinia and Okinawa

Sardinia is the second-largest island in the Mediterranean Sea. The land is mountainous, and they have hot summers and mild winters. Along with Italian, people also speak a distinct Sardinian language. The island is very popular with European vacationers, who come for its scenery, beaches, and gourmet food.

Okinawa is a small island that is part of Japan. It has a subtropical climate, with warm seawater and beautiful coral reefs. It's an important area for tourism in Japan. In the past, Okinawa was a separate nation, with its own distinctive language and culture. Karate was first developed there.

The reason is possibly that the men have a stress-free life working outside, while the women look after the house and the family money. "I do the work," says Tonino, holding his wife Giovanna around the waist. "My wife does the worrying."

OKINAWANS

Since I last visited Ushi five years ago, she's taken a new job, tried to **run away** from home, and started wearing **perfume**. Normal for a young woman, perhaps, but Ushi is 103. When I ask about the perfume, she **jokes** that she has a new boyfriend, then puts a hand over her mouth and laughs.

"Okinawans have one-fifth the heart disease, one-fourth the breast and prostate cancer, and one-third less mental health problems than Americans,"

says Craig Willcox of the Okinawa Centenarian Study. What's the key to their success? "*Ikigai* certainly helps," Willcox says. The word translates to "reason for living," and it may help to prevent stress and diseases such as high blood pressure.

Okinawans have a low-calorie diet. "A full plate of Okinawan vegetables, tofu, miso soup, and a little fish or meat contains fewer calories than a small hamburger," says Makoto Suzuki of the Okinawa Centenarian Study. "And it will have many more healthy nutrients."

When she's not watching sumo wrestling on TV, Yasu Itoman, 100, gets her own exercise by growing onions, tomatoes, carrots, and other herbs and vegetables in her garden. Her homegrown vegetables may help **prevent** cancer.

Bosa, Sardinia

Lifestyles 131

Reading Tip

Students can use a text's title and the photos with it to predict what it will be about. This helps create a context in the reader's mind and helps students make sense of the information they read. Call on students to guess what this article is about and ask them to explain their guesses.

After Reading

Assign each student to do research online to find three interesting facts about Okinawa or Sardinia and write them down. Then match them with partners who researched the other place and have them exchange information.

Evaluate Your Lifestyle

Communication

A • Go over the items in the list and elicit the questions needed to ask about each one. Write them on the board as necessary. For the first question, elicit follow-up questions and write them on the board; for example, *What sport do you play? How often do you play the sport?* Have students write follow-up questions for each item in their notebook.

• Have students move around the room asking the questions. They should only write the name of a person who answers *yes,* and find a different person for each item.

B • Call on each student to share something they learned about one of their classmates.

Writing

• Write 1–5 on the board and write notes for your answers to each question. Then have students help you start a paragraph about your lifestyle on the board: *I have a healthy lifestyle. I am happy in my job. I exercise four times a week. I go swimming, and I walk a lot.*

A • Tell students they are going to write about their lifestyle. Have them take notes for each question first. Then have them write their paragraph.

• Have students exchange papers with partners. Ask students to mark corrections and suggestions on their partners' papers.

• If desired, have students rewrite their papers, to be collected for grading.

B 🔁 **GOAL CHECK** ✔

• Have students work with partners to discuss their own health habits and make suggestions.

• Have several students tell the class the advice they gave their partner.

D **GOAL 4:** Evaluate Your Lifestyle

> Do you play a sport?

> Yes, I do.

> What sport do you play?

> Min-jun plays football.

> Seo-yeon has a stress-free life. She does yoga.

Communication

A 🔵 Go around the class and find someone who does each of the following. Write the names in the chart, and then ask a follow-up question.

Find someone who . . .	Name
1. . . . plays a sport.	
2. . . . has a stress-free life.	
3. . . . has a clear reason for living.	
4. . . . grows his or her own vegetables.	
5. . . . has a grandparent more than 70 years old.	

B 🔵 Report to the class.

Writing

A Write a paragraph about your own lifestyle. Answer the questions.

1. Do you lead a healthy lifestyle?
2. How often do you exercise?
3. What sort of food do you eat?
4. Do you get enough sleep?
5. How can you improve your lifestyle?

B 🔁 **GOAL CHECK** ✔ **Evaluate your lifestyle**

Discuss with a partner the good habits and the bad habits in your lifestyles. Take turns. Give each other advice.

132 Unit 10

Teacher Tip: "Fillers"

Here are some activities to "fill in" a few extra minutes at the end of a lesson:

• **The Blackboard Game** (if the board is filled with vocabulary and notes) Have a volunteer sit with his/her back to the board. Students take turns giving definitions of words on the board. When the volunteer says the correct word, you erase it. The game ends when all words are erased.

• **Error Quiz** On the board, write ten incorrect sentences that you have heard or seen in students' recent work. Divide the class into pairs to correct as many as they can in five minutes. When time is up, ask the class for corrections, and rewrite the sentences on the board.

• **Spelling Practice** Dictate 10 to 15 words that students find difficult. Let them compare answers with partners before you give the correct answers.

Traffic can be very stressful.

Before You Watch

A ⚡ Make a list of things that can cause stress. Discuss your list with a partner.

B Match the words and the definitions.

1. hormones _c_
2. physical stress _a_
3. mental stress _b_

a. stress on your body, like running
b. stress on your mind, like too much work
c. chemicals produced by your body

> **Word Focus**
>
> If you feel under **stress,** you feel worried and tense because of difficulties in your life.

While You Watch

A ▶ Watch the video. Circle **T** for *true* and **F** for *false*.

1. There are two types of stress: physical and mental.   ⓣ   F
2. Stress produces hormones.   ⓣ   F
3. When you exercise, you don't burn all the hormones.   T   Ⓕ
4. Long-term hormones can cause problems.   ⓣ   F

After You Watch

A ⚡ Discuss the questions with a partner.

1. What did you learn from this video?
2. Will it change your lifestyle?

Communication

A ❖ Work in groups of three or four. You have been assigned to design your school's or office's Anti-Stress Campaign. Make a list of four things you will do.

Lifestyles 133

For Your Information: The effects of stress

Stress is a normal reaction to things that threaten our well-being. When your body senses danger of some kind, it reacts to give you extra strength. But long-term stress every day can cause serious health problems because it affects all the physical systems of the body. Stress can cause or worsen heart disease, digestive problems, and skin conditions, and can lead to sleep problems and depression. Because stress hormones have such a strong impact on the body, it's important for our health to find ways to lessen stress and deal with it effectively.

Video Journal:
The Science of Stress

Before You Watch

A • Have students look at the picture and describe what they see. Introduce the idea of *stress*. Direct students' attention to the Word Focus box. Ask students, *Do you feel stressed today? How do you feel when you feel stressed?*

• Have students write a list of things that can cause stress and compare their list with a partner.

• Compare lists as a class and write a list on the board.

B • Have students match the words and definitions.

• Have students compare answers with a partner.

• Check answers.

While You Watch

A • Tell students to watch the video the first time and circle the answers.

• Play the video.

• Have students compare answers with a partner.

• Check answers.

After You Watch

A • Divide the class into pairs and have them answer the questions.

• Compare answers with the class.

Communication

A • Divide the class into small groups and explain the task. Because stress is bad for your health, your school or office has decided to run an Anti-Stress Campaign to make people healthier. Give/elicit an example of one way to do this. (For example: Play relaxing music.)

• Have each group make its list.

• Have each group present their ideas to the class.

• Discuss which ideas would work best.

Achievements

About the Photo

This photo was taken by John Burcham, an American photojournalist, who specializes in adventure and exploration photography. The photo shows a climber on the top of a mountain peak in Greenland. Climbing is both a challenging and exhilarating sport that requires a lot of strength and determination. The sense of achievement when the top of a mountain or high cliff is reached is extremely rewarding.

Greenland is a popular destination for climbers due to the vast number of mountains and different levels of challenge. Two of the most well-known are Gunnbjørns Fjeld and the cliffs at Tasermiut fjord, but there are thousands more.

- Introduce the theme of the unit. Explain that achievements are important things that people have done. Elicit examples, using famous people: *What was ____'s big achievement? She/He _____.*

- Direct students' attention to the photo. Have students describe what they see.

- Have students discuss the questions with a partner.

- Compare answers with the class.

- Ask these questions orally or by writing them on the board for students to answer in pairs: *What are things that most people achieve during their life? Which achievement in your life is the most important?*

- Go over the Unit Goals with the class, explaining as necessary.

- For each goal, elicit any words students already know and write them on the board; for example, vocabulary for chores, jobs, etc.

A single climber **stands** on a peak above the clouds in Greenland.

134

UNIT 11 GOALS	Grammar	Vocabulary	Listening
• Talk about today's chores • Interview for a job • Talk about personal accomplishments • Discuss humanity's greatest achievements	Present perfect tense ***Have** you **finished** your homework?* Present perfect tense vs. simple past tense *Claudio **has been** to many countries.* *He **went** to France last year.*	Chores Personal accomplishments	Listening for general understanding and specific details: A job interview

Unit Theme Overview

- Achievements come in all sizes. In the unit opener, students look at big personal achievements, such as climbing a mountain. But there are also small, daily achievements that build up to bigger things: finishing a tough workout at the gym or learning a long list of vocabulary words. This unit covers achievements on all different scales and introduces the language students need to talk about them.

- Students begin by looking at their daily tasks and practicing the present perfect tense to talk about the ones that have been completed. They move on to consider previous experiences and talk about them in the context of a job interview. They consider important milestones in one's lifetime and, finally, look at some of humanity's greatest achievements. Throughout the lessons, they consolidate their understanding of the present perfect tense and contrast it with the simple past tense.

UNIT 11 GOALS

1. Talk about today's chores

2. Interview for a job

3. Talk about personal accomplishments

4. Discuss humanity's greatest achievements

135

Speaking	Reading	Writing	Video Journal
Interviewing for a job Catching up with a friend **Pronunciation:** Reduced form of *have*	**National Geographic:** "Humanity's Greatest Achievements"	Writing about important human achievements	**National Geographic:** "Spacewalk"

Talk About Today's Chores

Vocabulary

Grammar

A | **GOAL 1:** Talk About Today's Chores

Vocabulary

A Label the pictures with phrases from the box.

pay the bills
buy the groceries
sweep the floor
cut the grass
walk the dog
vacuum
iron the clothes
put away the clothes

Word Focus

chore = A *chore* is a task that must be done, but that many people find boring or unpleasant.

1. buy the groceries 2. cut the grass 3. walk the dog 4. iron the clothes

5. pay the bills 6. sweep the floor 7. vacuum 8. put away the clothes

B In your notebook, write down which chores from exercise **A** you think are easy and which chores you think are difficult.

C In your family, who does the household chores? Discuss with a partner.

Grammar: Present perfect tense

Present perfect tense	
Statement	He **has ironed** the clothes.
Negative	I **haven't cooked** lunch yet.
Yes/No questions	**Have you finished** your homework?
Short answers	Yes, I **have.**/No, I **haven't.**
Wh- questions	What **have you done** today?

*The present perfect tense is formed with the verb *has/have* + the past participle of the verb.
*We use the present perfect tense to talk about an event that started in the past and continues in the present: *I have lived here all my life,* or an event that was completed at an unspecified time in the past: *I have read the book.*

*Some verbs have regular past participles. They end in *-ed*.		*Some verbs have irregular past participles.	
pass – passed	graduate – graduated	have – had	take – taken
clean – cleaned	travel – traveled	go – gone	pay – paid
iron – ironed	visit – visited	be – been	put – put

A Write the irregular past participles from the box next to the correct verb.

1. buy	_bought_	**5.** make	_made_	**9.** speak	_spoken_
2. do	_done_	**6.** meet	_met_	**10.** sweep	_swept_
3. drink	_drunk_	**7.** read	_read_	**11.** tell	_told_
4. eat	_eaten_	**8.** say	_said_	**12.** win	_won_

> read   spoken   drunk
> bought   swept   told
> won   said   made
> eaten   met   done

B Complete the conversation with the present perfect tense.

1. A: What (1) _have you done_ (you, do) today?

B: Nothing very exciting. I (2) _'ve cleaned_ (clean) the house, and I (3) _'ve cooked_ (cook) dinner. (4) _Have you had_ (you, have) an interesting day?

A: No, not really. (5) _I've been_ (I, be) sick. I (6) _haven't done_ (not do) anything.

2. A: Today, I (1) _'ve paid the bills_ (pay the bills) and I (2) _'ve bought the groceries_ (buy the groceries). (3) _Have you had_ (you, have) an interesting day?

B: Well, I (4) _'ve visited_ (visit) a friend. Then, I (5) _'ve bought_ (buy) some clothes for my new job.

C 🔁 Ask your partner questions using the present perfect.

Conversation

A 🔊20 Read the Real Language box and listen to the conversation. Has Lynn done her chores? yes

Mom: Hi, honey. I'm home.
Lynn: Hi, Mom.
Mom: Have you <u>walked the dog</u>?
Lynn: Yes, Mom. Of course I've walked the dog. And I've <u>vacuumed the living room</u>.
Mom: And <u>have you done your homework</u>?
Lynn: Mom! I've been busy <u>walking the dog</u> and <u>vacuuming</u>. I haven't had time.
Mom: Sorry, honey. It's just I've had a long day myself.

B 🔁 Practice the conversation with a partner. Switch roles and practice it again.

C 🔁 Replace the underlined chores and practice the conversation again.

D 🔁 **GOAL CHECK** ✔ **Talk about today's chores**

Talk to a partner about the chores you have done this week.

> Have you paid your electric bill this month?

Real Language

We use *of course* to show something is obvious.

Achievements   137

A • Have students work individually to write the past participle forms.
• Check answers. Go over the pronunciation of the past participles.

B • Have students work individually to fill in the verbs.
• Have students compare answers with a partner.
• Check answers.

C • Model the question, *Have you paid your electric bill this month?* Ask several students. Elicit the answers, *Yes, I have./No, I haven't.* Ask other questions and elicit more questions from students. Write some on the board to help students.
• Divide the class into pairs and have them ask and answer questions.
• Have several students tell the class about what their partner has and hasn't done.

Conversation

A • Have students close their books. Write the question on the board: *Has Lynn done her chores?*
• Play the recording. 🔊 20
• Check answers.
• Direct students' attention to the Real Language box.

B • Play or read the conversation again for the class to repeat.
• Practice the conversation with the class in chorus.
• Have students practice the conversation with partners and then switch roles and practice it again.

C • Have students work with a partner to make a new conversation.
• Call on student pairs to present their conversations to the class.

D 🔁 **GOAL CHECK** ✔

• Divide the class into pairs and have them take turns talking about their activities so far this week.
• Have several students tell the class what their partner has done.

Grammar Practice: Present perfect tense

Play "Find Someone Who . . . ." Dictate the following phrases for students to write down: *travel to another country/live in another city/climb a mountain/host a party/find some money/play basketball.*

• Tell students to find a person who has done each of these things by walking around the class and asking questions. Add more phrases if time allows.

• Model the activity by asking a student, *Have you ever traveled to another country? Have you ever lived in another city?* and so on, until the student answers "yes" to a question. Then write the student's name.

• Set a time limit (5 to 10 minutes). After finishing the game, ask the class, *Who has traveled to another country?* and so forth.

Interview for a Job

Listening

- Introduce the idea of a job interview. Ask students if they or someone they know has had one. What happens at a job interview?

A
- Tell students they are going to hear two people at interviews for a job. Have them read the ad and go over any unfamiliar words. Talk briefly about a tour guide's job and what is required. Tell students they should listen and write down Richard and Yuki's qualifications. Check understanding of qualifications and provide examples as necessary (high school diploma, college degree, language certificate, etc.).
- Play the recording. 🔊 21
- Divide the class into pairs and have them compare answers. Play the recording again.

B
- Have students complete the questions.
- Play the recording. 🔊 21
- Check answers.

C
- Tell students to listen again to the interviews and answer the questions.
- Play the recording one or more times. 🔊 21
- Have students compare answers with a partner.
- Check answers.

D
- Divide the class into pairs and have them discuss who should get the job and why.
- Compare decisions and reasons as a class.

B GOAL 2: Interview for a Job

Mesa Verde, Colorado, USA

NEEDED URGENTLY!
TOUR GUIDE
Mesa Verde
Professional appearance. Good interpersonal skills. Experience an advantage. Driver's license essential. Call 2356 9845.

Yuki

graduated from college

visited 8 countries

Richard

graduated from college

worked as a tour guide at Disneyland

has driver's license

Listening

A 🔊 21 Read the ad. Listen to Richard and Yuki at the interview. Use the boxes to take notes on their qualifications.

B 🔊 21 The interviewers asked the following questions. Complete the questions. Listen again to check your answers.

1. Have you _____*graduated*_____ from college?
2. Have you ever _____*worked*_____ as a tour guide?
3. Who is the most interesting person you have ever ____*met*____?
4. Have you ____*passed*____ your driving test?

C Answer the questions.

1. Has Richard ever traveled abroad? _____*no*_____
2. How many countries has Yuki visited? _____*eight*_____
3. Who is the most interesting person Yuki has met? ____*her father*____
4. Has Richard passed his driving test? _____*yes*_____
5. Has Yuki graduated from college? _____*yes*_____

D 🔄 Who should get the job? Discuss with a partner.

138   Unit 11

For Your Information: Job interviews

A job interview is a common step in getting a job in most countries, although the form of the interview may differ. Candidates may be interviewed one at a time or in a group. They may speak with only one interviewer or with a whole group of them. There are also differences in the kinds of questions that are asked. In the United States, for example, there are laws against job discrimination by age, religion, and marital status, so interviewers are not allowed to ask questions like *Are you married?* or *Don't you think you're too old to do this job?*

Pronunciation: Reduced form of *have*

A 🔊22 Listen to the examples. Notice the pronunciation of the reduced forms.

Full form	Reduced form
I have	I've
have you	/hæv-jə/
you have	you've
has he	/hæz-i/
she has	she's

B 🔊23 Listen to the sentences. Check (✓) the correct column.

	Full form	Reduced form
1. **Has she** left?	✓	
2. **Have you** finished?		✓
3. **Has he** read this book?		✓
4. **Have you** done your homework?	✓	
5. **I have** never been to the USA.		✓

C 🔊23 Listen again. Repeat the sentences.

Communication

A 🔁 Read the following ads. Then role-play an interview. For the first ad, **Student A** is the interviewer and **Student B** is the interviewee. Change roles for the second ad. When you are the interviewee, you can be yourself or pretend to be someone interested in the job.

═ WANTED! ═

Handyman for Kindergarten

Small kindergarten needs a person to help with maintenance—plumbing, carpentry, fixing our vehicles, etc. No experience with children necessary but must enjoy being around kids. Any age. $25 per hour.

LIFEGUARD

18–30 yrs old. You must be in very good shape. Must be able to swim 250 meters in 4 minutes and run 2,000 meters in 10 minutes. Experience an advantage. Some training offered.

Flexible hours.

B  🔁 **GOAL CHECK** ✓ Interview for a job

Think of another job. What is required? Write notes. Interview a partner. Switch roles and repeat.

Achievements **139**

Talk About Personal Accomplishments

Language Expansion

A • Point out the definition of accomplishment in the Word Focus box. Have students give examples of accomplishments. Go over the phrases in the box. Then have students work individually to write the correct phrase for each picture.

• Check answers.

B • Have students check the phrases in **A** that they have accomplished.

C • Divide the class into pairs and have them ask and answer questions about the accomplishments in **A**.

• Have several students tell the class about one of their partner's accomplishments.

Grammar

• Go over the information in the chart, contrasting the two tenses. Use examples from the accomplishments students talked about in **C**; for example, *Sylvia has passed her driving test. She took the test last year.*, etc.

C **GOAL 3:** Talk About Personal Accomplishments

get a promotion
travel abroad
pass your driving test
run a marathon
get a credit card
graduate from high school/college

Word Focus

accomplishment = something remarkable that a person has done

Language Expansion: Personal accomplishments

A Label the pictures with phrases from the box.

1. graduate from high school/college
2. run a marathon
3. travel abroad
4. pass your driving test
5. get a promotion
6. get a credit card

B Check (✓) the achievements in exercise **A** that you have done.

Answers will vary.

C 🔁 Ask a partner what he or she has achieved. Take turns.

> Have you passed your driving test?

Grammar: Present perfect tense vs. simple past tense

Present perfect tense vs. simple past tense	
The present perfect tense is used to show an action that happened at any time in the past.	The simple past tense is used to show an action that happened at a specific time in the past.
Claudio **has been** to many countries.	He **went** to France last year.

*We often use time expressions with the simple past tense, for example, *yesterday, last week, in 2010*.
*We use expressions like *just, never, ever, yet* with the present perfect tense.
 Have you **ever** been to another country?
 Nayla has **just** returned from France.
 I have **never** been there.
 I haven't graduated **yet**.

140   Unit 11

Word Bank: Personal achievements

get a better job
get in shape
give a speech
have children

have your name in the newspaper
lose weight
teach a class
win an award

Grammar: Present perfect tense vs. simple past tense

The present perfect tense describes events at any time in the past that have a connection with the present.

I've already graduated from college (so now I have my degree).

I've been to Mexico four times (so I know something about the country).

The simple past describes a completed action at a specific time.

I graduated from college in 2009. I went to Mexico last summer.

Past   Simple past tense   Now   Future

Present perfect tense

A Complete the sentences with the correct form of the verb in parentheses.

1. Last summer, we _____went_____ (go) to the Maldives.
2. I _____have lived_____ (live) in the same house all my life.
3. John _has never traveled_ (never travel) abroad.
4. Spain _____won_____ (win) the World Cup in 2010.
5. Brazil _____has won_____ (win) the World Cup five times.

B Complete the conversations with the correct form of the verb in parentheses.

1. **A:** _Have you passed_ (you pass) your driving test?
   B: Yes. I _____took_____ (take) it in January, and I _____passed_____ (pass) the first time.
2. **A:** _Have you been_ (you be) to Europe?
   B: Yes, I have. I _____went_____ (go) to Germany last year.

Conversation

A 🔊 24 | Listen to the conversation. Who has started his own business?

Pete

Alfredo: Hi, Pete. I haven't seen you for a long time. What's new?
Pete: Lots! I quit my job with <u>CompuSoft</u>, and I've started <u>my own computer business</u>.
Alfredo: Congratulations! When did you <u>open the business</u>?
Pete: Eight months ago, and it's going well.
Alfredo: Great!
Pete: And what about you?
Alfredo: Things haven't changed much. I'm still <u>working at the bank</u>. But I've <u>bought a new house</u>. It's right next to Central Park.
Pete: Wow! Nice area.
Alfredo: Yeah. You should come 'round and visit some time.
Pete: Will do, when I have some time.

B 🔄 Practice the conversation with a partner. Switch roles and practice it again.

C 🔄 Change the underlined words and practice the conversation again.

D 🔄 | GOAL CHECK ✔ **Talk about personal accomplishments**

Talk to a partner about your personal accomplishments or what you would like to achieve in the future.

A • Have students work individually to fill in the correct form of each verb —simple past or present perfect.
• Have students compare answers with a partner.
• Check answers.

B • Tell students to fill in the correct form of the verb—simple past or present perfect.
• Have students compare answers with a partner.
• Check answers.

Conversation

A • Have students close their books. Write the question on the board: *Who has started his own business?*
• Play the recording. 🔊 24
• Check answers.

B • Play or read the conversation again for the class to repeat. 🔊 24
• Practice the conversation with the class in chorus.
• Have students practice the conversation with partners and then switch roles and practice it again.

C • Have student pairs choose new ideas to replace the underlined words. Then have them practice their new conversation.
• Call on student pairs to present their conversations to the class.

D 🔄 | GOAL CHECK ✔

• Have students work individually to make a list of their accomplishments or what they hope they will accomplish during their lives.
• Assign new pairs and have them ask and answer questions about each other's lists.
• Have several students share one of their partner's accomplishments (past or future) with the class.

Grammar Practice: Present perfect tense vs. simple past tense

Write these questions on the board for students to discuss in groups:

What is the most unusual food you've ever eaten?
When/Where/Why did you eat it?

What is the best movie you've ever seen?
When/Where did you see it?

When groups have finished, ask them for any interesting/surprising information they heard from their classmates.

Discuss Humanity's Greatest Achievements

Reading

A • Have students look at the picture. Ask, *Where is this? Why are these pyramids incredible?* Write students' ideas on the board.

• Have students write a list of humanity's greatest achievements.

• Compare lists with the class and write a list on the board.

B • Have students read the article and find all the verbs in the present perfect tense.

• Check the verbs and write them on the board.

C • Have students read the statements. Point out the words in the Word Focus box. Have students read the article again and decide if the statements are *true* or *false.* Tell them to circle any words they don't understand.

• Have students compare answers with a partner.

• Check answers.

• Answer any questions about vocabulary.

D • Have students read the questions and write down their answers.

• Divide the class into groups of three or four and have them share their opinions.

• Appoint a secretary and a reporter in each group.

• Have the reporters share with the class the group's opinions.

D **GOAL 4:** Discuss Humanity's Greatest Achievements

Reading

A ⟳ What do you think are humanity's greatest achievements? Discuss with a partner. Answers will vary.

B Read the article. Circle all the verbs in the present perfect tense.

C Read the article. Circle **T** for *true* or **F** for *false.*

1. Humanity has lived on Earth for a long time.   T (F)

2. Many of humanity's greatest achievements are in science and technology.   (T) F

3. Antibiotics are machines.   T (F)

4. Art makes people happy.   (T) F

5. Humanity started to use fire a long time ago.   (T) F

D ⛒ Answer the questions. Give your own opinions. Share your answers with a group. Answers will vary.

1. Imagine life without electricity. How would it be different?

2. Many achievements have a negative effect. What are the negative effects of cars?

3. Do you think the Mona Lisa is a great achievement?

4. How would you define "great"?

> **Word Focus**
>
> **antibiotic** = a medicine that kills bacteria. Penicillin is an antibiotic.
>
> **printing press** = a machine that prints books

142 Unit 11

The Louvre, Paris, France

For Your Information: Humanity's greatest achievements

The Giza pyramids were built around 2560 BCE and took about 20 years to complete.

The first printing press was designed by Johannes Gutenburg in 1450.

The *Mona Lisa* was painted by Leonardo da Vinci between 1503 and 1506.

The term *electricity* was first used by William Gilbert in 1600.

Johann Sebastian Bach composed classical music in the 17th and 18th centuries.

Radio communication was invented by Guglielmo Marconi in 1895.

The first powered flight was by the Wright brothers, Orville and Wilbur, in North Carolina, in 1903.

The first television image was transmitted by Philo Farnsworth in 1927; it was a dollar sign.

HUMANITY'S GREATEST ACHIEVEMENTS

The Earth is 4.5 billion years old, but the human race (has lived) on it for just 200,000 years. In that short time, we (have achieved) some incredible things.

Many of humanity's great achievements are in science and technology. The list is almost endless. The invention of the airplane (has changed) our lives. The discovery of **antibiotics** (has saved) the lives of millions of people. Can you imagine living without electricity? What about the **printing press?** Without the printing press, you wouldn't be reading this. In the last 50 years, there (have been) astonishing achievements in communication, such as radio, TV, computers, the Internet, and smartphones. Could we live without these things? Probably, but would life be as interesting?

What about the arts? The arts (have brought) pleasure to many people, but are the Beatles and Bach more important than antibiotics? And is the *Mona Lisa* as important an achievement as going to space?

Finally, we must not forget humanity's early achievements, like the use of fire for cooking and heating, and the invention of the wheel. Can you imagine modern life without cooked food and cars?

What are humanity's greatest achievements? To answer the question, we need to decide what we mean by "great." Is it something that makes us rich or happy or saves lives? Or is it just something that makes us say "Wow," like the Pyramids of Giza? What do you think?

The Great Pyramids of Giza, Egypt

Have students write a paragraph about a person with an important achievement that they admire. Have them share their paragraphs with a partner or a group.

Have students research one of the achievements mentioned in the article and present the information to the class.

Penicillin, the first antibiotic, was discovered by Alexander Fleming in 1928.

The first electronic-digital computer was built by Professor John Atanasoff and graduate student Clifford Berry at Iowa State University between 1939 and 1942.

The microwave oven was invented by Percy L. Spencer in the mid-1940s.

The Beatles were the most popular band in the world in the mid-1960s.

The Internet was created by a group of universities and the U.S. Department of Defense in the 1960s.

The first mobile telephone was designed by Martin Cooper in 1973.

The World Wide Web (a system to share and organize information from any computer) was created by Timothy Berners-Lee in 1989.

Discuss Humanity's Greatest Achievements

Communication

A • Have students look at the pictures and describe what they see. Ask, *Why were these important achievements for humans?*

• Go over the list of achievements. Have students rank them in order of importance.

B • Have students compare their list with a partner, explain their reasons, and agree on an order.

C • Have pairs join to make groups of four and compare their lists. Have them try to agree on an order.

• Have each group share their list and agree on an order as a class.

Writing

A • Have students choose one of the achievements on the list. Write on the board: *When? Where? Who? How? Why?* Elicit ideas from the students for each question word and write notes on the board.

• Have students help you start writing a paragraph on the board about the achievement.

• Have students read the directions and choose an important human achievement. Have them make notes using the question words.

• Have students write a paragraph about the achievement they chose.

• Have students exchange papers with a partner to mark corrections and suggestions for improvements on their partners' papers.

• If desired, have students rewrite their papers, to be collected for grading.

B 🔁 **GOAL CHECK** ✔

• Assign new pairs and have them discuss the achievements they wrote about. Have them take turns asking and answering questions about the achievements.

D **GOAL 4:** Discuss Humanity's Greatest Achievements

An astronaut on the moon

▲ The *Mona Lisa*

Communication

A Here is a list of five important human achievements. Rank them in order of importance. Answers will vary.

_____ the use of fire

_____ walking on the moon

_____ the Internet

_____ electricity

_____ antibiotics

_____ art

B 🔁 Compare your list with a partner. Talk about your differences.

C 👥 Join another pair and compare your lists.

Writing

A Choose one important human achievement. It can be **any** achievement, not just from the reading. Write what you know about it, and say why you think it is an important achievement.

B 🔁 | **GOAL CHECK** ✔ **Discuss humanity's greatest achievements**

Talk with a partner about the achievements you wrote about. Ask and answer questions about the achievements you chose.

144   **Unit 11**

Teacher Tip: Fun with English outside of class

Encourage students to find language activities that they enjoy to get more practice outside of class. Some ideas:

• Sing along with English songs (lyrics can be found on the album liner or on Web sites).

• Speak in English with a friend or classmate outside of class time.

• Read an English comic book or a magazine on a topic that is well-known in the native language (for example, soccer or fashion).

• Watch English-language movies.

• Talk to yourself in English!

Before You Watch

A Read the summary of the video and fill in the blanks with words from the box.
Then watch the video and check your answers.

> weightless survive
> underwater oxygen
> solar panels

Video summary

In space, there is no _____oxygen_____. It is impossible to breathe. Sometimes astronauts have to make a

spacewalk outside the spacecraft. In order to _____survive_____, astronauts wear special space suits. They do

jobs like repair _____solar panels_____. It is dangerous work.

They prepare for their spacewalks _____underwater_____ in special tanks. It is like being _____weightless_____
in space but much safer.

While You Watch

A ▶ Watch the video and circle **T** for *true* or **F** for *false*.

1. It is always very cold in space.   T   (F)

2. Space suits are filled with oxygen.   (T)   F

3. The first person to walk in space was
   Edward White.   T   (F)

4. Astronauts fixed the solar panels
   on the Hubble Space Telescope.   (T)   F

After You Watch

A ⚡ Scientific achievements can be expensive. The National Aeronautics
and Space Administration (NASA) spent almost $18 billion in 2014. The
Large Hadron Collider (a huge scientific instrument), cost $4.6 billion.
Discuss these questions with a partner. Why do people spend a lot of money
on big science projects? Is it worth it?

Achievements 145

Video Journal:
Spacewalk

Before You Watch

A • Have students look at the picture
and say what it shows. Ask
students why it's dangerous to go
outside in space (there's no air; it's
hard to move).

• Go over the words in the box. Then
have students work individually to
complete the video summary.

• Have students compare answers
with a partner.

• Tell students to watch the video and
check their answers.

• Play the video.

• Check answers.

While You Watch

A • Tell students to watch the video
again and answer *true* or *false*.
Have students read the statements.

• Play the video.

• Have students compare answers
with a partner.

• Check answers.

After You Watch

A • Go over the information with
the class. If desired, give them
examples of important projects in
their country and how much they
cost.

• Divide the class into pairs and have
them discuss the questions and
give their opinions.

• Compare ideas with the class.

For Your Information: Weightlessness

Astronauts experience long periods of
weightlessness in space when their spacecraft is not
rotating or using its engines. It puts a lot of stress
on the human body and causes "space sickness,"
with nausea and vomiting, in about 45 percent of
people who experience it. Spending long periods of
time in space can seriously affect people's health,
because it weakens muscles and bones. Videos of
astronauts often show them enjoying things that
they can't do in Earth's gravity, such as lifting heavy
objects with one finger. But weightlessness also
makes their daily work much more difficult, and they
spend many hours training to do the simplest tasks.

Consequences

About the Photo

This photo shows stunning glaciers and the Goðafoss (Godafoss), a waterfall in Iceland. As can be seen from the rushing water in this photo, the glaciers are melting. According to studies, the glaciers that cover 10% of Iceland are losing 11 billion tons of ice a year.

In neighboring Greenland, the thick ice sheet that covers more than 70% of the country is melting by 80 cubic kilometers (approx. 50 cubic miles) every year. This change in climate has consequences. With the ice being thinner, it is harder for people to hunt and families are finding it difficult to support themselves using traditional methods. Furthermore, many animals are losing their habitats and food sources as the ice melts. But the effects of the ice sheet melting will not only impact Greenland and Iceland. As the ice melts, the sea level will rise around the world and coastlines will be affected.

- Direct students' attention to the photo. Have students describe what they see.

- Discuss the photo. Talk about what it shows. Introduce the idea of *consequences*—the results of things we do.

- Ask these questions orally or by writing them on the board for students to answer in pairs: *When have you made a bad decision? What were the consequences?*

- Go over the Unit Goals with the class, explaining as necessary.

- For each goal, elicit any words students already know and write them on the board; for example, vocabulary related to money, actions and consequences, etc.

Melting water from a glacier flows over a waterfall in Iceland.

146

UNIT 12 GOALS	Grammar	Vocabulary	Listening
• Talk about managing your money • Make choices on how to spend your money • Talk about cause and effect • Evaluate money and happiness	Real conditionals (or first conditional) *If they **borrow** some money, they **will be able to** buy a new house.*	Personal finances Animal habitats	Listening for specific details: At a travel agency

Look at the photo, answer the questions:

1 What does this photo show?

2 What is the cause and effect demonstrated by this photo?

Unit Theme Overview

- Many of the headlines in the news today are about the consequences of past actions. Industrial development and rapid economic growth have increased the production of carbon dioxide and other "greenhouse gases"—the consequences are global warming and severe weather. Old ethnic and national conflicts have never been resolved: The consequences are war and the displacement of millions of refugees. Even in our own lives, we can easily see the pattern of actions and consequences.

- In this unit, students begin examining the topic of consequences on a personal level by talking about money and financial decisions. They examine the possible results of different choices they might make. They move on to talk about consequences on a larger scale, by thinking about how people's actions affect animals and habitats. Finally, they look at how people's actions make them feel. All of these situations involve real possibilities and give students many opportunities to practice the use of the real (first) conditional form.

UNIT 12 GOALS

1. Talk about managing your money

2. Make choices on how to spend your money

3. Talk about cause and effect

4. Evaluate money and happiness

147

Speaking	Reading	Writing	Video Journal
Making decisions about spending money Talking about important issues **Pronunciation:** Sentence stress	**TED Talks:** "Michael Norton: How to Buy Happiness"	Writing an e-mail to a friend	**National Geographic:** "The Missing Snows of Kilimanjaro"

Talk About Managing Your Money

Vocabulary

A • Introduce the topic of managing your money. Ask students, *How do you manage your money? Do you make a plan? Or do you just spend as much money as you want to?*

• Have students read the article, paying special attention to the words in blue. If necessary, direct students' attention to the definition in the Word Focus box. Explain that in some countries, studying at a university is very expensive, and students must borrow money to pay for things, such as tuition, room and board, and books. They usually get all the money at the beginning of the school year.

B • Have students work individually to match the words in blue from the article with their meanings.

• Have students compare answers with a partner.

• Check answers.

Grammar

• Introduce the structure. Tell students (for example), *I'm going shopping this weekend. I want to buy a lot of things. If I have enough money, I'll buy some new clothes. If I have enough money, I'll buy some shoes.* Ask, *What about you? What will you buy if you have enough money?* Elicit answers from the class.

• Go over the information in the chart.

Word Focus

student loan = money that the government lends to students

A   GOAL 1: Talk About Managing Your Money

Vocabulary

A Read the article from a student magazine.

> **STUDENT LIFE**
>
> ## MANAGE YOUR MONEY
>
> Congratulations! You have received your first **student loan**. How are you going to spend it? Are you going to go out and buy that new cell phone or those cool sneakers? Well, don't!
>
> Before you spend a penny, you have to make a **budget** and plan your spending. First, write down your **income**—how much money you receive. Then calculate your **expenses** (rent, transportation, food). If your expenses are lower than your income
>
> you are on the right track! Now you know how much money you have left to spend each month. But don't **overspend** or you will have to **borrow** money. Borrowing money from the bank is expensive. **Interest rates** are high. You could check to see if a friend or family member can **lend** you the money.
>
> You also have to think about the long term. How are you going to pay for that spring break at the beach, or buy your family presents? You will have to **save** some money every month. So, that new cell phone can wait. Manage your money and maybe you'll be able to take that spring break at the beach—in Mexico!
>
> 21

B Write the words in blue next to the correct meanings.

1. the amount of money you spend _expenses_
2. to ask someone to give you money _borrow_
3. the amount of money you receive _income_
4. to spend too much money _overspend_
5. a spending plan _budget_
6. to give someone money _lend_
7. to put money in the bank for the future _save_
8. the percentage (%) charged when you borrow money _interest rate_

Grammar: Real conditionals (or first conditional)

If clause (simple present tense)	Result clause (future tense)
If I **buy** a new TV,	I **will** not **have** enough money to pay the rent.
If they **borrow** some money,	they **will be able to** buy a new house.

*We use real conditional sentences to express possible results of choices we make.
*When the *if* clause comes first, there is a comma between the *if* clause and the result clause.

148   Unit 12

Word Bank: Money

bank
checking account
credit card
deposit
online banking
savings account
transfer
withdraw

Grammar: Real conditionals

English has three types of conditional sentences with *if*.

1. Real situations (sometimes called the first conditional):
   If I study hard, I will get a good grade.

2. Unreal situations (sometimes called the second conditional):
   If I studied hard, I would get better grades. (but I'm lazy)

3. Unreal situations in the past (sometimes called the third conditional): *If I had studied hard, I would have gotten a better grade.* (but I didn't study)

A Match the *if* clauses to the correct result clauses.

1. If you borrow money from the bank, _d_
2. If you save some money every month, _e_
3. If you lend money to your sister, _a_
4. If your expenses are bigger than your income, _b_
5. If we eat at home instead of in a restaurant, _c_

a. she won't return the money until the end of the month.
b. you won't have enough money to pay the rent.
c. we will have enough money to go to the theater.
d. the interest rates will be high.
e. you will have enough money to buy a new computer.

B Unscramble the words to write conditional sentences. Don't forget the punctuation.

1. a bigger car   some money   we borrow   If   we can buy
   If we borrow some money, we can buy a bigger car.

2. a new job   more money   I will have   I get   If
   If I get a new job, I will have more money.

3. on vacation   we overspend   If   to go   we won't be able
   If we overspend, we won't be able to go on vacation.

4. you won't have to   I   use your credit card   If   lend you $100
   If I lend you $100, you won't have to use your credit card.

5. our car   sell   we will be able to rent   If we   a bigger apartment
   If we sell our car, we will be able to rent a bigger apartment.

Conversation

A 🔊 25 Listen to the conversation. What choice does Jim have to make? take a vacation or buy a new camera

Jim: I don't know what to do. I want to take a vacation, and I also want to buy a new camera.
Dave: I see. If you buy the camera, you won't have enough money for the vacation. Is that it?
Jim: You got it.
Dave: So, just take the vacation. Don't buy the camera.
Jim: But if I don't buy the camera, I won't be able to take any vacation photos.
Dave: OK, just buy the camera.
Jim: But if I buy the camera, I won't be able to take the vacation, and I won't need a camera.
Dave: Hmm . . . you have a problem.

> **Real Language**
>
> *to get* sometimes means *to understand*
> (Do you) get it? = Do you understand?
> You got it! = You understood.
> I don't get you/it. = I don't understand you/it.

B 🔄 Practice the conversation with a partner. Switch roles and practice it again.

C 🔄 Use the words in the box to make a new conversation.

D 🔄 **GOAL CHECK** ✔ **Talk about managing your money**

Work with a partner. Discuss how you manage your money. What are your expenses? Do you have a budget? Do you save?

> binoculars   bird watching
> weekend   glasses
> movies   bicycle
> cycling tour

Consequences   **149**

A
- Have students work individually to match the sentence parts.
- Have students compare answers with a partner.
- Check answers.

B
- Have students work individually to write the sentences. Remind students to add punctuation.
- Have students compare answers with a partner.
- Check answers.

Conversation

A
- Have students close their books. Write the question on the board: *What choice does Jim have to make?*
- Play the recording.   🔊 25
- Check answers.
- Direct students' attention to the Real Language box. Go over the expressions.

B
- Play or read the conversation again for the class to repeat.
- Practice the conversation with the class in chorus.
- Have students practice the conversation with a partner and then switch roles and practice it again.

C
- Go over the words in the box. Have student pairs use the words to make a new conversation. Then have them practice their new conversation.
- Call on student pairs to present their conversations to the class.

D 🔄 **GOAL CHECK** ✔

- Assign new pairs and have them talk about their money habits. Have them discuss the questions.
- Have several students tell the class something about their partner's money habits.

Grammar Practice: Real conditionals

Tell students they are going to make their own real conditional sentences about different situations—and then share the sentences with the class. Remind students that the clause with *if* has the verb in the present tense.

Write on the board: *We'll be very happy if _____*. Give students one minute to think of a sentence. Then go around the class quickly and have each student say his or her sentence.

Continue with: *I'll be very surprised if _____.*

We'll learn English faster if _____.

I'll save more money if _____.

Make Choices on How to Spend Your Money

Listening

A • Have students look at the photo and describe what they see.

• Tell students they are going to hear a conversation in a travel agency. Ask, *What do people do in a travel agency?* (plan vacations, buy plane tickets, etc.)

• Play the recording one or more times. 🔊 26

• Check answers.

B • Tell students to listen again to the conversation and answer the questions.

• Play the recording one or more times. 🔊 26

• Check answers.

• Ask the class, *How can a train go from London to Paris?* (through a tunnel) *If you go from London to Paris, how will you travel—by plane, train, or car?*

Pronunciation

• Remind students that our voices rise and fall when we say sentences. Practicing intonation will help them to sound more like native speakers.

A • Tell students to listen to the sentences and write arrows to mark the rising and falling intonation they hear.

• Play the recording one or more times. 🔊 27

• Have students compare answers with a partner.

• Check answers.

B • Play the recording again for students to repeat the sentences. 🔊 27

• Then have students practice reading the sentences to partners. Walk around helping with difficulties.

B | **GOAL 2:** Make Choices on How to Spend Your Money

London, England

Listening

A 🔊 **26** Listen to the conversation. Circle the correct answer.

The travel agent is in _____.

a. London   **b.** Paris   **c.** New York

B 🔊 **26** Listen again and answer the questions.

1. Is this the first time that the woman has visited England? _yes_
2. Why doesn't she want to take the plane? _She won't see anything._
3. Why doesn't she want to rent a car? _She will get lost._
4. How long does it take to go from Paris to London by train? _2 hours and 15 minutes_
5. How much does the train ticket cost? _$150_

Pronunciation: Intonation

A 🔊 **27** Listen to the sentences. Draw the arrows to show rise or fall.

1. If I buy a car, I won't be able to pay the rent.
2. If you take the bus, it will be cheaper.
3. If we borrow some money, we will repay it in a month.
4. If Sara leaves now, she will catch the seven o'clock train.
5. If we take the plane, it will be quicker.

B 🔊 **27** Listen again and repeat the sentences.

150   Unit 12

For Your Information: Eurostar

Eurostar is the name of the train service that runs from London to Lille, France and then to Paris and Brussels through a tunnel under the water of the English Channel. The project was planned in 1986, and service began in 1994. Long trains of 18 cars run at a speed of up to 186 mph (300 kph). In 2012, more than 10 million passengers traveled on Eurostar. More than 91 percent of the trains arrived on time.

Communication

A 🔄 Work with a partner. Plan a six-day visit to California. Each of you has $300 to spend on transportation. You will arrive in Los Angeles. You would like to visit Yosemite National Park, San Diego, and San Francisco.

Answers will vary.

> **If we take the train, will it be cheaper?**

> **If we take the plane, it will be quicker.**

> **If we take the bus, it will be cheaper.**

Yosemite National Park

	San Diego	San Francisco	Merced (for Yosemite)
Los Angeles	🚌 $40, 4 hours 🚂 $80, 3 hours ✈ $130, 1 hour	🚌 $60, 6 hours 🚂 $70, 8 hours (3 changes) ✈ $130, 1½ hours	🚌 $80, 7 hours 🚂 No service ✈ No service
San Diego		🚌 $135 return, 12 hours 🚂 No service ✈ $250, 1½ hours	🚌 $90, 10 hours 🚂 No service ✈ No service
San Francisco			🚌 $70, 4 hours 🚂 $60, 3 hours ✈ No service

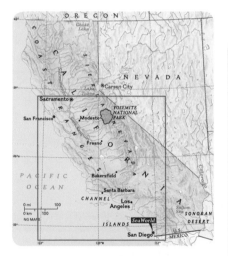

Itinerary	Transportation	Transportation costs
Day 1		
Day 2		
Day 3		
Day 4		
Day 5		
Day 6		

B ♻ **GOAL CHECK** ✔ **Make choices on how to spend your money**

Join another pair of students and explain to them how you decided to spend your transportation money.

Communication

A • Have students look at the picture and the map and describe what they see.

• Introduce the activity. Ask, *What are some famous places in California? Where do visitors like to go?* Ask if any students know of places other than the ones on the map.

• Divide the class into pairs and present the situation. They are going to visit California for six days, and they must decide how to travel to three places they want to visit. Each person has $300 to spend.

• Go over the chart that shows the means of transportation and prices.

• Tell students that they do not need to travel every day.

• Have students work with partners to make a plan for spending their time and money and complete the chart about their trip.

B 🔄 **GOAL CHECK** ✔

• Have students join another pair and talk about their decisions on how to spend their travel money.

• Have them take turns asking and answering questions about what they decided and why.

• Have several pairs tell the class what the other pair decided and why.

Expansion Activity

Have students work in pairs to make a similar plan for a six-day trip to three places in their country. You can assign three places or let them choose their own destinations.

Talk About Cause and Effect

Language Expansion

- Have students look at the pictures and say what they see.
- Direct students' attention to the Word Focus box. Go over the habitats in the pictures.
- Go over the names of the animals.

A
- Divide the class into pairs and have them talk about where each animal lives.
- Check answers.

B
- Have students work individually to complete the sentences with words from **A**. Remind them to use plural forms if necessary.
- Have students compare answers with a partner.
- Check answers.

Grammar

- Go over the information in the chart, reviewing what students learned about real conditionals in **Lesson A.**
- Point out that the result clause can also come first in real conditionals.

C GOAL 3: Talk About Cause and Effect

Language Expansion: Animal habitats

A Take turns. Make statements about animals and their **habitats**.

▲ desert   ▲ mountains   ▲ grasslands   ▲ rain forest   ▲ coral reef

▲ monkey *rain forest* ▲ camel *desert*   ▲ shark *coral reef*   ▲ mountain goat *mountains*   ▲ elephant *grasslands*

B Complete the sentences. Use the habitats and animals in exercise **A.**

1. Many countries near the equator have ___rain forests___ . They contain hundreds of different plants and animals, for example ___monkeys___ and colorful birds.

2. ___Camels___ can live without water for many days. They are perfectly adapted to live in the ___the desert___ .

3. The Great Barrier Reef in Australia is the biggest ___coral reef___ in the world. It is the home of ___sharks___ and many other kinds of fish.

4. Kenya is famous for its ___grasslands___ . Tourists come from all over the world to see the animals, like lions and ___elephants___ .

5. The highest ___mountains___ in the world are in Nepal. Not many animals live there. If you are lucky, you might see a ___mountain goat___ .

Grammar: Real conditionals

Result clause (future tense)	*If* clause (simple present tense)
The climate **will** change	if we **continue** to burn fossil fuels.
We **will** lose many valuable animals	if we **destroy** their habitats.
*Real conditionals can be written with the result clause first.	
*These conditionals do not need a comma.	

152   Unit 12

Word Bank:
Animals and habitats

coral reef: jellyfish, sea turtle

desert: rat, snake

grasslands: lion, zebra

mountains: mountain lion, wolf

rain forest: chimpanzee, gorilla

Grammar: Real conditionals

Look out for common errors, including wrong use of tenses (*If I ~~will~~ have enough money . . .*) and use of this structure for situations that are not real or possible (*If I ~~am~~ the president of this country . . .*).

A Use these cues to write conditional sentences.

1. children   suffer   if   don't take care of   animal habitats
   Our children will suffer if we don't take care of animal habitats.

2. fish   die   if   coral reef   die
   Fish will die if the coral reefs die.

3. visitors   not come   if   no   animals
   Visitors will not/won't come if there are no animals.

4. live longer   if   exercise more
   People will live longer if they exercise more.

5. go   beach   if   no   rain
   I will/I'll go to the beach if it doesn't rain.

B Complete the sentences using your own words.

1. Our coral reefs will die if _____ .

2. We will lose many useful plants if _____ .

3. _____ if you finish your work today.

4. _____ if more people use public transportation.

5. _____ if you cook dinner.

▲ Habitat destruction in a rain forest. Why is it important to save habitats like this?

Conversation

A 🔊 28   Listen to the conversation. What is Aya worried about? How can she help? *habitat destruction; go to work by bus*

Aya: I'm very worried about all we hear and read about habitat destruction. It's important, but how can I help?
Sharon: You go to work by car, right?
Aya: Yes.
Sharon: It will help if you go to work by bus.
Aya: How will that help?
Sharon: Buses carry lots of people. That means less gasoline is used per person. Less pollution, less climate change, less habitat destruction, right?
Aya: Yes, and I save money as well.
Sharon: Right!

B 🗪 Practice the conversation with a partner. Switch roles and practice it again.

C 🗪 | GOAL CHECK ✔ Talk about cause and effect

Work with a partner. Choose an important problem or environmental issue. Make a list of the things you can do to help. Tell your partner what positive consequences your actions will have.

Real Language
You can say *right?* (rising tone) at the end of a statement to check information. You can also use *right* (falling tone) to show you agree.

Consequences   **153**

A • Have students work individually to write sentences using the given words.
• Have students compare answers with a partner.
• Check answers.

B • Have students complete each sentence.
• Have students compare answers with a partner.
• Have several students share sentences and write them on the board. Have the class help you correct them as necessary.

Conversation

A • Have students close their books. Write the questions on the board: *What is Aya worried about? How can she help?*
• Play the recording. 🔊 28
• Check answers.

B • Play or read the conversation again for the class to repeat.
• Practice the conversation with the class in chorus.
• Have students practice the conversation with partners and then switch roles and practice it again.

C 🗪 | GOAL CHECK ✔

• Divide the class into pairs and have each pair choose one important problem. It can be a personal problem (such as being in bad shape) or a world problem (such as global warming). Have students brainstorm a list of ways to solve the problem and then talk about the consequences of each action.
• Call on student pairs to present their ideas to the class.

Grammar Practice: Real conditionals

On the board, write, *The population of our city increases to five million.* Ask the class, *What will happen if the population of our city increases to five million?* Elicit several sentences with consequences (for example, *If the population of our city increases to five million, we will build more houses.*) and write them on the board, linking them to the original sentence with an arrow. Then ask about the results of these events: *What will happen if we build more houses?* and write the possible consequences, linked to that event with an arrow. Continue in this way to explore the sequence of possible consequences. Then talk about other situations, such as *The Earth's climate gets warmer. Everyone in this country can have a free education.* And so forth.

Evaluate Money and Happiness

Reading

A • Have students look at the pictures and describe what they see. Have them predict what they will read about in the article.

• Have students read the list and decide which ones involve spending money.

• Compare answers as a class.

B • Divide students into groups of three or four. Have them discuss how they would feel after each of the situations in **A**. In the situations that involve spending money, have them discuss which one would make them feel better. Assign roles (leader, secretary, recorder, and reporter).

• Have the reporter for each group report back to the class about the group's discussion.

C • Have students read the statements. Point out the words in the Word Bank. Have students read the article and correct the false information. Tell them to circle any vocabulary they don't understand.

• Have students compare answers with a partner.

• Check answers.

• Go through the article answering any questions about vocabulary.

D **GOAL 4:** Evaluate Money and Happiness

Reading

A Read the list below. Make a check mark (✓) next to the items that describe spending money.

1. ___✓___ buying clothes for yourself
2. _____ spending time with a friend
3. _____ reading a book
4. ___✓___ buying a present for someone in your family
5. ___✓___ donating to a charity
6. ___✓___ going out to eat

B 👥 In a small group, take turns saying how you would feel after doing each of the things in exercise **A**. For the situations that deal with money, which would make you feel best? Why?

C Read the article. All the following statements are false. Correct the false information in your notebook. Write the correct sentences.

1. Many people believe that winning the lottery will ~~not~~ make them happy.

2. People that win the lottery ~~never~~ have problems with money.   *usually*

3. Michael Norton has done experiments to test how people feel after ~~exercising~~.
   spending money

4. Michael Norton's experiments show that spending money ~~does not make~~ people happy.   *on others makes*

WORD BANK
conflict problem
debt money that has to be paid
experiment test
lottery game of chance with cash prize
research exploration, investigation

TED Ideas worth spreading

Michael Norton Professor/Psychologist

HOW TO BUY HAPPINESS

The following article is about Michael Norton. After Unit 12, you'll have the opportunity to watch some of Norton's TED Talk and learn more about his idea worth spreading.

Michael Norton is a business school professor. He is interested in the effects of money on how people feel.

Some people believe that having a lot of money will make them happy. For example, many people think that if they win the **lottery,** they will be happy. However, many lottery winners overspend and have many **debts.** Also, they have **conflicts** because their friends and family want gifts of money, or loans. Debts and conflicts make people unhappy. This example about lottery winners shows that, "money can't buy happiness." But is that always true?

Norton believes that money *can* buy happiness. Why? He has done **experiments** on how people behave with money. In one experiment, some university students spent money on themselves and some students spent money on other people. Afterward, all the students were asked about their feelings. The students that spent money on themselves did not feel unhappy, but they did not feel happier, either. However, the **research** shows that students that spent money on others felt happier. Michael Norton did this type of money experiment all over the world, with people of all ages. Each time, the result was the same—spending money on others improved the happiness of the giver.

For Your Information: Michael Norton

Harvard Business School professor Michael Norton challenges the widely accepted view that money can't buy happiness. Norton is a social science researcher with a Ph.D. in Psychology who is interested in consumer behavior and psychology. His research on money and its relation to happiness has received a lot of interest, and his work has been published in several of the top academic journals, such as *Psychological Science* and the *Annual Review of*

Psychology. He is currently an associate professor of business administration in the marketing area at Harvard Business School, but has also been a visiting scholar at Stanford Graduate School of Business and the University of Pennsylvania. Based on his research, Norton argues that money *can* buy happiness, but it is *how* we spend our money that affects how happy we feel.

How you spend your money has an effect on your happiness.

"Maybe the reason that money doesn't make us happy is that we're always spending it on the wrong things."

— Michael Norton

155

Reading Tip

Have students guess what a text will be about beforehand. The point is not to get the answer right, but to get them thinking and ensure that they already have some ideas about the text. Students can use the pictures, captions, and headline to form their guesses.

After Reading

Have pairs of students look for more information about Michael Norton on the Internet. For example, *What is his other TED Talk, Labor and Love, about? What has he published?* etc. Assign students different aspects to research or let them choose. Have pairs present their information to the class.

Writing

A • Have students read the e-mail. Ask, *Who is it from? Who is it to? What did Samuel find? What does he want to do with it?* Have students complete the e-mail.

• Check answers.

B • Ask, *What are the consequences of Samuel's actions? What will happen if he buys music? What should Samuel do? How do we make suggestions?* Focus students' attention on the Writing Strategy box and the different ways of making suggestions.

• Have students write their reply to Samuel. Remind them to use information from what they read about spending and happiness to say what the effects of his actions will be.

• Have students exchange e-mails with a partner and identify the actions and consequences mentioned in the e-mail. Have students compare any differences between the actions and consequences in each e-mail.

• Have several students share their ideas with the class.

Communication

A • Have students write down five ways of spending the money.

B • Divide the class into pairs. Have them talk about each way to use the money and discuss any differences.

C 🔁 | **GOAL CHECK** ✔

• With the same partner, have students decide how they will spend the money. Focus their attention on the questions to help guide their discussion.

• Have pairs share how they will spend the money and what the consequences will be.

D **GOAL 4:** Evaluate Money and Happiness

Writing Strategy

Remember the different ways to make suggestions. You can use *could* to make a gentle suggestions. To give advice in a stronger way, use *should* or *ought to*.

Writing

A A friend sent you this e-mail. Complete the e-mail.

> I have some great news! I found some money on the street today. My sister's birthday is next week and I know she wants a scarf. Also, I want to buy myself some new music.
>
> If I buy the music, I __will__ not have enough money to buy the scarf. And if I __spend__ the money on music, I will not be able to buy the scarf. What do you think I should do?
>
> Samuel

B Write a reply to Samuel's e-mail using information from the article. Use real conditionals to talk about the effects of Samuel's choice.

Communication

A You won $100 in the lottery. Write down five possible ways to use the money.

B 🔁 Discuss your ideas with a partner. Talk about each way to use money and discuss any differences.

C 🔁 | **GOAL CHECK** ✔ **Evaluate money and happiness**

Work together to decide how to use the money. How much will you spend and what will you buy? Will you save or give away any of the money? What might happen as a result of how you spend the money?

Teacher Tip: Self-evaluation

At the end of the course, it's useful to have students spend some time reflecting on the progress they've made and their goals for future learning. One way to do this is by having them fill in a questionnaire in English and then (if time permits) having a brief meeting with each student to discuss his or her answers.

Here are some possible questions you could ask:

How much have you improved in these areas?
Speaking/Listening/Writing/Reading/Vocabulary/ Grammar
Write "a lot," "some," or "a little."

Which activities in class helped you the most?
Which activities didn't help you?
What will you do differently in your next class?

Mount Kilimanjaro

Before You Watch

A Read the chain of actions and consequences. Number the sentences below to make a similar chain.

Cars and airplanes produce carbon dioxide. > Carbon dioxide makes the atmosphere hotter. > The glaciers of Kilimanjaro melt.

___4___ Kilimanjaro's glaciers get smaller.   ___1___ People cut down trees.

___2___ There is less water in the atmosphere.   ___3___ There is less rain and snow.

While You Watch

A ▶ Watch the video. Fill in the numbers and datoo.

1. Kilimanjaro is nearly ___four___ miles high.
2. It is around ___220___ miles south of the equator.
3. The glaciers on Kilimanjaro are ___11,000___ years old.
4. Experts think that the glaciers could disappear by the year ___2020___.

B ▶ Watch again. Answer the questions.

1. Why are the glaciers of Kilimanjaro important to the people of Tanzania?
   They are an important source of water for drinking and farming.

2. Why are the glaciers disappearing? global warming and deforestation

> **Word Focus**
>
> **deforestation** = when trees and forests are cut down
>
> **glacier** = a large body of slowly moving ice
>
> **to melt** = to change from ice to water

After You Watch

A 🔁 Discuss this question with a partner: Is there anything that *you* can do to stop the melting of Kilimanjaro's glaciers?

Consequences 157

For Your Information: Mt. Kilimanjaro

Mt. Kilimanjaro is located in Tanzania, in East Africa, near the border with Kenya. The mountain is 5,895 meters (19,341 feet) above sea level. It is an inactive volcano, but hot gas still comes out of holes in the rock. The mountain was first climbed by three men in 1889. Because it is one of the "Seven Summits" (the highest mountain on each continent of the world), many people climb it every year. The climb doesn't require great skill, but many people suffer from altitude sickness on the climb, and every year about 10 people die on the mountain.

Video Journal:
The Missing Snows of Kilimanjaro

Before You Watch

- Have students look at the picture and describe what they see.
- Introduce the topic of the video. Ask what, if anything, students know about Mt. Kilimanjaro (the highest mountain in Africa).

A • Have students read the actions and consequences and then number the events in the order they occur.
- Have students compare answers with a partner.
- Check answers.

While You Watch

A • Direct students' attention to the Word Focus box. Tell students to watch the video the first time and find the numbers.
- Play the video.
- Have students compare answers with a partner.
- Check answers.

B • Tell students to watch the video again and answer the questions. Have the students read the questions.
- Play the video.
- Have students compare answers with a partner.
- Check answers.

After You Watch

A • Divide the class into pairs and have them brainstorm ways that they can help save the glaciers of Kilimanjaro.
- Compare answers with the class, making a list on the board.

How To Buy Happiness

Before You Watch

A • Have students read the list and check the ways they use money.

• Have students compare their list with a partner.

• Compare lists as a class. Do most students spend money on themselves or others? Do they donate money to charity? Lend money? What are the most common spending habits? Ask students why they spend money the way that they do.

B • Have students read the definitions and the sentences. Have them match the definitions to the words in bold in the sentences.

• Have students compare answers with a partner.

• Check answers.

C • Have students share what they remember about Michael Norton (from the Reading in Unit 12). Ask, *Who is Michael Norton? What does he do? What is he interested in?* Write students' answers on the board. Tell students they are going to watch a TED Talk where Norton talks about his research on money and happiness.

• Have students read the directions and write down what type of experiments they think they will see. Have them look at the list in **A** for ideas.

• Divide the class into pairs and have them compare their ideas.

• Compare answers with the class. On the board, write students' ideas about the experiments they think they will see in the TED Talk.

Before You Watch

A Read the list. Make a check (✓) next to the ways that you use money.

☐ pay bills

☐ buy things for yourself

☐ save money

☐ eat at a restaurant

☐ buy gifts for others

☐ spend money on expenses

☐ donate (give away) money

☐ lend money to others

B Read the sentences. Match the word in **bold** to its meaning.

a. give someone a reason to do something	**d.** helps others
	e. money spent for a future reward
b. good effect	**f.** scientific test
c. payment that is received	**g.** how well you work

1. If I don't sleep enough, I don't **perform** well at school. _g_

2. I like to get good grades in school; it **motivates** me to study. _a_

3. Alexandra decided to make an **investment** with her extra money. _e_

4. The **return** on the investment was small, only 20 dollars. _c_

5. Jack is working on an **experiment** about sunlight. _f_

6. Exercise has many **benefits**, such as being healthy. _b_

7. Being a volunteer is a **prosocial** activity. _d_

Michael Norton's idea worth spreading is that money *can* buy happiness! What matters isn't how much you have, but how you spend it. Watch Norton's full TED Talk on TED.com.

C You are going to watch a TED Talk about Michael Norton's experiments on how money makes people feel. What types of experiments do you think you will see? Talk about your ideas with a partner. Look at the list in exercise **A** for ideas.

While You Watch

A Watch the TED Talk. Complete the missing information in the chart as you watch. Answers may vary slightly. Suggested answers:

Experiment	How much money	Spent money on themselves	Spent money on others
college students	5 or _20_ dollars	did not feel happier	felt happier
sales teams	15 euro	did not sell more	sold more
dodgeball teams	did not say	did not win more games	won more games

B Read the photo captions on the next page. What quotes are you surprised by? Place a check (✓) next to the captions that you are surprised by. Then, in small groups, talk about why you are surprised.

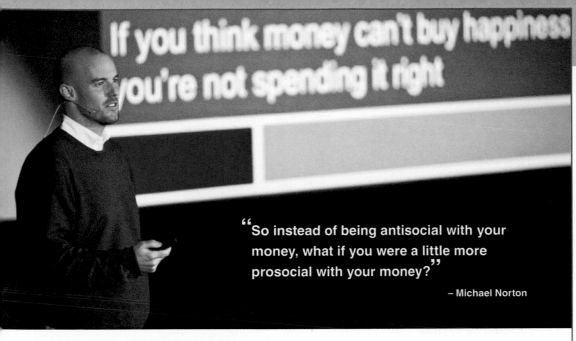

If you think money can't buy happiness
you're not spending it right

"So instead of being antisocial with your money, what if you were a little more prosocial with your money?"

– Michael Norton

□ "In fact, it doesn't matter how much money you spent. What really matters is that you spent it on somebody else rather than on yourself."

What they bought

Personal

Prosocial

□ "People who spent money on other people got happier. People who spent money on themselves, nothing happened."

And into companies

□ "One of the teams pooled their money and bought a piñata . . . very silly, trivial thing to do, but think of the difference on a team that didn't do that at all."

And beyond

□ "The teams that we give the money to spend on each other, they become different teams and, in fact, they dominate the league by the time they're done."

□ "And so I'll just say, I think if you think money can't buy happiness you're not spending it right."

Listen for Key Information

As you listen, you do not need to focus on every word you hear. Listen for specific words and phrases to get the information you need.

While You Watch

- Focus students' attention on the listening strategy box on the bottom of the page. Remind them that key words and ideas are usually emphasized in spoken English, so they should try to focus on these words and phrases as they listen. This will help them understand the main ideas. Remind them that it is also useful to take notes of these key words and ideas as they listen.

A • Tell students to look at the chart on page 158. Have them underline key words and phrases that they should listen for to get the information they need (for example, *experiment, amounts of money, spent on themselves, spent on others*). Tell them to complete the information as they watch the talk.

- Play the TED Talk.
- Have students compare answers with a partner.
- Check answers.

B • Have students read the photo captions and check the ones that surprise them.

- Divide the class into small groups. Have them compare their answers and explain their reasons.
- Compare and discuss reasons as a group.

159

TEDTALKS

After You Watch

A • Have students read the conditional sentence halves. Tell them to match any they can. Play the TED Talk again for students to confirm or complete their answers.

• Have students compare answers with a partner.

• Check answers.

B • Have students read each sentence and complete the ideas with information from the talk.

• Have students compare answers with a partner.

• Check answers.

C • Elicit from students what the different experiments were that Norton explained in the talk. Write notes on the board.

• Divide the class into pairs. Model the example with a student. Have students take turns saying something about one of the experiments and their partner guesses which experiment.

• Have different students make a statement and call on another student to guess the experiment.

D • Elicit advice for a happy, healthy lifestyle and write one or two ideas on the board. Elicit how we give advice (*should (not), must (not)*).

• Divide the class into small groups and have each group write a list of advice for a happy, healthy lifestyle. Remind them to use what they already know, as well as the ideas in the talk.

• Have each group share their advice. As a class, decide on the three most important pieces of advice and write them on the board.

TEDTALKS

Michael Norton Professor/Psychologist
HOW TO BUY HAPPINESS

This boy is buying food for his family. How do you think he feels?

After You Watch

A Watch the TED Talk again. Match the information to make sentences about what Michael Norton's experiments suggest.

1. _f_ If people on sports teams spend money on themselves,　　a. they will feel happier.
2. _a_ If students spend money on each other,　　b. they will not sell more.
3. _d_ If people on sales teams spend money on each other,　　c. they will win more games.
4. _e_ If students spend money on themselves,　　d. they will sell more.
5. _b_ If people on sales teams spend money on themselves,　　e. they will not feel happier.
6. _c_ If people on sports teams spend money on each other,　　f. they will not win more games.

B Complete these sentences.

1. To be prosocial with money means to spend it on _others/other people_.
2. People who are prosocial with money often feel _happier_ and perform _better_ at work or at sports.
3. Norton suggests that it is not important how _much_ money you spend on others; the benefits are the same.

C 🔁 Work with a partner. Take turns making statements about what you saw in the TED Talk. Your partner says which experiment you are talking about.

D 👥 Work with a group. Make a list of advice for a person who wants to have a happy and healthy lifestyle. Use what you already knew and what you learned in the TED Talk.

> You should . . .　　You must not . . .

160

E 👥 Interview three classmates about the last time they spent money on someone else. Follow the steps below.

- Write a list of questions, using *Who, What, How much,* and *Why.*

Questions	Names		
	_____	_____	_____
1.			
2.			
3.			
4.			
5.			

- Interview your classmates. Ask follow-up questions. Find out how your classmates felt after spending the money.
- Share what you learned with the class. Did what you learned from your classmates match what you learned in the TED Talk?

F 👥 With your group, look at the chart. Think about how you and your group spend money. Can you think of ways to spend money that are more prosocial? Think of a way to spend money that would be more prosocial and share your idea with the class.

Challenge! 👥 Place a check (✓) next to the **four** statements that represent the main ideas of Norton's talk.

_____ Money cannot buy happiness.

✓ Spending money in a prosocial way has a positive effect.

✓ Spending money on others often makes people feel happier, be more productive, and have stronger relationships.

✓ The important thing is to spend money on others —even a trivial amount can have a positive effect.

_____ Winning money makes people happy.

✓ The positive effects of spending money in a prosocial way seem to be the same all over the world.

_____ People should not buy things for themselves.

With a team, pick one idea and talk about ways people can work toward using the idea in their own lives. Come up with a plan of action and share it with the class.

161

E • Have students read the directions. Elicit possible questions and write one or two on the board; for example, *Who did you spend money on? What did you buy?* Have students write questions in their chart.

- For each question, have students write a follow-up question; for example, *Did ____ like the ____ you bought them? What did he/she say/do?*

- Have students interview three classmates. Remind them to also ask about how they felt after spending the money.

- Have different students share what they learned from interviewing their classmates and discuss whether it confirmed what they had learned in the TED Talk or not.

F • In the same groups they worked in for **E,** have students look at their charts and discuss how they spend money.

- Have each group write a list of ways to spend money that would be more prosocial.

- Have each group share one idea with the class.

Challenge

- Have students read the list and identify the four main ideas of Michael Norton's talk.

- Have students compare answers with a partner.

- Check answers.

- In the same small groups, have students choose one idea and discuss how people can apply it to their own life. Have each group create a plan of action to put the idea into practice.

- Have each group share their plan with the class.

Ideas Worth Sharing

- With books closed, have students share what they remember about Michael Norton. Ask, *What is his message? What does he believe people should do to be happier, more productive, and have better social relationships?* Write their ideas on the board.

- Have students read the information in the Ideas Worth Sharing box on page 158 again. Remind them that they can watch the whole talk at TED.com to help them develop their listening skills. Encourage them to look for more information about Michael Norton's work.

GLOSSARY

UNIT 1

boring: not interesting

chef: a cook in a restaurant

dancer: a person who earns money by dancing

dangerous: unsafe or harmful

doctor: a professional who helps sick or injured people

engineer: a person who plans the making of machines, roads, and bridges

happy: a joyful or cheerful feeling

interesting: something that is exciting or unusual

journalist: a person whose job is to collect news

photographer: someone who takes photos as a job

pilot: a professional who flies airplanes

police officer: a person who is trained to maintain law and order

politician: a person with a job in politics or government

poor: to not have a lot of money

rich: to have a lot of money

teacher: a person whose job is to instruct and educate others

travel agent: a person who plans trips and holidays

safe: not harmful or dangerous

unhappy: a sad feeling

UNIT 2

brush your teeth: clean your teeth with a small brush

catch the bus: get on a bus on time

celebrate: to do something special, like have a party, to mark an occasion

costumes: clothes worn by a person who is trying to look like a different person or thing

decorate: to make a place or object look beautiful or festive

eat breakfast: eat the first meal of the day, usually in the morning

eat out: eat at a restaurant

festival: a public celebration that takes place on special occasions

fireworks: colorful explosions of light in the sky, usually used for celebrations

fun: a good time

get up: wake up and get out of bed

go to bed: lie down to go to sleep

go to the movies: go to a theater to watch a film

masks: material worn on the face to hide one's identity

present: a gift

start work: begin your job

take a nap: sleep for a short time when it is not time for bed

take a shower: wash under a shower

watch TV: look at a TV

visit friends: go see friends

UNIT 3

airline ticket: a printed piece of paper bought for travel on an airplane

board the airplane: get on the airplane

buy duty free goods: buy goods at a store in an airport that do not add tax to the price

buy your ticket: use cash or credit cards to get a ticket

cash: paper money, like dollar bills, and metal coins used to buy things

check in: arrive and show your ticket

credit cards: a plastic card that allows a person to buy things by borrowing money

claim your baggage: pick up bags or suitcases after a flight

go through customs: when items brought into a country are checked by an official

go through immigration: have government workers check the passports and visas of travelers

go through security: have government workers check travelers to make sure no one has anything dangerous

international driver's license: a document that allows people to drive a car or motorcycle in foreign countries

pack your bags: put clothes and other things in bags

passport: a small book issued by a government to a citizen of a nation for travel

take a taxi: get somewhere using a car with a driver for hire

travel insurance: an agreement with a company in which you pay them money to cover costs and reduce the risk of travel

visa: a document that allows a person to travel to a country

UNIT 4

apple: a round fruit with firm, white flesh

bagel: a piece of bread that is round with a hole in the middle

banana: a long, curved fruit with yellow skin

beans: seeds that can be eaten

breakfast cereal: a breakfast food made from grain

broccoli: a vegetable with green stalks and green or purple heads

butter: soft yellow substance made from cream

cauliflower: large, round vegetable with a hard, white center

cheese: a solid food made from milk

chicken: the meat from a type of farm bird

coffee: a hot, brown, energy-giving drink made by water and coffee beans

customer: someone who buys goods or services

dairy products: different types of food that are made from milk

drinks: liquids that can be swallowed

egg: oval object made by birds, often eaten as food

fiber: a part of a plant found in many fruits and vegetables that is a part of a healthy diet

fish: the meat from an animal with fins that lives in the sea

fruits: the part of a plant that holds the seeds

hamburger: ground meat shaped into a flat circle

juice: a liquid that comes from a fruit or vegetable

lemon: a bright yellow fruit with sour juice

lettuce: a vegetable with large green leaves

meat: the flesh of animals

milk: a white liquid produced by some female animals such as cows

nuts: a fruit with a hard shell or its seed

onion: a round, layered vegetable with light brown skin

orange: a round juicy fruit with orange skin

pepper: a hollow vegetable with seeds inside

potato: round vegetables with white or red skins and white insides

protein: a substance found in meat, fish, and dairy foods that promotes growth

sausage: meat formed into a tube

shrimp: small shellfish with long tails

soda: a sweet carbonated drink

steak: a large piece of meat or fish

tea: flowers and leaves that are dried, shredded, and brewed into a drink

tomato: a soft, red fruit

tuna salad: a food that has chopped tuna meat and vegetables

turkey bacon: salted and smoked turkey meat

vegetables: different plants that can be eaten as food

waiter: a person who serves food and drink in a restaurant

water: clear liquid with no color or taste, people and animals need it to survive

UNIT 5

baseball: a game played on a field by nine players on each team using a small ball and a bat

climbing: a sport where a person moves upward over a vertical surface

diving: a water sport where a person jumps into water

fix the roof: repair the top of a house

football: a sport played by two 11-person teams, using an oval ball. In order to win one must pass or run the ball over the opponent's line

golf: an outdoors game in which people hit a small hard ball into a hole with a stick

go to the movies: (see Unit 2)

gymnastics: exercises that develop strength, coordination, and movement

hiking: taking a long walk in the country or up a mountain

ice hockey: ice-skating sport that uses curved sticks and a small round disk

jogging: running slowly as a form of exercise

lifting weights: a sport in which people try to lift very heavy objects

playing soccer: play a sport of two teams of 11 players, who kick a round ball into goals

skateboarding: a sport where people do tricks on a narrow board with four wheels

study: spend time learning about a subject

swimming: a sport in which people move through water by moving parts of the body

taking a break: taking time to relax

volleyball: a sport played with six players on each side of a net who score points by grounding the ball on the opponents' side

UNIT 6

buy souvenirs: buy objects to remember a place

check into the hotel: arrive at a hotel and get a room

emphatic adjectives: (See page 72)

pack suitcases: to place objects in bags or luggage in order to transport them during travel

unpack suitcases: to remove objects from a bag or luggage

rent a car: to pay money in order to use a car

take a bus tour: go on a bus that will visit places of interest and have a guide

take photos: take pictures with a camera

visit places of interest: go to famous places

UNIT 7

bad: unpleasant or harmful

dirty: not clean

e-mail: mail sent over the Internet

fax: a document that is sent electronically through telephone lines

green: the color of grass

hearing: listening to sounds through the ears

letter: a written or typed message sent by mail

loud: intense sound

newspaper ad: a printed advertisement that appears in a newspaper

salty: something that has the taste of salt

sight: the ability to see using your eyes

smartphone: a mobile phone that can access the Internet

smell: the feeling sensed through the nose

social media: websites and applications used for connecting with people on the Internet

soft: nice to touch

sweet: having a taste like sugar or honey

taste: the sense of flavor that comes from the tongue

text message: an electronic message sent through a cellular phone

touch: the ability to feel through the skin, especially with the fingers

TV: box-like device that shows pictures and sounds

wet: covered with, or full of, water or another liquid

UNIT 8

buy a new car: pay money to own a car

buy my own house: pay money to own a house

clean the house: to remove dirt and dust from a house

cloudy/overcast: covered with clouds; not sunny

cold/cool: having a low temperature; not warm

do the laundry: wash dirty clothes

get a new job: switch jobs

have children: start a family

hot/warm: having a high temperature; not cold

rain boots: shoes that are worn in the rain, usually made out of rubber or plastic

raincoat: a coat that stops a person from getting wet

rainy/wet: having a lot of rain

scarf: a piece of cloth worn around the neck

speak English fluently: to easily speak or write English

study for the next test: practice, read, and listen to get ready for a quiz

sun hat: a hat that protects the head and neck from the sun

sunglasses: eyeglasses that protect the eyes from the sun

sunny/bright/clear: brightly lit with sunlight; not cloudy

sweater: a warm piece of clothing worn over the upper body

swimsuit: a piece of clothing that is worn to go swimming

umbrella: a folding fabric used to protect someone from rain

windy/breezy: with a lot of wind

UNIT 9

belt: a strip of leather or cloth worn around the waist

blouse: a woman's shirt

cheap: goods that don't cost a lot

coat: warm clothing worn over other clothes

cool: a temperature that is low, but not too low

cotton: cloth made from the soft white fiber of a certain plant

expensive: costs a lot of money

gloves: a covering for the hand with separate parts for each finger

handbag: a woman's purse

hat: a clothing item which covers the head

heavy: something that weighs a lot; warm clothing

jacket: a short coat

jeans: informal pants made of denim

leather: animal skin used for clothing

light: something that does not weight a lot; clothing that is not warm

man-made fiber: fibers that are created by people

pants: a piece of clothing that covers the legs

rough: uneven and not smooth

shirt: a piece of clothing worn on the upper body

shoes: a covering for the foot

silk: cloth made from the fibers created by silkworms

skirt: a piece of women's clothing that covers the waist, hips, and part of the legs

smooth: with no roughness or holes

sneakers: a kind of shoe usually worn for sports or casual activities

socks: a piece of cloth worn over the foot and under a shoe

suit: a formal jacket and pants made from the same fabric

tie: a piece of cloth worn by men around the neck for formal occasions

t-shirt: a short-sleeved shirt worn over the upper body

warmth: amount of heat something makes

wool: cloth that is made from sheep's hair

UNIT 10

bad shape: not healthy and physically fit

cycling: to ride on a bicycle

eating a balanced diet: eating all of the important food groups

eating lots of sugar: eating foods and drinks that are sweet and unhealthy

good shape: healthy and physically fit

healthy: in good condition; strong, fit, in good shape

heartwarming: something that makes you happy

homegrown: produced in your own garden

homemade: not made in a factory

junk food: food that tastes good but is bad for your health

lifelong: all your life

lifestyle: a way of living

low calorie: not high in calories

mouth-watering: delicious; very good food

overworked: works too much

smoking: the use of tobacco, usually with cigarettes and cigars

stress-free: without worries or problems

sunbathing: to lie out underneath the sun

works out: exercises

watching lots of TV: spend a lot of time watching TV

UNIT 11

buy the groceries: purchase food and household things

cut the grass: use a machine to shorten grass

get a credit card: sign up for and receive a credit card

get a promotion: receive an advancement to a new and better job

graduate from high school/college: to receive a degree from an academic institution

iron the clothes: smooth out wrinkles on clothing

pass your driving test: pass an examination given to test a person's ability to drive

pay the bills: pay money for heat, electricity, and other household needs

put away the clothes: clean up and store clothes

run a marathon: run a race of over 26 miles (41.3 km)

sweep the floor: to clear a surface of dust or dirt using a broom or brush

travel abroad: travel out of the country

vacuum: to clean with a vacuum cleaner

walk the dog: to take a dog outside

UNIT 12

borrow: to receive something with the promise to return it

budget: an amount of money set aside for a purpose; a financial plan

camel: a large four-legged animal with a long neck and hump(s) on its back

coral reef: hard substance formed from the bones of tiny sea animals

desert: a very dry region with little or no rain

elephant: one of the largest land-mammals, with gray skin, a trunk, and long tusks

expenses: things that must be paid

grasslands: flat land covered with wild grass

income: the amount of money earned from working

interest rates: extra money that has to be paid back when you borrow money

lend: to allow the use of something for a period of time

monkey: a primate with thumbs, long tails, and human-like faces

mountain goat: a four-legged animal with horns that lives on mountains

mountains: a tall formation of land and rock higher than a hill

overspend: to spend too much money

rain forest: a forest with a lot of rainfall that has many different kinds of plants and animals

save: not to spend or use too much money in order to keep some for the future

shark: a meat-eating fish that lives in oceans and large rivers

SKILLS INDEX

giving advice, 33, 40, 125, 126
giving opinions and reasons, 32
job interviews, 139
making predictions, 38, 78, 101
naming objects, 165
role-playing, 32, 37, 47, 65, 105, 116, 139
trip planning, 113, 151

TED TALKS

How to Buy Happiness, 158–161
The Interspecies Internet? An Idea in Progress, 118–121
My Mind-Shifting Everest Swim, 78–81
A Virtual Choir 2,000 Voices Strong, 38–41

TEST-TAKING SKILLS

categorizing, 60
checking off answers, 18, 47, 59, 70, 90, 98, 99, 104, 105, 111, 139, 140, 154, 158, 161
circling answers, 7, 8, 9, 16, 18, 25, 37, 61, 70, 74, 86, 117, 126, 150
completing charts, 10, 31, 41, 76, 86, 87, 92, 101, 111, 120, 127, 132, 145, 151, 159, 161
definitions, 148
fill in the blanks, 4, 5, 6, 9, 13, 18, 49, 57, 61, 65, 69, 71, 77, 78, 110, 117, 118, 145, 157
labeling pictures, 16, 38, 56, 60, 62, 72, 80, 84, 108, 136, 140
matching, 5, 30, 64, 68, 72, 93, 96, 97, 108, 118, 120, 128, 133, 137, 149, 150
multiple choice, 18, 22, 25, 70, 80, 86, 117, 129, 149, 150, 159, 160
ordering pictures, 28
ordering sentences, 157
ranking answers, 116, 144, 157
rewriting questions, 101
sentence completion, 9, 17, 20, 24, 28, 29, 32, 38, 45, 49, 64, 72, 73, 77, 80, 89, 97, 100, 101, 108, 109, 113, 124, 128, 137, 138, 142, 152, 153, 156, 160
sorting answers into columns, 8, 12, 25, 46, 48, 52, 60, 68, 84, 96, 104, 124
true or false, 10, 13, 25, 30, 34, 37, 40, 53, 62, 70, 77, 90, 93, 98, 112, 133, 142, 145
underlining answers, 74, 102, 108
unscrambling sentences, 9, 21, 68, 85, 149
writing requests and predictions, 85, 101
writing questions, 33, 101, 129

TOPICS

Achievements, 134–145
Communication, 82–93
Consequences, 146–157
Destinations, 66–77
Food, 42–53
Going Places, 26–37
Lifestyles, 122–133
Moving Forward, 94–105
People, 2–13
Sports, 54–65
Types of Clothing, 106–117
Work, Rest, and Play, 14–25

VIDEO JOURNAL

Beagle Patrol, 37
Cheese-Rolling Races, 65
Dangerous Dinner, 53
The Last of the Woman Divers, 13
Machu Picchu, 77
Monkey Business, 25
The Missing Snows of Kilimanjaro, 157
The Science of Stress, 133
Solar Cooking, 105
Spacewalk, 145
Traditional Silk Making, 117
Wild Animal Trackers, 93

VOCABULARY

achievements, 140
activities, 56, 58
animals, 152
chores, 136
clothing, 100, 108, 112
communication methods, 84
compound adjectives, 128
countries and nationalities, 4
daily routine, 16
descriptive adjectives, 8
diets, 48
emphatic adjectives, 72
festivals and celebrations, 20
food, 44, 48
habitats, 152
habits, 124
money, 32, 148
numbers, 30
occupations, 4
party words, 20
people, 4
planning, 96
senses, 88
sports, 56, 60
travel, 28, 32, 68
weather conditions, 100

WRITING

advice, 125
answering questions, 64, 116, 132
e-mails, 64, 156
job descriptions, 12
letters, 156
list-making, 13
make suggestions, 156
paragraphs, 24, 76, 104, 116, 132, 144
recipes, 52
statements about the future, 104
text messages, 92
travel blog, 71, 76
travel tips, 36
word webs, 14

ILLUSTRATION

4: (t) National Geographic Maps; **7:** (1 to 6) Nesbitt Graphics, Inc.; **8:** (lt and lb) Nesbitt Graphics, Inc.; **44:** (t) Keith Neely/ IllustrationOnline.com; **45:** (b) Nesbitt Graphics, Inc.; **46:** (c) Nesbitt Graphics, Inc.; **48:** (t) Nesbitt Graphics, Inc.; **57:** (c) Rob Schuster; **88:** (t, tm, m, bm, b) Nesbitt Graphics, Inc.; **92:** (b) Rob Schuster; **108:** (t) Kenneth Batelman; **151:** (b) National Geographic Maps.

PHOTO

Cover Photo: Slow Images/Photographer's Choice/Getty Images

2–3: (c) Sigit Pamungkas/Reuters; **4:** (tl) Raul Touzon/National Geographic Creative, (bl) Robert George Young/Photographer's Choice/Getty Images, (tc) Robert Sisson/ National Geographic Creative, (tlc) Damien Meyer/AFP/Getty Images, (trc) jochem wijnands/Horizons WWP/Alamy, (tr) Zhang Meng/Xinhua Press/Corbis, (rc) Daj/Getty Images, (br) Paul Bradbury/OJO Images/ Getty Images; **6:** (tl) © iStockphoto.com/ Peter Close, (tr) © iStockphoto.com/ shotbydave, (blc) Simon Jarratt/ Fancy/ Corbis, (brc) © iStockphoto.com/yelo34; **7:** (tr) Roy Toft/National Geographic Creative; **8:** (tl) © iStockphoto.com/nicolesy, (tlc) Jupiterimages/Photos.com/Thinkstock, (trc) © iStockphoto.com/JLBarranco, (tr) © iStockphoto.com/diego_cervo, (bl) © iStockphoto.com/H-Gall, (blc) © iStockphoto.com/lmistock, (brc) © iStockphoto.com/Blue_Cutler, (br) © iStockphoto.com/epicurean; **9:** (tc) Michael Christopher Brown/National Geographic Creative; **10–11:** (rc) Kevin Fleming/National Geographic Creative; **11:** (tr) Priscilla Gragg/ Blend Images/Alamy, (tc) William Albert Allard/National Geographic Image Collection; **12:** (tc) Alex Treadway/National Geographic Creative, (lc) Steve Raymer/National Geographic Creative, (bl) Simon Jarratt/Ivy/ Corbis; **13:** (tc) Vincent Prevost/Hemis/ Terra/Corbis, (rc) He Lulu Xinhua News Agency/Newscom; **14–15:** (c) Stringer/ Reuters; **16:** (tl) © iStockphoto.com/ Juanmonino, (tc) © iStockphoto.com/Justin Horrocks, (tr) Bob Scott/Photodisc/ Thinkstock, (lc) Keith Brofsky/Photodisc/ Thinkstock, (c) Fuse/Getty Images, (rc) Andrea Chu/Photodisc/Thinkstock, (lc) © iStockphoto.com/BartekSzewczyk, (c) © iStockphoto.com/avdeev007, (rc) © Monkey Business Images/Shutterstock.com, (bl)

Fuse/Thinkstock, (bc) © iStockphoto.com/ Rich Legg, (br) © iStockphoto.com/DIGIcal; **17:** (br) Joe Raedle/Getty Images; **18:** (tc) Adam Crowley/Blend Images/Getty Images; **20:** (tc) India Picture/Collage/Corbis, (lc) Jupiterimages/Photos.com/Thinkstock, (bl) Scott Stulberg/Comet/Corbis; **22:** (l) Mike Pont/Getty Images Entertainment/Getty Images, (c) Roberto Serra - Iguana Press/ Getty Images Entertainment/Getty Images, (r) C Brandon/Redferns/Redferns/Getty Images; **23:** (c) James Duncan Davidson/ TED, (inset) Gallo Images/Getty Images News/Getty Images; **24:** (t) Chad Springer/ Corbis, (bl, bc, br) TED; **25:** (tc) Narong Sangnak/epa/Corbis Wire/Corbis; **26–27:** (c) Kani Polat/500px Prime; **28:** (tl) © iStockphoto.com/leezsnow, (tc) © iStockphoto.com/Neustockimages, (tr) © Galyna Andrushko/Shutterstock.com, (lc) © James Steidl/Shutterstock.com, (c) Hemera Technologies/Photos.com/Thinkstock, (rc) Bruno Domingos/Reuters/Corbis, (bl) Digital Vision/Getty Images, (bc) TongRo Images/ Harry Choi/Alamy, (br) Timur Kulgarin/ Shutterstock.com, (bl) Fuse/Thinkstock; **29:** (br) Skip Brown/National Geographic Creative; **30:** (tc) Bill Bachmann/Science Source; **31:** (tc) Mike Theiss/National Geographic Creative; **32:** (tl) © emilie zhang/ Shutterstock.com, (tlc) AP Images/Rebecca D'Angelo, (lc) Imagedoc/Alamy, (blc) © Oleksiy Mark/Shutterstock.com, (bl) Martin Shields/Alamy, (c) Andrew Woodley/Alamy, (rc) Alan Myers/Alamy; **33:** (br) Andria Patino/Encyclopedia/Corbis; **34–35:** (rc) Jimmy Chim/National Geographic Creative; **36:** (tc) Pola Damonte/Moment Open/Getty Images; **37:** (tc) Lauralea Lasher/National Geographic Creative, (rc) european pressphoto agency b.v./Alamy; **38:** (1) © Jonathan Lewis/Shutterstock.com, (2) © criben/Shutterstock.com, (3) © Aschindl/ Shutterstock.com, (4) © muzsy/ Shutterstock.com; **39:** (t) James Duncan Davidson/TED, (bl, br, t) TED; **40:** (t) TED; **41:** (t) Christian Vorhofer/imagebroker/ Corbis; **42:** (c) © Lucy Vaserfirer/500px Prime; **45:** (cl) © iStockphoto.com/ PaulCowan, (b) © iStockphoto.com/Andrea Skjold, (cr) © iStockphoto.com/1 design; **46:** (t) Jonathan Kingston/National Geographic Creative; **47:** (r) Chris Howes/ Wild Places Photography/Alamy; **48:** (1) © Dionisvera/Shutterstock.com, (2) © g215/ Shutterstock.com, (3) © zcw/Shutterstock. com, (4) © Gordo25/Shutterstock.com, (5) © iStockphoto.com/jaker5000, (6) © Elena Schweitzer/Shutterstock.com, (7) © iStockphoto.com/alex-mit, (8) © GVictoria/

Shutterstock.com; **50:** (l) Kevin Foy/Alamy, (inset) f4foto/Alamy; **51:** (tr) Dan Kitwood/ Getty Images News/Getty Images; **52:** (t) Rolf Nussbaumer/imagebroker/Canopy/ Corbis; **53:** (t) Brian J. Skerry/National Geographic Creative, (1) © Alexius Sutandio/Shutterstock.com, (2) lilithlita/ iStock/360/Getty Images, (3) Ben Horton/ National Geographic Creative, (4) Ben Horton/National Geographic Creative; **54:** (c) Courtesy Tim Kemple; **56:** (1) Lear Miller Photo/Image Source/Alamy, (2) © iStockphoto.com/isitsharp, (3) Francesco Tremolada/SOPA RF/Ramble/Corbis, (4) Tim McGuire/Comet/Corbis, (5) © iStockphoto. com/Mari, (6) JGI/Jamie Grill/Blend Images/ Getty Images, (7) © oliveromg/Shutterstock. com; **57:** (r) Jill Schneider/National Geographic Creative; **58:** (tl) © Monkey Business Images/Shutterstock.com, (tc) © Bull's-Eye Arts/Shutterstock.com, (tr) © Diego Cervo/Shutterstock.com, (bl) © Aspen Photo/Shutterstock.com, (bc) Jupiterimages/Stockbyte/Thinkstock, (br) © iStockphoto.com/buckarooh; **59:** (t) Michael Hanson/National Geographic Creative; **60:** (tl) © Mayskyphoto/Shutterstock.com, (tr) Koki Nagahama/Getty Images Sport/Getty Images, (bl) © Sergey_Peterman/ Shutterstock.com, (br) © Nikolpetr/ Shutterstock.com; **61:** (r) Keith Ladzinski/ alex-honnold-MR.pdf/alex-lowthe/Aurora/ Passage/Corbis; **62:** (tl, tr, bl, br) TED; **63:** (t) Darren Staples/Reuters, (c) AP Images/ MTI/Peter Komka, 63 (c) James Duncan Davis, 63 (inset) © 7382489561/ Shutterstock.com, (b) Ryan Pierse/Getty Images Sport/Getty Images; **64:** (t) © iStockphoto.com/DanielPrudek; **66:** (c) Jim Richardson/National Geographic Creative; **68:** (1) © Konstantin Sutyagin /Shutterstock. com, (2) © iStockphoto.com/Tempura, (3) © iStockphoto.com/ImagesbyTrista, (4) Richard Wong/Alamy, (5) © iStockphoto. com/1001nights, (6) © iStockphoto.com/ RiverNorthPhotography, (7) Max Alexander/ Dorling Kindersley/Getty Images; **69:** (r) Alison Wright/National Geographic Creative; **70:** (l) Joseph C. Justice Jr/Getty Images; **71:** (t) Beverly Joubert/National Geographic Creative, (b) Dmitry Rukhlenko/Travel Photos/Alamy; **72:** (tl) Jamie Grill/JGI/Blend Images/Alamy, (tr) Michael Hanson/National Geographic Creative; **73:** (r) Tim Laman/ National Geographic Creative; **74:** (b) Hiram Bingham/National Geographic Creative; **75:** (tr) Hiram Bingham/National Geographic Creative, (c) Micheal Melford/National Geographic Creative; **76:** (t) © WitR/ Shutterstock.com; **77:** (t) Johnny's photography/Moment/Getty Images; **78:** (tl) FRANS LANTING/National Geographic Creative, (tr) BORGE OUSLAND/National Geographic Creative, (bl) © 7382489561/Shutterstock.com, (br) MIKE THEISS/National Geographic Creative; **79:** (t) James Duncan Davidson/TED, (bl) MIKE THEISS/National Geographic Creative, (bc, br) TED; **81:** (t) RICHARD OLSENIUS /National Geographic Creative, (tl) RALPH LEE HOPKINS/National Geographic Creative, (tr) MIKE THEISS/National Geographic Creative, (bl) SKIP BROWN/National Geographic Creative, (br) PETE MCBRIDE/National Geographic Creative; **82:** (c) Petra Warner and Wolf Park; **84:** (1) © PaulPaladin/Shutterstock.com, (2) © iStockphoto.com/JaminWell, (3) © Steven Frame/Shutterstock.com, (4) Wavebreakmedia Ltd/Thinkstock, (5) Ingram Publishing/Thinkstock, (6) © Forest Badger/Shutterstock.com, (7) © Feng Yu/Shutterstock.com, (8) © bloomua/Shutterstock.com; **86:** (t) Nicole Duplaix/National Geographic Creative, (l) © StepStock/Shutterstock.com; **88:** (1) © iStockphoto.com/ALEAIMAGE, (2) © Edyta Pawlowska/Shutterstock.com, (3) © iStockphoto.com/cveltri, (4) © iStockphoto.com/jallfree, (5) © iStockphoto.com/Atlanta-Mike, (6) Fuse/Thinkstock, (7) © Monkey Business Images/Shutterstock.com, (8) Michael Blann/Digital Vision/Thinkstock; **89:** (t) David Coleman/Alamy; **91:** (c) James Duncan Davidson/TED; (inset) RALPH LEE HOPKINS/National Geographic Creative; **92:** (t) DAVID DOUBILET/National Geographic Creative; **93:** (t) RALPH LEE HOPKINS/National Geographic Creative; **94:** (c) XPACIFICA/National Geographic Creative; **96:** (1) © iStockphoto.com/Danila Krylov, (2) Top Photo Group/Thinkstock, (3) © iStockphoto.com/asiseeit/Steve Debenport, (4) © iStockphoto.com/Digitalskillet, (5) © iStockphoto.com/joxxxxjo, (6) Andrew Olney/Photodisc/Thinkstock, (7) © iStockphoto.com/YinYang, (8) Fuse/Thinkstock; **97:** (b) cotesebastien/iStock/360/Getty Images; **98:** (l) © MrKornFlakes/Shutterstock.com; **99:** (t) Bill Ross/Comet/Corbis; **100:** (1) © Alexander Shalamov/Shutterstock.com, (2) © Jozsef Szasz-Fabian/Shutterstock.com; (3) © iStockphoto.com/Floortje, (4) © Nikolay Postnikov/Shutterstock.com, (5) © iStockphoto.com/Oktay Ortakcioglu, 100 (6) © iStockphoto.com/evemilla, (7) © studioVin/Shutterstock.com, (8) © sunabesyou/Shutterstock.com; **101:** (b) Michael Melford/National Geographic

Creative; **102:** (c) MICHAEL MELFORD/National Geographic Creative; **104:** (t) Detlev van Ravenswaay/Picture Press/Getty Images; **105:** (t) Orjan F. Ellingvag/Dagens Naringsliv/Corbis News Premium/Corbis, (1) © vovan/Shutterstock.com, (2) © Alex Kuzovlev/Shutterstock.com, (3) © iStockphoto.com/WendellandCarolyn, (4) © iStockphoto.com/visdia, (5) Medford Taylor/National Geographic Creative; **106:** (c) Amy Toensing; **110:** (t) Cheryl Chan/Moment Open/Getty Images; **112:** (l) © iStockphoto.com/Jitalia17, (cl) © iStockphoto.com/AlexKalina, (c) © sagir/Shutterstock.com, (cr) © iStockphoto.com/itsjustluck, (r) Photos.com/360/Getty Images; **114:** (l) Luis Marden/National Geographic Creative, (r) oytun karadayi/E+/Getty Images; **115:** (c) Jason Edwards/National Geographic Creative; **116:** (t) Keren Su/Terra/Corbis; **117:** (t) Amy White & Al Petteway /National Geographic Creative; **119:** (t) James Duncan Davidson/TED, (bl, bc, br) TED; **120:** (t) AFP/Stringer/Getty Images; **122:** (c) DAVID DOUBILET/National Geographic Creative; **124:** (1) Jamie Grill/The Image Bank/Getty Images, (2) © iStockphoto.com/Silvrshootr, (3) © iStockphoto.com/enad, (4) © Lukasz Fus/Shutterstoc.com, (5) © iStockphoto.com/DanielBendjy, (6) © iStockphoto.com/digitalskillet, (7) © alicedaniel/Shutterstock.com, (8) ArkReligion.com/Art Directors & TRIP/Alamy, (9) © iStockphoto.com/bloodstone; **126:** (1) 101dalmatians/E+/Getty Images, (2) © iStockphoto.com/Brendan McIlhargey , (3) ©iStockphoto.com/lostinbids/jo unruh; **127:** (t) Brigitte Sporrer/Cultura/Getty Images; **128:** (t) Image Source/Getty Images; **129:** (r) Andersen Ross/Digital Vision/Getty Images; **131:** (r) Roberto Defraia - RobMcfrey/Moment/Getty Images, (inset) David McLain/National Geographic Image Collection; **132:** (t) Thomas Barwick/Iconica/Getty Images; **133:** Atlantide Phototravel/Corbis; **134:** (c) John Burcham/National Geographic Creative; **136:** (1) © Monkey Business Images/Shutterstock.com, (2) © katja kodba/Shutterstock.com, (3) © Sonya etchison/Shutterstock.com, (4) © Anne Kitzman/Shutterstock.com, (5) © iStockphoto.com/jwohlfeil, (6) © iStockphoto.com/Tomaz Levstek, (7) © iStockphoto.com/Klubovy, (8) Andrey Kekyalyaynen/Alamy; **137:** (b) Willie B. Thomas/E+/Getty Images; **138:** (t) IRA Block/National Geographic Creative; **139:** (b) Medford Taylor/National Geographic Creative; **140:** (1) © iStockphoto.com/GlobalStock, (2) Fang Chun Che/Dreamstime.com, (3) © Koh sze kiat /

Shutterstock.com, (4) © iStockphoto.com/Gene Chutka, (5) Eric Audras/PhotoAlto/Alamy, (6) wavebreakmedia Ltd/Thinkstock; **141:** (r) © Songquan Deng/Shutterstock.com; **142:** (inset) RICHARD NOWITZ/National Geographic Creative; **143:** (full) Kenneth Garrett/National Geographic Creative; **144:** (t) NASA/National Geographic Creative, (t) Corbis; **145:** (t) NASA/ESA/National Geographic Creative; **146:** (c) Joshua Holko www.jholko.com; **148:** (tl) Jim Richardson/National Geographic Creative, (c) Eric Audras/PhotoAlto/Alamy; **150:** (t) Towfiqu Photography/Moment/Getty Images; **151:** (tr) Marc Moritsch/National Geographic Creative; **152:** (1) © iStockphoto.com/Angel Herrero de Frutos, (2) © kavram/Shutterstock.com, (3, 4) FRANS LANTING/National Geographic Creative, (5) © marcoap1974/Shutterstock.com, (6) © iStockphoto.com/Ammit, (7) Richard Nowitz/National Geographic Creative, (8) © ShaneGross/Shutterstock.com, (9) Michael S. Quinton/National Geographic Creative, (10) © HonzaHruby/Shutterstock.com; **153:** (tr) FRANS LANTING/National Geographic Creative; **155:** (t) Justin Ide/TED, (inset) Pascal Deloche/Godong/Corbis; **156:** (t) Jeremy Woodhouse/Blend Images/Corbis; **157:** (t) Michele Burgess/Photolibrary/Getty Images; **159:** (t) Justin Ide/TED , (l, rt, rc, rb) TED; **160:** (t) Jason Edwards/National Geographic Creative.
T-216: David Madison/Getty Images; **T-231:** (1) das-foto/Shutterstock.com, (2) Tarasyuk Igor/Shutterstock.com, (3) jennyt/Shutterstock.com, (4) EM Arts/Shutterstock.com

TEXT

50–51: Adapted from "Bugs as Food: Humans Bite Back," by Maryann Mott: National Geographic News Public Website, April 16, 2004, **74–75:** "In the Wonderland of Peru," by Hiram Bingham: National Geographic Magazine, April 1913, **102–103:** Adapted from "Powering the Future," by Michael Parfit: National Geographic Magazine, August 2005, 114–115 Adapted from "Silk: The Queen of Textiles," by Nina Hyde: National Geographic Magazine, November 2005, 130–131 Adapted from "New Wrinkles on Aging," by Dan Buettner: National Geographic Magazine, October 1999

All TED Readings are adapted from information either within TED Talks or on the TED website.

UNIT 1

◀)) 3   **LESSON B, LISTENING**

TV Game Host: Hi, can you tell me something about yourself?

Kyoko: Sure. My name is Kyoko, and I'm Japanese. Actually, I'm from Tokyo.

Host: And what do you do?

Kyoko: I'm an engineer.

Host: Thank you, Kyoko. And here is our next contestant. Can you introduce yourself?

Luis: Yes. My name is Luis, and I'm a doctor. I'm from Lima in Peru.

Host: Thank you, Luis. And welcome to tonight's show.

Contestant Number 3, can you tell us something about yourself?

Jim: Yes, my name is Jim, Jim Waters. I'm a farmer.

Host: And where are you from?

Jim: I'm from a small town in Canada called Coldstone.

Host: Thank you, Jim. And welcome. And now our last contestant for tonight's show comes from Brazil.

Bianca: That's right. I'm Brazilian, my name is Bianca and, as you can see, I'm a musician. I'm from Rio de Janeiro in Brazil.

Host: Everybody ready? The first round is about nationalities. Kyoko, here is your first question. What nationality is a person from Jordan?

Kyoko: Umm ... Jordanese?

Host: No, sorry Kyoko. A person from Jordan is Jordanian.

Host: And now Luis. What nationality is a person from Germany?

Luis: German.

Host: Well done Luis. That's right. A person from Germany is German.

Host: Now Jim. Here's your question. What nationality is a person from Switzerland?

Jim: Hmm. A person from Switzerland is Swiss, I think.

Host: That's right. Swiss is the answer.

Host: And now you Bianca. What nationality is a person from Jamaica?

Bianca: OK. That's easy. Jamaican.

Host: Correct. A person from Jamaica is Jamaican.

◀)) 5   **LESSON B, PRONUNCIATION**

1. I am a teacher.

2. He's an engineer.

3. She's a nurse.

4. They are interesting.

5. You're welcome.

UNIT 2

LESSON B, LISTENING

Helen: Good evening, everyone. Welcome to *Sunday with the Stars*. You all know tonight's guest—it's Bob Hardy, the star of *Life on the Run*. Great to have you here, Bob.

Bob: Thanks, Helen. Great to be here.

Helen: OK, Bob. So, we know what you do during the week. You're a star! But on *Sunday with the Stars* we want to find out what you do in your free time. So, Bob, what do you do on Sundays?

Bob: Well Helen, the simple answer is that I do nothing.

Helen: Nothing! Come on, Bob.

Bob: Nothing. I don't play sports, I don't do any exercise. I just chill out.

Helen: OK, but what time do you get up?

Bob: I get up at about 9 o'clock and have breakfast around 10. In the week I don't have time for breakfast, so on Sunday I have a big breakfast.

Helen: Do you eat in or do you have breakfast in a restaurant?

Bob: I like cooking so I eat at home. Eggs, pancakes—the works! If it's nice out, I'll eat outside.

Helen: And then?

Bob: Then I often take a nap. In the afternoon, I sometimes watch sports on TV.

Helen: Do you like sports?

Bob: Yes. Basketball is my favorite—but I don't play—I just watch.

Helen: OK. So you don't leave the house at *all* on Sundays.

Bob: Oh yes. In the evening, I often go out for dinner with some friends. But I always try to go to bed early. I need to be ready for Monday morning and work.

Helen: OK, we'll go to a commercial break and when we come back, I'm going to find out more about these friends. Back in a minute.

UNIT 3

LESSON B, LISTENING

Conversation 1

Check-in clerk: Good morning. Can I see your ticket and passport, please?

Traveler: I have an e-ticket. Here is the confirmation number.

Check -in clerk: Thank you. Can I see your U.S. visa please?

Traveler: Here it is.

Check in clerk: Window or aisle?

Traveler: Excuse me?

Check in clerk: Would you like a seat next to the window or one next to the aisle?

Traveler: Oh, I see. A window seat, please.

Check in clerk: Do you have any bags to check in?

Traveler: Yes, this one's mine.

Check-in clerk: OK, here's your boarding pass. Your seat number is 18A. We will be boarding at gate number 5 at 2:30. Have a nice trip.

Traveler: Thank you.

Conversation 2

Officer: Good morning. Can I see your passport please?

Traveler: Good morning. Here it is.

Officer: Is this your first time in the United States?

Traveler: Yes it is.

Officer: What is the purpose of your visit?

Traveler: I'm here on vacation.

Officer: How long are you staying?

Traveler: For 2 weeks.

Officer: Where are you staying?

Traveler: I'm staying with friends in Los Angeles.

Officer: Place your left index finger here. Now, the right one. Thank you. Now please, look into the camera. Thank you. OK, that's fine. I hope you enjoy your vacation.

Traveler: Thank you.

Conversation 3

Receptionist: Good evening, sir. Can I help you?

Guest: Yes, I have a reservation. My name is Ken Lee.

Receptionist: Ah yes, Mr. Lee. Just for one night?

Guest: Yes, that's right. Just tonight.

Receptionist: Very good. Could you fill out this form, please?

Guest: Yes, of course.

Receptionist: OK, you have a single room. Number 303, on the third floor. Here is your room key.

Guest: Thank you.

Receptionist: Are those your bags?

Guest: Yes, and they are heavy.

Receptionist: Let me get a bell boy to help you.

Guest: Thank you.

Receptionist: You're welcome. Have a nice stay.

Guest: Thank you

UNIT 4

🔊 16 **LESSON B, LISTENING**

Waiter: Good evening, sir. My name is Walter and I am your waiter this evening.

Man: Good evening, Walter.

Waiter: Are you ready to order, sir?

Man: Can we order drinks first?

Waiter: Yes, of course.

Man: I would like an iced tea, please.

Woman: Do you have any mineral water?

Waiter: Yes, we do.

Woman: OK, I'll have a bottle of mineral water.

Waiter: And would you like an appetizer, madam?

Woman: No thank you, I'll just have a main dish. What would you recommend?

Waiter: The butter-baked chicken is excellent.

Woman: OK, I'll take the chicken.

Waiter: Butter-baked chicken. And for you, sir?

Man: Hmm let me see. Does the filet mignon come with salad?

Waiter: Yes, it does, sir.

Man: OK, I'll have the fillet mignon and the French dressing on my salad.

Waiter: Filet mignon. And how do you like your steak, sir?

Man: Medium, please.

Waiter: Anything else?

Man: No, I don't think so. Thank you.

◀))) 18   LESSON B, PRONUNCIATION

1. /djə æv/ a pen?
2. Would you like some more bread?
3. Do you have any paper?
4. /wʊd dʒə/ like some coffee?
5. /djə æv/ any change?

UNIT 5

◀))) 21   LESSON B, LISTENING

Conversation 1

Mai: Hi, Karen. What are you doing?

Karen: Hi! You'll never guess. I'm ice skating with Alan.

Mai: Ice skating! Wow! Alan doesn't like sports. You guys usually go to the movies on Fridays.

Karen: Not today!

Conversation 2

Lucas: Hi, Khaled. How's the studying going?

Khaled: I'm not studying.

Lucas: What! You usually study in the evening.

Khaled: No, today I'm taking a break. I'm playing basketball with some friends. Hey, can I call you back?

Lucas: Sure. Enjoy your game.

Conversation 3

Luis: Hi, Liam. What's up?

Liam: Hi, Luis. I'm fixing the roof.

Luis: You're fixing the roof! But you usually go to the ball game on Sundays.

Liam: Yes, but it's raining and the roof is leaking. So, no ball game this week.

Luis: Oh, well. Good luck.

🔊 23 **LESSON B, PRONUNCIATION**

1. What are you reading?

2. /wætʃə/ thinking?

3. /wætʃə/ playing?

4. What are you cooking?

5. /wætʃə/ writing?

UNIT 6

🔊 26 **LESSON B, LISTENING**

Mike: Hey, Chen. How was Orlando?

Chen: Great.

Mike: Come on then, tell me all about it! How many theme parks did you visit?

Chen: Hmm, three I think. Let me see. First we went to Disney World and then Universal Studios. Yes, and then Sea World. Yes, three.

Mike: Come on. Tell me more!

Chen: Well, Disney World was OK. I liked the Star Wars Show; that was cool. But I didn't like Sea World. Fish, fish, and more fish.

Mike: But what about Universal Studios? Did you go to the Spider-Man™ ride?

Chen: No, thanks. That's for kids. But I went to the Islands of Adventure. Now that was something. We took a ride called the Incredible Hulk Coaster. I can't describe it. You have to try it for yourself.

Mike: Oh, I would love to. You lucky, guy.

UNIT 7

🔊 3 **LESSON B, LISTENING**

Radio presenter: So that's it for today, folks. It was great to hear your views on the new traffic system in town. Next week's guest is John Parsons, the new chief of police and he'll be talking about his ideas on reducing crime. So why not call us on thirty-four, thirty-six, twenty-nine, eighteen, thirty-four. Do you want to write that down? Got a pen? Here we go—thirty-four, thirty-six, twenty-nine, eighteen, thirty-four.

You can also send us a fax on thirty-four, thirty, fourteen, seventy-six, twenty-two. One more time. That's thirty-four, thirty, fourteen, seventy-six, twenty-two.

We love to get your emails. Send us your views to Kingstownradio@coolmail.com. I'll say it again. It's Kingstownradio, that's all one word at coolmail dot com. OK one more time. Kingstownradio at coolmail dot com.

Send an SMS to 333 317 3476. That's three, three, three, three one seven, three, four, seven, six.

And that old snail mail still works. Our address is Kingstown Radio, 25 Main Street, Kingstown. Again, Kingstown Radio, 25 Main Street, Kingstown.

So, remember next week we'll be talking to the chief of police. I know he'll want to hear your views.

That's all for today from Community Call In. And it's back to the studio.

UNIT 8

◀)) 7 LESSON B, LISTENING

Jun: Hi, Pedro. Great to see you. Welcome to the show.

Pedro: Good to be on your show, Jun.

Jun: So, how's it going? Your last album was a big success. Do you have any plans for another album?

Pedro: Sure. I'm going to record a new album in January.

Jun: And when is it going to be in stores?

Pedro: It's not.

Jun: What! It's not going to be in stores?

Pedro: No. It's going to be Internet download only.

Jun: Wow! We're all looking forward to that. And then?

Pedro: And then I'm going to take a break in the summer.

Jun: So, you're not going to do another world tour?

Pedro: No, not this year. Alicia is going to have a baby in July.

Jun: Congratulations! So, you're going to be a father.

Pedro: Yeah. But it's not going to change my life. I'm still going to be recording and touring.

Jun: And I hear you're going to make a film. Is it true?

Pedro: I think we're going to start filming at the end of the year.

Jun: So, you're already a pop star, and you're going to be a film star and a father.
Nice going.

◀)) 9 LESSON B, PRONUNCIATION

1. When are you /ɡənə/ finish?

2. They're not going to like it.

3. We're going to leave at three thirty.

4. I'm /ɡənə/ take a shower.

5. Are you going to take a taxi?

6. What are you going to do this weekend?

7. I'm not /ɡənə/ go to the meeting?

UNIT 9

◀)) 12 LESSON B, LISTENING

Shop attendant: Can I help you?

Shopper: Yes, I'd like some blue shoes to go with these pants.

Shop attendant: Blue. Let me see. What about these?

Shopper: Do you have anything less formal?

Shop attendant: Yes, these are more casual.

Shopper: I like these. Can I try them on?

Shop attendant: Yes, of course. What size are you?

Shopper: I usually wear a 7 or 7 ½.

Shop attendant: Here we are.

Shopper: Oh! They're a little tight. Do you have a bigger size? An 8?

Shop attendant: Yes. How about these? Are they better?

Shopper: Yes. They're perfect. How much are they?

Shop attendant: They are $150.

Shopper: Hmm. Do you have anything less expensive?

Shop attendant: Something cheaper? Let me see. No, not in blue. What about black?

Shopper: Yes, black might be OK.

Shop attendant: What about these? They're on sale—$75.

Shopper: Hmm. I'm not sure.

Shop attendant: We have some white ones at $80. They'll go with your pants.

Shopper: White? No, I don't like white. I think I'll take the blue ones.

Shop attendant: Fine. Cash or charge?

Shopper: I'll put it on my card.

UNIT 10

LESSON B, LISTENING

Ben: Hi. My name is Ben, I'm 22 years old and I live and work in Los Angeles, California. I'm a very busy real estate agent. Sometimes clients want to see a house at 7 o'clock in the morning and sometimes at 10 o'clock at night, so I can never plan my meals. I just grab a hamburger or hot dog whenever I can and then run off to see the next customer.

I try to go to the gym on Sundays, but sometimes I don't make it. I know I should get more exercise, but I never have the time. And then of course, I smoke. I know I shouldn't and I keep trying to stop, but it's difficult.

Maggie: Hi, my name's Maggie and I'm 70 years old and I come from Winchester in England. In Britain, on your hundredth birthday, the Queen sends you a telegram. That's my ambition, to get a telegram from the Queen. So, I get up early, usually around 6 o'clock and I go to the pool. I love swimming. It's good exercise, but it also helps me to relax. I can plan my day and think through problems as I'm swimming. Then I come home and eat a big breakfast. I think breakfast is the most important meal of the day and I try to eat healthy foods, like whole meal bread, honey, yogurt, high fiber cereal.

The rest of the day I visit friends and take my dogs for long walks. However, I do have one bad habit. I love chocolate. I eat at least one chocolate bar every day. And then there's chocolate cake - mmm I love chocolate.

Anita: Hi, my name's Anita, I'm 35 years old and I have three kids. Bringing up three young kids is a lot of work and I also have a big garden where I grow organic vegetables to sell in the local market. With three kids and a big garden I don't have time to get any regular exercise. But of course, the work in the garden keeps me fit.

Needless to say, we eat a lot of fruit and vegetables from the garden and although we all eat meat, we don't eat much red meat, mainly chicken.

All in all, I think I have quite a healthy lifestyle. However, I do have one bad habit. I drink about 20 cups of coffee a day! I even drink coffee when I'm working in the garden. My husband says I'm just a machine for converting coffee into carrots. Well, at least the carrots are healthy even if the coffee isn't.

UNIT 11

◀)) 21 **LESSON B, LISTENING**

Interview 1

Interviewer: Good morning Miss Harmon. Thank you for coming to the interview.

Miss Harmon: My pleasure.

Interviewer: OK, let's begin. First, have you graduated from college?

Miss Harmon: Oh, yes. I studied English and History.

Interviewer: English and History. Very good. OK. Have you ever traveled abroad?

Miss Harmon: Yes, I think I have visited about eight different countries.

Interviewer: Eight! What is the most interesting place you have visited?

Miss Harmon: Venice! I love Venice. I've been there three times and I never get tired of it—the churches, the museums, the canals, the sense of history. It's amazing!

Interviewer: Very good. Have you worked as a tour guide before?

Miss Harmon: No, not really. I have taken friends around museums that I know well, but I haven't had a paid job as a tour guide.

Interviewer: OK. That's not a problem. Now a practical question: Have you passed your driving test?

Miss Harmon: No, but I've taken driving lessons. I'm going to take my test next month.

Interviewer: OK, and one final general question: Who is the most interesting person you have met?

Miss Harmon: Hmm, that's tricky. I've met a lot of interesting people. Possibly, my father.

Interviewer: Your father! Can you explain?

Miss Harmon: Well, he's worked in so many different places and he's read so much. I really admire him. But then I of course I would—he's my father!

Interviewer: Indeed. OK, thank you very much. We will get back to you on Tuesday. Thank you for coming.

Miss Harmon: Thank you.

Interview 2

Interviewer: Good morning, Mr. Reed. Thank you for coming to the interview.

Mr. Reed: Nice to meet you.

Interviewer: OK. So, let's begin. Have you graduated from college?

Mr. Reed: Yes. I majored in Chemistry.

Interviewer: Chemistry. OK. Now, have you ever worked as a tour guide?

Mr. Reed: Yes, I have. I worked in Disneyland last year. I was one of the guides on the Jungle Cruise. That was cool. I really liked meeting all those people.

Interviewer: Disneyland. Right. Speaking of people, who is the most interesting person you have ever met?

Mr. Reed: The most interesting person I have met. Well, I once met Earle Grave, you know the quarterback for the Bulls. Great guy. I really admire him.

Interviewer: Earle Grave. OK. And have you ever traveled abroad?

Mr. Reed: Er. Abroad? No, it's kind of expensive. But I'd like to.

Interviewer: OK. Have you passed your driving test?

Mr. Reed: Yes.

Interviewer: OK, thank you very much. We'll contact you next Tuesday. Thank you for coming.

Mr. Reed: Sure thing. Thank you for having me.

🔊 23 LESSON B, PRONUNCIATION

1. Has she left?
2. /ævjə/ finished?
3. /æz i:/ read this book?
4. Have you done your homework?
5. I've never been to the USA.

UNIT 12

🔊 26 LESSON B, LISTENING

Travel Agent: Good morning, can I help you?

Businesswoman: Yes. I'm going to Paris on business next month and when I'm there, I would like to visit some friends in London.

Travel Agent: OK, do you have your flight from New York to Paris? If we book both flights New York to Paris and Paris to London together, we can get you a better price.

Businesswoman: No, thank you. I have the New York to Paris flight. And I don't want any more planes! I've never been to England before and if I take a plane, I won't see anything. Just more airports.

Travel Agent: Well, you could rent a car or take the train.

Businesswoman: If I rent a car, I know I'll get lost. No, the train sounds better.

Travel Agent: OK. There are trains leaving Paris every hour.

Businesswoman: If I take the 6 p.m. train, what time will I arrive in London?

Travel Agent: Let me see. You'll arrive in London at 8:15 p.m.

Businesswoman: That sounds great. And how much will it cost?

Travel Agent: Hmm. That will be $175. But if you buy the ticket 2 weeks in advance, there is a discount. It will only cost $150.

Businesswoman: Great. I'll buy the ticket now. Thank you.

Travel Agent: OK, that will be $150.

UNIT 1

VIDEO JOURNAL *THE LAST OF THE WOMAN DIVERS*

NARRATOR: The island of Cheju off the coast of South Korea is famous for its natural beauty. It's also known for a group of women divers called *haenyos*.

These women dive into the sea every day to look for seafood. It's their job, and it's difficult and very dangerous work. They do not use oxygen tanks. They can hold their breath and stay underwater for up to five minutes!

For hundreds of years, the women of Cheju have made their living from the sea. They dive into the cold waters and catch octopus, abalone, and sea urchins. However, these women divers on Cheju may be the last. Things on this small island are changing.

Sunny Hong is different. She isn't a diver. She is a tour guide. She doesn't catch fish. She helps tourists that come to the island.

SUNNY HONG, Cheju tour guide: I wanted to find some kind of job which I can use my English, and also this kind of job is (how can I say) fit my aptitude.

NARRATOR: Sunny speaks English. She doesn't have to dive. However, all the other women in her family are divers.

HONG: This is my aunt, Ms. Hong. She's 63 years old and she started diving when she was thirteen, so almost fifty years now.

NARRATOR: Sunny's aunt and her friends have been diving nearly all of their lives!

HONG: They didn't have a choice. Also, they were born in sea village, so they had to be a woman diver, and there's nothing they can do except woman diver.

NARRATOR: The job is very dangerous. In Cheju, all the divers are women. Men are not divers.

The youngest diver on the island is 45 years old. The oldest is 75. These women dive for five to six hours every day! But, why do they keep diving?

The answer is easy. Sixty-year-old Song Ho has had a good day. She can make up to 300 U.S. dollars in a day! Diving is still a big business in Cheju. The women can use the money to educate their children.

HONG: I don't want to be a woman diver. I think I am lucky.

NARRATOR: The young people of Cheju have more opportunities. Sunny's aunt and her friends may just be the last of the Cheju women divers.

UNIT 2

VIDEO JOURNAL *MONKEY BUSINESS*

NARRATOR: Lopburi, Thailand is famous for its monkeys. Every year, on the last Sunday in November, the Lopburi Inn, a local hotel, sponsors a festival just for the resident macaque monkeys. And there are lots of them. For the Thai people, monkeys are very important. They believe that a monkey called Hanuman helped them in the past.

Nathanicha Kitwatananusont: We believe that Hanuman never dies, so he is a symbol of prosperity and good luck.

NARRATOR: The monkeys even walk around right next to the people. Every day the people from the town bring the monkeys food. But on the day of the festival, they bring a lot of food. The people watch while the monkeys eat all the food. Even the statues of monkeys get food—and a bottle of water.

NARRATOR: The sponsor of all this monkey business, Mr. Yungyut knows how to make an entrance. The first goal of the festival is to bring food to the monkeys.

Prof. Phibul: The second is for the tourists. Every year a lot of people, many people come to Lopburi to see the monkey party.

NARRATOR: The monkeys are very naughty. They eat and play all day and they never take a nap.

Nathanicha Kitwatananusont: You never get them to sit still, that's for sure.

TOURIST: I was kneeling down taking a picture of a monkey and all a sudden the monkey swiped my sunglasses off.

NARRATOR: The monkeys are a problem for the tourists and they are also a problem for the people of Lopburi.

POLICEMAN: I just frighten the monkeys. I don't kill them. Thai people like monkeys. They are not dangerous. But they sometimes cut the electric and telephone cables. That is the problem.

NARRATOR: But the people of Lopburi are happy to live with the monkeys. They like the monkeys and they give them food every day. The monkeys even take food from people's hands. People also wear costumes and decorate the city.

Nathanicha Kitwatananusont: When people come to visit here, you could see a smile on their face.

PROF. PHIBUL: Next year it will be bigger than this year. Sure!

NARRATOR: The people love the monkey party.

UNIT 3

VIDEO JOURNAL *BEAGLE PATROL*

NARRATOR: At the National Detector Dog Training Center in Orlando, Florida, every day has a noisy start.

BRENT HELDT: Hey Guys! Hey Guys! Hey!

NARRATOR: This is especially true for canine instructor Brent Heldt. A half a dozen beagles are waiting for their morning run. The first lucky dog is a beagle called Stockton.

HELDT: Go on, go get it! Go get it!

NARRATOR: Stockton is learning to become a detector dog. Before Heldt and Stockton start work, it is time for play.

HELDT: Come on get some! Come on! Come on!
   Their personalities are all very different. That's what makes this job so cool. I mean, every time I train these guys, I learn something different . . . every time.
We're going to work. Come on, Hoss. You big hoss!

NARRATOR: Detector dogs work in international airports and look for illegal imports like citrus fruits, mangoes, and apples that may carry diseases.
   They also sniff for meat products that may carry diseases. At twenty-one international airports around the United States every day, dogs help to find this food. But the dogs have to to do this without bothering passengers who are bringing home safe and legal gifts for their friends and family. That's where the National Detector Dog Training Center comes in.

HELDT: What we got here is a target box, it's called mixed. The reasons we call it that is because that's exactly what it is. It's mixed odor. We have some beef jerky. I have the beef odor, we have my apple odor, we have a citrus odor, and I have my mango odor. So should we try the bags now? Let's go try the hand bags. Come on.
   What we want the dogs to do, is work the seam of the suitcase because the odor comes out from the seam. What we teach the canine officers and the dogs, when we breathe the bag, odor is coming out of the bag.
   What have you got? Have you got something Stockton? Good boy! You found it, you found the meat! That's a good boy!

NARRATOR: Things don't always go so smoothly for Stockton though. On the next test he lies down when he is supposed to sit. On another, he gets too far ahead of Heldt.

HELDT: Where you going? Wait for me! Stockton, wait for me, Bud! You've got to work with me, I'm your partner remember?

NARRATOR: Even though it's serious work, it always has to be fun for the animal. So what does it take to be a detector dog?

HELDT: Obviously, number one, they have to be great with people and children, because when we work them in the airports, that's what we're working with—-the public coming from foreign countries. They've got to have real good food drive because they work for food. Anybody knows . . . who has a beagle . . . they love food. Even after they eat a big dinner, they're still ready to eat some more.

NARRATOR: However, even after all that training, not all of the dogs are good enough to become detector dogs.

HELDT: For some reason if they don't work out, we place them in homes. They stay with us until we can find a home that suits them and we have applicants on our adoption list all the time. And we screen them to make sure they're also a good fit for the dog that we have.

NARRATOR: But Stockton is learning quickly. Stockton's chances of becoming a detector dog look very good.

HELDT: His demeanor is really meek, he just rolls along kind of like a tortoise. Nothing kind of fazes him. He loves working. It's a game to him, which is really important.
Good job! Good job, very good!

NARRATOR: But when these two partners are working together, it's easy to see that it's not only Stockton who loves his work.

TED TALKS: ERIC WHITACRE, *A VIRTUAL CHOIR 2,000 VOICES STRONG*

NARRATOR: This is Eric Whitacre, a composer and conductor. He has written over 50 pieces of music. He is interested in how music can connect people around the world. Eric launched a project to bring together a "virtual" choir of individual voices from across the globe.

ERIC WHITACRE: Well a couple of years ago, a friend of mine e-mailed me a link, a YouTube link, and said, "You have got to see this." And it was this young woman who had posted a fan video to me, singing the soprano line to a piece of mine called "Sleep."

BRITLIN: Hi, Mr. Eric Whitacre. My name is Britlin Losee, and this is a video that I'd like to make for you. Here's me singing "Sleep." I'm a little nervous, just to let you know. ♪ If there are noises ♪ ♪ in the night ♪

ERIC WHITACRE: I was thunderstruck. Britlin was so innocent and so sweet, and her voice was so pure.
And I had this idea: if I could get 50 people to all do this same thing, sing their parts—soprano, alto, tenor and bass—wherever they were in the world, post their videos to YouTube, we could cut it all together and create a virtual choir. So I wrote on my blog, "OMG OMG." I actually wrote, "OMG," hopefully for the last time in public ever. And I sent out this call to singers. And I made free the download of the music to a piece that I had written in the year 2000 called "Lux Aurumque," which means "light and gold." And lo and behold, people started uploading their videos.

Now I should say, before that, what I did is I posted a conductor track of myself conducting. And it's in complete silence when I filmed it, because I was only hearing the music in my head, imagining the choir that would one day come to be. Afterwards, I played a piano track underneath so that the
singers would have something to listen to. And then as the videos started to come in. . .

This is Cheryl Ang from Singapore.
This is Evangelina Etienne from Massachusetts.
Stephen Hanson from Sweden.
This is Jamal Walker from Dallas, Texas.

There was even a little soprano solo in the piece, and so I had auditions. And a number of sopranos uploaded their parts. I was told later, and also by lots of singers who were involved in this, that they sometimes recorded 50 or 60 different takes until they got just the right take—they uploaded it. Here's our winner of the soprano solo. This is Melody Myers from Tennessee. I love the little smile she does right over the top of the note—like, "No problem, everything's fine."

And from the crowd emerged this young man, Scott Haines. And he said, "Listen, this is the project I've been looking for my whole life. I'd like to be the person to edit this all together." I said, "Thank you, Scott. I'm so glad that you found me." And Scott aggregated all of the videos. He scrubbed the audio. He made sure that everything lined up. This is "Lux Aurumque" sung by the Virtual Choir.

I'll stop it there in the interest of time. Thank you. Thank you. Thank you. So there's more. There's more. Thank you so much.

And I had the same reaction you did. I actually was moved to tears when I first saw it. I just couldn't believe the poetry of all of it—these souls all on their own desert island, sort of sending electronic messages in bottles to each other. And the video went viral. We had a million hits in the first month and got a lot of attention for it. And because of that, then a lot of singers started saying, "All right, what's Virtual Choir 2.0?" And so I decided for Virtual Choir 2.0 that I would choose the same piece that Britlin was singing, "Sleep," which is another work that I wrote in the year 2000—poetry by my dear friend Charles Anthony Silvestri. And again, I posted a conductor video, and we started accepting submissions. This time we got some more mature members. And some younger members.

That's Georgie from England. She's only nine. Isn't that the sweetest thing you've ever seen?
Someone did all eight videos—a bass even singing the soprano parts. This is Beau Autin.

And we just closed submissions January 10th, and our final tally was 2,051 videos from 58 different countries. From Malta, Madagascar, Thailand, Vietnam, Jordan, Egypt, Israel, as far north as Alaska and as far south as New Zealand.

And we also put a page on Facebook for the singers to upload their testimonials, what it was like for them, their experience singing it. And I've just chosen a few of them here. "My sister and I used to sing in choirs together constantly. Now she's an airman in the air force constantly traveling. It's so wonderful to sing together again!" I love the idea that she's singing with her sister. "Aside from the beautiful music, it's great just to know I'm part of a worldwide community of people I never met before, but who are connected anyway." And my personal favorite, "When I told my husband that I was going to be a part of this, he told me that I did not have the voice for it." Yeah, I'm sure a lot of you have heard that too. Me, too. "It hurt so much, and I shed some tears, but something inside of me wanted to do this despite his words. It is a dream come true to be part of this choir, as I've never been part of one. When I placed a marker on the Google Earth Map, I had to go with the nearest city, which is about 400 miles away from where I live. As I am in the Great Alaskan Bush, satellite is my connection to the world."

So two things struck me deeply about this. The first is that human beings will go to any lengths necessary to find and connect with each other. It doesn't matter the technology. And the second is that people seem to be experiencing an actual connection. It wasn't a virtual choir. There are people now online that are friends; they've never met. But, I know myself too, I feel this virtual esprit de corps, if you will, with all of them. I feel a closeness to this choir—almost like a family.

What I'd like to close with then today is the first look at "Sleep" by Virtual Choir 2.0. This will be a premiere today. We're not finished with the video yet.

But we do have the first three minutes. And it's a tremendous honor for me to be able to show it to you here first. You're the very first people to see this. This is "Sleep," the Virtual Choir.

Thank you very, very much. Thank you. Thank you very much. Thank you. Thank you.

UNIT 4

VIDEO JOURNAL *DANGEROUS DINNER*

NARRATOR: Japanese people eat a lot of fish. Every morning many people go to Tsukiji Seafood Market in Tokyo. The most expensive fish, and the most dangerous, is the puffer fish, or as the Japanese call it—*fugu*.

Parts of the puffer fish are poisonous. People who eat the poisonous parts of the fish can die.

However, you can find *fugu* on more than 80 menus in the Asakusa restaurant area of Tokyo. Although it is dangerous, people like to eat *fugu*.

Tom Caradonna is visiting Tokyo because he wants to try *fugu*. Tom and his friend Aki are eating at the Matsumoto restaurant. This famous restaurant is 120 years old. Everyone knows that the restaurant prepares the fish very carefully.

TOM: I've heard stories about people dying you know, trying the *fugu* but it hasn't really concerned me.

NARRATOR: Tom isn't worried but many have died because they ate the puffer fish.

At the Matsumoto restaurant, Chef Hayashi prepares the *fugu*.

CHEF HAYASHI: It'll be fine, don't worry. I've been doing this for 53 years. I took the exam in 1949 and passed it, This is my *fugu* chef license.

NARRATOR: After World War II, many people died from eating *fugu*. Many Japanese people were very hungry, and some looked for food in restaurant trash cans. Sometimes these people found pieces of *fugu*. They cooked the *fugu* and some of them died.

It was a serious problem. So, American General Douglas MacArthur, who led the U.S. forces in Japan, introduced a test. The *fugu* chefs had to take the test and get a license. Chef Hayashi took the test in 1949 and he still has his license. Nevertheless, *fugu* killed 2,500 Japanese people between 1945 and 1975.

HIDENORI KADOBAYASHI, Tokyo Health Department: About 70 percent of the poisonings happen in private homes, where people catch and prepare *fugu* on their own and get poisoned. That's most common.

NARRATOR: At the Tokyo University of Fisheries, Nagashima Tuji studies *fugu* poison carefully. He hopes to develop an anti-toxin, which is a medicine that will stop people from dying because of *fugu* poisoning.

NAGASHIMA: A tiger *fugu* has enough poison to kill 30 people. The poison itself, to give you an idea, is 1,000 times stronger than cyanide.

NARRATOR: *Fugu* toxin is a very strong poison. In fact, one milligram of the toxin is strong enough to kill a person. It kills by paralyzing people's nerves. This means that the person who has been poisoned can't move. It also paralyzes the lungs so that the person can't breathe.

Back in the Matsumoto restaurant kitchen, Chef Hayashi is preparing the *fugu* for Tom and Aki.

HAYASHI: These are the gills. They're poison.

NARRATOR: He warns. Chef Hayashi carefully cuts away the poisonous parts of the fish and throws them out. Then, he cuts the remaining flesh very thinly. Finally, he places the *fugu* on a plate and puts it in the shape of a chrysanthemum. The chrysanthemum is a beautiful flower that's popular in Japan.
   At the table, Aki and Tom are ready to try the *fugu*.

AKI: Still breathing?

TOM: I can still breathe!

NARRATOR: Replies Tom and he continues his meal. A *fugu* meal is usually eight different dishes. These dishes feature *fugu* that is prepared in different ways.

TOM: And I still feel fine.

NARRATOR: Tom's favorite course is the grilled *fugu*, and Aki agrees. At the end of the meal, Tom smiles; he's happy that he's still healthy and breathing.

UNIT 5

VIDEO JOURNAL *CHEESE-ROLLING RACES*

NARRATOR: Around the world there are many unusual sports but cheese rolling is one of the most unusual. Cheese rolling started about 200 years ago in the English town of Brockworth.
   First, the competitors come together at the top of Cooper's Hill. Then someone pushes a very large wheel of cheese down the hill. And after that? The competitors run after it! The cheese rolls down the hill at more than 60 kilometer per hour. The competitors go pretty fast, too! The first person to arrive at the bottom wins. What's the prize? The wheel of cheese—of course! The first winner of the day is Craig Brown, a pub worker. Craig's plan was simple.

CRAIG BROWN: Keep going...and try to get your balance back. It's steeper than you could ever think. You would have to run down there to really believe how steep it is!

NARRATOR: Many people enjoy the cheese rolling races, however they can be dangerous. A few years ago, 30 people were injured in an accident at a race. One of the cheeses rolled down the hill and went into the spectators. It's not just spectators who get injured, competitors do as well- especially when it's cold or there hasn't been much rain.

CHEESE-ROLLING SPECTATOR: It's when the ground is really hard . . . that's when the injuries are going to happen.

NARRATOR: So, why do people enter the race? Are they crazy? One cheese runner thinks they may be.

CHEESE RACER: It is dangerous. If I'm running down . . . must be crazy. Yeah, I must be crazy....

NARRATOR: These cheese racers may be crazy. But every year the crowds keep on cheering, and the competitors keep on running. Is it for the fame? Is it for the fun? We may never know, but it's that more than just cheese that makes people want to win Brockworth's annual cheese rolling race!

UNIT 6

VIDEO JOURNAL *MACHU PICCHU*

NARRATOR: This beautiful, quiet place is covered in sunshine and has mountains all around it. Its name is Machu Picchu. It's sometimes called the lost city of the Inca, and it's nearly 8,000 feet up in the Andes.

JULIO, Tour guide: It's a magic attraction that you can feel here. It's known all over the world that Machu Picchu is one of the magnetic centers of the ancient world.

NARRATOR: Machu Picchu is more than 500 years old. Today, it's a favorite place for visitors from all over the world.
   Even in the rain and fog, it's wonderful to walk through the ruins.
   When the Inca civilization ended, few people knew Machu Picchu existed. For a long time it was lost to the outside world. Then, in 1911, an explorer named Hiram Bingham found it again.
   At first, very few people visited Machu Picchu. But now, hundreds of tourists come here every day. They walk up the steps of the ancient city and climb over the ruins. Machu Picchu is no longer quiet. It's full of the sounds of tourists.

Some people in Peru hope that more tourists will come here. They think it will mean more business and money for the country.

However, some conservationists worry that more visitors won't be good for Machu Picchu. They say that tourism might not be good for the environment.

Jose, a local hotel owner says Machu Picchu and Peru can take a few more visitors.

Jose, Hotel owner: Why not be like the rest of the world? Why not expose and show Machu Picchu to the rest of the world? It's such a wonderful place, why keep it to a few?

NARRATOR: The truth is that parts of Peru are very poor, and tourists bring money to these communities.

Aguas Calientes is a town that grew suddenly near an area where visitors get on buses to get to the summit of Machu Picchu. The people here live completely on money from tourism. The town is just a group of stalls where local people sell art and things they have made to visitors

The Lost City is no longer lost. Tourists have found it. The modern world is coming closer to this ancient world every day.

Time may be running out for the Lost City of the Inca. More and more people are discovering it. In the end, it may be the modern world that forever changes this ancient city.

TED TALKS: LEWIS PUGH, *MY MIND-SHIFTING EVEREST SWIM*

NARRATOR: In 2007, Lewis Pugh swam across the North Pole. He was in water that was only 1.7 degrees Celsius (29 degrees Fahrenheit) for almost 19 minutes. The reason he did this was to bring attention to global warming and how it affects ecosystems. He told himself he'd never do another swim in water that cold again, but then another opportunity to bring attention to his cause presented itself.

LEWIS PUGH: And I remember getting out of the water and my hands feeling so painful and looking down at my fingers, and my fingers were literally the size of sausages because—you know, we're made partially of water—when water freezes it expands, and so the cells in my fingers had frozen and expanded and burst. And the most immediate thought when I came out of that water was the following: I'm never, ever going to do another cold water swim in my life again.

Anyway, last year, I heard about the Himalayas and the melting of the—and the melting of the glaciers because of climate change. I heard about this lake, Lake Imja. This lake has been formed in the last couple of years because of the melting of the glacier. The glacier's gone all the way up the mountain and left in its place this big lake. And I firmly believe that what we're seeing in the Himalayas is the next great, big battleground on this earth. Nearly two billion people—so one in three people on this earth—rely on the water from the Himalayas. And with a population increasing as quickly as it is, and with the water supply from these glaciers—because of climate change—decreasing so much, I think we have a real risk of instability. North, you've got China; south, you've India, Pakistan, Bangladesh, all these countries.

And so I decided to walk up to Mt. Everest, the highest mountain on this earth, and go and do a symbolic swim underneath the summit of Mt. Everest. Now, I don't know if any of you have had the opportunity to go to Mt. Everest, but it's quite an ordeal getting up there. 28 great, big, powerful yaks carrying all the equipment up onto this mountain—I don't just have my Speedo, but there's a big film crew who then send all the images around the world. The other thing which was so challenging about this swim is not just the altitude. I wanted to do the swim at 5,300 meters above sea level. So it's right up in the heavens. It's very, very difficult to breath. You get altitude sickness. I feels like you've got a man standing behind you with a hammer just hitting your head all the time.

And we walked up this pathway, all the way up. And to the right hand side of us was this great Khumbu Glacier. And all the way along the glacier we saw these big pools of melting ice. And then we got up to this small lake underneath the summit of Mt. Everest, and I prepared myself the same way as I've always prepared myself, for this swim which was going to be so very difficult. I put on my iPod, I listened to some music, I got myself as aggressive as possible—but controlled aggression—and then I hurled myself into that water.

I swam as quickly as I could for the first hundred meters, and then I realized very, very quickly, I had a huge problem on my hands. I could barely breathe. I was gasping for air. I then began to choke, and then it quickly led to me vomiting in the water. And it all happened so quickly: I
then—I don't know how it happened—but I went underwater. And luckily, the water was quite shallow, and I was able to push myself off the bottom of the lake and get up and then take another gasp of air. And then I said, carry on. Carry on. Carry on. I carried on for another five or six strokes, and then I had nothing in my body, and I went down to the bottom of the lake. And I don't where I got it from, but I was able to somehow pull myself up and as quickly as possible get to the side of the lake.

I got myself to the side of the lake. My crew grabbed me, and then we walked as quickly as we could down, over the rubble, down to our camp. And there, we sat down, and we did a debrief about what had gone wrong there on Mt.

Everest. And my team just gave it to me straight. They said, Lewis, you need to have a radical tactical shift if you want to do this swim. Every single thing which you have learned in the past 23 years of swimming, you must forget. Every single thing which you learned when you were serving in the British army, about speed and aggression, you put that to one side. We want you to walk up the hill in another two days' time. Take some time to rest and think about things. We want you to walk up the mountain in two days' time, and instead of swimming fast, swim as slowly as possible. Instead of swimming crawl, swim breaststroke. And remember, never ever swim with aggression. This is the time to swim with real humility.

And so we walked back up to the mountain two days later. And I stood there on the edge of the lake, and I looked up at Mt. Everest—and she is one of the most beautiful mountains on the earth—and I said to myself, just do this slowly. And I swam across the lake. And I can't begin to tell you how good I felt when I came to the other side.

But I learned two very, very important lessons there on Mt. Everest, and I thank my team of Sherpas who taught me this. The first one is that just because something has worked in the past so well, doesn't mean it's going to work in the future. And similarly, now, before I do anything, I ask myself what type of mindset do I require to successfully complete a task. And taking that into the world of climate change—which is, frankly, the Mt. Everest of all problems—just because we've lived the way we have lived for so long, just because we have consumed the way we have for so long and populated the earth the way we have for so long, doesn't mean that we can carry on the way we are carrying on. The warning signs are all there. When I was born, the world's population was 3.5 billion people. We're now 6.8 billion people, and we're expected to be 9 billion people by 2050.

And then the second lesson, the radical, tactical shift. And I've come here to ask you today: what radical tactical shift can you take in your relationship to the environment, which will ensure that our children and our grandchildren live in a safe world and a secure world, and most importantly, in a sustainable world? And I ask you, please, to go away from here and think about that one radical tactical shift which you could make, which will make that big difference, and then commit a hundred percent to doing it. Blog about it, tweet about it, talk about it, and commit a hundred percent, because very, very few things are impossible to achieve if we really put our whole minds to it. So thank you very, very much.

UNIT 7

VIDEO JOURNAL *WILD ANIMAL TRACKERS*

NARRATOR: In parts of South Africa, there are still big herds of wild animals like zebras, elephants, and giraffes. But today many of these animals are in danger because people are taking the land that animals need.

Conservationists are people who protect wildlife and nature. And many of them are now leading a fight to save these animals.

Louis Liebenberg is one of these conservationists.

LOUIS LIEBENBERG, Cyber Tracker Inventor: The most important thing is to try and get an understanding of what's happening out there.

NARRATOR: Liebenberg reports that people need to know more about animals. He says that people need to understand what happens to plants and animals over time. Are they increasing or decreasing in numbers? What plants are the animals eating?

For hundreds of years, African Bushmen have been very good wild animal trackers.

They know what the animals eat, where they go, and where they sleep. But, they don't always speak the same language as the conservationists so it can be difficult to communicate

Now, Liebenberg has brought an invention to the Karoo National Park. It's called the Cyber Tracker. He hopes that together, the Cyber Tracker and the Bushmen can help protect the animals.

Liebenberg explains that the Cyber Tracker is a small computer that helps collect information about animals with pictures, called icons, instead of words. That way, the Bushmen can record what they see even without words.

According to Liebenberg, the Cyber Tracker can collect very detailed and complicated information. And it can do it very quickly.

The Cyber Tracker also contains a global positioning device. Each time a Bushman sees something interesting about an animal or plant, he pushes a button. The Cyber Tracker records exactly where the man is. That way, even if the man can't read or write, he can record what he sees and where.

Liebenberg explains that the Cyber Tracker uses icons, or pictures, to communicate. There are pictures for drinking, walking, fighting, sleeping, eating, and other things. The user can report whether an animal is sick or dead, too. The Bushman can also record other meanings by pushing different buttons. With this option, they can name about 50 different plants.

BUSHMAN: Three females, three youngsters and one male.

NARRATOR: Liebenberg adds that the human factor is very important. A big part of using the Cyber Tracker is the Bushman's ability to understand and record what he sees.

When the trackers return to their base, they connect the Cyber Tracker to a personal computer. Then, Liebenberg uses the information to make maps. These maps show where the animal herds are, what they are eating, and what their health is like.

The Cyber Tracker project started five years ago. At first, the idea was to help a few animals in danger. Now, more and more people have started using the Cyber Tracker in African parks, and with different animals.

Recently, Liebenberg put the Cyber Tracker software on the Internet. Many conservationists around the world have started adding the technology to their conservation programs. Soon, the Cyber Tracker may be able to help wild animals everywhere!

UNIT 8

VIDEO JOURNAL *SOLAR COOKING*

NARRATOR: It's a cool, sunny day in Borrego Springs, California and Eleanor Shimeall is cooking food. She isn't using electricity, gas, charcoal, or wood to cook her food. Instead, Shimeall is using the sun to make her lunch.

ELEANOR SHIMEALL, Solar Cook: I'm going to check on this chicken and rice and see how it's cooking. Ah, it's doing a good job.

NARRATOR: In fact, she's made this entire delicious meal with solar power. A solar cooker needs only the light from the sun to cook meat, fish, grains, and vegetables—even if the air temperature isn't very hot. This method is popular with people who are worried about the environment. Solar cooking does not use fossil fuels and it does not cause pollution.

However, in developing countries, solar cookers can save lives.

DR. BOB METCALF, Solar Cookers International: With sunshine you have an alternative to fire. And that's important for two and a half billion people to learn about because they're running out of traditional fuels.

NARRATOR: Dr. Bob Metcalf is a microbiologist and a founding member of Solar Cookers International. Solar Cookers International promotes solar cooking worldwide, especially in the developing countries of Africa. Their goals are to stop deforestation and to make women's lives easier.

METCALF: They have to walk about two to three miles or so to collect wood. And then they have to tend the fire. And the smoke from that fire, it burns their eyes and chokes their lungs.

NARRATOR: According to the World Health Organization, smoke from wood fires causes the deaths of two million women and children each year. More than 22,000 families now cook traditional foods with the sun.

WENDY, Solar Cook: Oh, this is good. It's very good! The consistency is good; the texture is fine. No problem!

SCI WORKSHOP PARTICIPANT: We're all amazed that a cardboard box can cook.

NARRATOR: After each workshop, attendees get their own portable solar cook kits. The simple cookers cost about five dollars and last almost two years.

METCALF: Shiny things direct the sunshine onto a dark pot that then absorbs the sunshine, and changes that light energy into heat energy. And heat energy doesn't get out of the clear plastic bag; it doesn't get out of the window.

NARRATOR: SCI reports that solar cooking is also an effective way to make water pure and safe to drink.

METCALF: Six thousand people a day are going to die of waterborne diseases in developing countries. If you heat water to 65° Celsius, 149° Fahrenheit, you can pasteurize water and make it safe to drink.

NARRATOR: Solar Cookers International has developed a useful measuring tool that helps people to know when water is safe to drink.

METCALF: If the water gets hot enough to melt this wax, the water has reached pasteurization temperatures.

NARRATOR: From Nepal to Nicaragua, solar cooking projects are helping people in nearly every country in the developing world. Solar Cookers International's goal is to increase the use of solar cookers everywhere.

METCALF: Science is supposed to help and benefit all of mankind, and you've got something that is good science that could help two and a half billion people in the world. There's a great need for information that these things work.

SCI WORKSHOP PARTICIPANT: OK, solar cooker!

UNIT 9

VIDEO JOURNAL *HOW YOUR T-SHIRT CAN MAKE A DIFFERENCE*

Cotton is everywhere: in your furniture, in your food, in your wallet, in your closet. Cotton has a major impact on the planet. Take your favorite cotton T-shirt: It takes 2,700 liters of water to make one T-shirt, enough for one person to drink for 900 days. It also takes a lot of energy: to grow, manufacture, transport. Mostly, it needs energy to care of it. One load of drying takes 5x more energy than washing. One load of washing uses 40 gallons of water. Now think how often you wash and dry your T-shirt. Don't we have plenty of resources? Plenty of water? Yes, but . . . 97% is salty, nearly 2% is locked in snow or ice. That leaves less than 1% that we can access and 70% of that grows our crops. Cotton is a very thirsty crop. Now, think how many T-shirts are in your closet/city/country/on the planet. How many T-shirts do you need? How often do you need to wash and dry them? There is a solution. We can use less water & less energy. Skip the drying and ironing and save 1/3 of your T-shirt's carbon footprint. Choices make a difference. Make each choice count.

TED TALKS: DIANA REISS, PETER GABRIEL, NEIL GERSHENFELD, AND VINT CERF, *THE INTERSPECIES INTERNET? AN IDEA IN PROGRESS*

NARRATOR: Using mirrors, Diana Reiss proved that dolphins can recognize themselves and using computers she proved that dolphins can organize their own learning and use human technology to communicate. Does this mean that animals can communicate with humans or other animals? Let's pick up with Diana Reiss and then learn about her partners in a very exciting project called The Interspecies Internet.

DIANA REISS: Other animals are conscious. They're emotional. They're aware. There have been multitudes of studies with many species over the years that have given us exquisite evidence for thinking and consciousness in other animals, other animals that are quite different than we are in form. We are not alone. We are not alone in these abilities. And I hope, and one of my biggest dreams, is that, with our growing awareness about the consciousness of others and our relationship with the rest of the animal world, that we'll give them the respect and protection that they deserve. So that's a wish I'm throwing out here for everybody, and I hope I can really engage you in this idea.

NARRATOR: Peter Gabriel is a famous musician, who describes his amazing encounter with scientist Sue Savage-Rumbaugh and her research subjects, a type of ape called bonobo.

PETER GABRIEL: I make noises for a living. On a good day, it's music, and I want to talk a little bit about the most amazing music-making experience I ever had.

I'm a farm boy. I grew up surrounded by animals, and I would look in these eyes and wonder what was going on there?

What was amazing to me also was they seemed a lot more adept at getting a handle on our language than we were on getting a handle on theirs. I work with a lot of musicians from around the world, and often we don't have any common language at all, but we sit down behind our instruments, and suddenly there's a way for us to connect and emote.

So I started cold-calling, and eventually got through to Sue Savage-Rumbaugh, and she invited me down. I went down, and the bonobos had had access to percussion instruments, musical toys, but never before to a keyboard. At first they did what infants do, just bashed it with their fists, and then I asked, through Sue, if Panbanisha could try with one finger only.

SUE SAVAGE-RUMBAUGH: Can you play a grooming song? I want to hear a grooming song. Play a real quiet grooming song.

PETER GABRIEL: So groom was the subject of the piece.

So I'm just behind, jamming, yeah, this is what we started with. Sue's encouraging her to continue a little more.

She discovers a note she likes, finds the octave. She'd never sat at a keyboard before. Nice triplets.

SUE SAVAGE-RUMBAUGH: You did good. That was very good.

PETER GABRIEL: She hit "good."

So that night, we began to dream, and we thought, perhaps the most amazing tool that man's created is the Internet, and what would happen if we could somehow find new interfaces, visual-audio interfaces that would allow these remarkable sentient beings that we share the planet with access? And Sue Savage-Rumbaugh got excited about that, called her friend Steve Woodruff, and we began hustling all sorts of people whose work related or was inspiring, which led us to Diana, and led us to Neil.

NEIL GERSHENFELD: Thanks, Peter.

NARRATOR: Neil Gershenfeld is a scientist who works on combining the digital and physical worlds. He is one of the creators of the $1 web server, which has changed the way people use the Internet. It has allowed many people to do inexpensive but valuable research on health care and energy efficiency. His work has helped a lot of people.

NEIL GERSHENFELD: We started up this Interspecies Internet project. Now we started talking with TED about how you bring dolphins and great apes and elephants to TED, and we realized that wouldn't work. So we're going to bring you to them. So if we could switch to the audio from this computer, we've been video conferencing with cognitive animals, and we're going to have each of them just briefly introduce them. And so if we could also have this up, great.

So the first site we're going to meet is Cameron Park Zoo in Waco, with orangutans. In the daytime they live outside. It's nighttime there now. So can you please go ahead?

TERRI COX: Hi, I'm Terri Cox with the Cameron Park Zoo in Waco, Texas, and with me I have KeraJaan and Mei, two of our Bornean orangutans. During the day, they have a beautiful, large outdoor habitat, and at night, they come into this habitat, into their night quarters, where they can have a climate-controlled and secure environment to sleep in. We participate in the Apps for Apes program Orangutan Outreach, and we use iPads to help stimulate and enrich the animals, and also help raise awareness for these critically endangered animals.

NEIL GERSHENFELD: That's great. When we were rehearsing last night, he had fun watching the elephants. Next user group are the dolphins at the National Aquarium. Please go ahead.

ALLISON GINSBURG: Good evening! Well, my name is Allison Ginsburg and we're live in Baltimore at the National Aquarium. Joining us our 3 of our 8 Atlantic bottlenose dolphins: 20-year-old Chesapeake, who was our first dolphin born here, her 4-year-old daughter Bailey, and her half-sister, 11-year-old Maya. Here at the National Aquarium we are committed to excellence in animal care, to research, and to conservation. The dolphins are pretty intrigued as to what's going on here tonight.

NEIL GERSHENFELD: And the third user group, in Thailand, is Think Elephants. Go ahead, Josh.

JOSH PLOTNIK: Hi, my name is Josh Plotnik, and I'm with Think Elephants International, and we're here in the Golden Triangle of Thailand with the Golden Triangle Asian Elephant Foundation elephants. And we have 26 elephants here, and our research is focused on the evolution of intelligence with elephants, but our foundation Think Elephants is focused on bringing elephants into classrooms around the world virtually like this and showing people how incredible these animals are.

NEIL GERSHENFELD: Okay, that's great. Thanks Josh. And once again, we've been building great relationships among them just since we've been rehearsing. So at that point, if we can go back to the other computer, we were starting to think about how you integrate the rest of the biomass of the planet into the Internet, and we went to the best possible person I can think of, which is Vint Cerf, who is one of the founders who gave us the Internet. Vint?

VINT CERF: Thank you, Neil. That was beautiful. Forty years ago, Bob Kahn and I did the design of the Internet. Thirty years ago, we turned it on. Just last year, we turned on the production Internet.

When Bob and I did this design, we thought we were building a system to connect computers together. What we very quickly discovered is that this was a system for connecting people together. And what you've seen tonight tells you that we should not restrict this network to one species, that these other intelligent, sentient species should be part of the system too. This is the system as it looks today, by the way. This is what the Internet looks like to a computer that's trying to figure out where the traffic is supposed to go.

Well, you know where this is headed. The Internet of Things tell us that a lot of computer-enabled appliances and devices are going to become part of this system too: appliances that you use around the house, that you use in your office, that you carry around with yourself or in the car.

NARRATOR: With the Internet of Things, appliances and devices and other things are going to be connected to the Internet. People will want to communicate with all these devices, but using natural human language like everyday speech and gestures instead of through keyboards or mice. So, people are starting to explore communication with something that is not human. Thinking beings other than people will be connected.

VINT CERF: Now, there is a project that's underway called the interplanetary Internet. It's in operation between Earth and Mars. It's operating on the International Space Station. It's part of the spacecraft that's in orbit around the Sun that's rendezvoused with two planets. So the interplanetary system is on its way, but there's a last project, which the Defense Advanced Research Projects Agency, which funded the original ARPANET, funded the Internet, funded the interplanetary architecture, is now funding a project to design a spacecraft to get to the nearest star in 100 years' time. What that means is that what we're learning with these interactions with other species will teach us, ultimately, how we might interact with an alien from another world. I can hardly wait.

UNIT 10
VIDEO JOURNAL *SCIENCE OF STRESS*

ALYSSA: Hello, good morning . . . how was your sleep?

NARRATOR: Six o'clock in the morning and the stress of everyday life begins . . . Family . . . Home . . . Work . . . Over and over again . . . This kind of stress actually gives us energy to get through the day.

But doing it day after day can damage our bodies.

To find out what all that stress is doing to a body . . . let's go to the Neuro-endocrinology lab at Arizona State University.

Kathy Matt and her team of researchers are trying to find out what stress does to our bodies.

DR. KATHY MATT, Arizona State University: Stress good or bad is not just psychological, it's physiological as well.

NARRATOR: So, your body produces chemicals, called hormones, when you feel stress.

MATT: In these samples, we are measuring cortisol which is a stress hormone.

NARRATOR: The hormones that your body produces give you energy so that you can manage the stress.

Dr. Matt explains that there are two types of stress. Physical stress, like running and mental stress, like too much work. In physical stress your body burns the hormones. In mental stress your body doesn't burn all the hormones.

TECHNICIAN: Put this over your head.

NARRATOR: The effects of physical stress on the body are easy to measure . . .

TECHNICIAN: I'm going to take you up 2 ½ percent . . . ok?

NARRATOR: As the speed of the treadmill goes up, so does the heart rate and breathing.

TECHNICIAN: All right here we go. . .

NARRATOR: Right now the hormones in the blood are rising higher and higher.

TECHNICIAN: Here you go all you got . . .

NARRATOR: This woman is releasing many hormones and using all of the energy they create.

TECHNICIAN: Good job, way to go!

NARRATOR: So she passes the first test. Her body deals with physical stress pretty well. But what about mental stress?

TECHNICIAN: It's vital that you perform at your highest level for each of the tests.

NARRATOR: With the pressure on . . .

TECHNICIAN: Come on Alyssa as fast as you can . . .

NARRATOR: The heart races . . . The blood pressure soars . . .

TECHNICIAN: God I hate the 8s. I can't do the 8 times table.

NARRATOR: Again those stress hormones are kicking in.

ALYSSA: eight . . .

NARRATOR: When you are under long term mental stress, your body produces hormones all the time, but it doesn't burn the extra fuel . . . and that leads to all sorts of problems.

ALYSSA: I want you to put your fingers straight down.

TECHNICIAN: This machine checks if your bones are in good shape. If you have too many hormones in your blood, you can have problems with your bones.

Other studies show that long term stress can lead to diabetes, heart disease and neurological diseases.

TECHNICIAN: Here's your bone density. So you're really right on this norm.

NARRATOR: So far so good. She shows no long-term effects from mental stress . . . yet. But that doesn't mean she can just ignore it . . .

This means that if you do lots of exercise it will burn up the hormones and your body won't have so many problems from mental stress. And remember, not all stress is bad. Every now and then we need a good dose of those hormones to help us get to the end of the day.

UNIT 11

VIDEO JOURNAL *SPACEWALK*

NARRATOR: From inside a spacecraft, the Earth and space look beautiful. But outside the spacecraft—in space—it is a different and far more dangerous world. There is no oxygen to breathe and there is dangerous radiation. Also temperatures can drop to minus 120 degrees Celcius and rise to 120 degrees Celsius. But man has conquered this environment.

In order to survive in space, astronauts have to wear space suits. The space suits are made from a very strong material and it is filled with oxygen so the astronauts can breathe.

The first person to leave a spacecraft and "walk" in space was Soviet Cosmonaut, Alesksy Leonov, in 1965. He "walked" in space for 12 minutes. A few months later, astronaut Edward White became the first American to walk in space during the Gemini IV mission.

These early spacewalks were intended to discover if it is possible for man to survive in deep space. They were successful—man *can* survive in space. Now spacewalks are an everyday part of the space shuttle missions.

Astronauts take spacewalks in order to do jobs that they can't do from inside the shuttle. For example, they have fixed the solar panels on the Hubble Space Telescope and they are the construction workers for the International Space Station.

But still, spacewalks are dangerous. Astronauts work in pairs so if one astronaut has problems, the other astronaut can help. They are connected to the spacecraft so that they cannot float off in to space and lose contact with the spacecraft.

It is not easy to work in a space suit. It is difficult to hold tools in the big gloves. Also the astronauts are weightless and this makes it difficult to work as well.

So, how can the astronauts practice their spacewalks on Earth before they go into space?

The answer is—underwater. At NASA's Neutral Buoyancy Laboratory, the astronauts can practice jobs that they will later do in space. Their space suits are adjusted so that they do not sink to the bottom of the tank or float to the top of the water—they are weightless. They spend a lot of time practicing in the tank. For every hour that they will spend walking in space, they spend 10 hours practicing underwater.

As NASA moves forward on the maintenance and construction of the International Space Station, spacewalks will continue to be important.

UNIT 12

VIDEO JOURNAL *THE MISSING SNOWS OF KILIMANJARO*

NARRATOR: Mount Kilimanjaro is often called the roof of Africa. It rises 19,340 feet, or nearly four miles, into the sky and is the highest point on the African continent. Kilimanjaro is in northeastern Tanzania in East Africa. It lies almost exactly between the cities of Cairo, Egypt, to the north and Cape Town, South Africa, to the south. It's around 220 miles south of the equator, in a hot, tropical region of the world.

The impressive snow-covered peaks of Kilimanjaro have been an inspiration to visitors for a very long time. Over the years, thousands of people have traveled to Tanzania to climb this majestic mountain. Many others have come to view its famous glacier-covered peak. One of these visitors was an American writer named Ernest Hemingway. He wrote a story about the mountain that made it famous. The story, first published in 1936, is called 'The Snows of Kilimanjaro'. In the story, Hemingway describes the mountain's glaciers as "wide as all the world," "great," "high," and "unbelievably white in the sun."

Although the ice cap is fantastic to see, it does in fact have a much more important purpose. The glaciers were formed more than 11,000 years ago. They have become an important source of water for drinking and farming for people who live near Kilimanjaro. Unfortunately, for the last 100 years the snows of Kilimanjaro have been disappearing.

Since 1912, Kilimanjaro's glaciers have gotten more than 80 percent smaller. A NASA satellite has been taking pictures of the mountain's ice cap for more than 15 years. The pictures that were taken in 1993 are very different from those taken only seven years later, in the year 2000.

There are many ideas about why Kilimanjaro's snow is melting so quickly. For one thing, the mountain is in a tropical region, so the glaciers are at risk for the negative effects of climate change. One type of climate change that may be directly affecting Kilimanjaro is called global warming. This worldwide problem is causing a gradual increase in the earth's temperature. As the world's temperatures rise, the snows melt.

Deforestation is another possible reason why Kilimanjaro's glaciers are melting. When trees are cut down in large numbers, the effects can cause changes in the atmosphere and the climate. Trees keep the air cooler and help maintain the water levels in the atmosphere. This helps to create clouds and rain and snow. Less rain and snow and increased temperatures can cause the glaciers to melt.

Whatever the causes may be, the snows of Kilimanjaro are continuing to melt at a very fast rate. Experts now predict that the mountain's glaciers could completely disappear by the year 2020. The loss of Kilimanjaro's glaciers would likely cause many problems for the area around the mountain. It would remove an important source of water for the people who live on or near the mountain. It could also reduce the number of tourists who come to Tanzania to see the mountain, and the money that they bring to the country.

The missing snows of Mount Kilimanjaro may be a warning. They definitely show people all over the world the dangers of climate change and deforestation. Hopefully people will learn from the loss of Kilimanjaro's glaciers. Sadly, the majestic snows of Kilimanjaro may not be around forever for people to enjoy.

TED TALK: MICHAEL NORTON, *HOW TO BUY HAPPINESS*

NARRATOR: This is Michael Norton, a business school professor. He's interested in the idea that "money can't buy happiness." Is this true? Michael's research and experiments actually show that money actually show that money can buy happiness—if you spend it in certain ways.

Michael Norton: Maybe the reason that money doesn't make us happy is that we're always spending it on the wrong things, and in particular, that we're always spending it on ourselves. And we thought, I wonder what would happen if we made people spend more of their money on other people. So instead of being antisocial with your money, what if you were a little more prosocial with your money? And we thought, let's make people do it and see what happens. So let's have some people do what they usually do and spend money on themselves, and let's make some people give money away, and measure their happiness and see if, in fact, they get happier. So the first way that we did this. On one Vancouver morning, we went out on the campus at University of British Columbia and we approached people and said, "Do you want to be in an experiment?" They said, "Yes." We asked them how happy they were, and then we gave them an envelope. And one of the envelopes had things in it that said, "By 5:00 pm today, spend this money on yourself." So we gave some examples of what you could spend it on. Other people, in the morning, got a slip of paper that said, "By 5:00 pm today, spend this money on somebody else." Also inside the envelope was money. So some people got this slip of paper and $5. Some people got this slip of paper and $20.

We called them up at night and asked them, "What'd you spend it on, and how happy do you feel now?" What did they spend it on? Well these are college undergrads, so a lot of what they spent it on for themselves were things like earrings and makeup. One woman said she bought a stuffed animal for her niece. People gave money to homeless people. Huge effect here of Starbucks. So if you give undergraduates $5, it looks like coffee to them and they run over to Starbucks and spend it as fast as they can. But some people bought a coffee for themselves, the way they usually would, but other people said that they bought a coffee for somebody else. So the very same purchase, just targeted toward yourself or targeted toward somebody else. What did we find when we called them back at the end of the day? People who spent money on other people got happier. People who spent money on themselves, nothing happened. It didn't make them less happy, it just didn't do much for them. And the other thing we saw is the amount of money doesn't matter that much. So people thought that $20 would be way better than $5. In fact, it doesn't matter how much money you spent. What really matters is that you spent it on somebody else rather than on yourself. We see this again and again when we give people money to spend on other people instead of on themselves.

The specific way that you spend on other people isn't nearly as important as the fact that you spend on other people in order to make yourself happy, which is really quite important. So you don't have to do amazing things with your money to make yourself happy. You can do small, trivial things and yet still get these benefits from doing this.

Almost everywhere we look we see that giving money away makes you happier than keeping it for yourself. What about your work life, which is where we spend all the rest of our time when we're not with the people we know. We decided to infiltrate some companies and do a very similar thing. So these are sales teams in Belgium. They work in teams; they go out and sell to doctors and try to get them to buy drugs. So we can look and see how well they sell things as a function of being a member of a team. Some teams, we give people on the team some money for themselves and say, "Spend it however you want on yourself," just like we did with the undergrads in Canada. But other teams we say, "Here's 15 euro. Spend it on one of your teammates this week. Buy them something as a gift or a present and give it to them. And then we can see, well now we've got teams that spend on themselves and we've got these prosocial teams who we give money to make the team a little bit better. The reason I have a ridiculous piñata there is one of the teams pooled their money and bought a piñata, and they all got around and smashed the pinata and all the candy fell out and things like that. A very silly, trivial thing to do, but think of the difference on a team that didn't do that at all, that got 15 euro, put it in their pocket, maybe bought themselves a coffee, or teams that had this prosocial experience where they all bonded together to buy something and do a group activity. What we see is that, in fact, the teams that are prosocial sell more stuff than the teams that only got money for themselves. And one way to think about it is for every 15 euro you give people for themselves, they put it in their pocket, they don't do anything different than they did before. You don't get any money from that. You actually lose money because it doesn't motivate them to perform any better. But when you give them 15 euro to spend on their teammates, they do so much better on their teams that you actually get a huge win on investing this kind of money.

And I know that what you're all thinking about are dodgeball teams. This was a huge criticism that we got to say that if you can't show with dodgeball teams, this is all stupid. So we went out and found these dodgeball teams and infiltrated them. And we did the exact same thing as before. So some teams, we give people on the team money, they spend it on themselves. Other teams, we give them money to spend on their dodgeball teammates. The teams that spend money on themselves are just the same winning percentages as they were before. The teams that we give the money to spend on each other, they become different teams and, in fact, they dominate the league by the time they're done.

Across all of these different contexts—your personal life, your work life, even silly things like intramural sports—we see spending on other people has a bigger return for you than spending on yourself. And so I'll just say, I think if you think money can't buy happiness you're not spending it right. The implication is not you should buy this product instead of that product and that's the way to make yourself happier. It's in fact, that you should stop thinking about which product to buy for yourself and try giving some of it to other people instead.

UNIT 1 PEOPLE

Lesson A

A. 2. politician 3. dancer 4. chef 5. police officer 6. pilot 7. travel agent 8. journalist

B. 2. Jordanian 3. Irish 4. Japanese 5. Australian 6. Peruvian 7. Mexican 8. Answers will vary.

C. 2. I am from 3. you are 4. Are you 5. Are you 6. I am not 7. I am 8. are you 9. I am 10. That is *OR* Rio de Janeiro is

Lesson B

A. 2. Yes 3. Are you 4. I'm not 5. I am 6. years old *OR* blank 7. your name 8. I am 9. Are you 10. I'm not 11. Are you 12. it is

B. 2. she's 3. it's 4. you're 5. isn't 6. we're

Lesson C

A. 2. d 3. f 4. e 5. c 6. a

B. Answers will vary.

C. 1. My 2. Her 3. Their 4. your 5. His 6. his

D. 1. What is your name? 2. Where are you from? 3. What do you do? 4. Is your work interesting? Answers to the questions will vary.

Lesson D

A. 1. F 2. T 3. F 4. T 5. F 6. T 7. F 8. T

B. 1. Natsuko Mori 2. Moses Agba 3. Natsuko Mori 4. Michael Murphy 5. Shaukat Ali 6. Michael Murphy 7. Moses Agba 8. Shaukat Ali

C. Answers will vary.

D. Answers will vary.

REVIEW

A. Across 4. dangerous 6. rich 7. Canadian 10. Mexican 13. difficult 14. boring 16. are

Down 1. French 2. Korean 3. His 5. occupation 7. am 9. teacher 10. my 11. pilot 12. from 15. is

B. Answers will vary.

UNIT 2 WORK, REST, AND PLAY

Lesson A

A. 2. f 3. d 4. h 5. i 6. b 7. l 8. g 9. e 10. k 11. a 12. c

B. Answers will vary.

C. 1. at, in 2. in 3. on 4. on *OR* at 5. at, in 6. on

D. Answers will vary.

Lesson B

A. 2. What time do you get up on Sundays 3. What do you do in the morning? 4. Do you take a nap on Sunday afternoon? 5. Do you take a nap on Sunday afternoon? 5. Do you go to the movie in the evenings? Answers to the questions will vary.

B. Answers will vary.

C. Answers will vary.

Lesson C

A. 1. celebrate 2. decorate 3. present 4. mask 5. fireworks 6. costume

B. never, sometimes, often, usually, always

C. 1. I usually visit my family on Thanksgiving. 2. American Independence Day is always on July 4. 3. We never work on New Year's Day. 4. It is usually cold in winter. 5. We often give presents to our friends.

D. Answers will vary.

Lesson D

A. 1. The Netherlands, Iran, China 2. The Netherlands, China 3. The Netherlands, China 4. Iran, China 5. China 6. The Netherlands 7. The Netherlands, Iran, China

B. Answers will vary.

C. Answers will vary.

REVIEW

A. Across 3. goes 6. takes 7. catch 9. presents 11. in 12. free 13. eat 15. mask 16. on

Down 1. visits 2. watch 4. take 5. decorate 7. costume 8. festival 10. out 12. fun 14. at

B. Answers will vary.

UNIT 3 GOING PLACES

Lesson A

A. 1. buy 2. pack 3. take 4. check 5. go 6. buy 7. board 8. claim 9. go 10. go

B. Answers will vary.

Lesson B

A. 1. c 2. d 3. f 4. a 5. b 6. e

B. 1. Torres 2. Claudia 3. July 1, 1988 4. Buenos Aires 5. Argentinean 6. Argentina 7. Metro City 8. 118 Beach Road, Metro City 9. March 8th/March 12th 10. business

C. 2. passport, visa, and ticket. 3. get up, take a shower, and read the newspaper. 4. China, Japan, Korea, and Thailand

Lesson C

A. 1. passport 2. credit card 3. visa 4. airline ticket 5. international driver's license 6. cash 7. travel insurance

B. Answers will vary.

C. 1. Should I rent a car? 2. Should I take a warm coat? 3. Should I get travel insurance 4. Should I take lots of money? 5. Should I take a credit card? Answers to these questions will vary.

Lesson D

A. 1. F 2. F 3. T 4. T 5. F 6. F 7. F 8. T

B. 1. good idea 2. good idea 3. good idea 4. bad idea 5. bad idea 6. good idea 7. good idea 8. good idea

C. Answers will vary.

REVIEW

A. Across 2. them 3. pack 9. him 10. immigration 11. should 13. yours 14. Whose

Down 1. visa 2. take 3. passport 4. credit 5. through 6. mine 7. license 8. insurance 14. ours

B. 2. your 3. airline tickets 4. shouldn't 5. should 6. credit card 7. pack 8. check in 9. security 10. board.

UNIT 4 FOOD

Lesson A

A. 1. milk 2. coffee 3. lettuce 4. juice 5. apples 6. bananas 7. cheese 8. tea 9. steak 10. chicken 11. shrimp 12. potato 13. tomato 14. onions 15. fish 16. eggs

B. 1. some 2. any 3. any 4. a 5. any 6. some 7. any 8. some

C. Answers will vary.

Lesson B

A. 1. Are you ready to order? 2. What would you recommend? 3. The chicken is excellent. 4. Does the chicken come with salad? 5. Yes, it does. 6. I'll have the chicken and a baked potato. 7. Would you like anything else? 8. I would like a glass of mineral water.

B. Answers will vary.

Lesson C

A. 1. popcorn 2. bagel 3. broccoli 4. hamburger 5. cereal 6. nuts 7. hot dog 8. radish

B. Answers will vary.

C. Possible answers: 2. How many apples do you eat? 3. How much cereal do you eat? 4. How many bagels do you eat? 5. How much popcorn do you eat?

D. Answers will vary.

Lesson D

A. coddle, potatoes, shepherd's pie, boxty

B. 1, 2, 5, 4, 3

C. 1. F 2. T 3. T 4. F 5. T

D. Answers will vary.

REVIEW

A. Across 1. much 4. little 6. meat 7. some 10. dairy products 11. waiter 13. matter 14. diet 15. lots of 16. many

Down 2. customer 3. few 5. vegetables 8. fruit 9. protein 10. drinks 12. any 16. mind

B. Answers will vary.

UNIT 5 SPORTS

Lesson A

A. 1. hiking 2. climbing 3. taking a break 4. swimming 5. playing soccer 6. jogging 7. lifting weights

B. Possible answers: 2. What are they doing? / They're playing soccer. 3. What is she doing? / She's rock climbing. 4. What is he doing? / He's jogging. 5. What are they doing? / They are hiking. 6. What is he doing? / He is lifting weights.

C. Answers will vary.

Lesson B

A. 1. go ice skating 2. play basketball 3. watch a ball game 4. study 5. watch a movie 6. fix the roof

B. 2. On Mondays, Eric goes to his office. Today he is sleeping late. 3. On Mondays Ms. Tyson teaches classes. Today, she is swimming at the Sports Center. 4. On Mondays, Yuki and Yoko are studying English. Today, they are taking a break. 5. On Mondays, Mr. Kim drives a bus. Today, he is watching a ball game.

C. 1. am sitting 2. see 3. is working 4. am visiting 5. are looking 6. talking 7. is cooking

Lesson C

A. 1. football 2. volleyball 3. ice hockey 4. baseball 5. golf 6. gymnastics 7. diving 8. skateboarding

B. 2. am watching 3. do you like 4. don't know 5. are running 6. is throwing 7. are shouting 8. cost 9. don't want 10. hate 11. prefer 12. are you doing

C. Answers will vary.

Lesson D

A. *Row 1.* Soccer; of all ages, a ball, a place to play, an international
Row 2. Canada; ice hockey, drink hot chocolate, famous hockey teams on TV.
Row 3. Baseball; slow, interesting, friends, hot dogs
Row 4. China, Volleyball; school, offices, volleyball indoors or outdoors, expensive equipment

B. Answers will vary.

REVIEW

A. Across 2. break 3. go 5. cook 6. too 7. swimming 9. neither 13. indoor 15. climbing 16. am studying 17. know

Down 1. weights 4. team 5. costs 8. individual 10. equipment 11. prefers 12. jogging 14. play

B. Answers will vary.

UNIT 6 DESTINATIONS

Lesson A

A. 1. visit 2. take a 3. check in 4. rent 5. take 6. unpack 7. buy

B. 2. helped 3. took 4. asked 5. needed 6. flew 7. said 8. went 9. bought 10. traveled 11. knew 12. left 13. played 14. told 15. ate 16. learned

C. 2. We went to India. 3. Where did you fly to? 4. We Flew to New Delhi. 5. Then we took a train to Agra. 6. What did you do in Agra? 7. We visited the Taj Majal. 8. Did you like it? 9. We went to some great restaurants.

Lesson B

A. 1. went to the hotel. 2. On Tuesday, I visited the Eiffel Tower. 3. On Wednesday, I saw all the famous paintings in the Louvre Museum. 4. On Thursday, I took a boat trip on the Seine River. 5. On Friday, I watched artists in Montmartre and had dinner in a French restaurant. 6. On Saturday, I went shopping at a famous department store and bought souvenirs. 7. On Sunday I went to the airport. Then returned home.

B. Possible answers: 1. Where did you go? 2. How long did you stay? 3. What did you visit (or see) and eat? 4. What did you buy? 5. Did you like Buenos Aires?

Lesson C

A. 2. fascinating 3. horrible 4. spotless 5. exhausting 6. filthy 7. huge

B. Answers will vary.

C. 2. weren't, was 3. was, were 4. was, weren't 5. were, weren't

D. 1A. Was 1B. wasn't, was 2A. Were 2B. I wasn't, I was 3A. Was 3B. he wasn't, He was

Lesson D

A. 1. b 2. b 3. a 4. b

B. 1. ☺ 2. ☹ 3. ☺ 4. ☹ 5. ☹ 6. ☺ 7. ☺

C. Answers will vary.

REVIEW

A. Across 3. went 5. take 6. horrible 8. visit 11. huge 12. amazing 14. spotless 15. saw 16. said 17. filthy 18. fascinating

Down 1. left 2. rent 4. flew 7. exhausting 9. souvenirs 10. took 13. bought

B. Answers will vary.

UNIT 7 COMMUNICATION

Lesson A

A. 1. e-mail 2. text message 3. social media 4. fax 5. letter 6. smartphone 7. newspaper ad

B. Answers will vary.

C. 1. me 2. her 3. them 4. him 5. it 6. you 7. us

D. Answers will vary.

Lesson B

A. 2. eighty-four 3. twenty-three 4. ninety 5. forty-one 6. twelve 7. fifty-six 8. thirty-five 9. sixty-eight 10. eighteen 11. seventy 12. forty-three

B. 1. e-mail address 2. phone number 3. mailing address

C. Answers will vary.

Lesson C

A. 1. smell 2. taste 3. sight 4. hearing 5. touch

B. 1. g 2. c 3. d 4. e 5. f 6. b 7. h 8. a

C. 1. sounds 2. tastes 3. look 4. smells 5. feels 6. looks

D. Answers will vary.

Lesson D

A. They hear messages: dogs, cats, people, birds They see messages: bees They smell messages: wolves, dogs, cats They touch messages: horses, chimpanzees

B. 1. flowers and other places with food 2. smell 3. Cats 4. friends 5. sound

C. Answers will vary.

REVIEW

A. Across 5. bought 7. text 8. taste 10. sound 14. mailing 15. her 17. phone 18. look

Down 1. sent 2. wrote 3. found 4. got 6. hearing 9. touch 11. smell 12. him 13. sight 16. feel

B. 2. text message 3. e-mail 4. social media 5. smartphone

UNIT 8 MOVING FORWARD

Lesson A

A. 1. h 2. f 3. c 4. a 5. d 6. g 7. e 8. b

B. 2. They're not going to stay home. 3. They're going to pack their suitcases 4. They're not going to get to the airport late. 5. He's going to take an important test. 6. He's going to study very hard. 7. He's not going to play computer games. 8. He's not going to see his friends.

C. 1. What are you going to have for dinner? 2. Where are they going to be? 3. When is she going to leave? 4. Who is going to help you?

Lesson B

A. Possible answers: 2. They are going to take a bath. 3. I am going to eat breakfast. 4. I am going to go shopping. 5. They are going to watch TV. 6. We are going to have a party.

B. Possible answers: Questions: 2. Are you going to do anything special this weekend? 3. What are you going to do Saturday? 4. Where are you going to go on Sunday? 5. Who are you going to see this weekend? 6. What are you going to watch on TV? 7. Are you going to spend time with your family? 8. Are you going to study English this weekend?

C. Answers will vary.

Lesson C

A. 1. sunny, hot 2. it will be raining, windy 3. it will be overcast, cold

B. White Beach: sunhat, sun glasses, swimsuit. Metro City: umbrella, rubber boots, raincoat. Martinville: sweater, scarf.

C. 1. Will it be warm on your birthday? 2. No, it will be cold. 3. Then, you will not have your birthday party outdoors. 4. Of course, we will be outdoors. We will wear sweaters and scarves. 5. Okay! I will buy you a new scarf for your birthday.

D. Answers will vary.

Lesson D

A. homework, universities, classrooms, computers, jobs, lessons, tests

B. 1. No 2. Yes 3. Yes 4. No 5. No 6. Yes 7. Yes 8. Yes

C. Answers will vary.

REVIEW

A. Across 3. overcast 5. laundry 8. cold 10. going to 12. rubber boots 13. swimsuit 15. sweater 18. raincoat

Down 1. won't 2. wet 4. sunglasses 6. short-term 7. fluently 11. long-term 14. will 16. windy 17. hot

B. Answers will vary.

UNIT 9 TYPES OF CLOTHING

Lesson A

A. 1. jeans 2. blouse 3. pants 4. tie 5. suit 6. skirt 7. handbag 8. gloves 9. coat 10. belt 11. sneakers 12. jacket

B. 1. new 2. cheap 3. light 4. formal 5. hand-made 6. cool

C. 2. Sneakers are more comfortable than shoes. 3. These jeans are more informal than a suit. 4. This hat is better than that hat. 5. A shirt is thinner than a sweater. 6. This blouse is prettier than that blouse. 7. The black coat is cheaper than the blue coat. 8. Leather shoes are more expensive than plastic shoes.

Lesson B

A. 1. Can I help you? 2. What size are you? 3. What about this sweater? 4. How much is it? 5. Do you have anything a little less expensive? 6. Can I try it on?

B. 2. easier 3. more casual 4. larger 5. more interesting 6. more handsome 7. worse 8. more expensive 9. heavier 10. thinner 11. warmer 12. nicer

C. Answers will vary.

Lesson C

A. 1. wash 2. bleach 3. dry 4. iron 5. dry clean

B. Answers will vary.

C. 1. the easiest 2. the strongest 3. the smoothest 4. the most comfortable 5. the warmest 6. the worst

D. 1. I think it is the most beautiful place in our country. 2. It is the best restaurant in our city. 3. He/She is the best athlete in the world. 4. It is the most interesting show on TV now. 5. It is the biggest problem in the world today.

Lesson D

A. 1. a. see pictures of T-shirts 2. c. words and pictures 3. c. Customers 4. c. six 5. b. a week

B. 1. $22, 2. $18, 3. $14, 4. $28

C. Answers will vary.

D. Answers will vary.

REVIEW

A. Across 10. cotton 11. pajamas 12. most beautiful 14. bigger 16. better 17. thick 18. gloves

Down 1. best 2. nicest 3. worst 4. boots 5. handmade 6. expensive 7. prettiest 8. casual 9. hat 13. slippers 15. silk

B. Answers will vary.

UNIT 10 LIFESTYLES

Lesson A

A. 1. f 2. a 3. b 4. d 5. g 6. e 7. c

B. 1. suggestion 2. obligation 3. suggestion 4. advice 5. obligation 6. advice

C. Answers will vary.

D. Answers will vary.

Lesson B

A. 1. go, unhealthy 2. get, healthy 3. eat, unhealthy 4. spend, unhealthy 5. work, healthy 6. drink, unhealthy 7. play, unhealthy

B. Answers will vary.

Lesson C

A. 1. mouth-watering 2. home made 3. heart warming 4. life long 5. stress-free 6. over worked 7. low-calorie

B. 1. How old are you? 2. How long will you study English today? 3. How much junk food do you eat? 4. How often do you exercise? Answers to these questions will vary.

C. 1. often do you 2. How much do you play basketball every day? 3. Do you spend much time at home? 4. How old are you? 5. How many are in your family?

Lesson D

A. 1. no information 2. bad 3. no information 4. good 5. bad 6. good 7. no information 8. bad

B. Answers will vary.

C. Answers will vary.

REVIEW

A. Across 4. could 6. long 8. lifelong 11. stress-free 13. improve 15. often 16. much

Down 1. overworked 2. balanced 3. junk food 5. lifestyle 7. homegrown 12. should 15. ought 16. many

B. Answers will vary.

UNIT 11 ACHIEVEMENTS

Lesson A

A. 1. pay 2. cut 3. put away 4. buy 5. walk 6. iron 7. vacuum, sweep

B. 2. won 3. had 4. meet 5. go 6. swept 7. been 8. buy 9. taken 10. tell 11. pay 12. drunk 13. put 14. said 15. read 16. spoken

C. 1. haven't finished 2. Have you cleaned 3. I've vacuumed 4. haven't washed 5. haven't swept. 6. Have you done 7. I have 8. haven't walked

Lesson B

A. 2. Have you taken classes in business administration? 3. Have you had experience working in hotels? 4. Have you traveled to other countries? 5. Possible answer: Have you gotten (got) a driver's license?

B. 2. She hasn't taken any classes in business administration. 3. She has worked as a secretary. 4. She has lived in Italy for 5 years. 5. She has failed the driver's license test. 6. He has been a student at Eastern University. 7. He has majored in business administration. 8. He has worked in a restaurant. 9. He has traveled to Japan, Korea, and China. 10. Possible answer: He has gotten (got) his driver's license.

C. Answer will vary.

Lesson C

A. 1. c 2. f 3. d 4. a 5. b 6. f

B. 1. has traveled, went 2. has finished 3. passed 4. has met 5. have known 6. started 7. has written 8. ran

C. Answer will vary.

Lesson D

A. 1. scientist 2. ALS 3. wheelchair 4. computer 5. the beginning of the universe

B. 1. famous books/scientific papers 2. the greatest scientist in the world 3. written many important 4. prizes 5. been in 6. on television 7. traveled to countries 8. in space

C. Answer will vary.

REVIEW

A. Across 2. went 6. spoken 7. have seen 9. marathon 11. interview 13. groceries 15. graduate 16. promotion

Down 1. have had 3. taken 4. drunk 5. been 8. achievement 10. ever 12. eaten 14. abroad 15. gone 16. put

B. Answers will vary.

UNIT 12 CONSEQUENCES

Lesson A

A. 1. expenses 2. budget 3. lend 4. save 5. overspends 6. income 7. borrow 8. interest rates

B. 1. eat, will lose 2. lend, won't (will not) get 3. will learn, read 4. will get, work out 5. buy, won't (will not) have 6. won't (will not) be, doesn't save

C. 1. If I study hard I'll get a good grade. 2. If I go to bed late, I'll feel tired tomorrow.

Lesson B

A. 1. $1,185, 2. His income is less than his total budget. 3. rent, food in restaurants, and movies, concerts, and clubs. 4. Movies, concerts, clubs, and food in restaurants

B. Answer will vary.

C. Answer will vary.

Lesson C

A. 1. camel, desert 2. shark, coral reef 3. mountain goat, mountains 4. elephant, grasslands 5. monkey, rain forest

B. 2. If you travel in the desert, you won't need a raincoat. 3. If we cut down the rain forests, monkeys won't have a home. 4. If people use the grasslands for farms, elephants will have to live in zoos. 5. If you go to the mountains, you will see mountain goats.

C. 2. You won't need a raincoat if you travel in the desert. 3. Monkeys won't have a home if we cut down the rain forests. 4. Elephants will have to live in zoos if people use the grasslands for farms. 5. You will see mountain goats if you go to the mountains.

D. Answers will vary.

Lesson D

A. 1. Rainforest Hotel, Coral Reef Ship, Mountain Camp 2. Coral Reef Ship 3. Rainforest Hotel 4. Mountain Camp 5. Rainforest Hotel, Coral Reef Ship, Mountain Camp 6. Rainforest Hotel

B. Answers will vary.

C. Answers will vary.

REVIEW

A. Across 3. save 4. lend 5. will 7. consequence 14. grassland 15. shark 16. decide 18. transportation

Down 1. overspend 2. coral reef 6. income 8. expenses 9. habitat 10. borrow 11. budget 12. desert 17. If

B. Answers will vary.

Reasons for Writing

The Writing Program reinforces and complements the lessons in the Student Book. Writing gives students a chance to reflect on the English they've learned and to develop an indispensable academic skill.

The Writing Syllabus

The Writing Activities help students to develop all the building blocks of good writing: words, logical connectors, sentences, transitions, paragraphs, and short essays. As students progress through the levels of the **World English** series, the Writing Activities progress from the word and sentence level to the paragraph and composition level, allowing students to master the basics before they're asked to do more complex writing tasks.

The Writing Activities help students move from sentences to paragraphs as they show relationships between ideas and add detail and precision to their writing with descriptive adjectives.

Writing from Models vs. Process Writing

When students are provided with writing models—examples of completed writing tasks—they have a clear idea of what is expected from them as well as a model on which to base their own writing. Such models give students confidence and a sense of direction and can be found at all levels of the Writing Worksheets.

On the other hand, writers must also learn the writing process. They must generate ideas, plan their writing, perform the writing task, then polish their writing by revising and editing. The Writing Worksheets support process writing by providing activities to stimulate thinking, useful topics and vocabulary, graphic organizers for planning, and opportunities for students to share and refine their writing.

Ways to Use the Writing Program

In general, the Writing Activities are designed to be used after the class has covered all or most of a unit in the Student Book. The Writing Activities often contain grammar, vocabulary, and ideas from the units, which give students solid linguistic and conceptual ground to stand on.

On the other hand, it's not necessary to complete the Lesson D Writing task in the Student Book before using the Writing Activity for that unit. The worksheets complement the writing lessons in the Student Book, but can be used independently.

- **In-Class Discussion**

  Discussion is an important way to stimulate thinking and to help students generate ideas they can use in their own writing. When an activity contains a preliminary matching or listing activity, for example, ask students to share and explain their answers. Ask specific questions about the writing models in order to check comprehension and to elicit opinions about the topics. And be sure to take advantage of opportunities for students to discuss their writing with you and their classmates.

- **Homework**

  Most of the Writing Activities are appropriate for self-study as long as follow-up discussion and feedback are provided later.

- **Vocabulary Practice**

  Many of the Writing Activities contain target vocabulary from the corresponding unit in the Student Book. Ask students to locate vocabulary from the unit in the writing models, or check comprehension by asking students to explain vocabulary words in the context of the worksheet.

- **Grammar Reinforcement**

  Many of the Writing Activities require the use of grammar points found in the Student Book units, and using the grammar in context supports real language acquisition.

- **Pronunciation Practice**

  Although oral skills are not the focus of the Writing Activities, you can do choral repetition of the word lists in the worksheets or use the writing models to practice pronunciation points from the Student Book. Students can also do read-alouds of their finished writing in pairs or small groups while the teacher monitors their pronunciation.

- **Personalization**

  When students complete unfinished sentences, paragraphs, and essays, or when they do less controlled original writing, they bring their personal thoughts and experiences into the classroom and take ownership of the writing task as well as the language they are learning.

- **Real Communication**

  Since the real-world purpose of writing is to communicate, be sure to respond not only to linguistic and technical aspects of student writing, but also to students' ideas. Make comments and ask questions that show genuine interest, either in class or when you collect and give written feedback on the worksheets.

	Writing Tasks	Language Focus
UNIT 1 E-mail Message	• Use *be* in statements and questions • Identify countries, nationalities, and occupations • Use descriptive adjectives	*Are you a new student?* *I'm Chilean.* *Is this class interesting?*
UNIT 2 Describe a Celebration	• List daily activities • Use the simple present tense with *first, next, then,* and *finally* • Write about a celebration	*On my day off, I usually visit friends.* *In the evening, we watch fireworks.*
UNIT 3 Travel Tips	• Practice using pronouns to show possession • Use *should* and other expressions to give travel tips	*These are my keys. They belong to me.* *When you visit my country, you should always . . .*
UNIT 4 Restaurant Menu	• Use *some* and *any* to talk about eating habits • Answer questions with *How much?* and *How many?* • Create a restaurant menu	*In the morning, I usually eat some eggs.* *How much should the appetizers cost?*
UNIT 5 What Are They Doing?	• Use the present continuous and stative verbs to write about what people are doing	*Haley is walking on the beach. She prefers not to play sports.* *Jim is probably talking on the phone right now.*
UNIT 6 Describe a Place	• Write about your childhood • Describe a favorite childhood place	*When I was a child, I went to Cairo with my family.* *My favorite place was the park near our house.*
UNIT 7 Chain of Events	• Use verbs with direct and indirect objects to describe a chain of events • Use sensory verbs to give your opinion	*Tara sent an e-mail to Brian.* *To me, violin music sounds wonderful.*
UNIT 8 Plans and Predictions	• Use *be going to* to write about short-term and long-term plans • Use *will* to make predictions	*This afternoon, I'm going to write some emails.* *She will probably look for a job.*
UNIT 9 Similarities and Differences	• Compare clothing styles in the present and the past • Write a conversation about shopping for clothes	*My father wore tighter jeans than I do.* *Let's get Henri a sweater.*
UNIT 10 Lifestyle Advice	• Answer *How…?* questions • Write about ways to make your lifestyle healthier	*How much junk food do you eat?* *I should walk to school more often.*
UNIT 11 Bullet-Point List	• Write about past achievements • List the steps to a future goal • Use the present perfect tense to chart your progress	*My team won first place in a math competition.* *I have already applied to three universities.*
UNIT 12 Cause and Effect Story	• Write sentences using the real conditional • Use *so* to describe cause-and-effect relationships	*If you buy a camera, you won't be able to buy a plane ticket.* *Mike didn't want to rent a car, so they took the train.*

UNIT 1 PEOPLE

AN E-MAIL MESSAGE

A Read and complete the conversation.

Miguel: Hi, _____I'm_____ Miguel.

Jean: Hi, Miguel. I'm _____.

Miguel: Nice to meet you, Jean.

Jean: Nice to meet you, too. _____ you a new student?

Miguel: Yes, I am. I'm from Mexico.

Jean: Oh, you're _____! I'm from here. I'm Chilean.

Miguel: I see. Tell me, _____ this class interesting?

Jean: Yes, it is, and the teacher is nice.

Miguel: Oh, good. _____ is the teacher from?

Jean: Mr. Ortiz? He's _____ Argentina.

✓ Read the conversation again and complete the chart.

Name	Miguel		Mr. Ortiz
Country			Argentina
Nationality	Mexican	Chilean	
Occupation		student	teacher

✓ Write sentences about these people. Give the information in parentheses.

1. **(occupation) This is Mr. Ortiz.** _He's a teacher_____.

2. (nationality) This is Jean. _____.

3. (country) This is Miguel. _____.

4. (name) _____. She's from Chile.

5. (occupation) This is Miguel. _____.

6. (name) _____. He's Argentinean.

B Complete the e-mail message. Choose any descriptive adjective from the box.

> happy   interesting   boring   good   difficult   dangerous   bad

From: Miguel Hernandez
To: Alberto Ochoa
Subject: my new home

Hi Alberto,

Well, I'm in Chile, and I'm very _____! I really like the place and the people. On the first day of class, I talked to Jean. She's very _____. She knows a lot about my new school. We have a/n _____ teacher named Mr. Ortiz. His class is _____, but I like it. On the other hand, my sister doesn't like our new home. According to her, life here in Chile is _____. I hope she changes her opinion soon!

Your friend,

Miguel

UNIT 2 WORK, REST, AND PLAY

DESCRIBE A CELEBRATION

A What do you do on a work/school day? What do you do on your day off when you have free time? Use phrases from the box and some of your own phrases.

get up	go to school	take a nap	do homework	visit friends
catch the bus	go to work	go to bed	go to the movies	go shopping

On a work/school day . . .	On my day off . . .
• I get up at _____.	•
•	•
•	•
•	•

✓ Take turns. Ask a partner these questions. Answer with information from the chart.

1. What do you usually do on a work day?
2. What do you usually do on your day off?

✓ Write about your usual work day OR your usual day off.

On my usual (work day/day off), I do several things. First, I _____. Next, I _____. Then, I _____. Finally, I _____.

B Which festival or celebration do you enjoy? Answer these questions.

1. What's the name of the festival or celebration? (my birthday, Songkran, etc.)

   _____

2. What do you usually do during that festival or celebration . . . in the morning?
   _____ in the afternoon?
   _____ in the evening?

   _____

✓ Write about the festival or celebration.

One of my favorite things to celebrate is _____. In the morning, _____. Then, in the afternoon, _____. Finally, in the evening, _____.

It's a lot of fun!

UNIT 3 GOING PLACES
TRAVEL TIPS

A Fill in each blank with the correct pronoun. Use the pronouns for the words in the chart.

me	you	Bob	you and me	Melissa	Lynn and Steve
keys	a camera	a passport	plane tickets	a purse	a suitcase

1. These are _____my_____ keys. They're _____mine_____. They belong to _____me_____.
2. This is _____ camera. It's _____. It belongs to _____.
3. This is _____ passport. It's _____. It belongs to _____.
4. These are _____ plane tickets. They're _____. They belong to _____.
5. This is _____ purse. It's _____. It belongs to _____.
6. This is _____ suitcase. It's _____. It belongs to _____.

✓ Read the paragraph below and fill in each blank with the correct pronoun.

B Write a list of travel tips for someone who wants to visit your country.

When you visit my country

- You should always _____
- You should never _____
- It's a good idea to _____
- While you're here, you will need _____
- And don't forget to bring your _____
- Most importantly, you should _____

UNIT 4 FOOD
RESTAURANT MENU

A List some things you might eat and drink in one day.

morning	_____
afternoon	_____
evening	_____
night	_____

✓ Write sentences about your daily diet. Use the information from the chart.

1. In the morning, I usually eat some _____, and I usually drink some _____.

2. In the morning, I never eat any _____, and I never drink any _____.

3. In the afternoon, I usually eat some _____, and I usually drink some _____.

4. In the afternoon, I never eat any _____, and I never drink any _____.

5. In the evening, I usually eat some _____, and I usually drink some _____.

6. In the evening, I never eat any _____, and I never drink any _____.

7. At night, I usually eat some _____, and I usually drink some _____.

8. At night, I never eat any _____, and I never drink any _____.

B Imagine you are going to open a new restaurant. Answer these questions, then create a menu.

1. How many appetizers should be on the menu? _____

2. How much should the appetizers cost? _____

3. How many main dishes should be on the menu? _____

4. How much should the main dishes cost? _____

5. Should your menu have a few dishes for people on special diets? _____

6. Should your menu have a few desserts? _____

Menu

UNIT 5 SPORTS
WHAT ARE THEY DOING?

A What do you think the people are doing? Write a name next to each activity.

> Haley   Scott   Alejandro   Lucy   Aimi   Yi-Chen

_____ is walking on the beach.   _____ is playing soccer.

_____ is lifting weights.   _____ is taking a break.

_____ is swimming in the pool.   _____ is playing basketball.

✓ Write sentences about the people above. Use stative verbs and some of the words and phrases from the box. Use some of your own ideas, too.

stative verbs	**likes** (to be outdoors/indoor sports/quiet activities)
	has (a lot of sports equipment/a lot of free time)
	prefers (outdoor sports/individual sports/not to play sports)
	thinks (sports are wonderful/it's the best sport)
	seems (happy/tired/relaxed)
	feels (terrific/energetic/exhausted)

1. Haley *thinks* _____

2. Scott _____

3. Alejandro _____

4. Lucy _____

5. Aimi _____

6. Yi-Chen _____

✓ Put your sentences together. For example, write:

Haley is walking on the beach. She prefers not to play sports.

B Make a list of important people in your life. What is each person probably doing right now? Then complete the journal entry below.

> *Today is _____. I'm writing in my journal and thinking*
> *about people in my life. First, there's _____. (He/She) is probably*
> *_____ right now. Next, there's _____.*
> *Finally, there's _____. _____.*
> *I think _____.*

UNIT 6 DESTINATIONS

DESCRIBE A PLACE

A How was your life when you were a child?

When I was a child . . .

1. I wanted _____

2. I didn't want _____

3. I went

_____

4. I didn't go _____

5. I learned _____

6. I didn't learn _____

> **What did you want when you were a child?**

> **What did you not want when you were a child?**

✓ Take turns. Ask a partner questions about the sentences above.

B When you were a child, what was your favorite place to be? (e.g. your family's kitchen; a park near your house; your grandmother's farm; etc.) Answer these questions about that place.

1. What was your favorite place? _____

2. Why did you like that place? _____

3. How did you get there? _____

4. What did you do there? _____

5. What did you see, hear, and feel in your favorite place? _____

✓ Write about your favorite place when you were a child. Use some of the information above.

My Favorite Childhood Place

When I was a child, my favorite place was _____. I liked it because

_____. I usually went there _____.

While I was there, I usually _____.

I could (see/hear/feel) _____

and _____. It was wonderful to be there!

UNIT 7 COMMUNICATION
CHAIN OF EVENTS

A Look at the diagram below. How did Sanjay hear the news? Write sentences with indirect objects.
(In 1-4, write each sentence two different ways.)

Tara *sent an e-mail*	→	Brian *sent a text message*	→	Daniel *wrote a letter*	→	Sophia *told Melanie the news*	→	Melanie *gave a phone call*	→	Sanjay *heard the news!*

1. a. *Tara sent Brian an e-mail.*

   b. *Tara sent an e-mail to Brian.*

2. a. _____

   b. _____

3. a. _____

   b. _____

4. a. _____

   b. _____

5. a. _____

✓ Ask a partner questions about the sentences above. How did each person get the news?

How did Brian get the news?

Tara sent him an e-mail.

✓ Write a paragraph with the title: *How Sanjay heard the news.* Use these sequence words: *First, Next, Then, After that, Finally.*

B What's your opinion? Use adjectives from the box or your own ideas. Then write two new sentences.

wonderful	sweet	horrible	salty	bad	delicious	interesting	nice	terrible

1. To me, pizza tastes _____.

2. To me, running for an hour feels _____.

3. To me, violin music sounds _____.

4. To me, some modern art looks _____.

5. To me, gasoline smells _____.

6. To me, learning a new language feels _____.

7. To me, _____

8. To me, _____

UNIT 8 Moving Forward

PLANS AND PREDICTIONS

A What are your plans? Use some of the words from the box and some of your own ideas.

| graduate | eat lunch | buy a car | write some emails |
| do homework | get married | travel | go shopping |

my short-term plans	my long-term plans

✓ Write sentences about your plans. Use *be going to* and future expressions such as *Tonight, Next week, In two years, When I'm thirty*, etc.

I have several short-term plans. This afternoon, I'm going to _____

_____

_____

I also have some long-term plans. Next year, I'm going to _____

_____

_____

B What will probably happen? Make predictions using *will*.

1. Muriel needs some money. She knows how to program computers, and she's a very good cook.
What will she do? She will probably look for a job. Computer programmers make more money than cooks, so she probably won't look for a restaurant job.

2. Tony lives in London, but his family lives in Rome. He misses them. What will he do?

_____

_____

3. It's winter and you're in Antarctica. A major storm is moving across the ocean. What will happen when the storm hits? _____

_____

4. Paula is going to play soccer this afternoon. Last night, she didn't sleep. What will happen?

_____

_____

UNIT 9 TYPES OF CLOTHING
SIMILARITIES AND DIFFERENCES

A What do you usually wear? What did your parents wear at your age? Draw two pictures—one of you, and one of your mother or father at your age.

+------------------------+------------------------+
+------------------------+------------------------+

✓ Write sentences about the clothes in the pictures. What's the same? What's different? Use some of the words from the box and some of your own ideas.

| shorter | less expensive | more colorful | more old-fashioned | tighter |
| less formal | lighter | more modern | more beautiful | longer |

1. _My father wore tighter jeans than I do. I prefer looser jeans._

2. _____

3. _____

4. _____

5. _____

6. _____

B Henri's birthday is next week. Gina and Tom are shopping for a gift. Finish their conversation.

Gina: Let's get Henri a sweater. He's always cold.

Tom: I don't know. These sweaters are expensive. Let's _____.

Gina: That's a good idea, but _____.

Tom: You're right. How about some _____?

Gina: Hmm. I don't really like those.

Tom: Oh! Let's get him _____.

Gina: That's a great idea!

Tom: Henri will love (it/them) because _____.

UNIT 10 LIFESTYLES

LIFESTYLE ADVICE

A Answer these questions about your lifestyle.

Your Diet

1. How much junk food do you eat? _____

2. How often do you eat fruits and vegetables? _____

Your Exercise Habits

3. How much walking do you do? _____

4. How often do you get exercise or play sports? _____

Your Health Habits

5. How well do you handle stress? _____

6. How often do you spend time with family and friends? _____

B How could you improve your lifestyle? Write down some ideas.

suggestions (just ideas)	advice (recommendations)	obligation (necessities)
I could . . .	I should . . . I ought to . . .	I must . . . I have to . . .

C Write a page in your journal. Use the modals and some of your ideas from the chart in exercise **B**.

> Dear diary,
>
> I really want to make my lifestyle healthier, and I've thought of some things I can do. First, I
>
> _____.
>
> Second, I _____.
>
> In addition, I _____.
>
> Most importantly, I _____.
> These lifestyle changes will make me a healthier person, and they might help me live longer, too.

✓ Read your journal page to a partner. Then give each other suggestions for other lifestyle changes.

Those are great ideas!

You could also eat breakfast every day.

UNIT 11 ACHIEVEMENTS

BULLET-POINT LIST

A Write about your achievements. What are you proud of? When did these things happen?

Example: *In the 6th grade, my team won first place in a math competition.*

1. _____
2. _____
3. _____
4. _____
5. _____

B Check the things you hope to do in the future.

_____ buy a house   _____ get a credit card   _____ graduate from a university

_____ travel abroad   _____ have children   _____ start my own business

_____ get a job   _____ run in a marathon   _____ (other) _____ _____

✓ Choose one of your goals from the list above. Make a bullet-point list of things you must do in order to achieve that goal.

> **Goal:** _____
>
> **Things I must do to achieve my goal:**
>
> - _____
> - _____
> - _____
> - _____
> - _____

✓ Make a bullet-point list to show your progress. What have you already done to achieve your goal? What do you still need to do? Use the present perfect tense.

I have already . . .	**I haven't yet . . .**
• _____	• _____
• _____	• _____
• _____	• _____
• _____	• _____

UNIT 12 CONSEQUENCES
CAUSE AND EFFECT

A What will (or won't) happen? Finish the sentences.

Example: *If you buy a camera, you won't be able to buy a plane ticket.*

1. If you save your money now, you _____

2. If you take the train, you _____

3. If you argue with your friend, _____

4. If you eat a sandwich now, _____

5. If people continue to overfish, _____

6. If the number of people in the world continues to increase, _____

B We can use *so* to show causes and effects.

Example: <u>Riley bought a camera</u>, so <u>he doesn't have enough money for a plane ticket</u>.
        cause   **effect**

✓ Complete the sentences. Use *so* to show the effects.

1. Susan has a lot of money in the bank, so _____

2. We're going to take the train, so _____

3. I argued with my best friend, so _____

4. I ate a sandwich a few minutes ago, so _____

5. People are continuing to overfish, so _____

6. The number of people in the world is continuing to increase, so _____

C Write a story about two friends who took a vacation together. What did they do? Where did they go? Use your imagination, and use *so* to show causes and effects.

Example: *Mike didn't want to rent a car, so they took the train.*

WORLD ENGLISH COMMUNICATION ACTIVITIES

	Goals	Language Focus
UNIT 1 People	• Talk about people	*Her/his name is _____.* *S/he's from _____.* *S/he's a(an) _____.*
UNIT 2 Work, Rest, and Play	• Describe an unusual celebration • Share your ideas with the class	*It's called _____. It's for _____.* *People always . . . on _____.*
UNIT 3 Going Places	• Deciding what to take on a trip • Limiting travel needs to one suitcase	*I think we should take . . .* *Don't take . . .*
UNIT 4 Food	• Completing a menu • Ordering meals at a restaurant	*Do you have . . .* *Would you like . . .*
UNIT 5 Sports	• Planning a sports center • Organizing activities at a new sports center	*I think . . .* *I prefer . . .* *We need . . .*
UNIT 6 Destinations	• Improving a TV travel commercial with emphatic adjectives • Developing a TV travel commercial	*. . . was outstanding!* *. . . was fascinating/amazing enormous!*
UNIT 7 Communication	• Interpreting symbols • Creating signs from symbols	*What does this mean?* *It looks like a sign for . . .*
UNIT 8 Moving Forward	• Making predictions about the future • Choosing the best predictions	*_____ is going to . . .* *_____ will . . .*
UNIT 9 Types of Clothing	• Shopping for clothes in a store • Shopping for clothes online	*I'm looking for . . .* *This is _____ than that one.* *Are these _____?*
UNIT 10 Lifestyles	• Forming opinions about lifestyle habits • Sharing opinions about lifestyle	*I agree that . . .* *I disagree that . . .*
UNIT 11 Achievements	• Selecting a person for an achievement award • Explaining reasons for a choice	*I chose _____ because s/he has . . .* *_____ is a better choice because s/he has . . .*
UNIT 12 Consequences	• Considering consequences in planning a project • Offering different alternatives	*If we . . . we will . . .* *If we . . . we will be able to . . .*

UNIT 1 PEOPLE

A 🔁 Talk about the people in the pictures. Write your ideas. What are their names? How old are they? Where are they from? What do they do?

1. _____
_____
_____
_____

2. _____
_____
_____
_____

3. _____
_____
_____
_____

4. _____
_____
_____
_____

B 🔗 Get together with another pair of students. Share your ideas. Are they the same or different?

UNIT 2 WORK, REST, AND PLAY

A Look at these unusual celebrations. What do you think people do on these days?

September 5

Be Late for Something Day

July 20

National Ice Cream Day

January 3

Festival of Sleep

May 6

INTERNATIONAL NURSES' DAY

B Think of a new celebration. Answer the questions.

1. What is the name of your celebration? _____
2. Who is your celebration for? _____
3. When is your celebration? _____
4. What are three things people do for this celebration? _____
   _____
5. What are three things that people eat or drink for this celebration? _____
   _____
6. Why is your celebration fun? _____
   _____

C Tell the class about your celebration.

UNIT 3 GOING PLACES

A 🔁 You and your partner are going on a trip for one week. Choose the place you will go to.
Destination: _____

B Work alone. Look at this list and circle the things you want to take along.

sweaters	your passport	a swimsuit	a jacket	sunglasses
books to read	your camera	jeans	t-shirts	nice clothes to go out at night
a dictionary	credit cards	a video camera	lots of CDs	cookies and candy
dishes	an umbrella	a coat	boots	three pairs of shoes
magazines	a radio	skis	a tennis racquet	a laptop computer
cash	a driver's license	a guitar	a pillow	photos of your family
sandwiches	a smartphone	a tablet	_____	_____

C 🔁 Now work with a partner. The airplane is very small, so you can only take one suitcase—together! Which things on the list will you take? Remember, all the things must fit into one suitcase! Write your list.

_____
_____
_____
_____
_____

D ♻ Share your list with the class.

UNIT 4 FOOD

A 🔁 Read the menu. Fill in the spaces with foods you like.

Amy's Family Restaurant

Main Dishes	**Desserts**
Fried chicken ... $5.95	Ice cream ... $1.50
Baked fish ... $7.95	Fruit plate ... $2.00
Italian spaghetti ... $6.95	_____
_____	_____
_____	
Side dishes	**Drinks**
Salads: green, tomato, mixed ... $1.95	Mineral water, iced tea, coffee ... $1.50
Soups: chicken, _____,	_____, _____
_____ ... $2.50	

B 🔁 Practice this conversation with a partner.

Waiter:	Good evening. My name is Andy, and I'll be your waiter today. Are you ready to order?
Julie:	Yes, I am. I'd like the fried chicken, please.
Waiter:	OK . . . And would you like french fries or a baked potato with that?
Julie:	Hmm . . . I'll have french fries. And what kind of salad do you have?
Waiter:	We have green salad, tomato salad, and mixed vegetable salad.
Julie:	I'd like a green salad.
Waiter:	And what would you like to drink?
Julie:	Do you have iced tea?
Waiter:	Yes, we do. Small, medium, or large?
Julie:	Medium, please.

C 🔁 Look at the menu and make a new conversation with foods you like. Then change roles and make another conversation.

D ♣ Present your conversation to the class.

UNIT 5 SPORTS

 You and your group are going to plan a new sports center for all the people in your city. People can go there to play their favorite sports, and learn to play new sports. Talk together and decide about these things.

A What are five sports people can do or play in your sports center?

1. _____
2. _____
3. _____
4. _____
5. _____

B What are five things that people can learn at your sports center?

1. _____
2. _____
3. _____
4. _____
5. _____

C What are five special rooms in your sports center?

1. _____
2. _____
3. _____
4. _____
5. _____

D Give your sports center a name. _____

E Tell the class about your Sports Center!

UNIT 6 DESTINATIONS

A 🔄 Read this TV commercial for a travel destination out loud.

Actor #1:	Wow, you look so relaxed! How was your vacation at White Beach?
Actor #2:	Oh, it was very good.
Actor #1:	Tell me about your hotel!
Actor #2:	It was nice. Our room was big, and the view from the window was good.
Actor #1:	Did you like the beach?
Actor #2:	It was big and clean. We went swimming every day, and we took an interesting boat tour.
Actor #1:	Were you happy with your trip?
Actor #2:	Yes! White Beach is a good place for a vacation, and the weather there is nice every day.
Actor #1:	I should call my travel agent today—and take my next vacation at White Beach!

B 🔄 Make the commercial in exercise **A** more interesting. Cross out some of the adjectives and use emphatic adjectives from the box.

fascinating	enormous	excellent	outstanding
magnificent	amazing	spotless	huge

C 🔄 On another sheet of paper, write your own TV commercial for a place in your country. Use emphatic adjectives. Then practice your commercial with your partner.

D 🔆 Present your commercial to the class.

UNIT 7 COMMUNICATION

A 🔁 People use symbols to communicate without words. Look at the signs. What do these symbols mean in English?

1. _____ 2. _____ 3. _____

4. _____ 5. _____ 6. _____

B 🔁 Think of two new symbols for useful signs. Draw them on another sheet of paper.

C 🔁 Show your signs to other students. Can they understand them?

UNIT 8 MOVING FORWARD

A ⟳ Make predictions for ten years in the future, like the example.

1. your school _Our school is going to have a big, new building. It will be beautiful!_

2. your city _____

3. your teacher _____

4. a classmate _____

   Name: _____

5. a classmate _____

   Name: _____

6. your country _____

7. a sports team _____

8. a famous person _____

   Name: _____

B ⚙ Get together with another pair. Share your predictions.

C ⚙ Choose the three best predictions from your group. Read them to the class.

UNIT 9 TYPES OF CLOTHING

A 🔁 Read the conversation and fill in the words. Then practice the conversation with your partner.

> looking   take   on sale   price   fitting room

Clerk:	May I help you?
Customer:	Yes. I'm _____ for a warm sweater.
Clerk:	These sweaters are _____ this week. They're only $18.
Customer:	What are they made of?
Clerk:	They're 100% wool.
Customer:	$18 is a good _____ for a wool sweater. Do you have any in medium?
Clerk:	This green one is medium.
Customer:	Can I try it on?
Clerk:	Yes, the _____ is in the back of the store.

– – – –

Customer:	It's very warm. Do you have any other colors?
Clerk:	Let's see . . . We also have blue, brown, and black.
Customer:	Great! I'll _____ a green one and a black one, too.

B 🔁 Look at the advertisement and make two new conversations. Take turns buying things.

Gracy's Department Store

Big Winter Sale!

Leather jackets— only $125! Black, brown, or tan

Fashion jeans— just $40! 100% cotton denim in dark blue, light blue, or black

Winter ski parkas— $89! Warm, 100% man-made fiber, in red, blue, green, gold, or purple.

Snow boots— $35! Made of nylon in HOT colors to keep your feet warm. Blue, orange, green, or red

Cotton t-shirts— $10 In ten different colors

XS extra-small
S small
M medium
L large
XL extra-large

UNIT 10 LIFESTYLES

A Read the opinion survey and mark your answers.

Lifestyle Survey

1. Most people today don't sleep enough.

   ☐ I agree.   ☐ I disagree.   ☐ I don't know.

2. Traditional food in our country is healthier than modern food.

   ☐ I agree.   ☐ I disagree.   ☐ I don't know.

3. You can be healthy even with no exercise.

   ☐ I agree.   ☐ I disagree.   ☐ I don't know.

4. People must take vitamin pills to be healthy.

   ☐ I agree.   ☐ I disagree.   ☐ I don't know.

5. Life in the past was healthier than life today.

   ☐ I agree.   ☐ I disagree.   ☐ I don't know.

6. Eating a lot of junk food is worse than smoking.

   ☐ I agree.   ☐ I disagree.   ☐ I don't know.

7. Working too much is very bad for your health.

   ☐ I agree.   ☐ I disagree.   ☐ I don't know.

8. For good health, your genes are more important than your habits.

   ☐ I agree.   ☐ I disagree.   ☐ I don't know.

9. Most people worry about their health too much.

   ☐ I agree.   ☐ I disagree.   ☐ I don't know.

10. I eat a very healthy diet.

    ☐ I agree.   ☐ I disagree.   ☐ I don't know.

B Discuss your opinions with a group. Explain your reasons.

C Compare your answers with the whole class.

UNIT 11 ACHIEVEMENTS

A Your city is giving an Achievement Award to the person who has the most important achievements. Read about the four candidates.

Candidate 1: Alicia

Alicia got married after she graduated from high school, and had two children. Her husband died in a car accident. She went back to school and became a teacher. She teaches in a school for children with learning problems. She has helped more than 100 children learn to read and write.

Candidate 2: Jacob

Jacob can't walk. He has used a wheelchair since he was a little boy. He always loved his science and math classes. He is now studying to be a doctor, and he is the top student in his classes. He wants to help other people who can't walk.

Candidate 3: Kyra

Kyra's family had to leave their home country because of a war. When she was in high school, she worked at night to earn money for her family. After she graduated from high school, she started her own business. Her business has given jobs to more than 30 poor women.

Candidate 4: Rick

Rick is the oldest of ten brothers and sisters. He loves art, and he made beautiful drawings and paintings as a child. His parents didn't have money to pay for his education, so he worked in a factory for five years to study at an art school. He has given more than 100 paintings to hospitals to put in sick people's rooms.

B Talk with your partner. Choose two people to recommend for the award.

C Get together with another pair. Choose one person for the award, and make notes of your reasons.

D Tell the class about your decision. Explain your reasons.

UNIT 12 CONSEQUENCES

A Read the situation.

You are members of the City Council. All the schools in your city are old and crowded. Your city has bought some land to build a big new school. Workers are going to start building the school next week. Now scientists have found rare plants on the land. The plants are endangered, and they only grow around your city. The scientists say the plants contain an important medicine, and maybe they can cure diseases. The City Council must make a decision about the school.

B Talk about each of these plans and their consequences. Choose the best plan.

Plan 1: Build the school. Try to move the plants to another place.

Plan 2: Build the school. Don't worry about the plants.

Plan 3: Sell all the plants to a company to make medicine. Use the money for the city.

Plan 4: Don't build the school. Save all the plants.

Plan 5: Don't build the school. Sell the land. Use the money to buy other land.

Plan 6: (your own idea) _____

_____

C Present your decision to the class.

Unit 1: People

Lesson A

A Write the correct form of the verb *be*.

1. Pilar ____is____ Peruvian.

2. Li and Wei _____ Chinese.

3. We _____ Mexican.

4. They _____ dancers.

5. He _____ a journalist.

B Write the sentences again. Use contractions.

1. I am Mexican. I'm Mexican _____ .

2. They are Australian. _____ .

3. Leyla is Jordanian. _____ .

4. We are photographers from China. _____ .

5. You are a travel agent. _____ .

C Unscramble the sentences.

1. a / not / is / Ali / police officer. Ali is not a police officer _____ .

2. politicians. / are / They / not _____ .

3. are / We / Japanese. / not _____ .

4. am / I / a / chef. / not _____ .

5. not / You / French. / are _____ .

D Match the questions and answers.

1. Are you a journalist? __b__   **a.** No, she isn't. She's from Japan.

2. Is Jean-Luc French? _____   **b.** Yes, I am.

3. Is Yukiko Chinese? _____   **c.** No, they aren't. They're Australian.

4. Are they dancers? _____   **d.** Yes, he is.

5. Are the photographers Irish? _____   **e.** No, they aren't.

E Fill in the blanks with the correct form of pronoun + *be*, or contraction of pronoun + *be*.

1. **A:** __Are__ they Mexican?   **B:** Yes, they are _____ .

2. **A:** Are _____ French?   **B:** Yes, I _____ .

3. **A:** Are _____ Mexican?   **B:** No, they _____ . _____ Guatemalan.

4. **A:** _____ the politician Jordanian?   **B:** Yes, she _____ .

5. **A:** _____ the journalists French?   **B:** No, _____ Belgian.

Lesson C

A Complete the sentences with the correct form of *be*.

1. My friends _____ *are* _____ happy.

2. Eric's job _____ dangerous. He _____ a police officer.

3. Their jobs _____ interesting.

4. My English classes _____ difficult but they _____ interesting.

5. The politicians _____ rich.

B Circle the correct word or words to complete the sentence.

1. My uncle is (rich | (a rich) | an rich) man.

2. Carmen is (interesting | a interesting | an interesting) woman.

3. The assignment is (difficult | a difficult | an difficult) reading.

4. It is (dangerous | a dangerous | an dangerous) job.

5. Leo is (unhappy | a unhappy | an unhappy) child.

C Circle *a* or *an* to complete the sentence.

1. He is ((a) | an) boring person.

2. It is (a | an) interesting class.

3. France is (a | an) safe country.

4. It is (a | an) easy assignment.

5. She is (a | an) happy person.

D Write sentences using the cues and possessive adjectives. Follow the example.

1. Susan, German *Her nationality is German* _____.

2. you, Japan _____.

3. Luis, Peru _____.

4. NIna, Jordan _____.

5. Sofia and Jack, Australia _____.

E Complete the sentences using a possessive adjective.

1. My parents are journalists. _____ *Their* _____ jobs are interesting.

2. Enrique is a doctor. _____ salary is good.

3. Mei is a travel agent. _____ job is fun.

4. You are unhappy. _____ life is difficult.

5. I am a good student. _____ education is important to me.

Unit 2: Work, Rest, and Play

Lesson A

| go to bed | start work | take a nap | visit friends | ~~watch TV~~ |

A Complete the sentences. Use the correct form of the verbs in the box.

1. Diana and Jose _watch TV_____ in the evening.

2. Jun _____ in the afternoon after school.

3. I _____ at ten o'clock.

4. They _____ at eight o'clock in the morning.

5. We _____ on the weekend.

B Complete the negative sentences. Use the verbs in parentheses.

1. The baby (take a nap) _doesn't take a nap_____ in the morning.

2. We (go to the movies) _____ on Wednesdays.

3. They (eat out) _____ on the 4th of July.

4. I (catch the bus) _____ in the morning.

5. She (watch TV) _____ in the afternoon.

C Match the questions and answers.

1. Do you get up at seven o'clock? ___d___

2. Does Diego take a shower in the evening? _____

3. Do they catch the bus in the evening? _____

4. Do you eat out on Saturdays? _____

5. Does Nga eat breakfast in the morning? _____

a. No, they don't.

b. No, I don't. I eat out on Fridays.

c. Yes, she does.

d. Yes, I do.

e. No, he doesn't.

D Complete the questions and answers.

1. **A:** _____ eat breakfast _____ the morning?

   B: No, I _____ .

2. **A:** What time do you _____ in the morning?

   B: I catch the bus _____ eight thirty.

E Circle the correct preposition of time.

1. I get up (at | in | on) eight o'clock (at | in | on) Saturdays.

2. Davi takes a shower (at | in | on) seven o'clock (at | in | on) the morning.

3. Lorena starts work (at | in | on) nine o'clock (at | in | on) Mondays.

4. They watch TV (at | in | on) the evening and go to bed (at | in | on) eleven o'clock.

Lesson C

A Complete the sentences with *always*, *sometimes*, *often*, or *never*.

1. Independence Day in the USA is ____always____ July 4th.

2. Carnival is _____ in October.

3. New Year's Day is _____ January 1st.

4. Mihn is a doctor. She _____ works on holidays.

5. Carlos is a police officer. He _____ works on holidays.

B Unscramble the words to make sentences. Write the sentences.

1. is / always / Thanksgiving Day / a Thursday. / on _Thanksgiving Day is always on a Thursday._

2. sometimes / fireworks / We / on / New Year's Eve. / watch _____

3. sends / family / often / to / cards / her / She _____

4. eat / his birthday. / on / chicken / never / They _____

5. on / never / give / teachers / The / Mondays. / tests _____

C Fill in the blanks with *always*, *sometimes*, *often*, or *never*.

1. Martin doesn't read the newspaper. He ____never____ reads the newspaper

2. My mother catches the bus every morning. She _____ catches the bus.

3. I eat out three or four nights a week. I eat out _____ .

4. Nadia goes to the movies one or two times a month. She _____ goes to the movies.

5. My grandmother is afraid to drive. She _____ drives the car.

D Read about Thanksgiving. Circle the adverbs of frequency.

Thanksgiving is a big holiday in the United States. It is always on the last Thursday in November. The celebration is always a big meal. The main dish is usually turkey. Families often eat the meal in the afternoon. People never give gifts on Thanksgiving. People sometimes call family and friends on Thanksgiving.

E Read the paragraph in **D** again. Circle **T** for *true* and **F** for *false*.

1. Thanksgiving is sometimes on the last Thursday in November.   T   F

2. People often eat a big meal on Thanksgiving.   T   F

3. The meal is usually turkey.   T   F

4. People often eat the meal in the afternoon.   T   F

5. People sometimes give gifts on Thanksgiving.   T   F

Unit 3: Going Places

Lesson A

A Match the possessive phrases with the same meaning.

1. It's his bag. _____c_____   **a.** It's theirs.

2. This is your phone. _____   **b.** It's ours.

3. This is our house. _____   **c.** It's his.

4. It's their car. _____   **d.** They're mine.

5. They're my keys. _____   **e.** It's yours.

B Complete the conversations with possessive adjectives and pronouns

1. **A:** Is this your bag?

   B: Yes, it's _____ .

2. **A:** Is this Lisa's phone?

   B: No, _____ is a smartphone.

3. **A:** Are these _____ bags?

   B: No, ours are blue not black.

4. **A:** This is not _____ ticket. It's hers.

   B: Maybe she has _____ .

5. **A:** They can't find _____ bags.

   B: Are these _____ bags?

C Write the correct pronoun to complete the sentence.

1. The car belongs to them. It is _____theirs_____ .

2. The passports belong to us. They're _____ .

3. It belongs to him. It's _____ .

4. The bag belongs to me. It's _____ .

5. The keys belong to you. They're _____ .

D Answer the questions using *belong to* and a possessive adjective.

1. Whose bag is this? (Linda) It belongs to Linda. It's hers _____ .

2. Whose ticket is this? (me) _____ .

3. Whose sunglasses are these? (Laila) _____ .

4. Whose keys are these? (Mr. Webster) _____ .

5. Whose duty-free shopping is this? (them) _____ .

Lesson C

A Complete the sentences with *should* or *shouldn't*.

1. You ___should___ buy travel insurance.

2. They _____ buy their train tickets early to get the lowest price.

3. Duc _____ leave his credit cards at home.

4. Travelers _____ bring some cash.

B Read the answers. Write the questions.

1. **Q:** Should I print my ticket? _____.

   A: Yes, you should. Bring your printed ticket to check in for your flight.

2. **Q:** _____.

   A: Yes, you should. You will need your international driver's license in Mexico.

3. **Q:** _____.

   A: No, you shouldn't. Credit cards are safer than cash.

4. **Q:** _____.

   A: No, you shouldn't. You do not need a visa to enter the country.

C Unscramble the words to make sentences.

1. should / You / you / be careful / travel. / when

   You should be careful when you travel _____.

2. cash. / bring / shouldn't / too much / You

   _____

3. your / You / anyone. / credit card number / to / give / shouldn't

   _____

4. pack / should / one / You / bag.

   _____

D Write sentences using should for advice. Use words from the box.

> visa   credit card   airline tickets
> ~~international driver's licence~~

1. Linh is going to drive across the USA with a friend. What should she do?

   Linh should get an international driver's license _____.

2. Harry wants to go to Brazil. He needs a visa to enter the country. What should he do?

   _____

3. Asam does not want to bring cash on vacation. What should he do?

   _____

4. Airline tickets are cheaper online. What should travelers do?

   _____

Unit 4: Food

Lesson A

A Write the plural for count nouns. Put an **X** for non-count nouns.

Singular	Plural
pepper	peppers
water	
lettuce	
coffee	
egg	
bread	

Singular	Plural
tomato	
sausage	
chicken	
tea	
potato	
milk	

B Circle *some* or *any* to complete the sentences.

1. I don't want ((any) | some) milk.

2. The potato salad has (any | some) onions in it.

3. Eric bought (any | some) eggs at the store.

4. He doesn't drink (any | some) coffee in the morning.

5. Do you have (any | some) orange juice?

C Complete the sentences with *some* or *any*.

1. Do you want _____ lemon with your fish?

2. Alice shouldn't eat _____ salt.

3. Vegetarians don't eat _____ steak or chicken.

4. I need _____ lemons to make lemonade.

D Fill in the blanks with *How much* or *How many*.

1. How many _____ apples do you need for the pie?

2. _____ lemons do we have?

3. _____ milk does the baby drink?

4. _____ butter is in these cookies?

5. _____ potatoes would you like?

Lesson C

A Label the photos using quantifiers: *lots of, a few, a little.*

1. _____ 2. _____ 3. _____ 4. _____

B Circle *a little* or *a few* to complete the sentences.

1. There is (a few | (a little)) ice cream in the freezer.

2. I need (a few | a little) eggs to make a cake.

3. Rana needs (a few | a little) milk for her coffee.

4. Dave likes (a few | a little) French fries with his sandwich.

5. Karina shared (a few | a little) of her chocolate with me.

C Complete the sentences with *a few, a little,* or *lots of.*

1. Nadia needs _lots of_____ apples to make a big apple pie

2. Kamal drinks only _____ coffee in the morning.

3. Wei needs _____ oranges. Only two or three.

4. Scott drinks _____ water after playing soccer.

5. This soup is good. But it needs just _____ salt.

D Complete the conversations with *a few, a little,* or *lots of.*

1. **A:** Do you want some water?

   B: Just _a little_____ . I'm not very thirsty.

2. **A:** Buy some tomatoes, please. I'm going to make a sauce.

   B: How many do you need?

   A: I need _____ tomatoes. Buy ten or twelve.

3. **A:** How much chocolate do you eat each day?

   B: _____ pieces after dinner. About three.

Unit 5: Sports

Lesson A

| play | study | swim | talk | take a break |

A Complete the sentences with verbs in the present continuous tense. Use the words in the box.

1. Kevin and Leo _are playing_____ soccer.

2. Kim _____ to her teacher at the moment.

3. The joggers _____ now.

4. Rose _____ in the pool right now.

5. The students _____ in the library right now.

B Fill in the blanks with the present continuous tense. Use the cues.

1. They _are not taking a break_____ (not take a break) at the moment. They _are working_____ (work).

2. Sofia _____ (not watch TV) right now. She _____ (listen) to music.

3. Luis _____ (not lift weights). He _____ (drink) water.

4. Vincent _____ (not study) right now. He _____ (type) an e-mail.

5. My mother _____ (not cook) dinner now. She _____ (talk) on the phone.

C Write responses to the questions using the present continuous tense and the cues below.

1. What are you doing now? (take a break) _I'm taking a break._____

2. What is she doing? (call / friend) _____

3. What are they doing right now? (play / soccer) _____

4. What are you doing? (study / test) _____

5. What is he doing at the moment? (watch / movie) _____

D Write short answers to the Yes/No questions.

1. Are you watching the news right now? (yes) _Yes, I am._____

2. Is he jogging now? (no) _____

3. Are the kids swimming at the moment? (no) _____

4. Are you eating dinner at the moment? (yes) _____

5. Is she doing her homework now? (yes) _____

Lesson C

cost know like prefer think

A Complete the sentences with stative verbs in the correct form. Use the words in the box.

1. Many people _____think_____ skateboarding is dangerous.

2. Tickets for the football game _____ a lot of money.

3. Elroy _____ to play basketball outdoors.

4. My brothers _____ to watch diving. I _____ it's boring.

5. She _____ how to ice skate.

B Circle the correct form of the verb in parentheses.

1. I (am hating | (hate)) jogging.

2. Anwar (need | needs) a new skateboard.

3. Bryan (is preferring | prefers) basketball to football.

4. Ice hockey equipment (is costs | costs) a lot of money.

5. They (are knowing | know) how to ski.

C Write negative statements with stative verbs. Use the cues below.

1. She / not want / to dive / pool. _She doesn't want to dive into the pool_ .

2. We / not like / be / indoors _____ .

3. They / not know / play / golf _____ .

4. He / not think / sports / fun _____ .

5. I / not like / indoor sports _____ .

D Complete each question. Use the stative verbs in parentheses.

1. (you / prefer) _Do you prefer_ _____ indoor sports or outdoor sports?

2. (Miguel / prefer) _____ team sports or individual sports?

3. (skis / cost) _____ a lot of money?

4. (you /need) _____ a uniform to play basketball?

5. Why (you/ think) _____ some sports are dangerous?

E Write the correct form of the verb in parentheses.

1. Sonja _____likes_____ (like) to watch gymnastics on TV.

2. _____ (you prefer) swimming or jogging?

3. I _____ (hate) skiing on very cold days.

4. The children _____ (prefer) outdoor sports.

Unit 6: Destinations

Lesson A

A Complete the sentences with the simple past tense of the verb in parentheses.

1. They _____went_____ (go) to Mexico last year.

2. Vin _____ (take) his phone to class.

3. We _____ (eat) in a new Chinese restaurant.

4. You _____ (need) to make a reservation.

5. I _____ (buy) gifts for my family on vacation.

B Write the sentences again in the simple past tense.

1. He rents a car when he travels. _He rented a car when he traveled_ .

2. We eat pizza for lunch. _____.

3. We want to go to Italy for our vacation. _____.

4. The flight leaves at six o'clock in the evening. _____.

5. The teacher says the assignment is due on Friday. _____.

C Write the sentences again as negative.

1. We left class at one thirty. _We didn't leave class at one thirty_ .

2. He studied for the test. _____.

3. Carmen read two books during her vacation. _____.

4. My classmate helped me with the assignment. _____.

5. Sarah traveled to Japan last year. _____.

D Match the questions and answers.

1. Did you eat traditional foods? ___d___   **a.** Yes, she did.

2. Did Martine visit her family last year? _____   **b.** I went to Spain.

3. Did you see the Eiffel Tower? _____   **c.** No, he didn't.

4. Did Zach ask for directions? _____   **d.** Yes, they were delicious.

5. Where did you go for vacation last month? _____   **e.** Yes, I did!

E Unscramble the questions.

1. did / What / you / your / leave / house / time _What time did you leave your house_ ?

2. a / make / Did / reservation / you _____?

3. you / did / Where / live _____?

4. did / What / buy / you _____?

5. flight / arrive / on time / the / Did _____?

Lesson C

A Complete each sentence with *was* or *were*.

1. The movie __was__ fascinating.

2. The flight _____ exhausting.

3. Their hands _____ clean.

4. The museums _____ excellent.

5. The food _____ good.

B Answer the questions with short answers.

1. Was Machu Picchu fascinating? _Yes, it was_ .

2. Was the hiking exhausting? Yes, _____ .

3. Were they in Madrid? No, _____ .

4. Was the flight good? No, _____ .

5. Were the museums interesting? No, _____ .

C Match the questions and answers.

1. Was Bangkok fascinating? __b__   **a.** Yes, they were. They were spotless.

2. Was the flight terrible? _____   **b.** Yes, it was.

3. Were the hotel rooms clean? _____   **c.** Yes, they were huge.

4. Were the ruins big? _____   **d.** No, they weren't. I didn't talk to anyone!

5. Were the people friendly? _____   **e.** No, it wasn't bad.

D Read the answers. The write questions with *was* or *were*.

1. **A:** _How was your vacation?_ _____

   B: My vacation was excellent.

2. **A:** _____

   B: The food was good. The fresh fruit was amazing.

3. **A:** _____

   B: No, the flight wasn't tiring.

4. **A:** _____

   B: The city was so clean!

5. **A:** _____

   B: The ruins were enormous.

Unit 7: Communication

Lesson A

A Circle the indirect object and underline the direct object in the sentences.

1. Nicole bought (Ivan) a coffee.

2. Her parents gave her a smartphone.

3. He sent me a text message yesterday.

4. Claire sent her sister an email.

5. My grandmother sent me a letter.

B Unscramble the words to write sentences.

1. sent / the bank. / a fax / to / Yvonne _Yvonne sent a fax to the bank_ .

2. sent / an / my / I / e-mail. / teacher _____ .

3. a / gave / present. / his / Bruce / birthday / brother _____ .

4. a / sent / her / e-mail. / long / Her / friend _____ .

5. text message / Send / a / her _____ .

C Match the sentence parts to make requests.

1. I bought my sister ___e___   **a.** a cake

2. Mei faxed the university _____   **b.** an inexpensive hotel.

3. He sent his boss _____   **c.** her application.

4. My sister made me _____   **d.** an e-mail yesterday.

5. Greg found us _____   **e.** a nice gift.

D Circle the indirect object and underline the direct object in the requests.

1. Please make (me) a sandwich.

2. Give your sister a call.

3. Send your teacher an e-mail.

4. Write your aunt a letter.

5. Buy your parents a TV.

E Read the situations and make requests. Use the verbs in parentheses.

1. You need your friend's phone number. (give) _Give me your phone number_ .

2. You want your sister to buy a sweater for your mother. (buy) _____ .

3. You want your teacher to e-mail you the assignment. (send) _____ .

4. You want your friend to e-mail you a photo. (send) _____ .

5. You want a colleague to send you a contract. (fax) _____ .

Lesson C

feels   looks   smells   sounds   tastes

A Complete each sentence with a verb from the box.

1. The band _____ great.

2. The food _____ delicious.

3. The flower _____ nice.

4. The blanket _____ soft.

5. The floor _____ dirty.

B Circle the correct verb to complete the sentence.

1. The kitten's fur (feels | smells) soft.

2. My mother's cooking always (smells | sounds) delicious.

3. Your clothes (look | taste) wet.

4. I (feel | taste) cinnamon. Is there cinnamon in this cake?

5. The music (sounds | looks) too loud. Can you turn it down?

C Match the statements or questions and responses.

1. Do you hear the music? ___*b*___   **a.** It tastes very salty.

2. Did you see the flowers? _____   **b.** It sounds loud.

3. Taste the soup. _____   **c.** It feels so soft.

4. Feel this sweater. _____   **d.** It looks wet and rainy.

5. What's the weather?   **e.** They smell beautiful.

D More than one sensory verb can complete these sentences. Write the correct verbs on the lines.

1. A: The company is in trouble.

   B: I know. I read the e-mail from the director.

   A: The situation (___*looks*___ | _____) bad.

2. A: The meat isn't good to eat.

   B: How do you know?

   A: It (_____ | _____ | _____) bad.

Unit 8: Moving Forward

Lesson A

A Complete the sentences. Use the words in parentheses and *be going to*.

1. What <u>are you going to</u> (you) give Michelle for her birthday?

2. When _____ (they) buy a new car?

3. Today _____ (Chad) clean the house.

4. In the future _____ (I) buy my own house.

5. _____ (you) speak English fluently.

B Match the sentences.

1. Debbie didn't pass the test. __c__   **a.** She's going to do some laundry.

2. Jasmine's shirts are dirty. _____   **b.** We're going to buy a new car.

3. Juan is going to study English in London. _____   **c.** She's going to study more for the next test.

4. Our car is very old. _____   **d.** He's going to get a new job.

5. Tam doesn't like his job. _____   **e.** He's going to speak English fluently.

C Write negative statements with *be going to*. Use the cues.

1. Ahmed / arrive / tonight <u>Ahmed is not going to arrive tonight</u>.

2. The students / study / in the library _____.

3. Jana / buy / a smartphone _____.

4. My cousin / visit / next year _____.

5. Kris / cook / fish for dinner _____.

D Fill in the blanks in the conversation with *be going to* and the pronoun in parentheses.

A: What <u>are you going to</u> (You) study?

B: English. _____ (I) speak English fluently.

A: How _____ (you) do that?

B: _____ (I) study a lot. _____ (I) join conversation groups with English speakers. And _____ (I) try to study in an English-speaking country.

E Complete the questions. Use the words in parentheses and *be going to*.

1. <u>Are you going to visit</u> (You / visit) your sister this weekend?

2. When _____ (Hiro / clean) the apartment?

3. Where _____ (you / study) English?

4. How _____ (he / get) to San Francisco?

5. Why _____ (they / wait) for him?

Lesson C

A Unscramble the words to write sentences.

1. cold / be / It / will / tonight. _It will be cold tonight._

2. afternoon. / will / It / the / rain / in _____

3. will / Marta / soon. / arrive _____

4. few / in / Dinner / be / ready / a / minutes. / will _____

5. tonight / be. / will / There / snow _____

B Complete the negative sentences with *will*.

1. No, I _____ won't _____ drive you to the beach!

2. Sharon _____ eat her lunch today.

3. Study every day or you _____ do well on the test.

4. Oh no! My umbrella _____ open!

5. She _____ wear her new glasses to school.

C Write weather predictions using *will*. Use the cues.

1. (sunny / Spain) _It will be sunny in Spain_ .

2. (cloudy / Bogota) _____ .

3. (cold / Moscow / winter) _____ .

4. (hot / Sao Paulo / summer) _____ .

5. (windy / Boston / March) _____ .

D Rewrite the questions using *be going to*.

1. Will it be sunny at the beach? _Is it going to be sunny at the beach_ ?

2. Will it be windy on the boat? _____ ?

3. Will it be warm on the plane? _____ ?

4. Will the test be difficult? _____ ?

5. Will you call me when you get home? _____ ?

E Rewrite the questions using *will*. Then, complete the answers.

1. Is it going to be cold this winter? _Will it be cold this winter_ ? Yes, _it will_ .

2. Is the test going to be difficult? _____ ? No, _____ .

3. Am I going to like this movie? _____ ? Yes, _____ .

4. Are you going to do well on this test? _____ ? Yes, _____ .

5. Is it going to rain tomorrow? _____ ? No, _____ .

Unit 9: Types of Clothing

Lesson A

A Circle the correct comparative form of the adjective.

1. Formal clothes are ((more expensive) | expensive) than casual clothes.

2. Shoes are often (more cheap | cheaper) than boots.

3. My new handbag is (nicer | more nice) than my old one.

4. The black suit is (more better | better) than the gray one.

5. The pink blouse is (more beautiful | beautiful) than the white one.

B Complete the sentence. Use the comparative form of the word in parentheses and *than*.

1. Monica should buy the formal dress because it is _nicer than_____ (nice) the informal dress.

2. My father wants to buy a used car because it is _____ (cheap) a new one.

3. Ana is _____ (tall) her sister Eva.

4. The long coat is _____ (expensive) the short coat.

5. Is shopping online _____ (easy) than shopping in stores?

> good   ~~new~~   old   pretty   warm

C Complete each sentence with the comparative form of a word from the box and *than*.

1. Sam bought gloves yesterday. Sam's gloves are _newer than_____ mine.

2. Her jacket is _____ his. His coat is light.

3. Linda is _____ than Amanda.

4. The weather today is _____ yesterday.

5. Juro is _____ Kazuo. Kazuo is only seven.

D Write sentences using the comparative forms of the adjectives. Use the prompts.

1. (belt / cheap / boots) _The belt is cheaper than the boots_____.

2. (suit / expensive / sneakers) _____.

3. (belt / cheap / boots) _____.

4. (sweater / warm / shirt) _____.

5. (handmade clothes / good / machine-made) _____.

6. (jeans / formal / skirt) _____.

Lesson C

A Fill in the chart with the missing adjective forms.

Adjective	Comparative Form	Superlative Form
bad		
beautiful		
cheap		
expensive		
good		
heavy		
light		
nice		
pretty		
warm		

B Circle the comparative or superlative adjective to complete each sentence.

1. Leather handbags are the (more | (most)) expensive than cloth ones.

2. The new hat was (worse | worst) than the old one.

3. The woman bought the (more | most) beautiful dress in the store.

4. Kim bought the white belt because it was the (cheaper | cheapest) one.

5. It's hot out. You should wear the (lighter | lightest) clothes that you have.

C Complete the sentences. Use the superlative form of the word in parentheses and *the*.

1. _The cheapest_____ (cheap) clothes are not always _____ (good) quality.

2. The blue silk tie is _____ (nice) one.

3. The white pants are made of _____ (light) cloth.

4. _____ (long) coat is _____ (warm) coat.

5. _____ (pretty) blouse is the _____ (expensive) one, too.

D Complete the conversations with the comparative or superlative form of the adjective in parentheses.

1. **A:** Which sweater do you like _the best_____ (good)?

   B: The black one is _____ (good) the white one. But the red one is _____ (good).

   A: OK, I'll buy the red one. But it's not _____ (cheap)

2. **A:** Smartphones are expensive.

   B: Yes, but some phones are _____ (expensive) than smartphones.

   A: You're right. Smartphones are not the _____ (expensive) phones you can buy.

Unit 10: Lifestyles

Lesson A

A Read the sentences. Label each one *suggestion*, *advice*, or *obligation*.

1. Your phone bill is very expensive! You have to use it less often. _____obligation_____

2. You should walk to work. You need to exercise. _____

3. You could try talking to your sister about the problem. _____

4. You must be in class at 8 a.m. _____

5. You ought to leave now or you'll be late. _____

B Fill in the blanks with the correct modal. Use the cues.

1. You _____must_____ (very strong) use sunscreen at the beach.

2. You _____ (gentle) go to bed early to get eight hours sleep.

3. My brother _____ (strong) drink less coffee.

4. You _____ (gentle) eat salad for lunch.

5. You _____ (strong) drink lots of water after cycling.

C Write advice. Use modals and the cues in parentheses.

1. Tell your friend to stop at the red light. _You must stop at the red light_ (very strong).

2. Tell a classmate to study more often. _____ (strong).

3. Tell your sister to eat a balanced diet. _____ (strong).

4. Tell a friend to try cycling with you. _____ (gentle).

5. Tell your roommate to pay the bills this month. _____ (very strong).

D Read the conversation. Fill in the blanks with modals.
Van wants to be healthier. He is talking with a personal trainer about exercise and healthy habits.

Trainer: You _ought to_ (strong) do two things, Van. First, you _____ (very strong) eat a balanced diet. Second, you _____ (very strong) exercise every day.

Van: OK, I understand. I _____ (strong) stop eating lots of sugar. . . .

Trainer: No, Van. Not _____ (strong). _____ (very strong). You must stop eating lots of sugar. Your body needs a balanced diet to be healthy.

Van: And what about exercise?

Trainer: You should do exercise that you enjoy. You _____ (very strong) keep trying activities until you find one that you like. For example, you _____ (gentle) try cycling.

Van: I like running.

Trainer: Good. You _____ (strong) drink plenty of water before and after you run.

Lesson C

A Circle *How much* or *How many* to complete the sentence.

1. (How much | (How many)) books did you buy?

2. (How much | How many) coffee do they drink?

3. (How much | How many) potatoes did you cook?

4. (How much | How many) children do you have?

5. (How much | How many) money does he need?

B Match the questions and responses.

1. How long is the book? __c__   **a.** Every day.

2. How old is your son? _____   **b.** Two hours.

3. How often do you speak English? _____   **c.** It's 600 pages.

4. How much do you study each day? _____   **d.** Three.

5. How many classes do you have today? _____   **e.** He's seven.

> How long   How many   ~~How much~~   How often   How old

C Fill in the blanks with question words from the box.

1. _How much_ does a smartphone cost?

2. _____ do you visit your family?

3. _____ is your grandmother?

4. _____ did you live in Houston?

5. _____ cousins do you have?

D Write the questions.

Questions	Answers
1. How many hours does Fatima work ?	Fatima works 40 hours a week.
2. _____ ?	My brother is 24 years old.
3. _____ ?	I have two sisters.
4. _____ ?	It's three months.
5. _____ ?	The teacher gives homework every day.

Unit 11: Achievements

Lesson A

A Complete the chart with the irregular past participles.

Verb	Irregular past participle	Verb	Irregular past participle
be	(been)	read	
do		say	
eat		speak	
go		take	
have		tell	
make		pay	
meet		out	

B Circle the correct past participle to complete the sentence.

1. Jennifer has (make | (made)) breakfast this morning.

2. My teacher has (traveled | travels) to many countries in Asia.

3. Ines had (walked | walk) the dog before it began to rain.

4. Has he (finished | finishes) cutting the grass?

5. Rokuro had not (tell | told) Kenji to call him.

C Fill in the blanks with the present perfect tense of the verb in parentheses.

1. Iris _has done_____ (do) her homework.

2. Brazil _____ (won) the World Cup five times.

3. Cristina _____ (be) a teacher for twelve years.

4. My mother _____ (tell) me to be careful.

5. Marc _____ (read) the assignment.

D Answer the questions. Use short answers.

1. A: Has Rita been to an English-speaking country?   **B:** No, _she hasn't_____ .

2. A: Colin, have you met Ed?   **B:** No, _____ .

3. A: Tony, have you paid for the coffee?   **B:** Yes, _____ .

4. A: Have they spoken to their teacher?   **B:** Yes, _____ .

5. A: Has he made a decision yet?   **B:** Yes, _____ .

Lesson C

A Circle the correct form of the verb in parentheses.

1. Paola ((has traveled) | traveled) by airplane many times.

2. Yuan (has walked | walked) to class this morning.

3. My parents (have bought | bought) a new car last year.

4. Lisa (has started | started) a new job in January.

5. Kai (has seen | saw) this movie twice.

B Complete the sentences with the correct form of the verb in parentheses.

1. Last spring Justin _got promoted_____ (get promoted) to senior manager.

2. Justin _____ (be) happy with the promotion to senior manager.

3. He _____ (work) for the company for six years.

4. Justin _____ (begin) his career as an assistant manager.

5. He _____ (work) hard over the years.

C Complete the sentences. Use the words in parentheses to make expressions in the present perfect tense.

1. Mike _has just returned_____ (just, return) home from work.

2. Cecilia _____ (never, be) on an airplane.

3. The students _____ (just, graduate) from college.

4. My brother _____ (just, pass) his driving test.

5. My grandmother _____ (never, send) an e-mail.

D Complete the sentences. Use the words in parentheses to make negative expressions in the present perfect tense.

1. Our teacher _hasn't read_____ (not read) our compositions.

2. Fiona _____ (not, read) the book.

3. The students _____ (not visit) the museum.

4. Our bags _____ (not arrived) in baggage claim.

5. Han _____ (not be) to many countries.

E Write questions with the correct form of the verb in parentheses.

1. _Has Mila graduated_ (Mila, graduate) from college yet?

2. _____ (you, go) to class today?

3. _____ (they, live, ever) in a different country?

4. _____ (Jorge, take) the exam yet?

5. _____ (you, write, ever) a poem?

Unit 12: Consequences

Lesson A

A Match the *if* clauses to the correct result clauses.

1. __c__ If you save money,   **a.** you will feel better all day.
2. _____ If Claude leaves now,   **b.** you will do well in your career.
3. _____ If you eat breakfast,   **c.** you will have it for the future.
4. _____ If you listen in class,   **d.** he will be on time for class.
5. _____ If you work hard,   **e.** you will learn more.

B Complete the conditional sentences. Use the pronouns and verbs in parentheses.

1. If _we save_____ (we, save) money now, _we will be able to____ (we, be able to) take a trip in the summer.

2. If _____ (you, buy) a new laptop today, _____ (you, save) 10%!

3. If _____ (I, study) every night, _____ (I, learn) more vocabulary.

4. If _____ (you, put) money in the bank, _____ (you, earn) interest.

5. If _____ (he, borrow) money from the bank, _____ (he, pay) interest.

C Complete the real conditional sentences about studying in another country.

1. If _____ (you, study) in another country, _____ (you, miss) your friends and family

2. If _____ (you, live) in an English-speaking country, _____ (you, learn) English very quickly.

3. If _____ (you, are) a student at an international university, _____ (you, meet) people from all over the world.

4. If _____ (you, go) to another country, _____ (you, be) far from home.

5. If _____ (you, live) in another country, _____ (you, communicate) with friends and family by e-mail and online conversations.

D Complete the real conditional sentence with the words in parentheses.

1. If I speak English fluently, I _____ (work) for a multi-national company.

2. If I move to New York City, I _____ (visit) my family twice a year.

3. If I travel overnight, I _____ (be) very tired the next day.

4. If I miss the bus, I _____ (drive) to class.

5. If I finish my homework, I _____ (meet) you in park for a soccer game.

Lesson C

A Read the sentences. Add punctuation if needed.

1. If cities grow larger⊙more animals will lose their habitats.

2. We will lose important plants and trees if we build in too many places.

3. If we build in their habitats coyotes will come into neighborhoods to find food.

4. If we do not protect elephants they will all be gone soon.

5. We will lose many endangered species if we do not help save them now.

B Circle the *result clause* and underline the *if clause*.

1. (We will burn less fossil fuels) if more people use public transportation.

2. The planet will be safer if there is less pollution.

3. Jane will visit the Galapagos Islands if she can find an eco-friendly tour.

4. The coral reefs will rebuild if people do not disturb them.

5. More dolphins will survive if people do not catch them in fishing nets.

C Match the result clauses to the correct *if* clauses.

1. __d__ The elephants will disappear   **a.** if the glaciers melt[1].

2. _____ Pandas will survive   **b.** if they think it is important.

3. _____ The seas will rise   **c.** If the oceans heat up.

4. _____ People will care about the environment   **d.** if poaching[2] continues.

5. _____ Glaciers will melt   **e.** if they have more cubs[3].

[1] **melt** ice turns into water
[2] **poaching** killing elephants for their tusks
[3] **cubs** baby bears

D Complete the real conditional sentences about tourism to natural areas. Use the verbs and pronouns in parentheses.

1. Tourism to natural areas _____ (damage) the habitats if _____ (tourists, not be) careful.

2. Boats, cars, and planes _____ (pollute) the air if _____ (they are) used there.

3. Hotels, restaurants, and other services _____ (change) the area if _____ (people, not be) careful.

4. Some tourists _____ (pay) more for eco-friendly vacations if _____ (they, think) it is better for the environment.

5. Other people _____ (stay) at home if _____ (they, think) people should not visit natural habitats like the Galapagos Islands or the Arctic.

UNIT 1 PEOPLE

Lesson A

A. 1. is 2. are 3. are 4. are 5. is

B. 1. I'm Mexican 2. They're Australian. 3. Leyla's Jordanian. 4. We're photographers from China. 5. You're a travel agent.

C. 1. Ali is not a police officer. 2. They are not politicians. 3. We are not Japanese. 4. I am not a chef. 5. You are not French.

D. 1. b 2. d 3. a 4. e 5. c

E. 1. Are; they are 2. you; am 3. they; aren't; They're 4. Is; is 5. Are; they're

Lesson C

A. 1. are 2. is; is 3. are 4. are; are 5. are

B. 1. a rich 2. an interesting 3. a difficult 4. a dangerous 5. an unhappy

C. 1. a 2. an 3. a 4. an 5. a

D. 1. Her nationality is German. 2. Your nationality is Japanese. 3. His nationality is Peruvian. 4. Her nationality is Jordanian. 5. Their nationality is Australian.

E. 1. Their 2. His 3. Her 4. Your 5. My

UNIT 2 WORK, REST, AND PLAY

Lesson A

A. 1. watch TV 2. takes a nap 3. go to bed 4. start work 5. visit friends.

B. 1. doesn't take a nap 2. don't go to the movies 3. don't eat out 4. don't catch the bus 5. doesn't watch TV

C. 1. d 2. e 3. a 4. b 5. c

D. 1. A: Do you; in; B: don't 2. A: catch the bus; B: at

E. 1. at; on 2. at; in 3. at; on 4. in; at

Lesson C

A. 1. always 2. never 3. always 4. often *or* sometimes 5. often *or* sometimes

B. 1. Thanksgiving Day is always on a Thursday. 2. We sometimes watch fireworks on New Year's Eve. 3. She often sends cards to her family. 4. They never eat chicken on his birthday. 5. The teachers never give tests on Mondays.

C. 1. never 2. always 3. often 4. sometimes 5. never

D. Circle: always; always; usually; often; never; sometimes.

E. 1. F; Thanksgiving is <u>always</u> on the last Thursday in November. 2. F: People always eat a big meal on Thanksgiving. 3. T 4. T 5. F; People never give gifts on Thanksgiving.

UNIT 3 GOING PLACES

Lesson A

A. 1. c 2. e 3. b 4. a 5. d

B. 1. your; mine 2. hers 3. our 4. my; yours 5. their; their

C. 1. theirs 2. ours 3. his 4. mine 5. yours

D. 1. It belongs to Linda. It's hers. 2. It belongs to me. It's mine. 3. They belong to Laila. They're hers. 4. They belong to Mr. Webster. They're his. 5. It belongs to them. It's theirs.

Lesson C

A. 1. should 2. should 3. shouldn't 4. should

B. 1. Should I print my ticket? 2. Should I bring my international driver's license? 3. Should I bring a lot of cash? 4. Should I get a visa?

C. 1. You should be careful when you travel. 2. You shouldn't bring too much cash. 3. You shouldn't give your credit card number to anyone. 4. You should pack one bag.

D. 1. Linh should get an international driver's license. 2. Harry should get a visa. 3. Asam should bring credit cards. 4. Travelers should buy airline tickets online.

UNIT 4 FOOD

Lesson A

A.

Singular	Plural
pepper	peppers
water	x
lettuce	x
coffee	x
egg	eggs
bread	x

Singular	Plural
tomato	tomatoes
sausage	sausages
chicken	x
tea	x
potato	potatoes
milk	x

B. 1. any 2. some 3. some 4. any 5. any

C. 1. some 2. any 3. any 4. some

D. 1. How many 2. How many 3. How much 4. How much 5. How many

Lesson C

A. 1. a lot of oranges 2. a little milk 3. lots of milk 4. a few carrots

B. 1. a little 2. a few 3. a little 4. a few 5. a little

C. 1. lots of 2. a little 3. a few 4. lots of 5. a little

D. 1. B: a little 2. A: lots of 3. B: A few

UNIT 5 SPORTS

Lesson A

A. 1. are playing 2. is talking 3. are taking a break 4. is swimming 5. are studying

B. 1. are not taking a break; are working 2. is not watching TV; is listening 3. is not lifting weights; is drinking 4. is not studying; is typing 5. is not cooking; is talking

C. 1. I'm taking a break. 2. She is calling a friend. 3. They are playing soccer. 4. I'm studying for a test. 5. He is watching a movie.

D. 1. Yes, I am. 2. No, he isn't. 3. No, they aren't. 4. Yes, I am. 5. Yes, she is.

Lesson C

A. 1. think 2. cost 3. prefers 4. like; think 5. knows

B. 1. hate 2. needs 3. prefers 4. costs 5. know

C. 1. She doesn't want to dive into the pool. 2. We don't like to be indoors. 3. They don't know how to play golf. 4. He doesn't think sports are fun. 5. I don't like indoor sports.

D. 1. Do you prefer 2. Does Miguel prefer 3. Do skis cost 4. Do you need 5. do you think

E. 1. likes 2. Do you prefer 3. hate 4. prefer

UNIT 6 DESTINATIONS

Lesson A

A. 1. went 2. took 3. ate 4. needed 5. bought

B. 1. He rented a car when he traveled. 2. We ate pizza for lunch. 3. We wanted to go to Italy for our vacation. 4. The flight left at six o'clock in the evening. 5. The teacher said the assignment is due on Friday.

C. 1. We didn't leave class at one thirty. 2. He didn't study for the test. 3. Carmen didn't read two books during her vacation. 4. My classmate didn't help me with the assignment. 5. Sarah didn't travel to Japan last year.

D. 1. d 2. a 3. e 4. c 5. b

Lesson C

A. 1. was 2. was 3. were 4. were 5. was

B. 1. Yes, it was. 2. Yes, it was. 3. No, they weren't. 4. No, it wasn't. 5. No, they weren't.

C. 1. b 2. e 3. a 4. c 5. d

D. 1. How was your vacation? 2. How was the food? 3. Was the flight tiring? 4. Was the city clean? 5. Were the ruins enormous.

E. Ted: were; weren't **Juana:** was **Ted:** was **Juana:** was; was **Ted:** Was **Juana:** was; was

UNIT 7 COMMUNICATION

Lesson A

A. 1. Nicole bought (Ivan) a coffee. 2. (Her parents) gave her a smartphone. 3. (He) sent me a text message yesterday. 4. (Claire) sent her sister an email. 5. (My grandmother) sent me a letter.

B. 1. Yvonne sent a fax to the bank. 2. I sent my teacher an email. 3. Bruce gave his brother a birthday present. or His brother gave Bruce a birthday present. 4. Her friend sent her a long e-mail. 5. Send her a text message

C. 1. e 2. c 3. d 4. a 5. b

D. 1. Please make (me) a sandwich. 2. Give (your sister) a call. 3. Send (her) an e-mail. 4. Write (your aunt) a letter. 5. Buy (your parents) a TV.

E. 1. Give me your phone number. 2. Buy her a sweater. 3. Please send me the assignment. 4. Send me the photo. 5. Fax me the contract.

Lesson C

A. 1. sounds 2. tastes 3. smell 4. feels 5. looks

B. 1. feels 2. smells 3. look 4. taste 5. sounds

C. 1. b 2. e 3. a 4. c 5. d

D. 1. looks, sounds 2. smells, looks, tastes

UNIT 8 MOVING FORWARD

Lesson A

A. 1. are you going to 2. are they going to 3. Chad is going to 4. I am going to 5. You are going to

B. 1. c 2. a 3. e 4. b 5. d

C. 1. Ahmed is not going to arrive tonight. 2. The students are not going to study in the library. 3. Jana is not going to buy a smartphone. 4. My cousin is not going to visit next year. 5. Kris is not going to cook fish for dinner.

D. A: are you going to **B:** I'm going to **A:** are you going to **B:** I'm going to; I'm going to **I'm** going to

E. 1. Are you going to visit 2. is Hiro going to clean 3. are you going to study 4. is he going to get 5. are they going to wait

Lesson C

A. 1. It will be cold tonight. 2. It will rain in the afternoon. 3. Marta will arrive soon. 4. Dinner will be ready in a few minutes. 5. There will be snow tonight.

B. 1. won't 2. won't 3. won't 4. won't 5. won't

C. 1. It will be sunny in Spain. 2. It will be cloudy in Bogota. 3. It will be cold in Moscow in February. 4. It will be hot in Sao Paolo in summer. 5. It will be windy in Boston in March.

D. 1. Is it going to be sunny at the beach? 2. Is it going to be windy on the boat? 3. Is it going to be be warm on the plane? 4. Is the test going to be be difficult? 5. Are you going to call me when you get home?

E. 1. Will it be cold this winter? / Yes, it will. 2. Will the test going be difficult? / No, it won't. 3. Will I like this movie? / Yes, you will. 4. Will you do well on this test? / Yes, I will. 5. Will it rain tomorrow? / No, it won't.

UNIT 9 TYPES OF CLOTHING

Lesson A

A. 1. more expensive 2. cheaper 3. nicer 4. better 5. more beautiful

B. 1. nicer than 2. less expensive than 3. more beautiful than 4. more expensive than 5. better

C. 1. newer than 2. warmer than 3. prettier than 4. worse than 5. older than

D. 1. The belt is cheaper than the boots. 2. A suit is more expensive than sneakers. or Sneakers are less expensive than a suit. 3. A sweater is warmer than a shirt. 4. Handmade clothes are better than machine-made clothes. 5. Jeans are less formal than a skirt. or A skirt is more formal than jeans.

Lesson C

A.

Adjective	Comparative Form	Superlative Form
bad	worse	worst
beautiful	more beautiful	most beautiful
cheap	cheaper	cheapest
expensive	more expensive	most expensive
good	better	best
heavy	heavier	heaviest
light	lighter	lightest
nice	nicer	nicest
pretty	prettier	prettiest
warm	warmer	warmest

B. 1. most 2. worse 3. most 4. cheapest 5. lightest

C. 1. The cheapest; the best 2. the nicest 3. the lightest 4. the longest; the warmest 5. the prettiest; the most expensive

D. 1. A: better   B: better than; the best   A: cheapest 2. B: more expensive than   A: the most expensive

UNIT 10 LIFESTYLES

Lesson A

A. 1. obligation 2. advice 3. suggestion 4. obligation 5. advice

B. 1. must/have to 2. could 3. ought to/should 4. could 5. ought to/should

C. 1. You must stop at the red light. 2. You ought to study more often. 3. You should eat a balanced diet. 4. You could try cycling with me. 5. You have to pay the bills this month.

D. Trainer: ought to; must or have to; must or have to
Van: ought to/should
Trainer: ought to or should; Must or Have to
Van: N/A
Trainer: must or have to; could
Van: N/A
Trainer: ought to or should

Lesson C

A. 1. How many 2. How much 3. How many 4. How many 5. How much

B. 1. c 2. e 3. a 4. b 5. d

C. 1. How much 2. How often 3. How old 4. How long 5. How many

D. 1. How many hours does Fatima work? 2. How old is your brother? 3. How many sisters do you have? 4. How long is the semester? 5. How often does the teacher give homework?

UNIT 11 ACHIEVEMENTS

Lesson A

A.

Verb	Irregular past participle	Verb	Irregular past participle
be	been	read	read
do	done	say	said
eat	ate	speak	spoken
go	gone	take	taken
have	had	tell	told
make	made	pay	paid
meet	met	put	put

B. 1. made 2. traveled 3. walked 4. finished 5. told

C. 1. has done 2. has won 3. has been 4. has told 5. has read

D. 1. No, she hasn't. 2. No, I haven't. 3. Yes, I have. 4. Yes, they have. 5. Yes, he has.

Lesson C

A. 1. has traveled 2. walked 3. bought 4. started 5. has seen

B. 1. got promoted 2. was 3. has worked 4. began 5. has worked

C. 1. has just returned 2. has never been 3. have just graduated 4. has just passes 5. has never sent

D. 1. hasn't read 2. hasn't read 3. have not visited 4. have not arrived 5. has not been

E. 1. Has Mila graduated 2. Did you go 3. Have they ever lived 4. Has Jorge taken 5. Have you ever written

UNIT 12 CONSEQUENCES

Lesson A

A. 1. c 2. d 3. a 4. e 5. b

B. 1. we save, we will be able to 2. you buy, you will save 3. I study, I will learn more 4. you put, you will earn 5. he borrows, he will pay

C. 1. you study; you will miss 2. you live; you will learn 3. you are; you will meet 4. you go; you will meet 5. you live; you will communicate

D. 1. will work 2. will visit 3. will be 4. will drive 5. will meet

Lesson C

A. 1. If cities grow larger, more animals will lose their habitats. 2. No punctuation needed. 3. If we build in their habitats, coyotes will come into neighborhoods to find food. 4. If we do not protect elephants, they will all be gone soon. 5. No punctuation needed.

B. 1. We will burn less fossil fuels if more people use public transportation.
2. The planet will be safer if there is less pollution.
3. Jane will visit the Galapagos Islands if she can find an eco-friendly tour.
4. The coral reefs will grow if people do not disturb them.
5. More dolphins will survive if people do not catch them in fishing nets.

C. 1. d 2. e 3. a 4. b 5. c

D. 1. will damage; tourists are not 2. will pollute; they are 3. will change; people are not 4. will pay; they think 5. will stay; they think